Film Fatales

ALSO BY TOM LISANTI
AND FROM MCFARLAND

Pamela Tiffin: Hollywood to Rome, 1961–1974 (2015)

Glamour Girls of Sixties Hollywood: Seventy-Five Profiles (2008)

Hollywood Surf and Beach Movies: The First Wave, 1959–1969 (2005; paperback 2012)

Drive-in Dream Girls: A Galaxy of B-Movie Starlets of the Sixties (2003; paperback 2012)

Fantasy Femmes of Sixties Cinema: Interviews with 20 Actresses from Biker, Beach, and Elvis Movies (2001; paperback 2010)

ALSO BY LOUIS PAUL
AND FROM MCFARLAND

Tales from the Cult Film Trenches: Interviews with 36 Actors from Horror, Science Fiction and Exploitation Cinema (2008)

Italian Horror Film Directors (2005; paperback 2011)

Film Fatales

Women in Espionage Films and Television, 1962–1973

TOM LISANTI *and*
LOUIS PAUL
foreword by EILEEN O'NEILL

McFarland & Company, Inc., Publishers
Jefferson, North Carolina

The present work is a reprint of the illustrated case bound edition of Film Fatales: Women in Espionage Films and Television, 1962–1973, *first published in 2002 by McFarland.*

LIBRARY OF CONGRESS CATALOGUING-IN-PUBLICATION DATA

Lisanti, Tom, 1961–
Film fatales : women in espionage films and television, 1962–1973 / by Tom Lisanti and Louis Paul ; with a foreword by Eileen O'Neill.
p.   cm.

Includes bibliographical references and index.

ISBN 978-1-4766-6797-3
softcover : acid free paper ∞

1. Femmes fatales in motion pictures.   2. Spy films—History and criticism.   3. Motion picture actors and actresses—Biography—Dictionaries.   4. Actresses—Biography—Dictionaries.
I. Paul, Louis, 1960–   II. Title.

PN1995.9.F44L57   2017   791.43'028'082—dc21   2001008685

BRITISH LIBRARY CATALOGUING DATA ARE AVAILABLE

© 2002 Tom Lisanti and Louis Paul. All rights reserved

No part of this book may be reproduced or transmitted in any form or by any means, electronic or mechanical, including photocopying or recording, or by any information storage and retrieval system, without permission in writing from the publisher.

Cover photograph: Karin Dor in a promotional piece for *You Only Live Twice* (United Artists, 1967)

Printed in the United States of America

McFarland & Company, Inc., Publishers
Box 611, Jefferson, North Carolina 28640
www.mcfarlandpub.com

Tom dedicates this book to Ernie DeLia
for putting up with him and the starlets now and
to his mom Joan and siblings Joe, Lorraine and Donna
for putting up with him and the starlets then.

Louis dedicates this book to the women on screen
and in his life who have inspired him.

Acknowledgments

A number of people had a hand in helping us put together this book. First and foremost, we relay our thanks to these lovely ladies for their comments: Barbara Bouchet, Jean Hale, Gloria Hendry, Sharyn Hillyer, Kathy Kersh, Sue Ane Langdon, BarBara Luna, Deanna Lund, Arlene Martel, Marlyn Mason, Diane McBain, Salli Sachse, Tura Satana, Irene Tsu, Lana Wood, Celeste Yarnall, Francine York and a special thanks to spy gal extraordinaire, Eileen O'Neill. We would also like to thank Steve Swires for letting us use excerpts of his interviews with Martine Beswicke, Shirley Eaton and Elke Sommer.

We would like to express our gratitude to spy film expert Michael Monahan for lending photos from his collection, and to Jennifer Barnaby for all her Internet searching and scanning expertise. Also to author Tom Weaver for his expert advice, librarians Dan Patri and Jeremy Megraw (of the New York Public Library for the Performing Arts) and Shawn Chang for aiding with the Tina Louise and Joanna Pettet profiles. Thanks to Phil Palmieri for bringing Barbara Bouchet to his convention and allowing us to interview her. To Robert Taylor, curator of the Billy Rose Theatre Collection of the New York Public Library for the Performing Arts) for allowing us unlimited access to the vast film and television collections. To Sharon Peacocke from Down Under for her kindness and support in promoting our work on her web site *The Lively Set* (www.tripod.livelyset.com). Also thanks to the helpful staffs of the Margaret Herrick Library of the Motion Pictures Academy of Arts & Sciences and the Film Library of the Museum of Modern Art.

Louis would like to thank Heidi Stock for her inspirational guidance and helping him realize a dream and he would also like to thank Kevin Clement of Chiller Theatre.

Tom pays tribute to his family and friends for all their support with an extra special thanks to Ernie DeLia. His family: Joan Lisanti, Rose DeFeo, Joseph and Beth Lisanti, Lorraine and Richie Nicolo, Donna and Mike Cates, Joe Casamento and Barbara Klein, and the Reisingers: Al, Barbara, Paul and Lori Ann. His friends: Keith Aden, Jim Campbell, John Covelli, Teresa DeTurris, Matthew Fletcher, Scott Hannibal, Clyde Jones, Pete Kaiser, Tom Kazar, John Kelly, Phil Lindow, Jim McGann, Jim Napoleon, Steve Newell, Alan Pally, John Rowell, Mark Tolleson and Kevin Winkler.

Table of Contents

Acknowledgments ix
Foreword by Eileen O'Neill 1
Preface 5
Introduction 7

Profiles 31

Beverly Adams   33
Ursula Andress   36
Pier Angeli   39
Ann-Margret   41
Laura Antonelli   44
Claudine Auger   46
Tina Aumont   49
Barbara Bain   50
Alexandra Bastedo   53
Senta Berger   56
Martine Beswicke   60
Daniela Bianchi   63
Jacqueline Bisset   66
Honor Blackman   69
Erika Blanc   73
Dominique Boschero   77
Barbara Bouchet   79
Thordis Brandt   84
Anna Capri   86
Judy Carne   89
Hélène Chanel   91

Greta Chi   93
Tsai Chin   95
Joan Collins   98
Yvonne Craig   101
Doris Day   104
Lynda Day George   106
Danielle De Metz   109
Mimi Dillard   111
Karin Dor   113
Andrea Dromm   117
Shirley Eaton   118
Rossella Falk   121
Sharon Farrell   122
Barbara Feldon   125
Anne Francis   128
Eunice Gayson   131
Gila Golan   133
Shelby Grant   135
Alizia Gur   137
Jean Hale   140
Mie Hama   143

Susan Hart   145
Gloria Hendry   147
Sharyn Hillyer   150
Jill Ireland   153
Karen Jensen   155
Kathy Kersh   157
Sylva Koscina   160
Nancy Kovack   163
Nancy Kwan   166
Jocelyn Lane   169
Sue Ane Langdon   171
Daliah Lavi   174
Margaret Lee   177
Suzanna Leigh   181
Helga Line   184
Sue Lloyd   186
Beba Loncar   189
Tina Louise   191
Joanna Lumley   193
BarBara Luna   195
Deanna Lund   197

Table of Contents

Carol Lynley 200
Arlene Martel 203
Marlyn Mason 205
Lois Maxwell 208
Diane McBain 210
Marisa Mell 213
Donna Michelle 216
Mary Ann Mobley 218
Terry Moore 221
Rosalba Neri 223
Rosemary Nicols 227
France Nuyen 228
Eileen O'Neill 232
Luciana Paluzzi 236
Trina Parks 240
Joanna Pettet 242
Nyree Dawn Porter 245
Stefanie Powers 247
Dorothy Provine 250
Eva Renzi 252
Janine Reynaud 253
Diana Rigg 256
Salli Sachse 260
Jill St. John 261
Tura Satana 264
Jane Seymour 267
Nancy Sinatra 270
Sylvia Solar 272
Elke Sommer 274
Stella Stevens 278
Yoko Tani 282
Sharon Tate 285
Linda Thorson 287
Maggie Thrett 289
Marilu Tolo 291
Irene Tsu 293
Sigrid Valdis 296
Monica Vitti 298
Ira von Furstenberg 300
Lesley Ann Warren 301
Raquel Welch 304
Lana Wood 308
Celeste Yarnall 311
Francine York 314

Bibliography 319
Index 323

Foreword
by Eileen O'Neill

While movie theaters around the world were introducing Sean Connery as the omnipotent and debonair agent 007 in Ian Fleming's tome to film *Dr. No*, audiences were unanimously gasping, "Yes ... Yes ... YES!"

Harry Saltzman and Albert "Cubby" Broccoli, the film's producers, had successfully packaged the elements of danger, intrigue and that very salable commodity ... sex. James Bond certainly exuded it, as did the shapely and tantalizing "Bond" girls and the myriad of clones that followed. While Bond and his spy cohorts secretly copied enemy documents, we copied anything remotely Bond and/or secret agent. The influences of espionage also infiltrated the ancillary areas of fashion, cars, gadgets ... the list goes on. Nothing and no one could escape.

Living and working through the public birth of the heretofore "secrets" of international spydom and the blatant unveiling of sex captured as casually as ships passing in the night was eye opening to say the least. However, it is only now, in retrospect, that we can focus more clearly on the major impact of the spy genre. We were a far cry from *The Donna Reed Show* and *Leave It to Beaver*. Innocence was out ... worldliness was in.

As an actress performing during those days, I can't begin to tell you of the number of calls I received from my representatives at the William Morris talent agency saying, "Eileen, we just submitted you for a part in such and such ... it's a take-off on the James Bond films." This mantra applied to movies, television series, TV commercials and even to performances at celebrity-laced charity fund raisers.

One of the films was *A Man Called Dagger*, for which Steve Allen composed the musical score. Richard Kiel, one of the actors who appeared in this movie, also played the character "Jaws" whom we grew to know as the seven foot giant with razor sharp metal teeth in a number of Bond films. Recently, Richard and I were appearing at a celebrity autograph signing and we had great fun reminiscing about our performances in *Dagger*.

Many producers of television series created espionage episodes to keep up with the trend. Some of the ones in which I appeared include *Get Smart*, *The Beverly Hill-*

Trade ad promoting Eileen O'Neill's appearance on *Amos Burke, Secret Agent*. (*Courtesy of Eileen O'Neill*)

billies, *My Favorite Martian* and *The Double Life of Henry Phyfe*, where Red Buttons and I worked diligently on blowing up a safe while I pleaded for "one last kiss to remember my moment of greatness."

There was even a Max Factor television commercial where I was clad in a trench coat and drove an Aston Martin sports car just like James Bond's. After a hectic "good gal–bad guy" chase, the commercial concluded with me zooming down the driveway of a magnificent mansion in Pasadena, thus escaping the villain trying to capture the secret ingredients of my Max Factor 005 make-up.

Also, at that time I was on the Board of Directors of the Thalians, a charity for emotionally disturbed children, with our clinic adjacent to Cedars-Sinai Medical Center in Los Angeles. Debbie Reynolds was then—and still remains—the head of our organization, and many of the members, including Jack Haley, Jr. and Hugh O'Brian, were also in show business. The charity was formed as a way of "giving back" the many benefits we received as performers.

Each year we honored a celebrity with a formal star-studded fund raising gala. We also presented the honoree with our "Thalia" award, which Mr. Walt Disney designed for our exclusive use. Alex Romero, who choreographed many of Gene Kelly's wonderful dance sequences in MGM musicals, created our spy-oriented opening number. I can remember slinking onto the darkened stage to the now familiar James Bond theme while rhythmically shining flashlights over the audience's heads. As the stage lights brightened, it revealed our costumes of black trench coats. Our collars were seductively caressing our necks and the brims of our hats were tilted downward to conceal a portion of our faces. Naturally, we were wearing long black gloves. We danced and sang specially written "spy" lyrics. The audience showed great enthusiasm when we opened our trench coats to reveal tight sexy costumes and stiletto-heeled shoes. The evening was a success. The audience got what they wanted. They had their spy fix.

As we all know by now, the espionage epidemic swept not only the United States, but the entire world. It was the motivation behind producer Aaron Spelling and the American Broadcasting Company changing the format of the television series *Burke's Law*, in which I appeared as Sergeant Gloria Ames, with Gene Barry starring as Captain Amos Burke. The series was revamped from the limited arena of Los Angeles detectivedom and then retitled *Amos Burke, Secret Agent* so that the story lines could encompass worldwide situations and locations ... so that the art of creative deception could conquer the enemy who threatened world peace sans the battlefield of traditional war.

Through the use of encripted codes, electronic eavesdropping, covert operations, clandestine meetings and last, but not least, romantic interludes in exotic locations, the cold war remained just that ... cold! And although in the real world of espionage an agent as flamboyant as James Bond would have gotten caught and would have been permanently obliterated, we didn't seem to care that Hollywood altered that probability. As Agent John Q. Public, we could satisfy our most intimate voyeuristic desires from the safe obscurity of movie seats or our living room sofas.

Today the magic prevails, due to Tom Lisanti and Louis Paul, the secret agents of investigative research who spied into the fact files of that wonderful era. Thanks to these talented authors, you can share the experiences of those of us who were lucky enough to have lived and worked in the entertainment industry during those creative and intriguing years.

In our hearts, that wonderful *Dr. No* movie that started it all will forever remain "*Dr. Yes*."

As a point of coincidence, Eon (my very initials) Productions Ltd. created the Bond movies.

Preface

Our book is not all-inclusive in regards to the actresses profiled, and we don't pretend that it is. To include every actress that worked in a spy film and TV show from 1962 to 1973 would have made this tome far too voluminous. We decided to include a sampling of a vast array of American and foreign actresses who toiled in this very popular genre by limiting it to the "starlets" of the day. Due to space constraints, many European, Mexican, Indian and other international actresses could not be included. A vast number of actresses appeared on American TV spy shows, but, unfortunately, we did not have room for them all. We apologize to the fans of the actresses who were not included. Actresses' birth dates are included only if verified. We hope you enjoy our homage to 107 of the most beautiful women ever to bed James Bond, threaten Derek Flint, share a drink with Matt Helm, kiss OSS 117, or abet Diabolik.

Introduction

Spies—Fact and Fiction

Alluring, beautiful, dangerous, deadly, seductive, voluptuous—all these words and more describe the characters portrayed by the actresses profiled in this book. But to understand the sixties spy film genre, a little history lesson should be in order.

Fact: The Spy in History

Much of the image of the spy that the public imagines is one created by fiction and the cinema. More often than not, much of the world perceives the spy as a secret agent who valiantly penetrates the security forces of the enemy (whoever he, she or they are) and is single-handedly (or nearly) responsible for saving the world from potential mass destruction.

Of course, this is the spy as created by a host of writers, including Ian Fleming, John Le Carré and others, and bolstered by numerous cinematic interpretations of the writings of these authors and imitations of the same. In reality, the spy is neither a lawbreaker nor a common criminal. Working on the assumption that what they are doing is moral, sensible and of high national importance, these are people with unswerving, if sometimes misguided, loyalties. In reality, as opposed to the colorful exploits of a fictional spy, much real-life intelligence work is a slow, painstaking and often tedious affair.

The art of espionage is as ancient as human society itself. In the Bible, in the Book of Joshua, when the Israelites were about to conquer Palestine, their leaders sent out agents with orders to gain information about that country. During the Middle Ages and the Renaissance, intelligence gathering was interwoven with the ideas of diplomacy. By the time of the Royal Court of England and Queen Elizabeth I, spying was well on its way to becoming an international practice in obtaining information for political gain or national security. The same thing happened during much of the Revolutionary War.

In all the ancient and modern wars, espionage and information gathering, through the use of illicit and illegal means, played a major role, making its greatest strides during World War I, when intelligence gathering came into the "New Age." Before the U.S. entered this war, the American people exhibited a strong anti-war sentiment. However, after the Germans sank a number of U.S. ships, the U.S. quickly exhibited an overwhelming patriotic fervor, which quickly turned into a bit of wartime hysteria, aiding the operations of U.S. espionage agents in America to ferret out enemy agents in the U.S. and in Great Britain.

By World War II this practice became just one of many government undertakings, and often it was a joint-country assignment. It was not unheard of to have two countries joining forces, and sharing information and intelligence agents, working towards a common goal of gathering information that could lead possibly either to a better military defense for both countries or, better still, an early end to the war. During WWII, there were major technological advancements in the field of spying.

After World War II much of the globe's map was redrawn. With several Eastern European nations becoming Soviet satellites, travel between the west and the east made spying relatively easy for some. Espionage became a major undertaking for many nations during the Cold War, which lasted (depending on the interpretation of the events) from 1946 through 1990. Essentially, the world was drawn in half. The line divided what was known as the two superpowers, the Soviet Union and the United States, each with its own allies. However, with the dangerous economic stress of the late 1980s, Communism collapsed in Eastern Europe, and sometime in 1991 even the Soviet Union was being divided into territories.

A Brief History of International Spy Networks

Each country from World War II onwards created their own intelligence operations to combat their enemies. While many of these units were chiefly created for wartime use only, many of them still operate and exist to this day.

FRANCE: The Deuxieme Bureau, or French Intelligence for the High Command, was created in 1878. Its chief goal is to provide intelligence involving the fields of crime and espionage, and, in times of war (through its Special Services branch), work in counterespionage. As well, the French have the SDECE (Service de Documentation Extérieure et de Contre-Espionnage), or Department for Foreign Information and Counterespionage, which works much like the American CIA.

GREAT BRITAIN: MI5 (Military Intelligence, Department 5) was established in 1909. It is responsible for national security and operates much like the U.S. FBI. Unlike the FBI, MI5 handles no domestic criminal cases and has no authority to make arrests in international cases. In these cases, all arrests ordered by MI5 are arranged by Scotland Yard's Special Branch, which also presents all national evidence in court on behalf of MI5. MI6 (Military Intelligence, Department 6) evolved from the early British Secret Intelligence Service (SIS) in 1911. Its original director was known by the letter "C" rather than his last name. MI6 is most comparable to the American CIA, and gathers intelligence on a worldwide basis, conducting information gathering on all enemies and potential enemies of the crown. Special Branch is a Counterespionage Division of Scotland Yard, originated in 1883. Created to counter terrorism, one if its prime goals is to protect foreign dignitaries, and it often works with MI5.

THE SOVIET UNION: The KGB (Komitet Gosudarstvennoy Bezopasnosti), or The Committee of State Security, was actually established in 1917 in the Cheka (the Soviet Secret Police). But by 1954, as a direct result of the end of WWII and the beginning of the Cold War, the KGB became the official threat to the collective spy agencies of the world. The KGB combined the functions of foreign intelligence gathering, counterintelligence and domestic security. The GRU, or Central Intelligence Office, was another, better-funded organization which operated concurrently with the KGB, but its chief goal was the theft of industrial, technological, and scientific secrets from other countries. SMERSH (Soviet Assassination Division of the KGB) was a division of Soviet intelligence (in fact, the Ninth Division of the KGB, dedicated to Terror and Diversion) that was responsible for seeking out, blackmailing, kidnapping, and/or killing anyone who opposed the Communist regime, especially defecting Russians or Russians opposing Soviet ideals. Non-Russians as well were selected by SMERSH for assassinations, causing the agency to coin the phrase "Smert Shpionam," which literally means "Death to Spies!" British author Ian Fleming made SMERSH very popular in some of his James Bond adventures, where these agents proved to be deadly foils of the superspy.

THE UNITED STATES: The OSS (Office of Strategic Services) was created in 1942 because, prior to World War II, America actually had no official overall intelligence system beyond that operated by the FBI or the military. Until its reported demise in 1945, this agency was responsible for espionage and sabotage in countries occupied by the Germans, Italians, and Japanese. The CIA (Central Intelligence Agency) is the best known of the U.S. information gathering units. Created in 1947 under the National Security Act, it was originally assigned to operate and perform three basic tasks: Foreign intelligence gathering and evaluation, overseas counterintelligence operations, and secret political operations and psychological warfare in enemy countries. The NSA (National Security Agency), or Central Security Agency, is the largest of all the American intelligence organizations.

The FBI (Federal Bureau of Investigation) is a law enforcement and counterintelligence agency, chiefly made up of investigators, forensic experts, accountants, clerks, and other support personnel. Created in 1908, the agency has had many missions, but was very active during the two World Wars. J. Edgar Hoover, the director of the agency who was appointed in 1924, ran the organization until his death in 1972. In recent years the FBI has again been involved in counterintelligence.

Mata Hari

As hard as it is to believe nowadays, espionage has been with us for a very long time. As well, there have been a number of names bandied about, like Rudolf Abel, who headed a Soviet espionage network in the U.S.; Kim Philby, an infamous British double agent for the Russians; and Richard Sorge, a German national who spied for the Soviets while assigned to embassies in China and Japan. But perhaps one of the most famous spies in history was a woman named Mata Hari. She was, undoubtedly, the most celebrated female spy in history, and, questionably, the most well known secret agent of all time. Born Margaretha Gertrude Zelle in 1876, the Dutch girl was betrothed to a wealthy Naval man at a young age. A public scandal that paraded the couple's bizarre sexual practices before the country ended the marriage, and the bitter divorce that followed saw Margaretha struggling to make ends meet financially.

By 1903 she began using the Indian dances that she had studied in elaborately staged live shows that stunned Parisian nightlife. However, despite the strange appearance of her Eastern costumes and dance routines, no one seemed interested in hiring her as a major attraction. Margaretha found herself reduced to stripping off her clothes in seedy clubs. Within a year she had become a prostitute, and within a year afterwards was rumored to have moved to a sleazy bordello, servicing ten to twenty military men a day in order to make ends meet.

Returning to Holland, she begged many friends for cash. Amassing a substantial amount, she returned to Paris and, under the name Mata Hari, booked herself into the most expensive hotels and ate at the finest restaurants. Mata Hari made a stunning debut as a dancer in 1905 (where two years before she was begging for club owners to let her perform) and quickly became the darling of Parisian haute couture. Everywhere she went she was mobbed by wealthy men of all ages begging to experience Mata in the bedroom. One time the crowds became so violent that a riot ensued at the famed Casino de Paris. In just a few short years the young woman had gone from an innocent, to an experienced woman, to a downtrodden prostitute, to a sexual superstar.

As Mata Hari's interpretative dances became more praised, winning accolades from critics as well as her male admirers, so did her bedroom antics. It has been alleged that she made love to many different men from different countries in attempts to pry state, political and military secrets from them in the bedroom. Given citizenship by Germany, Mata Hari became a spy for that country.

By 1917, after years of infamous sexual escapades, Mata Hari was no longer in demand with males seeking sexual gratification. She was arrested in France as a spy and charged as being the deadly and seductive German agent H.21, who led many men to their end via their secrets whispered in the darkened bedroom. She was executed by a French firing squad, ending her decorous career as a secret agent.

Many of the women who appeared as venomous vixens and sultry spies in a number of the films and television shows discussed in this book owe a debt of historical gratitude to Mata Hari, for she certainly was one of the most prominent innovators (if not *the* most) of female spydom.

Another true-life spy in history was Ian Fleming, but the exploits of the popular fiction author did not come to light until many years after his death.

Fiction: Literary Espionage Precedents

Spy vs. Spy: The Espionage Novel vs. The Spy Thriller

Not everyone loves a good, exciting, violent read like an Ian Fleming novel. To some, the most serious and respected espionage novels seem to be the ones with very little action, fancied or otherwise. In the espionage novel, spies are supposed to keep their secrets, not tell them. The protagonist is morally ambiguous, and nearly everything is done in a formal and procedural manner. The life of a spy, as told in the books of Ambler, Le Carré and others, is one of a certain sense of loss, where the agent is solely responsible for the completion of an assignment, however mundane, and often has to deal with shady individuals with their own codes of honor, i.e. people interested in self preservation rather than the actual historical, moral and political motivations that beget spying.

One of the first espionage novels was *The Secret Agent* (1907) by Joseph Conrad. Actually a slow-moving tale about policemen, informants, and acts of political terrorism, this could be called an early and more historically accurate spy book. Thirty-one years later, Eric Ambler's *Epitaph for a Spy* (1938) told an unromantic tale of an agent assigned to track a suspected foreign element in his own country. Graham Greene's *Our Man in Havana* (1958) features an ordinary man who, through circumstances beyond his control, becomes a spy and a scapegoat for a political mess. By the time of author Len Deighton's 1962 novel *The Ipcress File*, an introduction to his Harry Palmer character, espionage and the Cold War was no longer a game played by stuffy shirts and men locked behind closed doors, sitting at tables piled high with secret papers. Instead, ordinary men were doing inordinate deeds, like risking one's life against one's own personal principles. When John Le Carré introduced the character of George Smiley to the public, most notably in *The Spy Who Came in from the Cold* (1963), he also one-upped Deighton by becoming infatuated with the bureaucratic intricacies of the spy game and the disillusionment with assignments, involving defections and mole hunts (the weeding out of traitors within one's own department).

The spy thriller, on the other hand, is usually graced with action, some of it fantastic or futuristic. The hero is often chauvinistic, sometimes morally bankrupt and, more often than not, totally oblivious to the harm caused to anyone in the completion of his mission.

Ian Fleming's James Bond character was much more than the real-life espionage agent that Fleming himself seems to have been (at least according to his biographers), for sitting behind a pile of papers stacked high on a desk filled with numerous refilled cups of coffee was not for this literary creation. Instead, Bond was a globe-trotting hero, a virile he-man who was known as 007, an identification number in the double-O section that mandated his license to kill, and who was seemingly ageless and had a nearly supernatural way of attracting women and loving them. Bond was a two-fisted agent who often disobeyed orders to get the assignment at hand completed, even if it meant numerous deaths along the way. During missions, he loved many women, and usually left them (or at least it seemed so, for they were absent from the next sequential novel in Fleming's writings) sated and rarely disappointed. Bond had an unusual preponderance for getting himself stuck in difficult situations, and often he nearly met his end at the hands of a veritable rogue's gallery of sadistic villains. In fact, in the first novel, *Casino Royale*, he was nearly emasculated for life due to the tortures inflicted upon him by the murderous Le Chiffre.

Ian Fleming: The Man Who Created James Bond

Although Ian Fleming (born 1908) was a British agent, he never really experienced the same type of life as his imaginary creation, James Bond. Fleming worked for the *London Times* and was sent to Russia as its correspondent during a politically sensitive trial involving espionage. In 1939 he joined British Naval Intelligence and served with that military espionage unit for several years. While stationed in Washington, D.C., Fleming became an operative for the SIS, another British Intelligence outfit, and he (otherwise known as Agent 17F) worked with many American espionage units and was reportedly instrumental in the forming of the American CIA. As an operative of Naval Intelligence, Fleming headed a special Royal Marines unit whose special mission was to decode enemy messages. After the war Ian Fleming returned to journalism and began writing and publishing the adventures of British secret agent James Bond in 1953. Although Fleming died in 1964, he managed to churn out 14 novels in 13 years, beginning with *Casino Royale*. He lived to see his James Bond character "fleshed-out" on the screen by virile Scottish actor Sean Connery, and was involved somewhat with the creation of the American *Man from U.N.C.L.E.* television series. The James Bond novels of Ian Fleming are examples of pulp writing at its best, with each book containing its own little world full of vile villains, sultry and deadly ciphers, and lovely and decorative innocents.

The James Bond novels at a glance:

Casino Royale (1953): Real-life Soviet assassination bureau SMERSH were the villains; Le Chiffre was the main antagonist and Vesper Lynde the seductive woman whom Bond loves.

Live and Let Die (1954): SMERSH returns, alongside Mr. Big, a New York–based gangster whom Bond tangles with when he briefly romances the innocent Solitaire.

Moonraker (1955): Bond battles Hugo Draxx, a flamboyant millionaire intent on destroying a key city with a nuclear holocaust. Gala Brand is Bond's seductive ally.

Diamonds Are Forever (1956): Bond tangles with the American syndicate and encounters jewel smuggling in this weak entry.

From Russia, with Love (1957): The best Bond book (and the best Bond movie) sees the secret agent (a.k.a. 007, so named for his Secret Service assignation as possessing a license to kill) doing battle with SMERSH again, facing off against devilish assassin Red Grant, and bedding the lovely Tatiana Romanova in a labyrinthine plot to assassinate the British agent because of all the trouble he has given SMERSH in the past.

Dr. No (1958): Bond tangles with Dr. Julius No, a sadistic 'free agent' with loyalties to no one, and manages to briefly become seduced by the lovely Honeychile Ryder, a woman with more vengeance in her heart than love.

Goldfinger (1959): Bond faces SMERSH operative Auric Goldfinger, the Masterson sisters and, eventually, the incredibly named Pussy Galore in a plot that sees the Russian freelancer (Goldfinger) seeking to seize the gold reserves of Ft. Knox.

For Your Eyes Only (1960): Bond appears in five tales—in "From a View to a Kill" he tackles vicious assassins sent by SHAPE (another Russian assassination outfit); in "For Your Eyes Only" he reluctantly assists a woman in her revenge plot; in "Quantum of Solace" he spends time reminiscing; in "Risico" he battles Kristatos, a villain in league with the Russians and involved in drug smuggling; and in "The Hildebrand Rarity" he battles a sadistic wife beater who may or may not have met his demise at the hand of the vacationing British agent.

Thunderball (1961): When Fleming and friends Jack Whittingham and Kevin McClory sat down to write a screenplay, they inadvertently created a deadlier threat than SMERSH, the purely fictional but much more dastardly SPECTRE. Fleming turned the ideas from this screenplay into a novel where chief villain Ernst Stavro Blofeld, the head of SPECTRE, turns his organization (made up of former members of SMERSH and other unsavory outfits) into a global killing machine bent on blackmailing much of Western civilization with a nuclear threat.

The Spy Who Loved Me (1962): Fleming (and Bond) at his most romantic, as seen from the view of a woman, a change of pace for the author.

On Her Majesty's Secret Service (1963): Fleming blows the lid off the Bond canon by having the character fall in love, marry and witness the death of his beloved, setting up a mano-a-mano death match with SPECTRE's Blofeld in a book to come.

You Only Live Twice (1964): Bond hunts down Blofeld (hiding under the pseudonym Shatterhand) and finally avenges the death of his wife.

The Man with the Golden Gun (1965): An

unfinished Fleming story about an ace assassin (with the comical name Pistols Scaramanga) sets the tone for the end of the literary series from Fleming.

Octopussy (1966): Also contains the short stories "The Living Daylights" and "The Property of a Lady," which were essentially all morality plays seemingly written by Fleming to make up for much of his hero's sadistic traits.

Since Fleming's death, other writers have dabbled in the Bond canon, some with varying degrees of success. Kingsley Amis (writing as Robert Markham) wrote *Colonel Sun* in 1968, which, true to Fleming's own style, upped the ante considerably as far as the violence was concerned and brought the character up to date with Red China's emergence as a significant foe.

In 1980 the Ian Fleming estate hired author John Gardner to continue the Bond stories, and he wrote a number of them, which also involved adding significant changes to the canon for the end of the millennium. *Licence Renewed* (1981) found the super agent battling a ruthless megalomaniac (as in the Roger Moore films of the seventies) hell-bent on mass destruction via a nuclear disaster. *For Special Services* (1982) saw Bond meeting his newest enemy, a revived SPECTRE, headed by Nena Blofeld, the diabolical daughter of his old arch rival. In *Icebreaker* (1983) the new Bond tackles the Neo Nazi movement and the NSAA (National Socialist Action Army). *Role of Honor* (1984) saw Bond fighting a New World Order and the remnants of SPECTRE. *Nobody Lives Forever* (1986) introduced a moribund action hero, at odds with the rough and tumble character of the past. In *No Deals, Mr. Bond* (1987) readers cringed at the re-emergence of SMERSH. In *Scorpius* (1987) a sinister comic book villain plots to rule the world via his 'brainwashed' religious followers. Gardner continued to churn out Bond books on a regular basis and, as he did so, the character evolved. Much of the brutal sarcasm of the Timothy Dalton film portrayals, and, later, shades of Pierce Brosnan's more urbane yet sadistic hired killer began to creep into the Gardner books, which, by the time of the publication of *Cold*, seemed to have become as influenced by the current film series as the original Fleming books. Other James Bond novels by Gardner include *Licence to Kill* (1989) [novelization of film script], *Win, Lose or Die* (1989), *Brokenclaw* (1990), *The Man from Barbarossa* (1991), *Death Is Forever* (1992), *Never Send Flowers* (1993), *SeaFire* (1994), *Goldeneye* (1995) [novelization of film script] and *Cold* (1996; a.k.a. *Cold Fall*).

Author Raymond Benson continued the James Bond chronicles in 1996 with a short story that appeared in the January 1997 issue of *Playboy* magazine. Titled *Blast from the Past*, the Bond author decided to bridge the Fleming and Gardner tomes by reviving the character of Irma Bunt (from *You Only Live Twice*), as well as introducing Bond's son (with Kissy Suzuki), who meets a sad demise. Benson's plots and characters (much like the later Gardner novels) stayed true to the current film series, even introducing the female M, the chief of the Secret Service division who gives Bond his assignments, who reads much like the character as portrayed by actress Judi Dench in the Pierce Brosnan Bond films.

Other Benson stories featuring James Bond include: *Zero Minus Ten* (1997), *Tomorrow Never Dies* (1997) [novelization of film script], *The Facts of Death* (1998), *Midsummer Nights Death* (1999) [*Playboy* magazine short story—January 1999], *High Time to Kill* (1999), *The World Is Not Enough* (1999) [novelization of film script], *Live at Five* (1999) [*TV Guide* short story—November 1999] and *Doubleshot* (2000).

Besides Ian Fleming, Len Deighton and Le Carré, other writers of note (although much less celebrated) who have had their works turned into cinematic interpretations of their words are Jean Bruce, Peter O'Donnell and Donald Hamilton. Bruce, a Frenchman who was born in 1921, authored 91 novels about the character Hubert Bonisseur de La Bath, an urbane, dandified French secret agent otherwise known by his code name: OSS 117. Bruce began writing the OSS 117 books in 1949, and his last was published in 1963. Josette Bruce continued the OSS 117 saga and wrote 142 stories, beginning in 1966. In 1987 Francoise and Martine Bruce continued the espionage hero's adventures, publishing stories until 1992. There have been at least seven films based on this character, some of them even garnering theatrical and/or television showings in the U.S.

Peter O'Donnell wrote a number of novels about Modesty Blaise, a female James Bond, with exciting plots and witty dialog. Of his dozen books penned about her, the first (*Modesty Blaise*) was turned into a film (and an unsuccessful television pilot in the seventies) of the same name.

Finally, Donald Hamilton penned a series of hard-boiled noirish thrillers about super spy Matt Helm. The brutal, sexy novels (which numbered 27) managed to gain a considerable following in readership, beginning with *Death of a Citizen* in 1960, and continued with *The Damagers* in 1993, his last published novel. Donald Hamilton died in his sleep on November 20, 2006. Unfortunately, the film version of the cold, ruthless killer agent became pop art extravaganzas fueled by nudge-nudge, wink-wink performances by actor-singer Dean Martin in the leading role. Although campy in style, the Dean Martin-Matt Helm movies managed to entertain audiences and are arguably some of the more successful Bond rip-offs of the sixties.

The Women, the Films, the TV Shows, 1962–1973

The Women

Without the women to allure, entice, seduce and sometimes destroy our heroes, where would the entertainment value be? A wide array of actresses graced many a spy film and television show during the sixties secret agent craze, which lasted approximately from 1962 through 1973. From international sex goddesses such as Ursula Andress, Elke Sommer and Senta Berger to long-forgotten American actresses Shelby Grant, Maggie Thrett and Thordis Brandt; from superstars Doris Day, Raquel Welch, Ann-Margret and Diana Rigg to European starlets Erika Blanc, Marisa Mell, Margaret Lee and Yoko Tani; for the most part women in the spy genre were used as mere window dressing. Bedecked in some of the most outrageously mod fashions and hairstyles of the sixties, it was hard to keep your eyes off them no matter how absurd the plot.

During this period the acting roles available for the women in spy films were limited to essentially four major types of characters:

1. *The helpful spy/secret agent/operative*—This character supports the hero. She is resourceful, helpful and independent, is good with a gun or karate chop, and (sometimes) carries a secret torch for the hero. Examples include France Nuyen in *Dimension 5* (1966), Dorothy Provine in *Kiss the Girls and Make Them Die* (1966), Joanna Pettet in *Casino Royale* (1967), Terry Moore in *A Man Called Dagger* (1967), Marisa Mell in *Diabolik* (1968) and Sharon Tate in *The Wrecking Crew* (1969). She usually aids or comes to the rescue of our hero, and sometimes pays for it with her life, i.e. Martine Beswicke in *Thunderball* (1965), Mimi Dillard

in *A Man Called Dagger* (1965) and Barbara Bouchet in *Danger Route* (1968). In a few films, most notably *Modesty Blaise* (1967) with Monica Vitti, *Caprice* (1967) with Doris Day, *Come Spy with Me* (1967) with Andrea Dromm and *The Doll Squad* (1973) with Francine York, the female agent/operative is the focus of the attention, and the male character is the support.

2. *The innocent*—This character is usually a civilian who inadvertently stumbles into the action, is mistaken for a spy, has secret information the enemy is after, or has revenge on her mind. She has no espionage background, so her crying, screaming and/or meddling becomes more of a burden and hindrance to our hero than help. She usually needs rescuing from the villains at least two times before the film's end. By fade out, this character usually has redeemed herself by aiding the super sleuth, which usually means that they will tumble into bed. Examples include Ursula Andress in *Dr. No* (1962), Margaret Lee in *Fury in Istanbul* (1965), Claudine Auger in *Thunderball* (1965), Stella Stevens in *The Silencers* (1966), Ann-Margret in *Murderer's Row* (1966) and Eileen O'Neill in *A Man Called Dagger* (1967). Sometimes, but very rarely, she meets a bad end: Tania Mallett in *Goldfinger* (1964), Karin Dor in *Target for a Killing* (1966), Diana Rigg in *On Her Majesty's Secret Service* (1969) and Lana Wood in *Diamonds Are Forever* (1971). In a rare, change-of-pace film, Raquel Welch's innocent skydiver used by good and evil agencies was the center of *Fathom* (1967).

3. *The bad-girl-turned-good*—When the

Pressbook art for *Dr. No* (United Artists, 1962).

film opens, this character is running the dirty tricks department. Her assignment is usually to kill our hero by any means possible. This is an indication to seduce the virile macho spy and assassinate him in bed. But one day of lovemaking turns them completely around as they join forces with the agent to combat the villains. Some of these deadly lovelies don't even make it into the boudoir but are redeemed with just a kiss, or two or five. Examples include Daniela Bianchi in *From Russia with Love* (1963), Honor Blackman in *Goldfinger* (1964), Gila Golan in *Our Man Flint* (1966), Senta Berger in *Bang! Bang! You're Dead!* (1966), Yoko Tani in *Desperate Mission* (1966), Jean Hale in *In Like Flint* (1967), Tina Louise in *The Wrecking Crew* (1969) and Jill St. John in *Diamonds Are Forever* (1971).

4. *The villainess/femme fatale/assassin*—This character has no redeeming qualities and is pure evil. She dispatches her victims easily and effortlessly without giving it a second thought. She can make life hell for our hero. Sometimes she is a double agent pretending to support him but waiting for the opportunity to pounce. Sometimes she is in the position to finish him off, but the intrigue of his manly sexuality gets the best of her and she gives in to her sexual longings. This character usually meets a grisly end at the hands of the villain she has rigorously helped or the hero. Examples include Luciana Paluzzi in *Thunderball* (1965), Daliah Lavi in *The Silencers* (1966), Elke Sommer in *Deadlier Than the Male* (1966), Erika Blanc in *The Spy Kills Silently* (1966), Rossella Falk in *Modesty Blaise* (1966), Karin Dor in *You Only Live Twice* (1967), Carol Lynley in *Danger Route* (1968), Nancy Kwan in *The Wrecking Crew* (1969), Beba Loncar in *Some Girls Do* (1969) and Gloria Hendry in *Live and Let Die* (1973).

The Films

The sixties spy craze unofficially kicked off when producers Harry Saltzman and Albert Broccoli (who purchased the rights to all but one of Ian Fleming's novels) released the first James Bond film, *Dr. No* (1962), starring Sean Connery as the suave agent 007. Though Connery dominated the first half of the movie with his dashing good looks, a whole new world of moviegoers sat open-mouthed when actress Ursula Andress (as Honey Ryder) arose from the ocean in a very skimpy white bikini and glided across the screen in vivid color. By using this attractive blonde newcomer and capitalizing upon her Amazonian figure, the producers of the film managed to stay fairly close to the character as described by Fleming. As far as appearances went, Andress set the mold for many of the spy girls to follow. For the next ten years a veritable potpourri of actresses would become stars (albeit fleetingly) by appearing in a James Bond film. Among the more memorable "Bond Girls" (as they were nicknamed) were Daniela Bianchi in *From Russia with Love* (1963), Honor Blackman and Shirley Eaton in *Goldfinger* (1964), Claudine Auger and Luciana Paluzzi in *Thunderball* (1965), Mie Hama in *You Only Live Twice* (1967), Diana Rigg in *On Her Majesty's Secret Service* (1969), Jill St. John and Lana Wood in *Diamonds Are Forever* (1971), and Jane Seymour and Gloria Hendry in *Live and Let Die* (1973). The only constant female in the James Bond series of films was Lois Maxwell as the loyal, devoted Miss Moneypenny, assistant to Bond's superior M, and who carried a torch for the secret agent.

Casino Royale was the James Bond novel "that got away." Charles Feldman produced the movie version in 1967, and when he couldn't get Sean Connery to star, he kept only the title and threw out the plot. Seven writers (including Terry

This pre-release "teaser" poster art for *On Her Majesty's Secret Service* (United Artists, 1969) keeps the identity of the new 007 (George Lazenby) a secret. (Courtesy of Michael Monahan)

Southern and Billy Wilder) had a hand in the screenplay, while five directors were responsible for different story arcs. Ursula Andress has the largest female role as James Bond, a.k.a. Vesper Lynd. Other gorgeous women to grace the film included Joanna Pettet, Daliah Lavi, Barbara Bouchet and newcomer Jacqueline Bisset. Though the film is convoluted it is highly amusing, and it is helped greatly by Burt Bacharach's light, upbeat score and the hit song "The Look of Love."

Concurrently, because of the worldwide box-office success of the James Bond films, European productions looking to jump on a financial cash cow and, hopefully, duplicate the success of the Bond series began production on their own similar and (in comparison to the lavish Bond films) lower budgeted productions. Soon such international spies as OSS 77, Agent Z55 and OSS 117 (played by various actors) were appearing in their own series of spy films throughout the world. Although these films drew in audiences abroad, very few of them received theatrical releases in the United States. Those that did usually faded quickly from theaters or were sold directly to U.S. television in syndication packages where they were shown quite often throughout the sixties, picking up many of their male admirers. The foreign spy films were dominated by a preponderance of bosomy, glamorous girls and heightened violence, and displayed a proclivity for using ridiculous gadgets in substitution for the larger budgets of the James Bond films, which many of these productions could not afford to approximate.

Some of the actors who appeared in the leading roles in these movies were either expatriate Americans (like Ken Clark, Lang Jeffries, Brett Halsey and Ray Danton) or European actors who found themselves cast for an uncanny likeness to Sean Connery (Spanish actor German Cobos in *Desperate Mission*, 1966)—or, in some cases, just a vague resemblance (as was the case with Italian actor Giorgio Ardisson in *Operation Counterspy*, 1965). Still other European film producers got on the bandwagon by casting Bond actresses in their own films, hence there is a considerable number of productions that featured these starlets and, in two cases, actors who were almost James Bond. Richard Johnson, who was nearly signed by Bond producers Broccoli and Saltzman for *Dr. No* (1962), starred in *Deadlier Than the Male* (1966), *Danger Route* (1968) and *Some Girls Do* (1969). John Gavin, who was originally signed to play James Bond in *Diamonds Are Forever* (1971)

Poster art for *Secret Agent Fireball* (AIP, 1965) starring Richard Harrison as OSS 77. (*Courtesy of Michael Monahan*)

but relinquished the role to allow Sean Connery to return to play Bond, had played a French super spy in *OSS 117 Murder for Sale* in 1968.

Some foreign-born actresses (such as Elke Sommer, Ursula Andress, Senta Berger, Sylva Koscina and Daliah Lavi) were recruited by Hollywood to grace American spy films. They traveled back and forth across the Atlantic, appearing in U.S. and continental films with equal felicity. When the roles began to dry up for them in American productions by the late sixties, it was back to Italy, France or Germany for international films of dubious merit.

For less-famous actresses remaining in Europe, gracing spy films were among the high points of their careers. These include Erika Blanc in *Operation Atlantis* (1965), Dominique Boschero in *Fury in Marrakesh* (1966), Helene Chanel in *Ring Around the World* (1966), Margaret Lee in *Secret Agent Super Dragon* (1965), Helga Line in *Mission Bloody Mary* (1965), Beba Loncar in *Some Girls Do* (1969), Rosalba Neri in *Upperseven: The Man to Kill* (1965), Janine Reynaud in *The Spy Who Came from the Sea* (1966), Sylvia Solar in *Danger: Death Ray* (1967), Yoko Tani in *Goldsnake "Killers' Company"* (1966), Marilu Tolo in *Espionage in Lisbon* (1965) and Ira Von Furstenberg in *Matchless* (1966).

With the popularity of the James Bond films reaching a fever pitch with *Thunderball* (1965) and *You Only Live Twice* (1967), American film producers began attempting theatrical spoofs of these films, spurred on by the success of their small screen counterparts, including *The Man from U.N.C.L.E.* and *The Saint*. Before Albert R. Broccoli teamed with Bond producing partner Harry Saltzman, he was in partnership with film producer Irving Allen, who did not find anything potentially profitable by making film versions of the Ian Fleming books. Years later Allen purchased the rights to author Donald Hamilton's Matt Helm character and cast actor-singer Dean Martin as Helm. The character in the films strayed far from author Hamilton's original penned creation, and the movies became little more than luxuriously budgeted spy spoof romps cast with a bevy of gorgeous and sexy American and European starlets (including Stella Stevens, Daliah Lavi, Nancy Kovack, Ann-Margret, Senta Berger, Sharon Tate, Elke Sommer, Nancy Kwan, Tina Louise and Beverly Adams as Lovey Kraveszit, Miss Moneypenny's amorous counterpart). The first movie in the series was *The Silencers* (1966), followed in quick succession by *Murderer's Row* (1966), *The Ambushers* (1967) and *The Wrecking Crew* (1969). The major difference between the women in the Helm movies, as compared to the Bond and later Flint films, was that the women, though portrayed in a comic book manner, were of stronger disposition and did not melt when kissed by the hero or immediately change their wicked ways.

Similarly, *Our Man Flint* (1966) and *In Like Flint* (1967), which starred James Coburn as Derek Flint, one of the planet's most intelligent men—a true bon vivant, a martial artist, and the best secret agent in the world—attempted to spoof the entire spy thriller genre. These films found critical favor and also were box office hits. Much of their success is due to Coburn's athleticism and natural charisma. However, the femme fatales (Gila Golan in *Our Man Flint* and Jean Hale in *In Like Flint*) start off determined (especially Golan as an assassin), but by the film's end they are rehabilitated due to the charming persuasiveness of the suave spy. The two films in the series found themselves occasionally attempting to be serious as well, although the treatment of women as Flint's own personal assistants (they manicure his nails, cut his hair, dress and cook for him, amongst other things) set women's rights back a number of decades.

Poster art for *Secret Agent: Super Dragon* (United Screen Arts, 1965). (Courtesy of Michael Monahan)

A Man Called Dagger (1967) was reminiscent of the low-budget European spy films being churned out almost monthly. Produced by Global Screen Associates, the film was originally supposed to be released by Cinema Distributors of America as *Why Spy?* in 1966, but when the deal fell through MGM picked up the distribution rights the following year. Briskly directed by Richard Rush, the movie features cinematography by Laszlo Kovacs and a music score by comedian Steve Allen. It was released to an

Dean Martin as boozing spy Matt Helm, with Duke Howard (Billy) and a scantily clad Ann-Margret (Suzie), in *Murderer's Row* (Columbia, 1966).

intrigued but ba∙ ed audience who may have thought the adult humor a bit much. Paul Mantee made a very sexy and macho super spy, and, as with the international spy films, *A Man Called Dagger* was peppered with some shapely lovelies, including Terry Moore as Dagger's partner, Sue Ane Langdon as the villain's paramour and Eileen O'Neill as the innocent caught up in nefarious doings.

In 1966, Monica Vitti starred as *Modesty Blaise*, a sexy secret agent who becomes involved in all kinds of intrigue and espionage when her nemesis Gabriel (Dirk Bogarde) and his psychopathic female sidekick (Rossella Falk) plan on creating a crisis in the Middle East. The following year, three spy films were released with an actress in the lead role. *Fathom* (1967) starred Raquel Welch as a beautiful skydiver tricked into retrieving the "Fire Dragon," which she thinks threatens U.S. security but is in fact a stolen piece of art. *Caprice* (1967) featured Doris Day as "the spy who came in from the cold cream" in a spoof on the cosmetics industry; and former model Andrea Dromm was agent Jill Parsons sent to the island of Jamaica to stop a madman from blowing up a U.S. carrier in *Come Spy with Me* (1967). None of these films were box office hits, so it took five years for another film to be released starring a woman as the lead agent, that being B-movie queen Francine York in Ted V. Mikels' *The Doll Squad* (1973).

As the sixties ended and the Bond series introduced a whole new leading man (*The Saint*'s Roger Moore), audiences and

James Coburn as suave, high-living agent Derek Flint is given a tour of Fabulous Face Spa by the bewitching Jean Hale (Lisa) in *In Like Flint* (20th Century–Fox, 1967).

viewers in the seventies found themselves much less interested in spydom. By this time, European film production had slowed dramatically due to the economies in a number of countries, and spy thrillers were no longer in vogue. In fact, they had stopped being so by the late sixties when they were supplanted by a resurgence of interest in the western and then the thriller film format.

As for the James Bond film series, Roger Moore continued in the role (after *Live and Let Die* in 1973) for 12 years (and seven films), to be replaced by Timothy Dalton in *The Living Daylights* (1987) and *Licence to Kill* (1989). Pierce Brosnan began to portray the character with *Goldeneye* (1995) and *Tomorrow Never Dies* (1997) through *Die Another Day* (2002). As for the women in the Bond films, changing mores and societal pressures deemed that they be treated more as equals and less as window dressing and sexual playthings. However, Denise Richards' nuclear weapons expert, Dr. Christmas Jones, in *The World Is Not Enough* (1999) was a giant leap back to the worst the sixties had to offer in terms of women's bimbo roles.

The TV Shows

But all the action, glamorous and otherwise, wasn't only on the big screen. Spydom came to television with a big bang when TV producers decided that the popularity of the Bond films and the rip-offs

Poster art for *Fathom* (20th Century–Fox, 1967), starring Raquel Welch, Tony Franciosa and Greta Chi.

warranted action on the small screen. The starlets who graced spydom's TV landscape series found themselves playing the same type of characters that their big screen counterparts played. Innocents, helpful agents and femme fatales dominated all small screen spy shows. Whereas some foreign actresses worked in both U.S. and European spy films, American gals were not a wanted commodity in Euro-spy flicks. So for the less-famous ones, TV offered them the roles that their B-movie counterparts were playing on the big screens throughout Europe. Sharon Farrell, Sharyn Hillyer, BarBara Luna, Arlene Martel, Marlyn Mason, Mary Ann Mobley and Celeste Yarnall were just some of the many actresses who guest starred on a myriad of TV spy shows but never made it to the big screen in an espionage adventure.

When Honor Blackman donned the tight-fitting black leather gear for *The Avengers* in 1962, she created quite a stir in England. When her replacement, Diana Rigg, did the same thing and then shifted to a mod style of clothing, karate chopping, heroic females became the *in thing* for adolescent males. Although the very first incarnation of *The Avengers* actually preceded the first of the James Bond films, by the time that *Dr. No* was in production, Blackman had already joined the series as Cathy Gale, a woman that did not often need assistance from her partner John Steed (Patrick Macnee), the urbane male member of the team who occasionally dabbled in fisticuffs with the series' villains. During this time *The Saint*, starring Roger Moore as Simon Templar, a sophisticated adventurer with an urge to rescue those in need of help, also premiered. Among the damsels in distress were such British starlets as Honor Blackman, Shirley Eaton, Eunice Gayson and Sue Lloyd. Both shows were relatively popular. But with the advent of the 1965-1966 seasons for each, they really took off—the adventures became grander, the episodes were filmed in color and the female guest stars were sexier.

The Man from U.N.C.L.E., which was, coincidentally enough, originally conceived by Bond creator Ian Fleming as *Solo*, a show about ace agent Napoleon Solo, who worked for a United Nations law enforcement unit, became one of the biggest hits on television during the 1964-65 season. The series really found its footing during the latter half of that season and the beginning of the next. Audiences were glued to their sets as the show safely stylized their fantasies (gorgeous women) and fears (THRUSH, a Cold War–like conglomerate of enemy agents). U.N.C.L.E.'s top agents were Solo (Robert Vaughn) and Illya Kuryakin (David McCallum), who both took orders from the fastidious bureau chief Mr. Waverly (Leo G. Carroll, who followed actor Will Kuluva as Mr. Allison in the pilot). Influenced by the wonderful technological space age gadgets on display in the Bond films, *The Man from U.N.C.L.E.* was a true delight for young viewers, especially men—as a number of sexy starlets, including Senta Berger, Yvonne Craig, Danielle De Metz, France Nuyen, Luciana Paluzzi, Diane McBain and Anna Capri, could be seen on the program. The show was so popular that a number of two-part episodes were re-edited, padded with new footage or outtakes, and rushed into theaters. During the show's first two years on the air, fans could see their favorite U.N.C.L.E. stars on the big screen in *To Trap a Spy* (1965), *The Spy with My Face* (1965), *One Spy Too Many* (1966) and *One of Our Spies Is Missing* (1966). Unfortunately, as the series began to become more of a spoof than a dramatic show by season three, the quality of the program suffered.

The Man from U.N.C.L.E. was such a hit after its first season that imitations soon followed (imitation is the sincerest form of flattery). The producers of the detective series *Burke's Law* jettisoned the series'

The Man from U.N.C.L.E. starred David McCallum (center) and Robert Vaughn (right) as U.N.C.L.E. agents Illya Kuryakin and Napoleon Solo, here pictured with guest star Carol Lynley (Annie) in the two-part episode "The Prince of Darkness Affair" (MGM-TV, 1967), which was released theatrically overseas as *The Helicopter Spies* in 1968.

supporting cast (Eileen O'Neill) so star Gene Barry could go from being the debonair head of homicide for Los Angeles to a debonair international agent in *Amos Burke, Secret Agent*. The change made the scope of the series broader, expanding Burke's base of operation from Los Angeles to worldwide locations. However, the revised format did not find an audience up against the more hip new espionage series *I Spy*. This light-hearted spy adventure featured two specific agents, played by Robert Culp and Bill Cosby as a playboy and athletic star, respectively, who journey around the world, undercover, to ferret out enemy agents. Cosby became the first black actor to co-star in a major network series and the first actor to win three consecutive Emmy Awards for his performance. His presence also allowed a number of black actresses (i.e. Cicely Tyson, Diana Sands, Leslie Uggams, Barbara McNair, Janet MacLachlan and Gloria Foster) entry into spydom, where for the most part they were shunned by other spy shows of the period.

But saving the world was not a job just for the men. *Honey West* premiered in the fall of 1965 and lasted only one season. Starring Anne Francis, Honey was a female private eye (it was the first drama series to

In an absurd twist, guest star Eileen O'Neill, a natural brunette, played a blonde agent who masquerades as a brunette in "Or No Tomorrow" on *Amos Burke, Secret Agent* (a Four Star Production–Barbety, 1965), with Gene Barry. ("He has a rather reserved look about him but underneath he is a sweetheart.") (*Courtesy of Eileen O'Neill*)

star an actress in the lead role) who was an expert in karate and usually investigated blackmail and murder. Far from possessing an espionage theme, the series was indirectly influenced by the Bond films due to the female lead's wardrobe and gadgets (including a tear gas–spraying fountain pen and a jeweled compact that hides a walkie-talkie). Also, this heroine did most of the fighting herself, leaving her adoring boyfriend (John Ericson) on the sidelines. Another one-season wonder was *The Man from U.N.C.L.E.* spin-off series *The Girl from U.N.C.L.E.* Debuting in the fall of 1966, it starred Stefanie Powers as U.N.C.L.E. agent April Dancer who, along with her partner Mark Slate (Noel Harrison), battles THRUSH agents throughout all corners of the globe. To keep the connection to its parent show tight, Leo G. Carroll made regular appearances on this show too, playing U.N.C.L.E. chief Mr. Waverly.

Spy series on television were not all tough action and deadly espionage games. The hit Emmy Award–winning comedy series *Get Smart* debuted in the fall of 1965, with Don Adams (as Maxwell Smart) and Barbara Feldon (as 99) playing agents employed by the secret organization called CONTROL. Week after week they tangled with Cold War refugees working for KAOS and their continuing plan to create a New World order or something like that. The jokes came fast and furious (Mel Brooks was one of the series' creators), but, more often than not, *Get Smart* made you smile and chuckle rather than eliciting any hearty laughs from the hardcore spy fan who demanded his spy spoofs be a bit more subtle.

Shortly after *Get Smart*'s debut, *The Double Life of Henry Phyfe* series appeared as a mid-season replacement series during the 1965-66 season. This was another small screen spy spoof however, it was no *Get Smart*. Red Buttons starred as Henry Wadsworth Phyfe, a mild-mannered accountant who is recruited by the CIS to impersonate murdered international agent U-31. However, nebbish Phyfe is nothing like his debonair bon vivant look-alike double, which causes him lots of trouble. Again a string of good-looking, voluptuous starlets, including Francine York, Nancy Kovack and Eileen O'Neill, made guest appearances. This sitcom lasted but one season, as the tide began to turn away from spy series with subtle comedic overtones and more toward serious espionage fare.

The Wild Wild West debuted in 1965, and this program combined the two most popular themes on television at the time, the western and spies. Secret service agents Jim West (Robert Conrad) and Artemus Gordon (Ross Martin) report directly to President Grant in this odd show that took place at a time just before the turn of the century. The athletic West and master of disguise Gordon often met a number of unusual enemy agents, mad scientists and megalomaniacs bent on world domination (or at least the United States in the 1800s). The series is remembered fondly for its then-odd combination of a western milieu and Bond-like gadgetry, beautiful female guest stars (including Yvonne Craig, Diane McBain, BarBara Luna, Jocelyn Lane and Sue Ane Langdon) and sometimes sadistic violence (Conrad was often seen with his torso bare, trussed up and tortured in many episodes). As the program continued through its four-season run, it delivered a number of entertaining episodes filled with above average scripts and thrills.

Just when it seemed that comedy and spoofing would be the only way to see an espionage program on television, relief came in the form of the Emmy Award–winning *Mission: Impossible* in 1966. This series provided a bold new twist to the by now standard espionage plot device by having a highly secretive team of operatives assigned to specific international tasks. Their mission: to right wrongs being committed by enemy agents from both within and without

Robert Conrad, as secret service agent James West, finds himself in another tense situation accompanied by a beautiful woman, guest star Francine York (Dr. Sara Gibson), in "The Night of the Pelican" on *The Wild Wild West* (Paramount Television, 1968).

an Eastern European or Third World country. Martin Landau was cast as Roland Hand, the world's foremost magician and master of disguise, and Barbara Bain was cast as Cinnamon Carter, a globetrotting model and sometime film actress with special abilities. Bain's smart, chic, resourceful character stood out from the typical spy roles women were playing on the small screen. She went on to acquire three consecutive Emmy Awards for her performance. It was during her acceptance speech for her third award that she quit the series, shocking her producers, who were sitting in the audience. During the series' fourth season a number of actresses who made guest appearances (including Dina Merrill, Anne Francis, Lee Meriwether and BarBara Luna) vied for a regular slot, but it surprisingly went to a twenty-something Lesley Ann Warren, who was brought on to attract a younger audience. Warren debuted during the fifth season as the hip, with-it Dana. After only a season, cool blonde Lynda Day George, as Casey, replaced her.

From 1968 through 1973 a number of spy series came and went. The spy craze begun in 1962, which peaked in 1967, was waning fast. *It Takes a Thief* (which starred Robert Wagner) took an urbane super thief, sprung him from prison and indoctrinated him into spying by transforming him into a member of an elite force. *The Delphi Bureau* (with Laurence Luckinbill as an operative answerable only to the President of the United States) and *Assignment: Vienna* (with Robert Conrad as an agent masquerading as the operator of a bar and restaurant) managed to briefly capture audiences before disinterest and low ratings set in. *Search* was another one-season spy show, and it featured three rotating actors (Hugh O'Brian, Tony Franciosa and Doug McClure) playing agents working for the Probe Division of World Securities. What distinguished these agents from others was the fact that they had transmitters implanted in an ear, enabling them to be in constant contact with their base of operations. The major networks saw the trend in spy shows changing, so Gene Barry's new spy series *The Adventurer* was relegated to syndication in 1972.

Master thief Robert Wagner as Al Mundy, accompanied by guest star Celeste Yarnall (Ilsa Malenska), is recruited to pull off another heist, all for the good of mankind, in "Locked in the Cradle of the Keep" on *It Takes a Thief* (Universal Television, 1968).

In the UK, popular espionage series like *Department S* (with Peter Wyngarde, Joel Fabiani and Rosemary Nicols as Interpol operatives), *The Protectors* (with Robert Vaughn, Nyree Dawn Porter and Tony Anholt as private detectives working for a worldwide organization) and *The Persuaders* (with Roger Moore and Tony Curtis as wealthy adventurers) managed to keep viewers watching for a season or more. Though they drew international audiences, their rejection by U.S. television viewers sealed their fates, as these shows were nothing like classic British spy television series that preceded them. Hence, the return of *The Avengers* as *The New Avengers* in the mid-seventies; but that show's insistence on occasional harsh violence, and the lack of star chemistry between the returning Patrick Macnee (as John Steed) and younger cast members Joanna Lumley and Gareth Hunt, failed to keep the show in production for more than two seasons.

Flashing forward to the dawn of a new millennium, three recent spoofs, *Austin Powers: International Man of Mystery* (1997), *Austin Powers: The Spy Who Shagged Me* (1999) and a second sequel released in 2002, successfully recreated the comical adventures, gadgetry and beautifully coiffured women in dangerous situations from sixties spy films. Of course, nothing is as it seems in an *Austin Powers* film. Its creator and star, Mike Myers, goes to great lengths to ensure our extreme titillation whenever he deems it necessary by recreating the swinging London of the sixties, returning us to a time when women were mini-skirted secret agents, femme fatales and voluptuous vixens.

Profiles

Beverly Adams

To the general public, Canadian actress Beverly Adams is best known as Beverly Sassoon, beauty consultant and ex-wife of hair stylist Vidal Sassoon. However, to the legions of spy film fans, the former Columbia contract player is remembered as "Lovey Kravezit," the amorous secretary to Dean Martin's super sleuth Matt Helm in the spoofs *The Silencers* (1966), *Murderers' Row* (1966) and *The Ambushers* (1967). Bedecked in the latest sixties hairstyles and fashions, Adams made Lovey one of spydom's most memorable female characters. Miss Kravezit was to Matt Helm what Miss Moneypenny was to James Bond. However, while Moneypenny yearned to be Mrs. Bond, Lovey seemed to enjoy her romantic interludes with her boss with no strings attached.

Beverly Adams was born on November 7, 1945, in Edmonton, Alberta. Her father was in the U.S. army, so the family moved from Canada to Illinois, back to Canada and then California. With Beverly being a very bright child and somewhat of a bookworm, her parents wished for her to get a medical degree. During the summer after her first year in college, Adams worked in a dress shop and did some modeling on television. This led to a commercial and a meeting with Ozzie Nelson, who immediately gave her a lead guest role on his popular series. More TV work followed, including appearances on *Burke's Law*, *My Three Sons*, *The Red Skelton Hour* and *Channing*. Adams landed a recurring role as a nurse on *Dr. Kildare*, but frustrated with her limited part, quit after her ninth episode. She entered Columbia Pictures' New Talent Program and was signed to a contract. She played a snow bunny in the teen-oriented *Winter a Go-Go* (1965) and was loaned out to AIP to play a beach bunny in *How to Stuff a Wild Bikini* (1965).

Purportedly, producer Dino De Laurentiis spotted Adams at a party in 1966 and offered her a role in the Italian–Portuguese production *Kiss the Girls and Make Them Die* (a.k.a. *Se Tutte Le Donne Del Monda*), which was released in the U.S. by Columbia Pictures in 1968. In the film, Adams appears briefly as Karin, one of a bevy of beauties (including Margaret Lee, Marilu Tolo and Nicoletta Machiavelli) industrialist Mr. Ardonian (Raf Vallone) plans to repopulate the U.S. with after his satellite emitting ultrasonic waves has destroyed the sex drive of the world's population. Karin suffers the wrath of Ardonian when she decides to get married to

Beverly Adams in a publicity pose as Matt Helm's secretary Lovey Kravezit in *Murderers' Row* (Columbia, 1966).

another man. Before the nuptials can take place, she is killed by a boa constrictor concealed in a beautiful frilly white boa given to her as a wedding gift from Ardonian.

Adams was next cast as agent Matt Helm's secretary, Lovey, in the film *The Silencers* (1966). The movie opens with retired spy cum photographer Matt Helm (Dean Martin) lying in his revolving bed as he gets a phone call from his former boss (James Gregory) at ICE, who asks Helm to return to duty and prevent Tung-Tze (Victor Buono) from destroying a vital atomic testing base. Ignoring his plea, Helm hangs up on him as his bed lifts up and gently slides him into a huge bubble bath occupied by his beautiful auburn-haired secretary (Adams), who greets him with a kiss. Helm responds, "Good morning. The soap please, Miss Kravezit." As she reaches for a big bar of soap, inside which is hidden a small bottle of booze, Miss Kravezit requests that he call her by her first name. When Helm inquires what that is, she answers, "It's Lovey." Helm says in astonishment, "*Lovey Kravezit!?!* Oh, that's some kind of name." After they emerge from their bath and towel off, Helm gets a photograph assignment in Acapulco and invites Lovey along. However, they never make it, as Helm is coaxed into helping ICE.

Beverly Adams returned as the loyal, sexy Lovey Kravezit in *Murderers' Row* (1966) and *The Ambushers* (1967), two of the three follow-ups to *The Silencers*. The sequels offered her prominent billing and a sexy mod wardrobe but not much more to do (though it was enough for exhibitors to vote her a 1966 "Star of Tomorrow" in *The Motion Picture Herald*, where she placed ahead of actress Sandy Dennis in the poll). While Adams is shown in the bath and wearing only a towel during her scenes in *The Silencers*, Adams wears one of the more outlandish outfits designed by Moss Mabry for *Murderers' Row* (1966). In 1966 Adams told columnist Kathleen Carroll, "Prior to making the sequel, my mother asked, 'You're not going to wear anything more revealing than you wore in the first movie?' I replied, 'No, mother, the dress I'm wearing has a turtle-neck collar and long sleeves.'" What Adams failed to mention was that she wore a mini-dress—sheer between yellow bands of fabric in the middle of the dress and at the hemline—with matching dangling ball earrings as she aided Matt Helm in scheduling his calendar models, nicknamed the Slaygirls, for their photo shoot. After Helm is presumed killed in an explosion orchestrated by one of his Slaygirls, enemy agent Miss January (Corinne Cole), Adams and the other Slaygirls attend his funeral (at a saloon, natch) dressed in black.

After returning from shooting a movie in London, Beverly Adams told *The New York Post* in 1968, "When I was in England making *Torture Garden* [1967] the director told me: 'No one must have a Sassoon haircut,' and I asked, 'What's that?'" She quickly found out. Not only did she wind up with a stylish new look, she also landed a steady boyfriend in salon owner Vidal Sassoon.

Adams' final film appearance was in the deadly serious Bond imitation *Hammerhead* (1968), directed by David Miller on location in London and Lisbon. Vince Edwards stars as stoic American secret agent Charlie Hood, who poses as a dealer of pornographic art to infiltrate the realm of collector Hammerhead (Peter Vaughn), who is after NATO's nuclear secrets. Adams plays Ivory, one of Hammerhead's mistreated mistresses. Hood first encounters the scantily clad girl on Hammerhead's yacht as the drunken Ivory dances in her cabin. As the music becomes louder and her "prayer dance" reaches a fever pitch, she tries to seduce Hood. However, he rejects her advances and she becomes enraged. Ivory only appears in the scenes on the yacht, and her purpose to the plot is suspect. When the action shifts to land she is nowhere to be found. However, Ivory pops up at the end of the film as part of a group of hippies attending a happening on the shoreline as Hood and the other agents close in on Hammerhead. As Ivory witnesses Hammerhead's helicopter whisking him away in his rope-suspended sedan perch, she grabs a spear and shoots him through the heart. As his body plunges into the ocean, Ivory remarks, "Bye baby ... and thanks for everything!" She then nonchalantly rejoins the dancing. As usual, Adams looks marvelous in her mod sixties hairstyles and outfits (she was *born* for this decade) and received good notices. Gordon Gow, writing in *Films and Filming*, commented, "Plenty of girls are around to console or provoke him [Hood]: the best of same being Beverly Adams who performs a hippy (as distinct from hippie) prayer dance while drinking several glasses of whiskey."

After marrying Vidal Sassoon in 1968, Beverly Adams retired from acting and became the spokesperson for Vidal Sassoon, Inc. Their marriage lasted 13 years and produced four children. Never out of the limelight, Adams returned to acting in the eighties using her married name and guest starred on a few series, including *Quincy* and *CHiPs*. Today she can be seen on QVC where she recently launched her line of pet care products called the Beverly Sassoon Pet Care System.

Other films include: *The New Interns* (1964), *Roustabout* (1964), *Birds Do It* (1966), *The Devil's Angels* (1967) and *Mind Games* (1996).

Ursula Andress

Born on March 19, 1936, in Berne, Switzerland, to German parents, Ursula Andress first sought out film work while on a holiday in Rome. After a string of low budget Italian film productions, such as *An American in Rome* (a.k.a. *Americano a Roma*, 1954) and *The Adventures of Casanova* (a.k.a. *Le Avventure di Giacomo Casanova*, 1954), Andress was brought to the U.S. as the "New Dietrich." In 1957 she married actor John Derek, who supervised every aspect of her career (until their divorce in 1964), much in the same way he would later "mold" the career of future wife Bo Derek.

According to an early '60s issue of *Movie Life Yearbook*, her height was given as 5'6" and her measurements as 36-24-36. She won her first major role, purely by accident, at age 25. It had been reported that the producers of *Dr. No* (1962) were nearly set on Julie Christie for the role of the sensuous Honey Ryder but had decided that she did not appear voluptuous enough on screen. Then, resuming their talent search, they made a discovery—Andress' portrait was the only one in a batch of photographs on the desk of *Dr. No* co-producer Albert R. Broccoli that showed a young woman with her hair all wet. In an Avco-Embassy press release touting a seventies Andress film, Broccoli is quoted as saying, "She looked very attractive ... wet, like a sea lion." There and then he sought her out and sent her to Jamaica for a screen test as the character Honey Ryder.

In *Dr. No*, the first of the James Bond series films starring Sean Connery, she is first glimpsed as a shapely blonde bikini-clad amazon (she reportedly designed the skimpy white bikini herself) emerging Venus-like out of the Caribbean sea onto the beach where Bond is waiting to spot the henchmen of the villainous title character, Dr. No (Joseph Wiseman). It wasn't known at the time, but she was the very first in a historic bevy of beauties that the

Ursula Andress poses seductively on the set of *Dr. No* (United Artists, 1962).

famous British super spy would encounter over the course of the next 20 films, lasting into the new millennium. In *Dr. No* Andress's vocal performance had been overdubbed by another actress named Nikki van der Zyl (rumored to be the same mysterious voice talent who also lent similar assistance to Daniela Bianchi in *From Russia with Love*). Van Der Zyl managed to mimic Andress' natural speaking voice quite well.

In the original Ian Fleming novel, her character of Honey Ryder's first appearance was described as being "Not quite naked. She wore a broad leather belt around her waist with a hunting knife in a leather sheath at her right hip. The belt made her nakedness extraordinarily erotic.... The skin was a very light uniform café au lait with the sheen of dull satin. The gentle curve of the backbone was deeply indented, suggesting more powerful muscles than is usual in a woman and the behind was almost as firm and rounded as a boy's was. The legs were straight and beautiful ... her hair was ash blonde.... She was Botticelli's Venus, seen from behind." Obviously, the film's producers had made a real casting coup by hiring such a striking looking woman to embody the screen version of the fictional character.

Due to this role, Andress became an international sensation. Within a year she was sharing billing with Frank Sinatra, Dean Martin and Anita Ekberg in the western caper film *Four for Texas* (1963), and with singer-actor Elvis Presley in *Fun in Acapulco* (1963). In 1963 Andress was a co-winner of the Golden Globe Award for "Most Promising Newcomer–Female" (sharing the award with fellow actresses Tippi Hedren and Elke Sommer), and was named a "Star of Tomorrow." Andress was then cast as the lead in the Hammer Films production of *She* (1965), the ninth film version of the H. Rider Haggard adventure about a lost civilization in the desert, its ageless queen (Andress) and a flame of eternal life. That same year she appeared in the comic espionage adventure film *The Tribulations of a Chinaman in China* (a.k.a. *Les Tribulations d'Un Chinois en Chine*) as Alexandrine Pinardel, the love interest of star Jean-Paul Belmondo. The movie, filmed in France, Hong Kong, India, Malaysia and Switzerland, remains one of the undiscovered gems of the sixties. Andress would also have a lengthy off-screen relationship with the French matinee idol for several years. Also in 1965 she appeared with Marcello Mastroianni in the pop-art science fiction thriller *The 10th Victim* (a.k.a. *La Decima Vittima*) as Caroline Meredith, one of the last contestants in a futuristic, televised game of assassination.

Andress returned to the world of James Bond in the unofficial Bond entry *Casino Royale* in 1967. As the devilishly seductive Vesper Lynd, Andress appeared in two of the episodic film's stories. This film, which was co-financed by a producer (Charles Feldman) who claimed to have purchased the only book that Bond author Ian Fleming wrote that was not at the time owned by Albert R. Broccoli and Harry Saltzman, was quickly rushed into production with the aid of five directors (Val Guest, Ken Hughes, John Huston, Joe McGrath and Robert Parrish), assisted by a veritable army of acting talent. Unfortunately, the film varies greatly from the major plot of the original, thrilling and sadistic Fleming book, and at times revels in its sixties pop art psychedelic influences. Today it has gained great appeal as a cult film.

In the movie the criminal empire SMERSH is developing rapidly as a danger to world peace. The American, British, French and Russian forces combine to ask retired secret agent James Bond (David Niven) to reconsider going back into service to save the world. Confusing the audiences is the fact that other actors (including Peter Sellers) also play characters named James Bond. Andress' character Vesper Lynd (a SMERSH agent) romances and then attempts to kill Sellers. *Casino Royale* co-composer Burt Bacharach was so taken with her visage in this film that he wrote that movie's big hit song "The Look of Love" for her. In the book *Songwriters on Songwriting* he wrote, "It wasn't really a love theme as much as a kind of very understated sexual theme written for her body and face."

After this film, celluloid appearances by Ursula Andress became sporadic. She claimed to be coolly indifferent to being regarded as one of the world's most recognizable sex symbols, despite two much touted appearances in the men's magazine *Playboy* in 1965 and 1966. Andress returned to the screen in the adventure film *The Southern Star* (a.k.a. *L'Etoile du Sole*, 1969), in which she co-starred with Orson Welles, and the comic heist picture *Perfect Friday* (1970), in which she appeared with Stanley Baker. *Red Sun* (1971) was a much-hyped western featuring Andress cavorting with French action star Alain Delon, Charles Bronson and Toshiro Mifune.

Andress relocated to Italy, where for the next several years she appeared in a number of varied films, like the comic espionage movie *Loaded Guns* (a.k.a. *Colpo in Canna*, 1974), in which she starred as Nora Green with Marc Porel; *Safari Express* (a.k.a. *Africa Express*, 1975), in which she starred as Madeline Cooper, a female secret agent who is joined by an American (Giulliano Gemma) who is running an arms smuggling business in Africa, as both battle villain Jack Palance; and the lurid crime melodrama *The Last Chance* (a.k.a. *L'Ultima Chance*, a.k.a. *Stateline Motel*, 1975), in which she revealed much in the role of a sensuous but deadly cipher in a battle between criminals Eli Wallach and Fabio Testi.

Appearances in sexy comedies like *The Loves and Times of Scaramouche* (a.k.a. *Le Avventure e Gli Amore di Scaramouche*, 1976) and *The Sensuous Nurse* (a.k.a. *L'Infirmiera*, 1976) followed, but a career lowpoint, some would say, would be in Sergio Martino's cannibal epic *The Mountain of the Cannibal God* (a.k.a. *The Slave of the Cannibal God*, 1978), where, as Susan Stevenson, Andress spends much of the film being chased by crazed, flesh-hungry natives before she is captured, made their Queen, stripped naked and covered in a strange slimy secretion.

In 1979 Ursula Andress met the American actor Harry Hamlin during the filming of the fantasy epic *The Clash of the Titans* (1981), and the two not only became a romantic item but also spawned a child, Dimitri. The short-lived romance seemed to have affected Andress' outlook on life, and her roles since this film (in which she played, appropriately, the Goddess Aphrodite) became less frequent.

Andress was seen on U.S. television screens in brief roles in the popular eighties programs *Falcon Crest* (1981), the short-lived science fiction—adventure show *Manimal* (1983), the mini-series *Peter the Great* (1986) and *Man Against the Mob: The Chinatown Murders* (1989), where she reunited with *Blue Max* (1965) co-star George Peppard.

Recently, Andress was seen on Italian television screens as the evil Queen Xellesia in the multi-part series *Fantaghiro II, III, IV* (a.k.a. *The Cave of the Golden Rose*, 1993–1995), directed by Lamberto Bava, and in the independent film *Cremaster 5* (1998) as "The Queen." In a January 1999 issue of *Playboy* magazine she ranked number 19 on the magazine's list of the "100 Sexiest Stars of the Century."

Other films include: *Doppio Delitto* (1978), *Liberte, Egalite, Choucroute* (1985), *Klassazamekunft* (1988), *Il Professore Diva* (1989) and *In 80 Jahren um die Welt* (2001—TV).

Pier Angeli

Pier Angeli was born Anna Maria Pierangeli on June 19, 1932, in Calgari, Sardinia, Italy. Anna and her sister (Marisa Pavan) were both interested in films and dreamt of becoming actresses. In 1948, at the age of 16, Anna won her first part in a film, but was uncredited when the now obscure movie was released to theaters. The next year she received her first billed part, as Mirella, a young student who experiences the pangs of first love in the Italian production *Tomorrow Is Too Late* (a.k.a. *Domani e Troppo Tardi*, 1949). Her dark hair and piercing eyes may have seemed too harsh for many of the 'Glamour Girl' roles available at the time, so Anna spent the years 1949 through 1951 performing in a variety of Italian stage productions, cast in minor roles.

However, Hollywood moguls who caught her performance in a number of poorly received Italian films took notice of her, changed her name to the more exotic Pier Angeli, and gave her a prominent part in the film *Teresa* in 1951. Critics took note of her fragile beauty and talent, and the

Pier Angeli in a rare MGM starlet pose.

Hollywood Foreign Press awarded her a Golden Globe for her performance in this film as "Most Promising Newcomer–Female." She appeared in a number of forgettable Hollywood films, including *The Silver Chalice* (1954) starring newcomer Paul Newman. During this time she also befriended another American actor, James Dean; she became infatuated with him, and the two were romantically linked in the tabloids before Anna was suddenly married to singer Vic Damone (the two were divorced four years later). Angeli reunited with Paul Newman (playing the role of Norma Graziano) for the biographical film *Somebody Up There Likes Me* in 1956, about the real-life American boxer.

A drought of good roles followed, and she soon found herself in Italian costume epics like *White Slave Ship* (a.k.a. *L'Ammutinamento*, 1961) and *Sodom and Gomorrah* (1962) before appearing onscreen in her first espionage film, *Panic in Bangkok for OSS 117* (a.k.a. *Banco a Bangkok Pour OSS 117*, 1964), as Lila. In this exciting adventure movie, Dr. Sinn (Robert Hossein), the head of a criminal organization, plans on using his secret virus weapon on the world. Secret agent OSS 117 (Kerwin Mathews) is sent to the Far East to stop him and to avenge the murder of a fellow agent. Along the way, our hero falls in love with the beautiful Lila, who assists him in foiling the plans of Dr. Sinn.

Angeli returned to the big screen the next year in a pivotal role as Louise in the international co-production *The Battle of the Bulge* (1965), but the good notices she received for her role of a war torn town whore, did little to further her career. It was back to spy movies for *Spy in Your Eye* a.k.a. *Berlino Appuntamento per le Spie* (1965), where she played Paula Krauss. In this film, a U.S. agent (Brett Halsey) has a secret transmitter planted on him which hinders the efforts of a criminal organization and enemy agents to get a secret formula willed to the daughter of dead scientist. The secret agent battles a Russian spy organization bent on ruling the world with deadly laser ray weapon that can be built with the secret formula. Angeli's appearance in the film took a backseat to the macho posturing of the cast members as well as hilarious anti-Communist rhetoric spewed by the cast members.

In *M.M.M. 83* a.k.a. *Missione Mortale Molo 83* (1965), she had a much more important role. In this film, a British scientist is murdered in Sicily and agent Morris (Fred Beir) of the Secret Service finds a briefcase from the murder scene that contains stolen documents re: synthetic jet engine fuel. His French counterpart (Gerard Blain) may be a double agent who has been romantically partnered with Angeli (who begins to fall for Morris).

Angeli appeared as Marie in the seldom seen espionage film *Code Name Red Roses* a.k.a. *Rose Rosse Per Il Fuehrer* (1968) and then appeared in a sparse number of films like the Italian crime melodrama *Cry Chicago* (a.k.a. *Viva America*, 1969) and the thriller *In the Folds of the Flesh* a.k.a. *Nelle Pieghe della Carne* (1970). She was reunited with *Panic In Bangkok for OSS 117* co-star Kerwin Mathews for the abysmal no budget American horror movie *Octaman* in 1971 and then committed suicide just after the production wrapped. Anna Maria Pierangeli died at the age of 39 on September 10, 1971 in Beverly Hills, California of an overdose of barbiturates. Shortly before her death she commented on the lack of good roles that plagued her during her career, her failed romances (especially with James Dean) and marriages.

Other films include: *The Devill Makes Three* (1952), *The Story of Three Loves* (1953), *The Flame and the Flesh* (1954), *Meet Me in Las Vegas* (1956), *Merry Andrew* (1958), *The Angry Silence* (1960), *S.O.S. Pacific* (1960), *The Renegade Gunfighter* (a.k.a. *Per Mille Dollari Al Giorno*, 1966), *One Step to Hell* (1967) and *Addio, Alexandra* (1969).

Ann-Margret

A true sixties icon, Ann-Margret (born Ann-Margret Olsson on April 28, 1941, in Valsjobyn, Sweden) did it all during that groovy decade. With her wild mane of red hair and curvaceous figure, Ann-Margret acted, sang, and danced in comedies, musicals and dramas. She made her film debut in *A Pocketful of Miracles* (winning a Golden Globe for "Most Promising Newcomer–Female"), and her second film, *State Fair* (1962), got her voted a "Star of Tomorrow" that same year. But it was her lively performance in *Bye Bye Birdie* (1963) that catapulted her to the top. She followed this with an equally good performance opposite Elvis Presley in *Viva Las Vegas* (1964). After playing the *Kitten with a Whip* (1964), Ann-Margret was typecast as a sexpot—loved by her fans and despised by the critics—in a number of fun but forgettable films. It was during this period that she made her lone excursion into the mod world of spies in *Murderers' Row*, the sequel to *The Silencers*, which introduced Dean Martin's droll agent Matt Helm to the world. No expense was spared as *Murderers' Row* featured elaborate sets, colorful, outlandish costumes (most of them worn by A-M), and convincing backdrops of the French Riviera. Released in December of 1966, *Murderer's Row* grossed over six million dollars and was the eleventh highest grossing film of 1967.

In *Murderers' Row* Ann-Margret played Suzie, the swinging daughter of kidnapped scientist Dr. Norman Solaris (Richard Eastham), who has invented a helio-beam capable of destroying the world using the sun's rays. Arch villain Julian Wall (Karl Malden) plans to use it to decimate Washington, D.C. ("Operation Scorch"). He orders his top agent, Ironhead (Tom Reese), to orchestrate the assassinations of all of ICE's agents, including Helm. However, Matt survives the explosion rigged in his home. Presumed dead, he poses as a hit man named James A. Peters and heads for the Riviera, where he discovers that his

Showing that the pop art sixties was indeed a wild time, the modly attired Ann-Margret as Susie, a scientist's daughter, frets for her life in *Murderers' Row* (Columbia, 1966). (*Courtesy of Michael Monahan*)

contact has been murdered and stuffed into her refrigerator. As he leaves her apartment he meets Suzie who asks, "Are you a friend of Dominique's? I don't think she's in today." Helm deadpans, "No, she's *out*." Later they run into each other at a local discotheque where Ann-Margret (wearing a striped midriff with matching colored polka-dotted bellbottoms) gyrates to the sounds of Dino, Desi and Billy. Matt is arrested for Dominque's murder, but Suzie lies to get him sprung from jail. Later she confesses that Solaris is her father and that she believes Wall and his girlfriend Coco Duquette (Camilla Sparv) are responsible for his disappearance. After Helm convinces Wall and Coco that he is a thug from Chicago, he blows his cover to save Suzie from an exploding broach she received as a gift purportedly from him. As she dances vigorously to a wild rocking beat at the discotheque, Helm enters, rips her mini-dress off and throws it at a wall (on which is hung Frank Sinatra's picture). They then make their way to Wall's fortress island. After a series of car chases, fistfights, explosions (caused by Suzie's hairpin) and a hovercraft pursuit, Ironhead, Coco and Wall are killed, Solaris is rescued, and Washington, D.C., is saved. The film ends with Matt Helm and Suzie taking the plunge from his bed into his enormous bathtub.

Though Ann-Margret tries hard, her performance in *Murderers' Row* is not one of her best. She seems miscast as Suzie and lacks chemistry with Dean Martin. *Box Office* magazine found her "flat voiced," while Robert Salmaggi, of the *New York World Journal Tribune*, described A-M as "romping around with mile-long eyelashes, last-word mod gear and fronting her sticky-sweet professional virgin demeanor." Even her dancing is embarrassing. *Variety* remarked, "Ann-Margret is notable for some abandoned choreography and a chance to use both of her expressions—the open-mouthed Monroe imitation and the slinky Theda Bara bit." Her over-the-top gyrating and shimmying may have been director Henry Levin's way to distract the audience from the "singing" of the group Dino, Desi and Billy, led by Dean Martin's son.

By 1970 Ann-Margret's acting career had plunged to such depths that she accepted the lead role opposite Joe Namath in the biker flick *C.C. and Company*. However, the following year she landed the role of an aging fashion model in Mike Nichols' *Carnal Knowledge* (1971), and her performance was so breathtaking that she received a Golden Globe Award and an Academy Award nomination for "Best Supporting Actress." Her acting comeback was sidelined in 1972 when she went into a coma and needed facial reconstruction after falling off the stage while performing her nightclub act in Las Vegas. Ann-Margret made a complete recovery and received a second Golden Globe Award and Academy Award nomination for her fiery role in the The Who's rock opera *Tommy* (1975). Since then, Ann-Margret has never lacked for work, and one of her more recent popular roles was as the boozy mother of football team owner Cameron Diaz in Oliver Stone's *Any Given Sunday* (1999).

Other films include: *The Pleasure Seekers* (1964), *Bus Riley's Back in Town* (1965), *Once a Thief* (1965), *The Cincinnati Kid* (1965), *Made in Paris* (1966), *R.P.M.* (1970), *The Train Robbers* (1973), *Joseph Andrews* (1977), *The Cheap Detective* (1978), *Magic* (1978), *Who Will Love My Children?* (1983—TV), *A Streetcar Named Desire* (1984—TV), *Twice in a Lifetime* (1985), *52 Pick-Up* (1986), *The Two Mrs. Grenvilles* (1987—TV), *Newsies* (1992), *Grumpy Old Men* (1993), *Grumpier Old Men* (1995), *The Last Producer* (2000) and *Interstate 60* (2002).

Laura Antonelli

Laura Antonelli was born Laura Antonaz on November 28, 1941, in Pola, a coastal town in Yugoslavia. The family moved to Italy, where they relocated first to Genoa, then to Venice, finally settling in Naples. As a young child Laura Antonaz was interested in education. As an adult she sought out a career as a mathematics teacher but settled for a degree as a gymnastics instructor instead. In 1979 she remarked to *The New York Times* regarding her childhood, "My parents had made me take hours of gym classes during my teens ... they felt I was ugly, clumsy, insignificant and they hoped that I would at least develop some grace. I became very good, especially in rhythmical gym, which is a kind of dance."

With her instructing diploma in hand, Antonelli set off for the Italian capital of Rome and a position as a high school gym teacher. It was in Rome where she met a number of people involved in the entertainment industry and got her first paying job as a model in television commercials hawking beverages and bed sheets. A failed attempt as a television news commentator followed, but more success with commercials brought her to the attention of a film producer, who cast her (uncredited) in a movie titled *Le Sedicenni* (1965).

She fared better in another small but provocative role in the comic spy spoof *Dr. Goldfoot and the Girl Bombs* (a.k.a. *La Spie Vengono dal Semifreddo*, 1966) as Rosanna, one of the deadly girl-bombs invented by Dr. Goldfoot (Vincent Price). In this film Dr. Goldfoot teams with Red Chinese agents to start a war between the Russians and the U.S. An FBI agent (Fabian Forte) and two Italians (Franco Franchi and Ciccio Ingrassia) team up to battle Goldfoot, who plans on using his beautiful, robotic servant women to kill major military figures on both sides of the cold war and start World War III. While the film was not well received in the U.S. (its campy, broad humor finding little audience empathy on American screens), it did quite well in its native Italy where co-stars Franco and Ciccio were household names. Sort of the Dean Martin and Jerry Lewis of Italian comedy, the duo appeared in numerous films before and after this movie until their break-up in the seventies.

Antonelli followed this role with a brief appearance in the sex comedy *Scusi, Lei e Favoravole O Contrario?* (1967) and then a larger one in the then controversial film *The Sexual Revolution* (a.k.a. *La Rivoluzione Sessuale*, 1968). It is with this movie that she also changed her familial surname to Antonelli. Roles in *Fellini's Satyricon* (1968), a sex comedy titled *L'Arcangelo* (1969) and a crime melodrama *Un Detective* (1969, uncredited), followed. But it was with *Devil in the Flesh* (a.k.a. *La Malizie di Venere*, a.k.a. *Venus in Furs*) in 1969, that she met head-on with controversy. In this film version of the Sader-Masoch novel about illicit love, Antonelli, as Wanda, the film's protagonist, finds herself in a variety of sexually explicit (for the time) situations. In June of 1969 the U.S. customs office seized theatrical prints of the movie intended for exhibition in American theaters, citing possible "obscenity violations" of the moral code. The film was brutally cut by U.S. and British censors (sometimes by as much as 45 minutes) and released without fanfare. Laura Antonelli was then only 22 years old and already making international headlines.

Laura Antonelli as Rosanna, a seductive but deadly female robot in *Dr. Goldfoot and the Girl Bombs* (AIP, 1966).

Laura Antonelli met French action star Jean-Paul Belmondo on the set of the costume adventure *Swashbuckler* (a.k.a. *Les Maries de Le'An II*, 1971), and the two co-starred again in *High Heels* (a.k.a. *Doctor Popaul*, 1972) and developed a romantic relationship that lasted into the early eighties.

During this period Antonelli appeared in the Italian thriller *Without Apparent Motive* (a.k.a. *Sans Mobile Apparent*, 1972), the comedic horror spoof *The Eroticist* (a.k.a. *All'Onorevole Piacciono del Donne*, 1972) and the career turning-point *Malicious* (a.k.a. *Malizia*, 1973), a sexy comedy drama about the coming of age of a young man as he and his widower father are enticed and seduced by a housekeeper (Antonelli). By now she was edging ever so slightly towards a full figured woman, and her often-unclothed performances were bringing in tons of money for the Italian producers of her films.

In an interview published in *Andy Warhol's Interview* magazine in 1979, Antonelli commented, "I have lots of fantasies and the possibility to express them through acting gives me an incredible sense of satisfaction.... I had to build my career all by myself. I never had a production company, or a producer, or a husband behind me and this is very rare in Italy. Second, I think I gave the best of myself in what I did, but of course, the situation was limited and now I'm tired of acting..."

In recent years Laura Antonelli appeared occasionally onscreen (*Malicious 2000* [a.k.a. *Malizia 2000*] in 1992 is her last known credit). Laura Antonelli passed away on June 22, 2015. The heyday of Italian sex comedies and dramas seems to have peaked, and until a revival, fans of Laura Antonelli can watch her seldom-matched catalog of erotica.

Other films include: *Peccato Veniale* (1973), *How Funny Can Sex Be?* (a.k.a. *Sessomatto*, 1973), *Till Marriage Do Us Part* (a.k.a. *Mio Dio Come Sono Caduta in Basso*, 1974), *Simona* (1974), *The Divine Nymph* (a.k.a. *Divina Creatura*, 1976), Lucino Visconti's *The Innocent* (a.k.a. *L'Innocente*, 1976), *The Black Journal* (a.k.a. *Il Gran Bollito*, 1977), *Wifemistress* (a.k.a. *Mogliamante*, 1977), *Inside Laura Antonelli* (1979), *Tigers in Lipstick* (a.k.a. *Letti Selvaggi*, 1979), *Collector's Item* (a.k.a. *La Gabbia*, 1986), *The Venetian Woman* (a.k.a. *La Venexiana*, 1986), *Rimini, Rimini* (1987) and *L'Avaro* (a.k.a. *The Miser*, 1989).

Claudine Auger

Born as Claudine Oger (pronounced "Oh-Zay," literally the same pronunciation as Auger) on April 26, 1942, in Paris, France, she was an alumnus of the St. Joan of Arc College and then later the National School of Dramatic Arts, where she performed dramatic roles in plays by Moliere, Racine and Shakespeare. Auger can speak several languages, one of them being, of course, English, which she quickly learned during her scholastic years.

The brunette actress made her screen debut at the age of 17 in 1960 while still at school. Jean Cocteau, who was looking for someone to play a tall ballerina in his film *The Testament of Orpheus* (a.k.a. *Le Testament D'Orphee*), discovered her. Although uncredited, this was the first taste of life as a screen actress for the young woman, who returned to her studies at the National Theatre Conservatory (also known as the Paris Drama Conservatory). She became "Miss France" in 1961 and then married the renowned French writer-director Pierre Gaspard-Huit (she was 18 and he 43). She explained her relationship to an Associated Press journalist in 1966, "I had just won the 'Miss France' contest with all its publicity and one of the prizes was a role in one of Pierre's pictures, it was love at first sight."

Acting roles in Gaspard-Huit's film and other movies followed. She had a part in the costume film *The Iron Mask* (a.k.a. *Le Masque De Fer*) in 1962 and the epic adventure *Kali Yug, La Dea Della Vendetta* (a.k.a. *The Vengeance of Kali*), which was filmed as a two-part movie and released to European theaters in 1963.

Five years after her first film experience with Jean Cocteau she played the role of Domino Derval in the fifth James Bond film, *Thunderball* (1965). The formerly thin actress had now grown into a voluptuous woman and as she related to a *New York Journal American* correspondent in November of 1965, it was a tumultuous journey: "When I was thirteen I wasn't very pretty. I was slim, how you say, like a matchstick..." Now, at age 23 she had grown into a striking woman with auburn hair, brown eyes, a height of 5'8", and measurements of 36-23-37. Auger got her role in the film by pure chance. Doing some underwater swimming while vacationing in Nassau, she surfaced the same time as *Thunderball* co-producer

Kevin McClory, who promptly signed her for the film. Other actresses considered for the part at the time were Julie Christie, Faye Dunaway and Raquel Welch, who almost appeared in the role but was released from her contract to star in *Fantastic Voyage*. In *Thunderball* Auger plays Domino Derval, the sister of a man murdered by Largo (Adolfo Celli), a sinister mastermind of an ingenious plan to hold for ransom the most powerful countries in the world. Largo is one of the most trusted agents of S.P.E.C.T.R.E. (The Supreme Organization for Extortion, Counterespionage, Revenge and Murder) and its leader, the seldom-seen, enigmatic Blofeld.

During the film's lengthy running time, it transpires that Domino's brother assisted Largo in his plan but was murdered. She is Largo's mistress but actually knows nothing of his other life as a criminal agent. Largo plans to use stolen atomic bombs (from a downed aircraft in the ocean) as the ransom in a convoluted extortion plot. British agent James Bond (Sean Connery) is assigned the task of locating the weapons and stopping the villains. However, once he spots a photo of Domino (Auger) in the special dossier on her brother, he sees a way to enjoy his dangerous mission—by romancing the woman. Ian Fleming describes Bond meeting Domino for the first time in the original *Thunderball* book: "She had a gay, to-hell-with-you face that, Bond thought, would become animal in passion. In bed she would fight and bite and then suddenly melt into hot surrender. He could almost see the proud, sensual mouth bear away from the even white teeth in a snarl of desire and then, afterward, soften into a half-pout of loving slavery. In profile, the eyes were charcoal slits ... fierce and direct with a golden flicker in the dark brown hair that held much the same message as the mouth ... a soft, muddled Brigitte Bardot haircut ... the sunburn was not overdone ... her breasts, high and riding and deeply V-ed.... The general impression, Bond decided, was of a willfull, high-tempered, sensual girl..."

With its beautiful location scenery (shot mainly in the Mediterranean and in Jamaica), wonderful gadgets, frenetic fight scenes and explosive undersea battle between hordes of British and American agents and S.P.E.C.T.R.E. henchmen, the film went on to be the top moneymaker of 1965. It also won an Academy Award for its special effects. During a whirlwind, worldwide press tour to support the film, Auger explained to a *New York Daily News* columnist in December 1965 about the extensive underwater shooting for the film: "...I was never frightened of it. I took to it like a fish. It's beautiful down there and peaceful and I get a sense of freedom I don't get on land or in the air. One has to be more careful skin diving in the Caribbean than in the Mediterranean because of sharks ... close to shore there are lazy sharks and we were assured they wouldn't attack us if we remained calm. Fortunately, I didn't meet one to test my nerve."

At the time of its U.S. release, while she was doing extensive publicity for the film, she also said to the *New York Journal-American* reporter about her character: "...Domino's a continental girl and the girlfriend of the villain. I become Bond's ally and fall in love with him.... I am so delighted with *Thunderball*. We filmed it in Jamaica and London. It's my first showcase to American audiences. I hoped I am liked, it's important to my future." Following this film, to promote the movie she appeared semi-nude in *Playboy* magazine and made a guest star appearance on American television in a Bob Hope special.

Auger returned to the espionage cinema in the spy spoof *The Man from Marrakech* (a.k.a. *L'Homme de Marrakech*, 1966); she played Lila in this film about an American adventurer (George Hamilton) involved

Claudine Auger preparing for the fast-paced action in *Thunderball* (United Artists, 1965).

in a gold bullion robbery and danger in the Moroccan desert and Portugal. The next year she appeared (along with co-star Yul Brynner) in the more serious espionage drama *Triple Cross* (1967). She co-starred in *Killing Game* (a.k.a. *Jeu De Massacre*, a.k.a. *Comic Strip Hero*), a pop-art melodrama movie with slight espionage overtones, in 1967. As Jacqueline, she became the fatal romantic interest for a man who may be a secret agent, a mass murderer, or just some confused daydreamer.

During the following years Auger appeared in a variety of films, like Italian horror genre director Mario Bava's *Bay of Blood* (a.k.a. *Antefatto*, a.k.a. *Carnage*, a.k.a. *Twitch of the Dead Nerve*, 1971), the crime melodramas *Summertime Killer* (a.k.a. *Un Verano Para Matar*, 1972) and *Ricco* (a.k.a. *Un Tippo con Una Faccia Strana*, 1972), and the stylish thriller *The Black Belly of the Tarantula* (a.k.a. *La Tarantola dal Ventre Nero*, 1972). She also appeared with Alain Delon in the crime adventure film *Cop Story* (a.k.a. *Flic Story*) in 1975. In 1981 Auger co-starred in a BBC television production, and then in a German espionage-themed miniseries that same year where she played the wife of a brilliant biochemist. She continues to act, and most recently she has been seen on British and American television screens in "The Three Gables" episode of *The Memoirs of Sherlock Holmes* (1994) with the late Jeremy Brett, and on French television in *Rouge et le Noir* in 1997.

Other films include: *L'Arcidiavolo* (1966), *I Bastardi* (1968), *Il Triangolo delle Bemude* (1978), *Viaggio con Anita* (1979), *Black Jack* (1980), *Aragosta a Colazione* (a.k.a. *Lobster for Breakfast*, 1982), *Secret Places* (1984), *Un Amore di donna* (1988) and *Salt on Our Skin* (a.k.a. *Desire*, 1992).

Tina Aumont

Born Maria Christina Aumont on February 14, 1946, in Hollywood, California, Tina Aumont's contribution as an actress to spy cinema is small, but her contribution to the Continental film genre as an actress often seen in various stages of undress, if not entirely nude, has made her a cult figure to European film audiences and genre movie aficionados who appreciate the female form.

Aumont was born as the result of a union between the sultry Dominican-born singer-actress Maria Montez and French matinee idol Jean-Pierre Aumont. Although lithesome and thin at a height of 5'7", the brunette actress with the seemingly large eyes and seemingly innocent, come hither look exuded sensuality even at the early age of 20. She married the French actor Christian Marquand when she was 17 years old (and he was 38). In 1966 she made her film debut (credited onscreen as Tina Marquand) playing Nicole in director Joseph Losey's bizarre cinematic interpretation of the then-popular comic character Modesty Blaise in the film of the same name. In Modesty Blaise (1966) super agent Modesty Blaise (Monica Vitti) becomes involved in all kinds of intrigue and espionage when arch villain Gabriel (Dirk Bogarde) and his psychopathic female executioner sidekick (Rossella Falk), using a cache of stolen diamonds, plans on creating a crisis in the Middle East. The British government asks Modesty Blaise to return to active service, which she considers for a high fee. Blaise is weary of being the "Queen of International Adventure," with its accompanying elegance and luxury. Aumont commented to a Los Angeles Times reporter in March 1966 about her role in this film: "I went to England for this picture ... my first. The part was small—an inexperienced young spy who falls in love with Terence Stamp and gets killed."

Although her role was minor in Modesty Blaise, Aumont was noticed and managed to gain an important part (as Lonetta, an Indian maiden) in the western Texas Across the River (1966), starring Dean Martin and Alain Delon. She followed that film with roles in internationally produced films like Scusi, Lei e Favorevole O Contrario? (1967), the western Man, Pride and Vengeance (a.k.a. L'Uomo, L'Orgoglio, La Vendetta, 1967), Fellini's Satyricon (1968) and Tinto Brass' The Howl (a.k.a. L'Urlo, 1968). Tina Aumont also posed semi-nude for Playboy magazine in July 1969.

Tina Aumont displays a sweet and seductive smile.

Aumont appeared in the graphic Italian thriller *The Bodies Bear Traces of Carnal Violence* (a.k.a. *I Corpi Presentano Tracce di Violenza Carnale*, a.k.a. *Torso*, 1973) and then began a long run in erotic films with her near-controversial performances in *Malicious* (a.k.a. *Malizia*, 1973), *Fellini's Casanova* (1976) and *The Divine Nymph* (a.k.a. *La Divina Creatura*, 1976).

As stardom as an actress in more critically acclaimed films eluded her, Aumont continued her appearances in erotic films with *La Principessa Nuda* (1976), the controversial *Salon Kitty* (1976) and the lurid *Holocaust 2: The Memories, Delirium and the Vendetta Part Two* (a.k.a. *Holocaust—I Ricordi, I Deliri, La Vendetta*, 1980).

Tina Aumont married French actor and television producer Francois Ferrial in January 1985, and she was seen in French horror filmFiles are combined but without a TOC there is no way to check the order. Amy D. notified to get one for me. director Jean Rollin's *The Two Orphan Vampires* (a.k.a. *Les Deux Orphelines Vampires*, 1997) and in the French television film *Victoire, Ou la Douleur des Femmes* (2000). She passed away on October 28, 2006.

Other films include: *A Matter of Time* (1976), *Il Messia* (1978), *Le Marquis De Slime* (1997), *La Mécanique des femmes* (2000) and *Cinématon* (segment "1985," 2000).

Barbara Bain

Barbara Bain was born on September 13, 1931, in Chicago, Illinois. Unsubstantiated sources claim that her real and familial name is actually Millie Fogel. Growing up as the daughter of Russian immigrants who got into the wholesale grocery business, she studied sociology as a student and graduated from the University of Illinois with a BA in that field. Bain journeyed to New York to try her hand at a variety of jobs whilst studying modern dance with Martha Graham and her company. To help pay her rent and tuition, she found success as a model and in a short time appeared in the pages of *Harper's Bazaar*, *Mademoiselle* and *Vogue*. Bain told *People* magazine in 1976, "I wasn't as good as I wanted to be ... and dance was then too remote from the rest of the world. It became lots of misery."

Being a strong-willed woman, the ash-blonde Bain then decided on either a career in academics with her sociology degree or a career in the arts; she chose an acting career and gave it her all. Barbara Bain studied at the famed Actor's Studio and the Neighborhood Playhouse beginning in 1956. She told *People* magazine, "When my feet landed on that stage I felt like I was touching home. I was terrible, but I loved it." At the Actor's Studio she met fellow student and teacher Martin Landau and fell under his tutelage. Martin Landau recalled in a June 1976 issue of *People* magazine, "[It was a] little, dirty and terrible loft.... I thought she was an empty-headed model, a magazine cover wired for sound." A short time later they were married (in 1957) and then toured the country in the Paddy Chayefsky play *Middle of the Night*. The play's tour ended on the West Coast and the Landaus decided to stay there, as Bain was now getting offers to appear on television programs like *Bonanza*, *The Dick*

Van Dyke Show, Wagon Train and The Greatest Show on Earth (in which Landau and his wife both appeared). She also appeared as Alma Sutton in the "KAOS in Control" episode (10/30/65) of Get Smart, where she played a suspected double agent who has stolen the "Retrogresser Gun," which can regress the minds of brilliant scientists to those of eight year olds.

In the mid–1960s, when producer Bruce Geller was developing Mission: Impossible as a television series, he thought of a bold new twist to the by now standard espionage plot device by which a highly secretive team of operatives would be assigned to specific international tasks. Their mission—to right wrongs being committed by enemy agents both from within and without an Eastern European or Third World country. Bain told TV Guide magazine in November 1997, "It all had to do with outfoxing the other people and getting them to do themselves in. We didn't do them in. Mission was a fantasy. People saw it as a fantasy. And that's how it was geared. Nobody for a minute at that time thought any of that stuff was [really] going on." Martin Landau was cast as Rollin Hand, the world's foremost magician and master of disguise, and Barbara Bain was cast as Cinnamon Carter, a globetrotting model and sometime film actress with special abilities. But donning elaborate disguises was not one of them, for, unlike Landau's Hand character and some of the other characters on the show, Bain seldom acted in a disguise because she is claustrophobic and could not be "contained" within much of the heavy latex involved. In the program, Bain's physical appearance came across on television screens as a thin, coarse model type who, when on a modeling assignment, could look glamorous, and when called upon to seduce and destroy a target during a Mission: Impossible mission, could appear slinky and seductive, with a killer "come hither" gaze. The show quickly became the antithesis of many standard American spy programs, which, unfortunately, were more often than not comical spoofs (Get Smart, for example). Whilst many of Mission: Impossible's weekly plots were definitely out-there in terms of complicated story lines and arcs within episodes that sometimes confounded viewers, each episode of the initial three year run of the show consistently delivered to television viewers a high standard of acting. Barbara Bain went on to win three Emmys in a row (then unprecedented) as "Best Actress in a Drama Series."

By Mission: Impossible's fourth year it became apparent that the writers were struggling to keep the show's originality afloat, and, amidst cries of poor scripts and creative challenges, some of the original cast members began to press the producers to keep the former level of excellence seen in previous seasons alive. Landau left the show for several episodes, finally to return mid-season to fulfill his contract, but Bain shocked television (and the show's producers) when she accepted her third straight Emmy win for the program and announced on television that she would not be returning in the role. According to a news item in the Courier-Journal & Times of Kentucky in the fall of 1971, Bain "blasted the management of the studio to the stunned silence in the auditorium, then stumbled offstage into the arms of her husband, Martin Landau, the third consecutive Emmy she'd won from her performances as Cinnamon Carter on the show clutched to her bosom."

In 1975 Martin Landau and Barbara Bain were invited to England to co-star in what was advertised at the time as the most expensive science fiction program made for television, Space: 1999. Rejected by all three of the major U.S. networks, Space: 1999 floated around in syndication for two years before it was canceled.

In the years since the cancellation of

The second season cast of the series *Mission: Impossible* (Paramount Television, ca. 1966): (*clockwise from top left*) Barbara Bain (Cinnamon), Peter Graves (Jim Phelps), Martin Landau (Rollin), Greg Morris (Barney) and Peter Lupus (Willy).

Space: 1999 there has been a short-lived (two-season) revival of *Mission: Impossible* with original star Peter Graves and cameos or supporting parts played by previous members of the I.M.F. (Impossible Mission Force) team, but not any appearances by Bain or Landau. They separated and divorced. Barbara Bain continues to act to this day by appearing in the occasional film like *Trust Me* (1989), where she played a dishonest art dealer, and the comic movie *Spirit of '76* (1990). More recently, she and Landau were rumored to be slated to appear in cameos for the feature film revivals of the *Mission: Impossible* television show that starred Tom Cruise, but no such roles were offered in any of the sequels. Bain did recreate the role of Cinnamon Carter in an episode of the Dick Van Dyke mystery series *Diagnosis: Murder* in the fall of 1997 (also on this same episode was Patrick Macnee, Robert Vaughan and Robert Culp, three male stars from some of sixties television's greatest spy programs, *The Avengers*, *The Man from U.N.C.L.E.* and *I Spy*, respectively). She told *TV Guide* magazine, "I've been asked to recreate the role many times and I didn't want to. But, *Diagnosis: Murder* came up and it was kind of the right moment to consider it."

Today Barbara Bain is more interested in helping to educate children through a program that she has helped develop where actors read stories and classic literature to underprivileged children. She told *Drama-Logue* magazine about the program: "I started with the books in my attic from my own kids. I started in Venice [California]. Now, I'm in Watts. It is very informal. I prefer just sitting on the floor. We are often in the library." Does her three-year stint on *Mission: Impossible* still follow her? She told *Drama-Logue*, "No question. There is kind of a fix on me in a certain way. The sophisticated, cool sort of thing."

Other films include: *Murder Once Removed* (1971—TV), *The Harlem Globetrotters on Gilligan's Island* (1981—TV), *Bel Air* (2000) and *American Gun* (2001).

Alexandra Bastedo

Alexandra Bastedo was born in East Sussex, England, on March 9, 1946. At the young age of three she wanted to be the "Elephant Lady" in the local traveling attraction, *Billy Smart's Circus*. At 14 years of age she wanted to be a veterinarian. As a young teenager she had been "discovered" by a joint Columbia Pictures and *London Evening News* contest that was hoping to find a young new starlet. The contest, dubbed "The Teenage Diplomat for Great Britain," garnered Alexandra Bastedo a co-starring role (as a character named England) in William Castle's thriller comedy *13 Frightened Girls* (1963). In this film, 13 girls in a Swiss boarding school become involved in espionage when a Russian spy is found murdered nearby. Due to this part, she received offers from the *Alfred Hitchcock Presents* and *The Donna Reed Show* programs in the U.S. However, her parents sent her back to school, quickly deflating her newfound film career.

Becoming a popular student, her quick glimpse of Hollywood set her on a different course. Several years later she was selected to compete in the "Miss United Kingdom" contest, where she also used her knowledge of the French, Italian and Spanish languages to assist in the interviewing of other contestants in their own languages and helped to translate their words to the audience. Her interest in acting began to grow and she started studying drama in earnest. In 1965 she appeared on the popular television program *The Saint* in the episode "Crime of the Century" (3/4) and returned to that show two years later in "The Counterfeit Countess" (3/3/67). Following that, an uncredited role in the spy movie *The Liquidator* (1965), and a minor one in *Casino Royale* (1967), ensured her path as a starlet, but leading roles eluded her until she was offered the third lead in the 1968 British television series *The Champions*.

The Champions was one of the strangest European-produced adventure programs ever made; and while its collective 30 episodes (over two years) did not successfully approach the often surreal level of fantasy featured in other spy-oriented programs like *The Avengers* and *The Prisoner*, years after its cancellation it has gained a cult following of its own.

The Champions' premise was simple yet effective. It involved a trio of secret agents, Craig Sterling (Stuart Damon), Richard Barrett (William Gaunt) and Sharron Macready (Bastedo), who suffer a near fatal plane crash in the Himalayan mountains while returning from a mission. Rescued by a mysterious Tibetan Monk and endowed with special powers, they are then returned home, where they put these new abilities to work for their Geneva-based organization, Nemesis. The special powers shared by the three agents include super strength, telepathy, ESP and a heightening of all their natural senses.

Their chief at Nemesis, Tremayne, is unaware of their new powers as he assigns them to a variety of seemingly impossible missions. In spite of their newly acquired powers, the "Champions of Law, Order and Justice" are by no means invincible, needing to work together as a collective team. The program was often a mixed bag of hardcore espionage stories sprinkled with some unusually adventurous situations (some involving grave danger to the cast by having them perform a variety of feats to display their supposed powerful strength). Behind the scenes, *Avengers* production people, like that show's creator, Brian Clemens, and one of its best directors, Roy Ward Baker, contributed to *The Champions*' success in England. But when American television stations declined to pick up the complete first season of *The Champions* (opting to only show ten episodes in 1968 on NBC), the future and the fate of *The Champions* was sealed, and the ITC series was canceled in 1969.

Alexandra Bastedo went on to appear in other British espionage series in the following years. On *Department S* she played Nicole in the episode "The Man Who Got a New Face" (10/15/69), where the team of Department S investigates the mysterious death of a wealthy man who collapses after someone attaches a grotesque mask to his face that he could not remove. Bastedo was also seen in the obscure TV series *Codename* in 1970, and appeared as Alexandra, a Russian agent masquerading as a Swedish journalist who's sent to entice information from Jason King (Peter Wyngarde) regarding his supposedly dead friend, a double agent, in "Variations of a Theme" (10/20/71) on *Jason King* (a *Department S* spin-off). She also guest starred on the American syndicated series shot abroad called *The Adventurer* starring Gene Barry. Her episode, entitled "Action," aired in 1972.

Bastedo then journeyed to Spain where she starred in the cult horror film favorite *The Blood Spattered Bride* (a.k.a. *La Novia Ensangrentada*, 1972), which was based in part on Sheridan Le Fanu's *Carmilla*, a

Alexandra Bastedo prepares to either seduce or murder a young victim in *The Blood Spattered Bride* (Morgana Films, 1972).

tale of lesbian vampiric lust. She then appeared in the strange *I Hate My Body* (a.k.a. *Odio Mi Cuerpo*), a sex change shocker thriller.

A featured role in the old-fashioned British thriller *The Ghoul* (1975), alongside veteran Hammer Films favorite Peter Cushing, was a clear attempt to return to the fold of more dramatic acting, but the failure of that hackneyed horror film (with gory murders) to find an appreciative audience sent Bastedo back to Spain, where she appeared in thrillers like *Estigma* (1979) and *La Verdad Oculta* (1987).

Retiring from show business, Alexandra Bastedo returned to an early love, animals. In recent years she has written three books; the latest, *Cat Care and Cuisine*, was published in 1998. Bastedo is also the President of the British RSPCA, Vice President of the Brent Lodge Bird Hospital and a patron of the Animal Welfare Trust, as well as other organizations. She maintained her own animal sanctuary until her death on January 12, 2014.

Other films include: *I Can't ... I Can't* (1969), *Kashmiri Run* (1970), *Find the Lady* (1976) and *Draw* (1984—TV).

Senta Berger

Senta Berger was born May 13, 1941, in Vienna, Austria. It has been reported in press release materials in the seventies that she was born while Vienna was under siege by invading German forces during World War II and that her family home was bombed four times before she was five years old. As a young child of six she enrolled in a ballet school. However, ten years later she was asked to leave because her body had developed too greatly for her to continue as a ballet student, which was fine for her since she had now shifted her personal interest towards the theater. She studied drama at the Reinhardt Seminar in Vienna and became one of the youngest persons to be admitted into the permanent ranks at the elite Theatre in der Josefstadt, another dramatic school. She performed onstage twice a week in a variety of productions throughout her scholastic years there, and was not that eager to leave the confines of the German stage for a film career. Earning a paltry $12 for her biweekly stage appearances, Berger would travel to school from her home and back via a bicycle. In fact, she told this story to the *Newark New Jersey Evening News* in November of 1960: "I felt that it would be nice to earn more money but I reasoned that at my age [at the time], training was more important. I lived at home with my parents, so $12 was enough to get by on. I rode a bicycle to the theater…"

Then the cinema came calling, and Senta Berger's film career began in 1957 when a director came around the school with the intent of casting actual schoolgirls, or drama students who could pass for young schoolgirls, in roles for his next film, *Die Lindenwirtin Vom Donaustrand* (1957).

Berger told a reporter for the Associated Press in the Spring of 1966, "After three weeks [of filming] my mother found out and gave me a slap." Afterwards, other roles were offered to her, but many of them, like *Die Unentschuldigte Stunde* (1957), did little to further her dramatic career, and she found herself often cast as the young voluptuous woman that she was in real life. Berger remained with the drama school and stage acting whilst she was filming these seemingly inconsequential (for her) films. Then one day her life changed when American actor Richard Widmark was casting for a new espionage film that he was co-producing and which would be filmed in Germany. Recalled Widmark to Associated Press journalist James Bacon in the fall of 1960, "Someone told me that the Josefstadt Theatre had a girl with the kind of figure Marilyn Monroe would like to have had. That's what I was looking for … acting ability was secondary."

Widmark went to the Josefstadt Theatre and, legend has it, saw his new discovery and co-star riding to school on her bicycle. The movie, *The Secret Ways* (1961), became the 20-year-old Berger's first American film. Even without the good word of mouth, chances are that Widmark would have probably spotted her anyway, given that by this time the young actress had become quite a head-turner with her 5'4" height, natural brunette hair, deep blue eyes (which appear gray-green in some films) and 37-24-38 measurements. In *The Secret Ways* Berger played a minor but pivotal role as Elsa, a woman that Widmark's character comes in contact with. In the film, a cynical American adventurer (Widmark) is paid to convince an aging underground leader (Walter Rilla) to leave Budapest. Widmark poses as a newsman to infiltrate the Iron Curtain, only to learn that the Communists are expecting an American agent posing as a newsman to try to enter the country. Widmark ends up in prison with Rilla and tries to get them both out of Eastern Europe. Today fans of the spy film genre consider it to be one of the underrated gems of the early sixties and comparable to another noir-ish, hard-boiled film, *The Spy Who Came in from the Cold*. For Senta Berger fans, the film is a real treat; costumed in a tight-fitting blouse and skirt two sizes too small for her frame, she appears to be literally busting out all over the screen whenever she appears.

For Senta Berger herself, the acclaim that the film bought her in the U.S. (*The Newark Evening News* declared her a "Siren Who Acts," and the *New York World-Telegram and Sun* mentioned "People Kept Staring") also brought her better, more prominent roles in Europe. Later on she claimed to an Associated Press reporter while promoting the film that her journey to Hollywood could have occurred earlier: "A famous director offered me a good role in a Hollywood movie when I was only 16 ... but first he wanted to take me on a holiday in the south of France to, as he put it, discuss the part. I declined and told him quite honestly that he was too old to be making such propositions to young girls."

As a result of Berger's work in *The Secret Ways*, she won a prominent part in the German espionage film *Operation Caviar* (a.k.a. *Es Muss Nicht Immer Kaviar Sein*, a.k.a. *It Doesn't Always Have to Be Caviar*, 1961) about a bank clerk who is forced against his will to work as a spy during the closing days of World War II. Another role at this time was in a German-produced thriller based on a mystery novel by British author Edgar Wallace, *The Secret of the Black Trunk* (a.k.a. *Das Geheimnis Der Schwarzen Koffer*, 1961). When Hammer Films directing veteran Terence Fisher entered into a co-production with a German film company, Berger was cast in the pivotal role of Ellen Blackburn in the Sherlock Holmes thriller (starring Christopher Lee) *Sherlock Holmes and the Deadly Necklace* (a.k.a. *Sherlock Holmes und das Halband des Todes*, 1962).

Espionage was the name of the game in the thriller *The Testament of Dr. Mabuse* (a.k.a. *Das Testament des Dr. Mabuse*, a.k.a. *Terror of the Mad Doctor*, 1962), in which she was cast as Nelly in this exciting and unusual remake of the Fritz Lang classic. After relocating his underworld base, the criminal mastermind Dr. Mabuse (Wolfgang Preiss) again plans more world domination, with police agencies on his trail. Minor roles followed until Berger was cast in the World War II adventure film *The Victors* (1963), which again brought her to the attention of American audiences and producers. As a result, Columbia Pictures signed her to a multiple picture contract in 1964. She said at the time to a reporter for the *New York World-Telegram and Sun*, "I cannot understand why, when I see so many beautiful girls in Hollywood." That same year she also appeared in the U.S. TV show *Walt Disney's Wonderful World of Color* in a two-part program, *The Waltz King*, which was released as a feature overseas.

Senta Berger's next role in a spy film was in the little seen *Spy Hunt in Vienna* (a.k.a. *Schusse Im Dreivierteltakt*, a.k.a. *Shots in ¾ Time*, 1964), in which a secret agent (Pierre Brice) travels all over Eastern Europe to track down a stolen device for a missile guidance system. The film also co-starred Daliah Lavi and perennial villain Anton Diffring.

Nineteen sixty-five was an important year in her career, as she had lead roles in two major films, *The Glory Guys* with Tom Tryon, and *Major Dundee* with Charlton Heston. Berger won the hearts of exhibitors, who voted her a "Star of Tomorrow." She was back on television in the spy pro-

Senta Berger as femme fatale Serena aims a deadly weapon in *The Spy with My Face* (MGM, 1965).

me, in a way ... and sometimes I feel like Alice in Wonderland" (*New York World-Telegram and Sun*, June 1964).

For espionage fans, Berger's next five films were all in the then-popular spy craze vein. The influence of the James Bond films just grew and grew and roles for beautiful, seductive and athletic women became available by the truckload. In *Bang! Bang! You're Dead!* (a.k.a. *Our Man in Marrakech*, 1966) Berger plays the love interest (as well as a spy) who becomes involved with an American innocent (Tony Randall) involved with a murderous spy ring in Morocco. In *To Commit a Murder* (a.k.a. *Peau D'Espion*, 1966) she plays the part of Gertraud Sphax, lover of the film's hero, a writer and war hero (Louis Jourdan) who

gram *The Man from U.N.C.L.E.* in a two-part episode, "The Double Affair" (11/17/64), that was released to theaters in the U.S. and abroad as *The Spy with My Face*. As a voluptuous femme fatale named Serena, Berger wasn't straining for Shakespearean dialog, but the role did help to make her a familiar face with American audiences who may have remembered her appearance in *The Victors*. The next year she achieved acclaim in the role of an Israeli soldier who falls in love with American Colonel Kirk Douglas in the politically charged film *Cast a Giant Shadow*. She said of her popularity at the time, "Columbia Pictures invented turns into a spy to battle sinister Chinese agents. During the course of the film, Jourdan is assigned to prevent a French scientist, working on a secret laser weapon, from defecting to China. She has a cameo role in the all-star *The Poppy Is Also a Flower* (a.k.a. *The Opium Connection*, 1966). This international co-production (funded by the United Nations) also features Yul Brynner, Angie Dickinson, Trevor Howard, E.G. Marshall and others.

One of Berger's most dramatic performances was in the brutal espionage film *The Quiller Memorandum* (1966), as Inge, a treacherous potential double agent. In the film, U.S. Agent Quiller (George Segal) battles a rising Neo-Nazi movement in contemporary Berlin. In one of the best of Dean Martin's Matt Helm movies, *The Ambushers* (1967), Berger nearly stole the show as Francesca Madeiros, an often undraped deadly femme fatale who assassinates her victims while clad in bra and panties. In this spoofy spy adventure she was more than just another of "Helm's girls" (actually modeled on the female assistants in James Coburn's Flint series)—she was a deadly adversary, as Helm (Martin), one of the U.S. Government's best secret agents, does battle with a nefarious criminal organization.

On American TV Berger found herself (as an enemy agent) playing second fiddle to former Miss America Mary Ann Mobley in the tele-feature *Istanbul Express* (1968). Gene Barry was top billed as a spy posing as an art dealer traveling on the Trans-Europa Express to Istanbul to bid for some valuable papers from a dead scientist. Berger also made two notable appearances on the espionage-themed television program *It Takes a Thief*, starring Robert Wagner as Al Mundy. In the series 90-minute premiere episode, "A Thief Is a Thief Is a Thief" (1/9/68), master thief Al Mundy is paroled from prison early to use his "expertise" for the S.I.A., a government agency involved with protecting the security of the U.S. Munday must steal a briefcase containing information on American agents from a Middle Eastern courier. Berger played Claire Vickers, and other guest stars included John Saxon and Susan Saint James. In "Flowers from Alexander" (10/23/69) Berger portrayed Laurie James, an old friend of Mundy's who asks him to accompany her to Rome, unaware that she is delivering secret information to her lover, an enemy agent and the only man to ever give her flowers.

Just as Senta Berger's international film career was busting out, so to speak, she began to work mainly in European films and was seldom seen on American screens thereafter. Roles in the twisty thriller *Diabolically Yours* (1967), with French matinee idol Alain Delon (later remade as *Shattered* with Tom Berenger and Bob Hoskins), and the notorious bomb *De Sade* (1969) (which was rated X in America because of its nudity and subject matter of the Marquis De Sade) did little to further her career.

In 1968 she married German writer-director Michael Verhoeven (no relation to the renowned Dutch film director Paul Verhoeven) and they have two children, Luca and Simon. Verhoeven has also directed his wife in at least four of his feature films. It became apparent that Berger was attempting to project a different kind of image for herself as a woman and as an actress. "Women are very much more exhibitionistic than men. I'm sure I'd have posed nude if I didn't happen to be married to a man who doesn't want me to expose myself," she commented to *The New York Post* columnist Earl Wilson in 1969. She must have changed her personal opinions about nudity when she began appearing *au naturel* in a variety of unusual films, including the controversial Italian prehistoric sex comedy *When Women Had Tails* (a.k.a. *Quando le Donne Avevano le Coda*, 1970), its sequel *When Women Lost Their Tails* (a.k.a. *Quando le Donne Persero la Coda*, 1971), an Italian sex comedy cum political allegory called *Roma Bene* (1971), the obscure French espionage drama *The Cobra* (a.k.a. *Saut d'Ange*, 1971) and the Italian thriller *Man Without a Memory* (a.k.a. *L'Uomo Senza Memoria*, 1974), where, as Sara Grimaldi, she wields a mean chainsaw in a deadly, nasty duel the same year that *The Texas Chainsaw Massacre* appeared on screens.

Senta Berger ended the seventies with appearances in Sam Peckinpah's highly regarded *Cross of Iron* (1976), about German soldiers during World War II and the incestuous love story *Portrait of a Bourgeois in Black* (a.k.a. *Ritratto di Borghesia in Nero*, a.k.a. *Nest of Vipers*), in which she raises the ire of her academic son by seducing his equally young schoolmate. In the spy thriller *The Swiss Conspiracy* (1977) Berger looked as glamorous as ever. In this film, a former American justice official (David Janssen), who now works as a Private Detective in Switzerland, is hired by a Zurich bank to protect its customers from blackmailers.

Senta Berger has never stopped acting; as a matter of fact, she has made at least one film nearly every year since *The Swiss Conspiracy*, her last appearance before American film audiences, and she has appeared in close to 100 movies. Working in television primarily nowadays, she has made at least four appearances in mini-series and films in Germany in 1999 alone, with *Zimmer mit Fruhstuck* (1999) being among the latest productions.

Other films include: *Killing Cars* (1985), *Oceano* (1989-Italian TV), *Bella Ciao* (1996—Italian TV) and *Probieren Sie's Mit Einem Jungeren* (2000—TV).

Martine Beswicke

Born September 26, 1941, in Port Antonio, Jamaica, Martine Beswicke is fondly recalled by spy film aficionados as Zora, one of the two Turkish Gypsy girls who wind up fighting over 007 in *From Russia with Love* (1963), and as Paula Caplan, an agent for the British government stationed in the Bahamas who assists Bond in a later assignment in *Thunderball* (1965). What many people probably do not know is that the actress also screen-tested for the role of Honeychile Ryder in the first James Bond film, *Dr. No*, in 1962.

In 1954 Martine moved to London, England, with her mother and younger sister. The next year she dropped out of high school to secure a paying position to help with the bills at home, becoming a secretary at the age of 16. Returning to Jamaica in 1956, her dark sultry looks gained her appearances in short promotional films made by the local tourist board. In 1961 she became "Miss Jamaica" after winning the island's prominent beauty contest and used the money awarded to her as the winning contestant to return to London.

Returning to England with her beauty title in hand, Beswicke managed to garner a position as a model in both fashion shows and magazine advertisements. Small roles in short films followed. One of them, in which she co-starred with a then up and coming popular singer, was seen by British film director Robert-Hartford Davies, who cast her in a bit part in his film *Saturday Night Out* in 1962. It was a role (as a barmaid) with only one line of dialog, but for Beswicke it was a start in the cinema. As a result, a talent agency looked over her resume, took a look at her short film roles and sent her on an audition for a leading role that was being cast for a new film titled *Dr. No*.

It has been reported that Terence Young, the director of the first James Bond adventure, was very impressed by Martine Beswicke's physical appearance but thought that her acting experience lacked bite.

Encouraged by the screen test for the Honey Ryder role, Beswicke enrolled in acting classes. The following year Young recalled her screen test and hired her for the role of Zora, a Turkish Gypsy hellcat in the second James Bond film, *From Russia with Love* (1963).

In this film, the second Bond movie with Sean Connery as secret agent 007, Beswicke stood out as one of the two Turkish Gypsy girls who fight over a local man and who then vie to share the night with Bond after a cataclysmic fight with Russian spies. Of the part, she recalled to interviewer Steve Swires in *Fangoria* magazine in July of 1986, "I was a very nice girl, but Alizia Gur (who played Vida, the other Gypsy girl) was a cow.... We had terrible clashes and I was disgusted with her. I had a lot of anger inside me, so that scene was the perfect way to work it out. We rehearsed the fight for three weeks, but when we shot it, Gur was really fighting. Everyone encouraged me to fight back, so I did. We got into a real scrapping match." If what Beswicke says here is true, then that explains the catfight ferocity that fuels this scene, one of the most memorable in the Bond cinematic canon. (This was corroborated in the now deleted audio commentary by Bond producers and director Young for the Criterion laser disc release of the film in 1993.) As a side note, *From Russia with Love* won a British Academy Award for "Best Cinematography." It was the first and only James Bond film to win one up to 1973.

Beswicke returned to the world of James Bond in 1965 for the fourth film in the franchise, *Thunderball*. As Paula Caplan, an agent assigned to the Bahamas, she assists Bond (Connery) as he romances the seductive Domino (Claudine Auger) while avoiding the treacherous lure of Luciana Paluzzi's femme fatale character and attempting to prove that multi-millionaire Largo is in fact an enemy agent working for S.P.E.C.T.R.E.–head Blofeld. Beswicke also recalled this role for Swires in the same *Fangoria* interview in 1986: "That was absolutely one of the greatest filmmaking experiences of my life. Although I only worked for a few days, I was in the Bahamas for two months. We completely took over the island and had everything that we wanted. Since the other actresses were working much more than I was, I got to do all the publicity." That same year she appeared in *Danger Man* (a.k.a. *Secret Agent*) in an episode titled "Such Men Are Dangerous."

Beswicke was then cast as the second female lead in the Hammer Films prehistoric action hit *One Million Years B.C.* (1966), opposite Raquel Welch. As Nupondi she competed with Welch for leading man John Richardson (who she won in real life, for Martine and Richardson subsequently lived together for seven years). As a side note, John Richardson had screen tested (among other actors vying for the role) to replace Sean Connery for *On Her Majesty's Secret Service* (1969), but the role went to Australian model George Lazenby. In *The Penthouse* (1967) Beswicke was featured as the female member of a trio of British psychopaths who terrorize a philandering couple. Finally garnering a leading role, she was cast as Queen Kari in the film *Prehistoric Women* (1967), a sort of follow-up to the successful *One Million Years B.C.* As the seductive and deadly leader of a tribe of lost Amazons, Beswicke had one of the great roles of a lifetime. Unfortunately, the production was plagued by indifferent direction, a low budget and the fact that it was following up a gargantuan worldwide box-office hit, without that film's scope and original leading actress.

Roles in the European westerns *A Bullet for the General* (a.k.a. *Quien Sabe?*) and *John the Bastard* (both 1967) followed, as well as two appearances on the American espionage television show *It Takes a Thief* (she appeared in the "Blue, Blue Danube"

Martine Beswicke as Zora, the Gypsy girl, prepares to entice Sean Connery (James Bond) in *From Russia with Love* (United Artists, 1963).

[as Maria, 10/30/69] and "The Galloping Skin Game" [as Christine Leland, 12/3/68]). A small role (as the original assistant to blind detective James Franciscus) in the 1970 pilot of the underrated American television show *Longstreet* (1970) followed, but when the series was picked up she was replaced by Marlyn Mason.

Returning to England and to Hammer Films, Beswicke starred in the controversial *Dr. Jekyll and Sister Hyde* (1971). However, the success of this film did not translate into better roles for the actress, and she ended up appearing in Oliver Stone's low budget cult film debut, *Seizure* (1973), as "the Queen of Evil," and in the Italian sexploitation film *Ultimo Tango a Zagarol* (1973) as a prostitute. She ended the seventies by appearing in low budget trash films like *Devil Dog: The Hound from Hell* (1978—TV) and *The Happy Hooker Goes to Hollywood* (1980), her first starring role in a decade.

Martine Beswicke has spent the better part of the last 20 years trying to regain her former glory as an in-demand actress. Despite appearing in small roles in such prominent films as Jonathan Demme's *Melvin and Howard* (1980), and in popular direct-to-video action and horror titles like Fred Olen Ray's *Cyclone* (1987) and *The Offspring* (a.k.a. *From a Whisper to a Scream*, 1987) which seemed designed primarily for cult film audiences, she has seemed to have had a difficult time. Recently she has contributed (onscreen) commentary for the DVD re-release of *From Russia with Love*.

Other films include: *Crime Club* (1975—TV), *Strange New World* (1975—TV), *My Husband Is Missing* (1980—TV), *Balboa* (1986), *Miami Blues* (1990), *Evil Spirits* (1990), *Wide Sargasso Sea* (1993) and *Night of the Scarecrow* (1995).

Daniela Bianchi

Daniela Bianchi was born on January 31, 1942, in Rome, Italy. As a young girl she studied ballet. But as she grew into womanhood she found herself becoming a voluptuous young lady and, therefore, unable to go forward with that dream. She became one of Italy's top fashion models, and in 1960 her modeling career went international when she became the first runner-up in the "Miss Universe" contest (although she did win the prize as "Miss Photogenic" in the overall contest). In 1962 she was crowned "Miss Italy," and television producers began to pay attention to her 5'7" height, light brown hair, golden-brown eyes and that fabulous frame. She appeared on Italian television in a small role alongside Rossano Brazzi, and this led to her cinematic career and her first major film, with a supporting role in *Always on Sunday* (a.k.a. *Una Domenica D'Estate*, 1962). She followed with another supporting role in the Italian-Spanish costume adventure *The Sword of El Cid* (a.k.a. *La Spada Del El Cid*, 1962).

In 1963 Daniela Bianchi was cast as the leading lady in the second James Bond film, *From Russia with Love*, after the Bond filmmakers had already seen 200 hopefuls throughout Europe; they settled on her after they came across her face adorning an Italian glamour magazine. As Tatiana

Romanova, she became the second major love interest for the Bond character, then played by Sean Connery, and a fitting successor, at least physically, to the previous film's leading lady, Ursula Andress.

In the film, her character lures Bond to the boudoir (not an uneasy task, given the proclivities of the womanizing hero), with the promise of assistance in acquiring a special Russian decoding device for his country in exchange for asylum. Tricked by her own countrymen and KGB agent Rosa Klebb (Lotte Lenya) into becoming a double agent, Tatiana becomes an unwilling and unknowing pawn in an elaborate plan to trick the British government into assigning Bond to a special mission only to have a superbly deadly assassin (Robert Shaw) assigned to his demise. Described by Bond author Ian Fleming in the original book, her character has "...pale soft skin with an ivory sheen at the cheekbones. Wide apart, level eyes of the deepest blue ... the lips were full and finely etched." This aptly describes Bianchi's facial features. Of course, Fleming could not have expected the producers to also make such a wide-waisted, hip-swinging, bosomy find as her to bring his Tatiana to life, making his character even more three-dimensional.

Unfortunately, rumors persist to this day that much of her vocal performance in the film was dubbed by another actress because of Bianchi's trouble with the English language. The audio commentary (now since deleted), long out of print, of the Criterion laser disc edition of the film released in the early nineties had Bond producers and director Terence Young uncomfortably joking that they often had to film the actress from the waist upward due to her awkward walk and wide hips. Whatever the truth, Bianchi's appearance was tantalizing enough to the filmmakers that they filled the movie with risqué double entendres. In one scene her character tells Bond (just before a long kiss) that her mouth is too big; he replies "It's the right size, for me that is..."

The next year Bianchi was working in

The beautiful Daniela Bianchi poses on the set of *From Russia with Love* (United Artists, 1963).

the United States in a special three-part episode of the television show *Dr. Kildare*. Titled "Rome Will Never Leave," the special episodes were intended to show a new romantic love interest for *Kildare* star Richard Chamberlain's hard-working physician. However, in a November 1964 interview in *TV Guide* magazine she seemed to have trouble with the English language, telling of her inability to comprehend the labyrinthine Los Angeles Freeway and exclaiming, "I want to be a big star!"

She returned to the big screen and more espionage fun in the French spoof *The Tiger Likes Fresh Blood* (a.k.a. *Le Tigre Aime La Chair Fraiche*, 1964), where The Tiger, a.k.a. Louis Rapire (Roger Hanin), a French Secret Service agent, guards the wife and daughter (Bianchi) of a Turkish diplomat targeted for assassination by enemy agents. In 1965 she was back in the spy game in *Mission Bloody Mary* (a.k.a. *Agente 077: Missione Bloody Mary*), an obscure but exceptional action film produced in Europe. Like many of the European Bond clones of the period, *Mission* was a low budget but earnest and enjoyable knock-off of the more elaborate Bond films. The plot, in particular, for this film demanded attention: When an atomic bomb is stolen by the Chinese in a plan for world domination, American secret agent Dick Malloy (Ken Clark) is assigned to the case. The CIA itself (or a renegade faction) may actually be responsible for the theft. Bianchi, as the leading lady, plays the love interest in this film.

It seemed that Bianchi's career became firmly entrenched in espionage and melodramas, as is shown by her next role in the film *Slalom* (1965). In this unusual movie, the hero (Vittorio Gassman) is a newlywed on his honeymoon who becomes involved with a gang of counterfeiters led by (*Thunderball* villain) Adolfo Celli, employed by the Chinese to flood the world with false currency. Bianchi is the hero's bride.

In the bizarre spy spoof *Operation Oro* (a.k.a. *Baleari Operazione Oro*, a.k.a. *The Balearic Caper*, 1966), she appears alongside co-star Jacques Sernas, Marilu Tolo and *Goldfinger* villain Harold Sakata. A wonderful leading role as a villain and then as the heroine in *Special Mission Lady Chaplin* (a.k.a. *Missione Speciale Lady Chaplin*, 1966)— playing Lady Arabella Chaplin—brought Bianchi good notices in the European press. It also helped that the film was a medium budgeted, above average action movie about Secret agent Dick Malloy (Ken Clark), who investigates the disappearance of an atomic submarine, the murder of important individuals and a secret organization that uses a deadly liquid to destroy. The film also featured Helga Line and Jacques Bergerac in its cast.

Bianchi was cast in the violent and sadistic *Requiem for a Secret Agent* (a.k.a. *Requiem per un Agente Segreto*, 1966) as Evelyn. In this film, spy John "Bingo" Merrill (Stewart Granger) is employed by the British Secret Service when he is not moonlighting as a double agent or an adventurer. Merrill looks into the murder of a fellow agent by foreign spies in Morocco. As he investigates, he uncovers a criminal organization that arranges assassinations, corrupt political activities and war; he also teams with Israeli agents hunting a former Nazi war criminal (Peter Van Eyck) who may be the gang's leader. When Granger learns of Bianchi's duplicity (she is in league with the villains), he shoots her dead in cold blood.

A more lighthearted entry is *Operation Kid Brother* (a.k.a. *O.K. Connery*, 1967). When James Bond (referred to, but not actually named) is presumed to have been killed in an airplane accident, Dr. Neil Connery (played by Neil Connery, brother of Sean Connery), the brother of James Bond(!), is asked to join the spy service (by Bernard Lee and Lois Maxwell, who played M and Moneypenny respectively in the "real" 007 series) as a villain (Adolfo Celli, playing a mix of the *Goldfinger* and *Thunderball* villains) plots to rule the world with powerful weapons, etc., assisted by a traitorous femme fatale (Bianchi). Neil Connery's secret is that he is a supreme martial arts master and a world renowned hypnotist, and he uses both talents to defeat the criminal empire of Celli, known here as Thanatos. In bed with hero Connery (Neil that is), Bianchi has the juicy line: "Your brother was never like this!"

In *Dirty Heroes* (a.k.a. *Dalle Ardenne all'Inferno*, 1968), a World War II film with espionage overtones, Bianchi has one of her best roles: Towards the end of World War II, two American GIs (one of them Frederick Stafford, an Austrian actor who himself starred in a number of spy films in Italy in the sixties), who had been Chicago underworld figures before the war, plan to steal a valuable treasure from the German military command. While they also attempt to assist the Nazi-fighting Partisans in Italy, one of the men (Stafford) falls in love with the Jewish medical assistant wife (Bianchi) of a German tank squad commander (Curt Jurgens).

Bianchi's last film to date was *The Last Chance* (a.k.a. *Scacco Internazionale*, 1968), in which Michael Rennie stars as a NATO agent who recruits American newsman Tab Hunter in Europe to help battle Russian spy ring led by Mr. X. She retired from acting after marrying an Italian shipping magnate during the early seventies, and they have one son.

Recently, Daniela Bianchi contributed onscreen commentary to the special edition DVD release of *From Russia with Love* issued in late 2000.

Other films include: *L'Ombrellone* (1966) and *Troppo per Vivre ... Poco per Morire* (1967).

Jacqueline Bisset

A leading lady of the late sixties through the eighties, stunning actress Jacqueline Bisset (born Winnifred Jacqueline Fraser-Bisset on September 13, 1944, in Surrey, England) started out as a model before landing a bit role in *The Knack ... And How to Get It* (1965). In 1967 she delivered two performances that got the critics and Hollywood talking. In *Two for the Road* she played a vacationing schoolgirl who comes down with measles. The other role was that of Giovanna Goodthighs in the ornate, overdone James Bond spoof *Casino Royale*, Bisset's first foray into the spy genre. Considering all the competing shapely female forms displayed in *Casino Royale* (including those of Ursula Andress, Joanna Pettet, Daliah Lavi, and Barbara Bouchet), it was an impressive feat for this newcomer to get noticed. However, with brown-auburn wavy hair, full lips and penetrating green eyes, it is not too surprising she stood out. Bisset was truly a stunner. Though only on screen for a short period of time, Bisset was so dazzling she snagged a contract with 20th Century-Fox. Stardom was just around the corner.

In the convoluted *Casino Royale* (1967) a retired Sir James Bond (David Niven) returns to service to save the world from

SMERSH, who is killing the top agents from all over the world. To confuse the enemy, a number of agents are re-named James Bond and are sent into the field. Jacqueline Bisset appears briefly in scenes directed by Joe McGrath and Robert Parrish as the seductive Giovanna Goodthighs. (She told the *New York Post* in 1968 that, "I thought this name would do for me what the name Pussy Galore did for Honor Blackman in another James Bond movie.") Bisset is very enticing as Miss Goodthighs, who is sent by the head of SMERSH, Le Chiffre (Orson Welles), to terminate bungling agent Evelyn Tremble (Peter Sellers), one of many spies masquerading as James Bond. As he enters his hotel suite, the beautiful spy, scantily clad in a man's shirt and holding a champagne bottle, greets him. Startled, Tremble fires a shot from his gun. "You missed, Mr. Bond. I'm Miss Goodthighs." Tremble deadpans, "I can see that." After explaining that she and the champagne are compliments of the hotel, she makes her way over to his bed and comments, "Very sexy pants you're wearing, James." He answers proudly, "Yes, they're the new Double 0 fronts." As they roll around the bed, Goodthighs drugs his champagne, but Tremble drops an antidote pill into it. He gets woozy, stumbles out of bed, and collapses in the bathroom, only to be awakened by the lovely Vesper Lynd (Ursula Andress). After complaining about why the antidote pill didn't give him 24-hour protection as promised by the real James Bond, he wonders what happened to Miss Goodthighs. Vesper replies intently, "Don't worry. I took good care of her." Unfortunately for the film, that is the last we see of Bisset's character.

According to Chris Strodder, writing in *Swingin' Chicks of the '60s*, Bisset did not like the name "Miss Goodthighs" because she felt it drew attention to her weakest feature. Also, since she so impressed the film's producers after her scenes were completed in two days, she remained on the set for ten weeks playing one of Orson Welles' many gang members.

Also in 1967, Bisset landed one of her first leading roles in the obscure spy movie *The Cape Town Affair* (1967), co-starring James Brolin and Claire Trevor, which was a remake of *Pickup on South Street*. Filmed on location in South Africa, the movie features Brolin as a thief who steals a purse containing a reel of microfilm from a woman named Candy (Bisset)—the unknowing courier for a Communist spy ring. *The Cape Town Affair* was barely noticed in 1967, as Brolin and Bisset were unknowns then, but due to their later star power it is now available on video.

Jacqueline Bisset had a banner year in 1968 co-starring in two box office hits—*The Detective* with Frank Sinatra and *Bullitt* with Steve McQueen. And she received a Golden Globe nomination for "Most Promising Newcomer–Female" for her role as a promiscuous out-of-work actress in *The Sweet Ride* (1968) starring Michael Sarrazin. After playing a pregnant stewardess in the glossy all-star blockbuster *Airport* (1970), Bisset gave one of her finest performances, as a naïve woman who abandons her family for the glamour of Las Vegas in *The Grasshopper* (1970). She continued impressing the critics with roles in the Academy Award winning drama *Day for Night* (1973) and *The Thief Who Came to Dinner* (1973). However, her most popular role was as a scientist in the underwater adventure film *The Deep* (1977). Fans were attracted to the film not to immerse themselves in Bisset's acting prowess but to see her clad only in a wet T-shirt. These shots were so popular that a poster of Bisset from the film became one of the biggest sellers of the seventies, while *Newsweek* voted her "the most beautiful film actress of all time."

Jacqueline Bisset's film career cooled by the late eighties, and she has become a

Jacqueline Bisset lives up to her name as Miss Goodthighs in *Casino Royale* (Columbia, 1967).

permanent fixture in expensive international made-for-TV productions. One of her most recent small screen ventures, *Joan of Arc* (1999), won Bisset Emmy and Golden Globe nominations for "Best Supporting Actress." Still a talented beauty, Bisset seems ready to tackle many more roles to come.

Other films include: *Cul-de-Sac* (1966), *Secret World* (1969), *Secrets* (1971), *The Mephisto Waltz* (1971), *The Life and Times of Judge Roy Bean* (1972), *Murder on the Orient Express* (1974), *The Spiral Staircase* (1975—TV), *St. Ives* (1976), *The Greek Tycoon* (1978), *Who Is Killing the Great Chefs of Europe?* (1978), *When Time Ran Out* (1980), *Rich and Famous* (1981), *Class* (1983), *Under the Volcano* (1984), *Anna Karenina* (1985—TV), *Napoleon and Josephine: A Love Story* (1987—TV), *Scenes from the Class Struggle in Beverly Hills* (1989), *Wild Orchid* (1990), *End of Summer* (1997—TV), *Let the Devil Wear Black* (1999), *Britannic* (2000—TV), *Sex and Mrs. X* (2000—TV), *New Year's Day* (2000) and *Heart of Stone* (2000).

Honor Blackman

Honor Blackman was born on August 27, 1927, in London, England. Legend has it that a film producer spotted the blue eyed blonde riding a motorcycle as a courier for a wartime blood donor service. This led to her professional film career and a contract with the British film production company, the J. Arthur Rank Organization, where she and other young hopeful starlets, were groomed for fame. In actuality, the Rank Organization signed many a young and pretty aspiring actress to their roster in order to decorate their entries into the UK's postwar film boom with these lovely ladies in primarily walk-on roles, but some graduated to speaking parts and better.

Among Blackman's first documented film appearances was a bit part in *Fame Is the Spur* in 1946. Four years later she graduated to a supporting role in the espionage film *The Conspirator* (1950), with Robert Taylor as a double agent and Elizabeth Taylor as his wife who stumbles upon her husband's secret. Blackman continued toiling in forgettable low-budget programmers, but one credit of interest was in an episode of *The New Adventures of Charlie Chan* (1958), a short-lived, Poverty Row–budgeted British television program. She then received good notices for her role in the film *A Night to Remember* (1958) as Miss Liz Lucas. This film was a melodramatic but earnest recreation of the events leading up to the disaster that befell the cruise ship *Titanic* after the turn of the century. Until the 1998 James Cameron–directed version of the film, this would be regarded as the best cinematic interpretation of the story.

However, despite good press, film stardom still eluded Honor Blackman, and she returned to British television for a supporting role on the program *The Four Just Men* (based on the best-selling Edgar Wallace mystery) and a leading role in *Probation Officer* in 1959. Her role as a tough-talking but attractive female probation officer, a masculine woman if you will, paved the way for her role in *The Avengers*. Other popular espionage programs of the time in which she appeared were *Danger Man* (called *Secret Agent* in the U.S.), in the episode "Colonel Rodriguez" (telecast in America on 4/21/61), and *The Saint*, in the "Arrow of God" episode (telecast in the U.S. on 5/7/65, but filmed in 1962). In this tale, Simon Templar (Roger Moore) investigates the death of a man at a house party and learns that every single guest had a reason to murder him, including the victim's wife (Blackman).

In 1961 the popular British television program *Police Surgeon* was suffering a crisis when leading star Ian Hendry (who played Dr. Martin King) announced that he was leaving the program, catapulting co-star Patrick Macnee into the leading role. The show's producers searched for a suitable co-star for Macnee's John Steed character and, in the process, changed the format entirely from a policier into an espionage drama. Blackman was cast as Cathy Gale (after original choice Nyree Dawn Porter was unavailable for the role, even after numerous successful screen tests), and in her two years on the program she helped to change the way that British television audiences would face the world. At the height of her fame with *The Avengers*, Blackman's Cathy Gale was thought of (in the same way as were The Beatles) as a contributing factor in the

Honor Blackman poses in her skin-tight leather on the set of the television program *The Avengers* (EMI Film Distributors, Ltd., ca. 1962).

breakdown of social mores and the newfound expression of sexual morality. Cathy Gale was a rough and tumble secret agent, a woman who felt comfortable in a slinky, sexy leather dress as well as a skin-tight leather pantsuit. Highlighting the ample actress' wardrobe was a seldom-doffed pair of high-heeled black leather boots. The leather craze that Blackman had inadvertently started was due to an idea to wear such garments to make her character seem more menacing; it became a fashion style. Even a usually staid London *Sunday Times* television critic commented (in 1964), "I'm sure Ms. Gale's taste in clothes is a boon to innumerable fetishists and deviationists."

For the (sometimes live) rushed production schedule of the series, Blackman had to endure all sorts of bruises and bumps rehearsing the show's elaborately choreographed stunt fights. She told a reporter for the New York World Telegram and Sun in December 1964, "For two years I had black and blue marks all over me and purple shoulders. I hated to wear a dress because of the great mass of bruises on my legs."

As the show's popularity with audiences, particularly male viewers, grew, so did the program's element of kinkiness and unusual charm. Blackman's character was spending so much screen time saving co-star Macnee and kicking male villain butt that she had few moments to be the sensuous woman that the real-life Blackman claimed to be. Seeking a way to introduce a kinder, gentler Cathy Gale to UK audiences met with derision by the show's producers, and she stayed in the role of the judo-chopping Cathy Gale until 1964. She told the same New York World Telegram and Sun reporter in 1964, "One night as I was bashing around on the mat taking my judo instruction, I asked my instructor what he thought about Cathy having a lover [on the show]. He analyzed it perfectly. He said that men watching the show didn't want to see Cathy being mauled by anyone else [besides the villains]."

She explained further to a British Associated Press journalist in 1969, "Men still get belligerent in my company. Half of them seem to be afraid that I'll pick them up and throw them out the window. The other half seem to want me to try." The show's popularity was such that in early 1964, months before Blackman left the show, she and Patrick Macnee recorded a single for Decca Records. On one side was the song "Kinky Boots," the other "Let's Keep It Friendly." Neither television star could actually sing, but the record was devised as a novelty to commemorate the black shiny leather boots worn by Blackman's Cathy Gale character. The recording stiffed, but, oddly enough, 25 years later, with the retro-sixties craze in full swing due to the immense popularity of the American secret agent spoof *Austin Powers: International Man of Mystery* (1996), the single was re-released and crept up the charts to become something of a minor sensation. The small disaster of the failure of the original release of the "Kinky Boots" single to chart did not faze Blackman, who promptly recorded an album as well, *Everything I've Got*, in 1964. In between co-starring on the television show she found time to appear in the feature films *A Matter of Who?* (1962), an obscure thriller with espionage overtones, and as the Goddess Hera in the mythological adventure *Jason and the Argonauts* (1963).

Before informing *The Avengers'* producers that she would not be returning to the show, as her contract was about to run out for the current season, there occurred a bit of media attention surrounding Blackman. Apparently, during a rehearsal for an elaborate, violent fight scene, she had thrown a stuntman into a shallow grave and actually knocked him unconscious. There began a number of British tabloid stories that claimed that Ms. Blackman was becoming a little too associated with the fictional character of Cathy Gale. This feat of strength impressed the producers of the James Bond films and they signed her for one of the leading roles in the third James Bond entry, *Goldfinger* (1964). As Pussy Galore, one of Ian Fleming's most devilish femme fatales, Blackman would have the role of a lifetime. The fact that her real-life training for *The Avengers* had garnered her an Orange Belt in Judo had helped as well, especially in some of the fight sequences on the Bond film. She revealed to a *New*

York World columnist in 1964, "They provided me with a double for the scene where I fly through the air and land in the hay, but I preferred to do it myself. They gave me a mattress under the hay to land on. I never had it so good." Adding to the producers' worries that Blackman's character in both the original Fleming novel (also called *Goldfinger*) and the film was written with some subtle and some not-so-subtle lesbian references was concern over her character's name; for a brief time they considered changing it to Kitty Galore.

Goldfinger is considered by Bond buffs to be among the long-running series' best entries. With its tale of a European megalomaniac named Auric Goldfinger (Gert Frobe) who plans on sabotaging the entire Gold Reserve supply of the United States in an elaborate robbery leading to a sinister world domination scheme, the film also takes the series into new territory, that of the fantastic, with its deadly laser beam weapons, sensuous, voluptuous, but treacherous femme fatales and nearly unstoppable killer henchmen, exemplified in this film by Harold Sakata's deadly Odd Job. Like the Ian Fleming story, Bond (Sean Connery) finally beds the butch Pussy Galore and seemingly cures her of any other possible sexual tendencies outside of heterosexuality. In the end, Bond saved the world, and to most closed-minded people packing theater auditoriums in 1964, he saved it from more than just the villain Goldfinger and his world domination scheme.

As for Honor Blackman, the role of Pussy Galore would haunt her for years. While she would garner good reviews for roles in films as diverse as *Life at the Top* (1965) and *The Secret of My Success* (1965), the kind of media attention and success that accompanied her earlier seemed to have vanished. She retreated to the stage (she acted in the leading role in the macabre thriller *Wait Until Dark* in England in 1967) and her family life (she had married actor Maurice Kaufman in 1961, and they adopted a son and a daughter to complete their home).

Blackman reunited with Connery for the strange western *Shalako* (1968) and then appeared in the underrated adventure film *A Twist of Sand* (1968). She briefly danced with controversy when she appeared nude in the film *The Virgin and the Gypsy* (1970), an adaptation of a steamy D.H. Lawrence novel. Smaller roles in exploitation films like *Revenge* (1971) and an uncredited appearance in Richard Lester's all-star *The Three Musketeers* (1973) followed. Genre film aficionados might recall her appearance in the next to last Hammer Film of the seventies, *To the Devil—A Daughter* (1975), and as the villainous Susan Sillsby in Radley Metzger's above average remake of *The Cat and the Canary* (1978).

Recently, Honor Blackman has been seen as a regular on the British television program *The Upper Hand* (1990–1993), in *Talos, the Mummy* (1999), where she portrayed a police chief and in the films *Bridget Jones' Diary* (2001) and *Jack Brown and the Curse of the Crown* (2001).

Other films include: *Something Big* (1971), *The Secret Adversary* (1982) and *The Sight* (2000).

Erika Blanc

Erika Blanc was born Enrica Bianchi Colombato on July 23, 1942, in Gargnano in Brescia, Italy. As a young child she spent her early years growing up near the shores of Lake Garda, one of Italy's most scenic lakes, located in the northern section of the country. When she grew into a young woman, Blanc studied in a school in France and then continued her scholastic education in a special school in Geneva, studying costume design, as one of her goals was to become a dress designer. While in Geneva she was offered a contract to be a model for an advertising firm.

Before returning to Italy, Blanc also spent a short time as a journalist for the fashion magazine *Le Femme d'Aujourd Hui* and the journal *La Tribune de Geneve* reporting on current events and fashions. Returning home, Blanc was spotted one day walking near Lake Garda by an Italian producer named Bruno Gaburro, who asked the 20 year old to appear in a documentary about the lake region. Infatuated with her now striking adult features, very high cheekbones and eerie, piercing eyes, all set upon a pale, nearly unreal mannequin-like face, Gaburro asked her to marry him and she obliged.

The couple moved to Rome, Italy's capital, where they lived a tough, financially strained life, causing Blanc to find work as a waitress, then as an erotic dancer in a nightclub. Erika Blanc then appeared in a number of fashion magazine layouts and the occasional television commercial as an extra. Striking up a friendship with the film crew of a Rossano Brazzi and Maureen O'Hara romantic film titled *Villa Fiorita*, she gained a small role. She was soon signed by famed producer Dino De Laurentiis to test for roles in some of the peplums, or sword and sandal movies of the time, that were very popular in Italy and the overseas countries to which they were exported. But these appearances never came to be, as she quickly lost parts to the scores of other actresses in the area. During this time one of Blanc's more prominent early roles (although uncredited) was in director Tinto Brass' science fiction comedy *Il Disco Volante* (1964), a film that also featured the then new screen sensation Monica Vitti in the role of Dolores.

During this time Blanc appeared in a very successful photo-story magazine, which was sold at newspaper stands. In it she appeared in a continuing story told through cartoon style dialogue balloons and still photographs featuring her as the heroine in melodramatic moments. It was most likely this series of photo books, which featured the actress in a number of identities, like "Erika Brown" and "Erika White," that bought her even greater attention.

She was signed to a larger role than usual in one of the early Italian James Bond–style films, titled *Operation Atlantis* (a.k.a. *Agente 003 Operazione Atlantide*, 1965). This film told the tale of a Special Science Organization (The R.I.U.) that invites Secret Agent S 03 (John Ericson) to a nuclear base in the Middle East (named Atlantis) to investigate possible sabotage. Blanc appeared as a contact for Ericson's agent, only to be killed off by a rival spy. "That was my [real] film debut," remembers Erika Blanc. "I played a spy. I had to meet the secret agent, dressed as a prostitute not to be exposed, but since the cameras were placed very far, it had to be a long shot, passing cars were stopping me for real! I had never heard

Erica Blanc, starlet of a number of European espionage films.

such four-letter words before, let's say I was a bit naïve and these passers-by covered me with obscenities. Dear me, my very first [major] scene in a movie and I was dressed like a whore, waiting for that damn secret agent."

Blanc had a slightly larger role (as Miss Perry) in her next film, *Mission Bloody Mary* (a.k.a. *Agente 077: Mission Bloody Mary*, (1965). In this enjoyable, kinetic and violent movie, Blanc's talents and growing erotic presence onscreen were used as a brief diversion for the main plot, which involved a stolen atomic bomb by Communist Chinese agents who plan to use the weapon in a scheme for world domination. Secret agent Dick Malloy (American actor Ken Clark) is assigned to the case. A mole in the CIA (which Malloy works for) may actually be involved in the theft. "Every-thing they offered, I accepted it," recalled Blanc. "In *Bloody Mary*, I was the secretary."

In the Italian-Spanish co-production *Espionage in Lisbon* (a.k.a. *Mision Lisboa*, a.k.a. *Mission Lisbon*, 1965) where secret agent 077 (Brett Halsey) is sent after a formula that neutralizes electricity, Blanc was billed as the "girl in a bikini." Nevertheless, although this was a smaller role for her in this film, which is chiefly remembered for its script by the Spanish genre filmmaker Jess Franco and its jaunty music by frequent Franco collaborator Daniel White, Blanc made enough of an impression on Italian film producers to allow her to make the jump to leading roles.

In *The Vengeance of Lady Morgan* (a.k.a. *La Vendetta di Lady Morgan*, 1965), she appeared as an evil, corrupting governess who, together with a sadistic brute, plans to drive the actual owner (Barbara Nelli) of a recently inherited castle to madness and suicide. Coming to the heroine's aid is a male vampiric ghost who thwarts the plans of the villains.

Blanc returned to the spy genre for an appearance in *A Million Dollars for an Assassin* (a.k.a. *Un Millione di Dollari Per Sette Assassini*, 1966). In this convoluted espionage movie, an American criminal named Michael King (Roger Browne) is drafted to become an adventurer and rescue the misguided son of a wealthy Middle Eastern man from a band of criminals. Instead, the former master thief finds action when he contends with villainous spies and murderers.

Blanc's biggest break came via a starring role in director Mario Bava's *Kill, Baby, Kill* (a.k.a. *Operazione Paura*, a.k.a. *Operation Fear*, 1966), in which she played the part of a young woman returning to her ancestral home, plagued by a murderous ghostly child. "Bava did things that no other adult could," said Blanc. "Look, I don't mean he acted like a child, because he was an incredibly intelligent man, very polite as well, it's just that he had this playful attitude as it were. He made us all feel the atmosphere of the story, got us involved in this big game that we were playing."

More spy films that she appeared in during this period are *The Spy Kills Silently* (a.k.a. *Le Spie Uccidono in Silenzio*, 1966), which is about an Interpol agent (Lang Jeffries) working with Scotland Yard who investigates a criminal gang terrorizing the scientific peace progress community. She played a drug-addicted villainess in this film: "I remember shooting in Beirut with five different actors, each speaking his own language, in the same scene ... a disaster! They put liquid in my eyes for a scene in which I had to look as if I had been drugged or something like that. They called a doctor who gave me this liquid to make my eyes black, there were no contact lenses then and I did the scene with my pupils completely dilated. Moreover, the lights they were using for the scene were not as they are nowadays, they were enormous. It was terrible, believe me, my eyes kept watering. Nevertheless, thank God, I still have good sight and don't wear glasses."

In the obscure action movie *A Fistful of Diamonds* (a.k.a. *L'Uomo Dal Pugno D'Oro*, 1966), Blanc appeared as a femme fatale diverting audiences from the convoluted plot at hand about enemy agents who plan to drop radioactive dust on a major American city, bringing retired agent Danny Moon, a.k.a. Agent Z55 (German Cobos), back into action. In the German-Italian co-production *Target: Frankie* (a.k.a. *Feuer Frei auf Frankie*, 1967), an American scientist (Joachim Fuchsberger) is killed in Europe, setting off a plot wherein the CIA sends the deceased man's playboy lookalike brother (also Fuchsberger), who has been recruited to become an agent, to escort the dead scientist's assistant (Blanc) safely back to America. The agent and the woman he is protecting encounter the sinister spy organization "the Rainbow." Blanc had a more villainous turn in *Target Gold Seven* (a.k.a. *Tecnica di una Spia*, 1967) as Erika Brown. In this film a secret agent (Tony Russell) investigates the theft of uranium at sea and finds the hidden base of a criminal organization. Blanc appeared in a much more glamorous role (as the girlfriend of the lead) in *Tom Dollar* (1967). In this enjoyable mix of the standard Bond film formula and Blake Edward's Inspector Clouseau/Pink Panther series (the hero is always assisted by his martial artist assistant), a private investigator, Tom Dollar (Maurice Poli), investigates uranium smuggling in Iran.

A much more prominent role for Blanc was in the film *Kill Panther Kill* (a.k.a. *Kommissar X–Drei Blaue Panther*, a.k.a. *Commissioner X–Three Blue Panthers*, 1968). In this hyperactive action film (an entry in a series of six movies, spanning seven years) Interpol inspector Captain Rowland (Brad Harris) and his New York–based private eye best friend Joe Walker (Tony Kendall, real name Luciano Stella) become involved with gangsters, spies and femme fatales, all after stolen gems, when an assassination takes place at the Canadian Expo '67 in Montreal. A gangster boss, who had been imprisoned, escapes and meets up with his twin brother (an atomic scientist) at the '67 Expo, kills the twin and impersonates him. Blanc plays Liz Hillary, the wife of the scientist/gangster.

Her final role in this type of film was in *The Magnificent Tony Carrera* (a.k.a. *El Magnifico Tony Carrera*, 1968), where she appeared in the part of Antonella. In this obscure action movie about a former famous thief (now a well known race car driver and inventor of a powerful new fuel, engaged to be married to an heiress) named Tony Carrera (Thomas Hunter), she appears as an attractive diversion to the plot, which had our anti-hero coerced to steal NATO defense plans that enemy agents are after.

The relaxation of censorship in many European countries, coupled with the ever-changing political climate and the open sexual revolution, were just some of the ingredients that made the Italian thriller genre so popular. This genre of film (which became known as the "Giallo" for the yellow colored paperback covers of lurid crime and melodrama pulp novels that initially beget the thriller's cinematic incarnation in Italy) would eventually be represented by nearly 100 titles during its heyday, which lasted until the early eighties. Erica Blanc's later career was boosted by appearances in these films.

So Sweet, So Perverse (a.k.a. *Cosi Dolce ... Cosi Perversa*, 1969) featured Blanc in the role of a murderous woman seeking to drive former American starlet Carroll Baker crazy. This Umberto Lenzi thriller is fondly recalled today, chiefly for its use of psychological terror rather than a graphic, physical one. Blanc's svelte and shapely body were finally showcased in the softcore sex film *I, Emmanuelle* (a.k.a. *Io, Emmanuelle*, 1969), in the title role of Emmanuelle. This, the very first film incarnation of the story (predating by several years the French film series by Just Jaekin) is little more than a melodramatic sex movie, forgotten by most genre scholars due to the much more graphic cinematic interpretations of the character to follow. Few people know that Blanc inherited the leading role from fellow popular Italian starlet Edwige Fenech (who was originally signed but obviously did not get to make the movie), but the indifferent direction by Cesare Canavari relegated the film to obscurity.

More prominent was her role as the delectable and deadly Susan in *The Night That Evelyn Came Out of the Grave* (a.k.a. *La Notte Che Evelyn Usci Dalla Tomba*, 1971). However, *The Devil's Nightmare* (a.k.a. *La Terrificante Notte del Demonio*, 1971) contains Blanc's most memorable film appearance. As an undead succubus, she appears in the guise of two characters, one a seemingly innocent female presence who lives in an ancestral castle with a former Nazi baron who experiments with alchemy, and the other, a deadly and devilish Satanic killer who presents a number of victims with their deaths as represented by each one's vice— a sort of death by the "Seven Deadly Sins," with Blanc as the server of one's comeuppance.

During the next few years, roles followed Blanc in Italian gangster films, thrillers and many a western. But she is most remembered for a small role in the action comedy *The Stranger and the Gunfighter* (a.k.a. *La Dove Non Battle il Sole*, 1974) as the "American Lady." As the seventies wore on, more roles in sexy comedies, which contained a number of graphic nude scenes, followed, including *L'Ammazzatina* (1975, as a stripper named Erika), *La Portiera Nuda* (1975) and *L'Amantide* (1976).

As the eighties came, Blanc turned her attention to the stage once again, but this time as an actress instead of an erotic dancer, as in her youth. She retired from acting briefly before appearing in Lamberto Bava's thriller *Body Puzzle* (1991) in a very small role as a psychiatrist. She resumed her retirement from acting until she made cameos in two Italian television films, *L'Edera* (1992) and *Leo e Beo* (1997). Recently, Erika Blanc has appeared on British television, being interviewed at length about her appearances in a number of genre films and about the European sex and horror film industry of the sixties and seventies. This series, entitled *Eurotica*, was shown on British television in 1999 and 2000, and showed a still lively Erika Blanc vividly recalling and remarking upon that which made her a name. Erika Blanc is also the mother of Italian actress Regina Franchi.

Other films include: *Spara, Gringo, Spara* (1970), *The Revenge of the Godfather* (a.k.a. *L'Amico del Padrino*, 1972), *The Long Arm of the Godfather* (a.k.a. *La Lunga dal Padrino*, 1972), *The Red Headed Corpse* (a.ka. *La Rossa Dalla Pelle Che Scotta*, 1972), *Mark of the Devil Part 2* (a.k.a.

Hexen Geschandlet und Zu Tode Gequalt, a.k.a. Witches: Violated and Tortured to Death, 1972), No Way Out (a.k.a. Tony Arzenta, a.k.a. Big Guns, 1973), La Bambola (1973—Italian TV), A Dragonfly for Each Corpse (a.k.a. Una Libela Para Cada Muerto, 1974), Sogno di una Notte D'Estate (1983) and Le Fate ignoranti (a.k.a. The Ignorant Fairies, 2001).

Note: Quotes used are from the book 99 Donne by Manlio Gomarasca and Davide Pulici (Nocturno Press, 1999).

Dominique Boschero

Dominique Boschero (born in 1937) was a French model whose face adorned the cover of Paris' premiere fashion magazines in the late fifties and early sixties. The tall, voluptuous and dark-haired Boschero appeared in her first film, Printemps a Paris, in 1957. Her notoriety as a model garnered her work abroad, and in 1962 she appeared in the Italian costume adventure The Three Avengers (a.k.a. I Tre Magnifici). Roles in similar costume epics followed, among them The Golden Arrow (a.k.a. L'Arciere Delle Mille e Una Notte, 1962), where she co-starred with Tab Hunter.

Her first appearance in a spy film was in the West German co-production Hong Kong Hot Harbor (a.k.a. Heisser Hafen Hong Kong, 1962), a rather obscure title about a journalist who investigates the death of a friend and finds a secret microfilm document containing research plans for a new deadly weapon, resulting in tangles with enemy agents also after the document. Boschero became lost in the shu· e of French, German and Italian actors who were vying for their screen time in the film, partly shot on location in the Orient. She fared better in The Secret of the Chinese Carnation (a.k.a. Das Geheimnis der Chinesischen Nelke, 1964), another international co-production. This time she appeared as a sensuous femme fatale in a deadly plot about three different groups of agents, all of them chasing after a microfilm containing a secret formula for a new rocket fuel.

In 1965 Boschero co-starred in the bizarre Italian espionage film Borman (1965). This odd entry, about a CIA agent named Bob Gordon (Robert Kent, real name Sandro Moretti) sent to South America to discover the truth about the cloning of evil Nazi Martin Borman, was seen by few people during its initial Italian release, and by fewer today. Its combination of historical facts, spy theatrics, femme fatales and low, low budget sets and locations (with a lot of actors speaking their lines in front of bare walls) contributed to the film's obscurity.

Dominque Boschero was again plagued by another no-budget Italian film (a sequel of sorts to Borman) in OSS 77: Operation Lotus Flower (a.k.a. OSS 77–Operazione Fior di Loto, 1965). In this title, a Secret Service agent (Robert Kent again) is assigned to save a famous Chinese scientist who escaped from an atomic power station in Pakistan. Russian MIG jets shot down the plane, and our hero must save both an injured pilot and the scientist, who are also being stalked by a neo–Nazi spy ring called "NZ 2." In the midst of all these colorful espionage shenanigans, Boschero once again becomes lost in the shu‑ e and seems to virtually disappear entirely from the film probably the result of the filmmakers' budgetary concerns, or maybe she disappears from the film unexplained because she realized what a low point this production was.

Boschero finally won a coveted leading role in the exciting *Fury in Marakesh* (a.k.a. *Furia a Marrakech*, a.k.a. *Death Pays in Dollars*, 1966). In this film, a secret agent (Stephen Forsythe) investigates rogue agents involved with a criminal organization that has discovered the hiding place where Hitler has buried millions of dollars. Forsythe tracks them to the 1964 New York World's Fair, then to Europe. Boschero has an interesting part as a woman who robs one of the gang's henchmen of counterfeit money, which in a roundabout way leads the hero to their lair. What kept the film from being more popular with international audiences and spy film fans was the sometimes-draggy pace and non-performance from male model turned actor Forsythe.

An attempt to showcase her growing acting talents arose in *Ring Around the World* (a.k.a. *Duello Nel Mondo*, 1966). Here she portrayed a haggard showgirl who had an affair with a man being investigated by an insurance company agent (Richard Harrison). The agent becomes involved in researching the strange deaths of his company's clients and becomes the target of a macabre assassin who kills with bullets made of ice. *Secret Agent Fireball* (a.k.a. *Le Spie Uccidono a Beirut*, a.k.a. *The Killers Are Challenged*, a.k.a. *077 Challenge to the Killers*, 1966) is a far more entertaining and less serious spy film. Echoing the levels of the

Dominique Boschero is deadly and alluring with a gun.

fantastic that the official Bond films were themselves toying with in such films as *Goldfinger* and *Thunderball*, this film, set in the Far East, has a secret agent (Richard Harrison) investigating a missing Russian scientist and valuable microfilm of a new atomic bomb formula. Along the way, our hero does battle with a nefarious criminal ring that imitates S.P.E.C.T.R.E.

The ultimate screen performance by Dominique Boschero came with her screen-stealing turn in the bizarre, uninhibited, wacky, wild and completely unbelievable secret agent-super hero hybrid known as *Argoman, the Fantastic Superman* (a.k.a. *Come Rubare la Corona d'Inghilterra*, a.k.a. *How to Steal the Crown Jewels of England*, 1967). In this film, Argoman (Roger Browne), a man with incredible super powers (hypnotic, flying and levitation, among others), is also a part-time thief for pleasure who battles a worldwide criminal ring with a deadly laser weapon bent on world sterilization and then domination. In between being the prissy, dandy millionaire alter ego and bedding voluptuous women, Argoman puts on his red suit to fight evil. Boschero at first appears as a seemingly lost woman whose recreational hovercraft is levitated by Argoman onto his own private island where they engage in sex. Afterwards, Argoman rewards her with fabulous riches, unaware that she is actually a mastermind villain who fronts a vast criminal empire. By the film's climax, clad in colorful plumes in an elaborate costume, Boschero tortures Argoman and seeks to remove his magic powers permanently. It's an incredible sight as she smiles with glee while poor Argoman finds his strength draining away at the hands of a woman who earlier in the film he took enjoyment from. It was rare in these French, German and Italian spy films that a woman would take on the leading role of the villain and become such a sadistic character. That the film featured a super hero-criminal-good guy as its central protagonist doomed it as a hard sell to theaters at the time of its production. The predominant attention paid to risqué dialogue and visuals, as well, made sure that children were not the intended audience for this film.

Concentrating full time on her acting, Boschero, unfortunately, was unable to duplicate the success of becoming a leading lady that she had had with this role. Subsequent appearances in Italian thrillers like *Libido* (1967), *The Unnaturals* (a.k.a. *Il Contronatura*, 1968), *Iguana with a Tongue of Fire* (a.k.a. *L'Iguana dalla Lingua di Fuoco*, 1971) and *Who Saw Her Die?* (a.k.a. *Chi L'Ha Vista Morire*, 1972) did little to propel her career forward, and often she was used for decorative purposes, or worse, her character reached her demise before the end credits.

Finally, one of her last film credits is the abysmal, controversial and tasteless espionage-sleaze-mondo film *Faccia di Spia* (1975). In this ridiculous hybrid of genres, an Italian spy is sent to South America to investigate white slavers and mercenaries involved in political insurrection. After what seems like an eternity filled with awful acting by the cast, the film suddenly veers into exploitation territory with (faked) footage of atrocities committed upon female cast members held in slavery. Sensing this nadir of her acting career, Boschero returned to France in 1976 to act in *Tous le Chemins Menent a L'Homme* (1976), a film of which little is known.

Other films include: *La Mortale Trappola di Belfagor* (1967), *La Signora e Stata Violenta* (1973) and *Je Suis un Call-Girl* (1973).

Barbara Bouchet

Barbara Bouchet was born Barbel Goutscher on August 15, 1943, in Reichenberg, Sudetenland, Germany (now the area is known as Liberac, Czech Republic). She was the eldest of a family of siblings that included two sisters (Eileen and Annette) and two brothers (Peter and Wolfgang). The family moved to Munich when she was ten. Fritz, her father, a photographer by profession, secured a position with the Viewmaster Company. Ingrid, her mother, was an actress. But it was another actress, Christine Kaufmann, who impressed the young blonde. Kaufmann's appearance in the film *Der Schweigende Engel* (1954) as a deaf ballet dancer made such an impact on Bouchet that she decided to pursue a career as a ballet dancer.

As a young teenager, Barbara Bouchet studied classical ballet before moving to America with her parents, where the Goutscher family endured hardships as immigrants to the New World. Then one day Bouchet gave a photo of herself to a male admirer, who sent the picture to a talent search contest. Winning the "Perfect Gidget Contest," Bouchet's first taste of Hollywood was a screen test (that resulted in no parts) and a date with the actor James Darren (for publicity purposes). Still continuing her dancing academics, she roomed with a female friend in Los Angeles and began taking modeling lessons, finally abandoning her interest in ballet. She won her first beauty contest at the age of 14 when she became "Miss China Beach." Other wins in beauty contests followed, as well as acting lessons (at the Hollywood Professional School). Bouchet began making commercials and was spotted by Doris Day's husband, who gave the young woman a walk-on role in a film. Her rising fame as a model garnered her magazine covers and more prominent television commercial work, leading to bit parts in such films as *A Global Affair* (1964), *John Goldfarb, Please Come Home* (1964) and *Bedtime Story* (1964), as one of Marlon Brando's adoring girlfriends. Unfortunately for her, and fortunately for the male audience members, she was usually cast as the beautiful girl in the bikini.

Bouchet appeared as the voluptuous, bikini clad Ava Vestock in the low budget American spy film *Agent for H.A.R.M.* (1965). In this near–Poverty Row production (that, coincidentally, wound up satirizing the European Bond rip-offs instead of the Bond films themselves), an agent named Adam Chance (Peter Mark Richman), who works for H.A.R.M. (Human Aetiological Relations Machine), is assigned to protect a defecting Eastern European scientist from attacks by enemy agents. Making matters more complicated, the scientist has developed a super weapon that destroys flesh. Whenever you find yourself chuckling at the straight-faced histrionics of the cast (including genre veterans Robert Quarry and Wendell Corey), you can always admire Bouchet's fine form. During this period she also appeared on *The Man from U.N.C.L.E.* in "The Project Deephole Affair" (3/18/66). As the aptly named THRUSH agent Narcissus Darling, she gets to tangle with U.N.C.L.E. agent Napoleon Solo (Robert Vaughn) over schlmo Buzz Conway (Jack Weston), whom THRUSH believe is a geologist with an earthquake-making device.

A screen test for the film *In Harm's Way* (1965) led to an association with tyro producer-director Otto Preminger, who not only signed her to play Kirk Douglas' ill-fated philandering wife, but also to an exclusive seven year contract. However, since Preminger's cinematic output was approximately one film every one or two years, Bouchet was stuck doing nothing and getting paid for it. Unfortunately for cinemagoers, it kept her out of the public eye for almost a year until she asked Preminger to release her from the contract and he later obliged. Bouchet commented, "After I did *In Harm's Way*, Preminger used to get a lot of fun out of telling me that so and so had asked about me for a film role, and he said 'No, she belongs to me!' He pays you every week and you belong to him.... You belonged to the producers at that time and they could do with you whatever they wanted. If they wanted to loan you out and make money on you, they could. Preminger didn't want to loan me out, which just left me sitting there." A determined Bouchet desperately wanted her independence, so "I got on a plane and I flew to New York. I spoke to him [Preminger] in German. He liked that, when I spoke to him in German. I said, 'Otto please let me out. I don't want to be under contract anymore. I want to move on,' and he just let me go."

Returning to Europe, an abortive screen test for Michelangelo Antonioni's film *Blow-Up* brought her into contact with independent film producer Charles K. Feldman who was then casting actresses for his film version of the James Bond adventure *Casino Royale*. Bouchet recalls, "It just happened that I ran into Charles Feldman at the Cannes Film Festival. I was there to meet Michelangelo Antonioni about a film and I met Charley Feldman on the plane on the way down there. He was just starting up production on *Casino Royale*. He said 'I'd like for you to be Ms. Moneypenny.'"

Apparently, Feldman had secured the film rights to the Ian Fleming novel of the same name from the author years before Bond producers Albert Broccoli and Harry Saltzman purchased the film rights to the other books in the series. In effect, Feldman was allowed to make his own James Bond film called *Casino Royale*, and the producers of the Sean Connery series (at that time) could do nothing about it.

Since the film was being directed by five filmmakers simultaneously (John Huston, Val Guest, Ken Hughes, Robert Parrish and Joe McGrath), and the script written and constantly re-written by as many, if not more, screenwriters, much of the storyline became hard to follow and seemed to ramble on. Bouchet's sequences were primarily directed by Val Guest, a veteran of many British thrillers and science fiction films, but the chaotic shooting schedule dragged on for a year (which did not seem laborious for her since she was also tied to Feldman with a multi-year contract at the time).

Essentially this film version of *Casino Royale* (there was one before it, an American production done for the CBS television network that aired once on October 21, 1954) is a chaotic but delightful affair. As a whole, the film concerns an attempt to thwart a threat to the free world. The criminal organization S.M.E.R.S.H. is a danger to world peace; the American, British, French and Russian forces combine to ask retired secret agent James Bond to reconsider going back into service to save the world and defeat the evil Genius Dr. Noah.

Bouchet's segment is called by Bond film aficionados the "Moneypenny's Daughter" sequence. As the daughter of the original Miss Moneypenny, the longtime secretary to the late spy agency head M (John Huston in the film's prologue), Bouchet's role as the new Moneypenny is to take up the mantle from her mother. She assists James Bond (David Niven) in selecting a new A.F.S.D. (Anti-Female Spy Device) that will combat a rash of recent secret agent assassinations. What this device *is*, is never actually explained, but Moneypenny (Bouchet) lines up the best of Bond's newest protégées and kisses each one, fully on their lips, to test their stamina. Moneypenny decides that the studly Agent Cooper (Terence Cooper) is the man for the job. But the next segment of the film reveals that the mild-mannered author of books on card tricks, Evelyn Tremble (Peter Sellers), has been selected for the job, being the newly recruited agent with the A.F.S.D. Bouchet turns up later in the film before the chaotic pop art climax.

"*Casino Royale* took a year and a half to complete," remembers Bouchet. "We had five directors shooting in London all the time. The sets got built up, and then they got torn down all the time, they must have had money to spend like I don't know what.... I remember that I just got tired of being in London all the time, there was

Barbara Bouchet, as Miss Moneypenny, shares a moment with David Niven (James Bond) in *Casino Royale* (Columbia, 1967).

hardly any sunshine. When there was, I used to go to the park, and once I got arrested because you don't go there in your bathing suit."

Bouchet remained in England to act in the deadly serious espionage film *Danger Route* (1968). In the role of Mari, she comes into contact with a British agent (Richard Johnson) sent to kill a Russian scientist who has defected to the Americans. That same year she guest starred on the seminal science fiction show *Star Trek* in the episode "By Any Other Name."

The sudden death of producer Charles Feldman released Bouchet from her contract with him, and she found a prominent role in the film *Sweet Charity* (1969) as Ursula, the satin mini-dress and mini-mink stole wearing socialite fiancée of a Latin movie idol. The film co-starred Shirley MacLaine, Sammy Davis, Jr., Ricardo Montalban and others. But the changing mores of the sixties found that cinematic versions of Broadway musicals were becoming passé, and the film had little life beyond its initial box-office theatrical run and cult interest.

Bouchet journeyed to Italy where, accepting the invitation of an Italian producer (who was originally intent on luring American actress Candice Bergen), she was signed to a contract performing in films that he would produce. She co-starred in the violent crime melodrama *Colpo Rovente* (1969) and followed that with a role in the sexy historical film *L'Asino D'Oro: Processo per Fatti Strani Contro Lucius Apuleius Citta-*

dino Romano (1970). In *Il Debito Conjugale* (1970), another sexy comedy, she was allowed to showcase her seldom acknowledged knack for physical comedy, and in the ribald softcore sex comedy *Calde Notti di Don Giovanni* (1971) she left little to the imagination in a role that flaunted her often nude body.

The early seventies were busy years for Bouchet as an actress. She starred or co-starred (in supporting roles) in a number of violent crime movies and erotic thrillers. Among them, she appeared in the politically charged thriller *The Man with the Icy Eyes* (a.k.a. *L'Uomo Dagli Occhi di Ghiaccio*, 1971), about a journalist (Antonio Sabato) who becomes immersed in a labyrinthine plot involving the assassination of a U.S. Senator. In the film, Bouchet played Anne Saks, a promiscuous model who becomes involved in the web of corruption. In *Amuck!* (a.k.a. *Alla Ricera del Piacere*, a.k.a. *Replica of a Crime*, 1972), she co-starred as Greta Franklin, a woman searching for the answers in the mysterious disappearance and death of her childhood friend, becoming entangled in a bizarre web of erotic mind games masterminded by the mentally corrupt Farley Granger (assisted by Rosalba Neri as his devilish, bisexual companion Eleonora). Bouchet's acting expertise is showcased as never before as she must contend with unwanted erotic advances, drugs, pornography and murder.

Many new fans were introduced to the star when *Sex with a Smile* (a.k.a. *40 Gradi All'Ombra del Lenzuolo*, 1976) was released. In this sexy comedy, a wealthy Swiss woman (Bouchet) is coerced into sleeping with a complete stranger for several million dollars; her episode was just one of many interesting moments in this sexy multi-story comedy that became a worldwide financial hit. Bouchet also appeared in a similar role in the equally popular follow-up, *Sex with a Smile 2* (a.k.a. *Spogliamoci Cosi Senza Pudor*, a.k.a. *Love in Four Easy Lessons*, 1976). Bouchet's last memorable role in a genre film was in Sergio Bergonzelli's crime melodrama *The Diamond Connection* (a.k.a. *Diamanti Sporchi di Sangue*, 1977). In 1979 her career was rewarded with the Italian "Valentino" award, which was bestowed upon her as recognition for her work in the Italian film industry. As her roles on the big screen became more infrequent, she was seen more often on television. In the eighties she co-hosted the Italian program *The Beauty Centre Show* and became a spokeswoman for a European health spa. Barbara Bouchet finally returned to the U.S. and co-starred (with Gregory Peck) in the mini-series *The Scarlet and the Black* (1983). After a retirement that lasted for over 15 years, Barbara Bouchet returned to the screen in Martin Scorsese's *Gangs of New York* (2002).

Other films include: *The Red Queen Kills Seven Times* (a.k.a. *La Dama Rossa Uccide Sette Volte*, 1972), *House of 1000 Pleasures* (a.k.a. *Finalmente ... Le Mille E Una Notte*, 1972) *Don't Torture a Duckling* (a.k.a. *Non Si Sevizia un Paperino*, 1972), *The Black Belly of the Tarantula* (a.k.a. *La Tarantola dal Ventre Nero*, 1972), *Cry of a Prostitute* (a.k.a. *Quelli Che Contano*, 1972), *La Ragazza Tutta Nuda Assassinata Nel Parco*, 1972), *Ricco* (a.k.a. *Un Tippo Con Una Faccia Strana*, 1972), *Murder in Paris* (a.k.a. *Casa d'Appuntamento*, a.k.a. *The House of Appointments*, 1973), *La Badessa di Castro* (1974), *The Surabaya Conspiracy* (1975), *Death Rage* (a.k.a. *Con la Rabbia Agli Occhi*, 1976).

Thordis Brandt

Thordis Brandt was born in West Germany of Norwegian and German descent, and grew up in Canada. After completing her degree in nursing, the statuesque blonde relocated to Santa Monica with two companions. After six months her friends returned home while Brandt remained in California. Between private nursing jobs she took dancing lessons and made three appearances on *Art Linkletter's House Party* demonstrating the art of the Watusi. Encouraged by her friends, she acquired an agent and began getting bit roles in films. Though a curvaceous, statuesque, flaxen haired beauty, Brandt never progressed from supporting roles to leads and was frequently cast as voluptuous spies and treacherous enemy agents in espionage movies and TV shows during the decade.

One of Brandt's first film roles was in the Marty Allen and Steve Rossi comedy *The Last of the Secret Agents?* (1966). She played helpful spy Fred Johnson, who is a man disguised as a seductive woman. Johnson rendezvoused with Allen and Rossi's inept tourists on a Paris-bound train as they are trailing members of the organization THEM who are planning to steal the Venus di Milo. In this film, Brandt is only seen and not heard, since a male actor dubbed her lines.

As one of the Amazons working at Fabulous Face in *In Like Flint* (1967), Brandt received more screen time and the use of her own voice. However, she is indistinguishable from the other spa attendants, with their pulled-back hair under a powder blue cap and matching uniforms. Brandt's character is the one who discovers that their brainwashing technique hasn't been working on Derek Flint's (James Coburn) female assistants. She goes to her boss Lisa (Jean Hale) with her discovery. Tipped off that Flint is on his way to Fabulous Face, Lisa orders Brandt to freeze the girls in the crynology lab. After completing her task begrudgingly ("I hated to do that—they're nice; what a pity they're so hard to convince"), Brandt's character comments about Flint's influence on the girls to another attendant and says, "Does it ever make you wonder—when you see what girls like that feel?" So it is not too surprising when she and the other ladies side with Flint against General Carter (Steve Ihnat) and his men, and organize Operation Smooch to stop their plan of world domination.

In 1967 Brandt turned up on three small screen spy shows. She was part of the evil Prince Boriarsi's (Eduardo Ciannelli) plot to loot the Vatican treasury in "The Catacomb and Dogma Affair" (1/24/67) on *The Girl from U.N.C.L.E.* Then in "Casanova from Canarsie" (3/29/67) on *I Spy* she played Valentine, one of two shapely agents (the other being Joan Marshall) sent by Kelly and Scott to prevent a mild-mannered Pentagon clerk (Wally Cox) from revealing top secret information to enemy agent Consuelo (Leticia Roman), who is enticing him to defect. And in the second half (aired on 10/9/67) of the two-part "The Prince of Darkness Affair" on *The Man from U.N.C.L.E.* (released theatrically overseas as *The Helicopter Spies*), Thordis Brandt appeared as Miss Zalamar. With her flaxen hair pulled back and her form-fitting mini-dress, Brandt is a knockout as the assistant to Bradford Dillman's maniac Luther Sebastian, the leader of the Third Way. When Sebastian orders her to check the next day's schedule, she responds, "Yes, sir!" He

Publicity photograph of Thordis Brandt (*second from right*) and the other "Amazons" backstage on the set of *In Like Flint* (20th Century–Fox, 1967).

then says, "I like the way you said that. It has a nice tone of respect. Efficiency." "Yes, *sir*," replies Miss Zalamar with a smitten look on her face. She then eagerly aids him in his plan to launch the thermal prism into space to control the world, which, of course, is foiled by U.N.C.L.E.

Between spy roles, Brandt could be seen as a Ziegfeld Girl in *Funny Girl* (1968) and a model in the Elvis Presley musical *Live a Little, Love a Little* (1968). And she continued as a private duty nurse. She commented to Aleene MacMinn in the *Los Angeles Times*, "When I started ... I looked after Patricia Neal. Well, acting people got to know me from that and now when their friends get sick, they call me. I've sort of become the actor's nurse."

Thordis Brandt was next cast in the low-budget horror opus *The Witchmaker* (1969). As Tasha, Brandt's character joins a team investigating a series of bizarre murders linked to a witch's coven in the swamps of Louisiana. At the height of idiocy, her character decides to sunbathe in a skimpy bikini, making her the prime target of the coven's warlock (John Lodge). After making a few more TV guest appearances (i.e. *Mannix*, *Hogan's Heroes*, *Dragnet*)

Brandt retired from acting. She currently resides in Beverly Hills.

Other films include: *The Oscar* (1966), *Way ... Way Out* (1966), *Spinout* (1966), *The Split* (1968) and *Up Your Teddy Bear* (1970).

Anna Capri

This Hungarian blonde was born Anna Marie Nanasi on July 6, 1945, in a displaced-persons camp in West Germany. Her father, a doctor, was able to bring his family to the United States in 1950 with the help of a refugee organization. Little Anna began modeling as a child, and when the family relocated to Hollywood her mother enrolled her in a professional school for children. She progressed from TV commercials through bits in TV and movies. Warner Bros. signed her to a contract in 1959 and promptly re-christened her Anna Capri after the Isle.

After appearing in a number of Warner Bros.–produced television series (including *Cheyenne*), Capri landed the role of Mary Rose, the 16-year-old adoptive daughter of Andrew Duggan and Peggy McCay in the short-lived situation comedy *Room for One More* in 1962. She was voted a Hollywood Deb Star for 1962, but this baby-faced ingenue yearned to play the femme fatale. She told *TV Guide* in 1964, "I want to play the love object, the kind that comes in like a hurricane and goes out like a whirlwind."

After playing precocious good girls in *Kisses for My President* (1964) and *The Girls on the Beach* (1965), Anna Capri got her wish when she was cast as the bad girl in "The Bridge of Lions Affair" (2/4 and 2/11/66) on *The Man from U.N.C.L.E.* This two-part episode was also edited into the feature *One of Our Spies Is Missing* (1966) and rushed into theaters. Resembling a cross between Sandra Dee and Joey Heatherton, Capri energetically portrayed high fashion model Do Do, who was no dodo and was as beautiful as she was deadly. Working for Madame De Sala (Vera Miles) at her salon, she is in cahoots to protect a rejuvenation drug that Da Sala has a scientist working on for her elderly husband. Do Do helps drown model Lorelei Lancer (Dolores Faith) and pulls a knife on U.N.C.L.E. agent Napoleon Solo (Robert Vaughn) as they begin fighting. The feisty hellcat bites his ear and scratches his eyes. Solo gets his rematch high on an empty theater's catwalk, and the innocent-looking blonde plunges to her death after being accidentally shot by one of De Sala's cohorts.

Capri's other two appearances on *The Man from U.N.C.L.E.* were less menacing. In "The Birds and the Bees Affair" (1/21/66) she played Tavia Sandor, who helps U.N.C.L.E. agent Illya Kuryakin (David McCallum) stop THRUSH agent Mozart (John McGiver) from releasing a strain of small, deadly bees. And in "The Maze Affair" (12/18/67) Capri was paired this time with Robert Vaughn's Napoleon Solo as her character, Abbe Melton, is the "innocent" who gets caught up in Solo's efforts to stop THRUSH from blowing up U.N.C.L.E. headquarters.

In "Will the Real Good Guys Please

A publicity shot of Anna Capri (Tavia Sandor) and David McCallum (Illya Kuryakin) in "The Birds and the Bees Affair" on *The Man from U.N.C.L.E.* (MGM-TV, 1967).

Stand Up?" (11/2/66) on *I Spy*, Capri played Jolie Gagni, the daughter of a rocket scientist (Henry Wilcoxon) whom two enemy spies (Lee Philips and Hari Rhodes) posing as agents Kelly (Bill Cosby) and Scott (Robert Culp) attempt to kidnap. In "The Night of the Hangman" (10/20/67) on *The Wild Wild West*, Capri played Abigail Moss, an eyewitness to the murder of rich rancher Amos Rawlins. She fingers innocent farmer Lucius Brand (Harry Dean Stanton), who is sentenced to hang in two days. It turns out that sweet Abigail Moss' real name is Jennifer Colt, and that she is wanted in four states. Agent Artemus Gordon (Ross Martin) realizes that she was paid to lie when he is informed by her landlady (Jesslyn Fax) that Moss skipped town because "some uncle left *our bird of passage* a fortune in jewels. That's her story. But if you ask me, she has more than her share of *uncles*." Disguised as a jeweler, Artemus finds Abigail on the next stagecoach out of town and convinces her that her diamond broach is a fake. When she returns to town she unknowingly leads Gordon's partner James West (Robert Conrad) to the real killers—Rawlins' wife in cahoots with the town's banker.

Anna Capri gives a very effective performance as the headstrong Marsha, a stenographer working for the S.I.A., in "Beyond a Treasonable Doubt" (3/16/70), the second-to-last episode of *It Takes a Thief*. When thief-turned-government spy Al Mundy (Robert Wagner) is charged with treason, he goes to Marsha to find out who supplied the evidence against him. He professes his innocence, but she refuses to help and says sternly, "You'll assume I'll believe that, don't you? Women always believe Al Mundy. It's always been that way. Whenever you're in a jam there's always a girl falling all over herself to help you out. You really expect me to think of a convincing patsy and help you switch the guilt?" Marsha seems to be speaking for the whole sixties generation of spy girls used and discarded by chauvinistic men. Marsha later has a change of heart and aids Al in locating the real traitor. The episode ends with Marsha and Al in front of a roaring fireplace as Marsha rehashes Al's checkered past as a thief. She muses, "All together, with a record like that you could easily be involved with treachery of any kind. Especially when I think how you've acted toward women. Come to think of it, so many women." Marsha then slaps him across the face and says, "Thanks. I needed that." Al reaches over and kisses her and responds, "Thanks. I needed *that*." The episode closes with them in a romantic clinch. As usual, Al Mundy gets his girl.

Capri's final TV spy appearance was on the short-lived spy series *Search*. This series featured three rotating actors (Hugh O'Brian, Tony Franciosa and Doug McClure) playing agents working for the Probe Division of World Securities. What distinguished these agents from others was that fact that they had transmitters implanted in an ear, enabling them to be in constant contact with their base of operations. In Capri's episode, entitled "The Clayton Lewis Document" (2/14/73), Probe agent Nick Bianco (Franciosa) searches for the person attempting to blackmail a Presidential aide into revealing information regarding top-secret disarmament talks. Also guest starring were Craig Stevens, Rhonda Fleming and Julie Adams.

In the early seventies Capri returned to the big screen and was billed as Ahna Capri. She remarked to *The Hollywood Reporter* in 1969, "Too many people pronounce 'Anna' with a flat 'a' and it comes out an ugly Aaaana. I want my name more musical sounding, with a broad 'a,' like Ahna, so I'm spelling it that way." Using her new moniker, Capri co-starred with Strother Martin in the creepy horror film *Brotherhood of Satan* (1971), about a town whose children are being snatched by a devil cult. In the Bruce Lee classic *Enter the Dragon* (1973), a sort of combination spy, blaxploitation and kung fu movie, Capri, as the insatiable Tania, physically stood out as the only Caucasian actress in the cast. The exploitation classic *The Specialist* (1975) gave Capri a starring role as an enticing assassin; however, she retired from acting shortly thereafter. Ahna Capri continued to reside in Los Angeles making autograph convention appearances until her death on August 19, 2010.

Other films include: *Target: Harry* (1969), *Darker Than Amber* (1970), *Company of Killers* (1970—TV), *Payday* (1972), *Piranha, Piranha!* (1972), *The Bingo Long Traveling All-Stars and Motor Kings* (1975) and *Nowhere to Run* (1978—TV).

Judy Carne

To most television fans actress Judy Carne is only remembered as the original Sock-It-to-Me girl on *Rowan and Martin's Laugh-In*. But the bouncy, auburn-haired British lass (born Joyce Audrey Botterill on April 27, 1939, in Northampton, England) had a prolific career on television before she literally made a splash on that hit variety series. The daughter of a London fruit merchant, she danced with the Bush-Davies ballet and made her stage debut in the 1956 revue *For Amusement Only* in the West End. Before Carne headed for the U.S. she was a panelist on *Juke Box Jury* and a regular on the sitcom *The Rag Trade*.

Judy Carne was first introduced to American audiences as Heather Finch, a British exchange student who comes to stay with an American family in the first hour-long comedy series, *Fair Exchange*, in 1962. She next played the rich Barbara Wyntoon, daughter of the snobbish Cecil Wyntoon (John Dehner), in love with the poor Jim Bailey (Les Brown, Jr.) on the long forgotten sitcom *The Baileys of Balboa* during the 1964-65 season. And on the big screen she had a small role as one of the three "nameless broads" (the others being Janine Gray and Kathy Kersh) who are found in bed with James Coburn in the comedy *The Americanization of Emily* (1964).

With the advent of The Beatles in 1964, all things British were in during the mid-sixties, so Carne, with her cute looks and mod dress, was perfect for the spy genre. In "The Ultimate Computer Affair" (10/1/65) during *The Man from U.N.C.L.E.*'s second season, Carne essayed the role of prim Salty Oliver. An international prison inspector, she begrudgingly allows U.N.C.L.E. agent Napoleon Solo (Robert Vaughn) to pose as her husband to sneak him into a Latin American penal colony to find his partner Illya Kuryakin (David McCallum) and destroy a super computer that is being assembled to program all of THRUSH's operations. Carne was once again the innocent in the fourth season episode "The Gurnius Affair" (11/27/67), which featured David McCallum in a dual role. As photographer Terry Cook, Carne (with dyed blonde hair) is witness to the escape of Nazi war criminal Von Etske (Will Kuluva). He plans on joining his THRUSH counterparts Zorgon Gurnius (George Macready) and Nexor (McCallum) to release a mind-control ray on the President of the United States. Illya intercepts Nexor and is shocked to see his lookalike. He then masquerades as Nexor and, with Solo and Terry, journeys to the Nazi's South American base to sabotage their scheme.

In between U.N.C.L.E. appearances, Judy Carne landed her third TV series, called *Love on a Rooftop* during the 1966-67 TV season. She played newlywed Julie Hammond Willis, the pampered daughter of a rich used car dealer, who is married to struggling architect David (Peter Deuel) and living in a tiny windowless apartment that sits on the roof of a building with a wonderful view of the San Francisco Bay area. Though warm and original, critical kudos could not compensate for dismal ratings and the show was cancelled.

Judy Carne (Terry Cook) as a swinging photographer who gets involved with Nazi war criminals in "The Gurnius Affair" on *The Man from U.N.C.L.E.* **(MGM-TV, 1967).**

Shortly after her last appearance on *The Man from U.N.C.L.E.*, Carne found "overnight" fame on the innovative new variety series *Rowan and Martin's Laugh-In*, beginning in January 1968. Though Carne had comedic talent, she is best remembered as the Sock-It-to-Me girl, in which she would invariably get doused with a bucket of water. Also memorable were scenes of Carne gyrating in a bikini as the camera zoomed in on phrases and slogans painted in Day-Glo colors on her body. Carne stayed with the series for two years and left part way through season three. She told *TV Guide* in 1969, "Frankly, it has become a big bloody bore." In 1991 she remarked to *The Advocate* that, "My managers were greedy and I thought I should be doing Vegas and Broadway for 16 grand a week. I don't place the blame on anyone but myself, but if I had good managers, who knows what would have been?"

Post *Laugh-In*, Judy Carne landed a one-year gig on *The Kraft Music Hall*, starred on Broadway in *The Boy Friend*, did a number of TV guest shots and movies-of-the-week (most notably *QB VII* in 1974), and was a regular performer on the talk and game show circuits. The mid-seventies, however, really did sock it to Carne. She made headlines in the road company of *Absurd Person Singular* for an altercation with co-star Betsy von Furstenburg, who reportedly purposely spilled a glass of water on Carne during a performance. A nightclub act she put together failed miserably, and purportedly she even performed in a dive in Mexico whose opening act was a cockfight. Her sixties experimentation with drugs developed into full-blown heroin addiction. In 1978 she was busted for illegal prescription drugs (she was acquitted) and suffered a broken neck in a car accident.

In 1985 Carne co-authored (with former boyfriend Bob Merrill) her heartbreaking autobiography *Laughing on the Outside, Crying on the Inside: The Bittersweet Saga of the Sock-It-To-Me Girl*. She candidly revealed details of her tumultuous three-year marriage to Burt Reynolds, her admitted bisexuality, her love affair with singer Lana Cantrell, life on *Laugh-In* and her drug addiction. The book put her back in the spotlight for a short period, and to capitalize on her newfound notoriety she put together a cabaret act entitled *Only I....* Her show ran for a few months at the Duplex in Greenwich Village during the early nineties, and she caught the attention of radio shock jock Howard Stern appearing on his radio and TV shows.

Judy Carne returned to her home town of Northampton, England. Her last words to *The Advocate* were, "I'm a '60s flower child who has refused to grow up. *Mature* and *responsible* are words I don't understand. For me, work equals [staying] clean, and keeping myself together is most important to me." She died on September 3, 2015.

Other films include: *A Pair of Briefs* (1962), *All the Right Noises* (1969), *Dead Men Tell No Tales* (1971—TV), *Someone at the Top of the Stairs* (1973—TV) and *Only with Married Men* (1974—TV).

Hélène Chanel

Hélène Chanel was born in France as Hélène Stoliaroff. She is of partly French and partly Russian descent. As a young teenager her striking appearance—jet black bob-cut hair over large, liquid eyes with seemingly endless oversized irises—made her the target of modeling agencies in her native France. Finally succumbing to their offers, she began a career that led to film roles. When she began acting in 1959 the publicity office of her first film, *Detournement de Mineurs*, thought her real name was not commercial enough. They changed it to Chancel (which means "lucky" in French), but an Italian publicity agent misspelled it to Chanel and it has stayed that way ever since (though she was sometimes billed as Helen Chanel and Sherill Morgan in her movies). She journeyed to Italy that very same year, and claims that she made many films in that country in order to avoid returning to her native France. Her first Italian film was *Genitori in Blue-Jeans* (1959). Among her initial film roles in Italy was an appearance in one of the better peplums, titled *Samson and the Seven Miracles of the World* (a.k.a. *Maciste Alla Corte del Gran Khan*, a.k.a. *Maciste at the Court of the Great Khan*, 1961).

More roles in similar productions followed. Riccardo Freda's *Maciste in Hell* (a.k.a. *Maciste All'Infierno*, a.k.a. *The Witch's*

Curse, 1962), one of the most respected of Italian sword and sandal films, featured a larger role than Chanel had ever had before on the screen, but not without a certain amount of hard physical work on the part of the actress.

Other roles followed, including a few appearances onscreen with popular Italian comedians Franco & Ciccio, most notably in *Cinque Marines per Cento Ragazze* (1962), which was about bumbling spies (the star comedians) chasing after a secret formula. According to Chanel, she was almost chosen for an important role in *From Russia with Love* (1963) but lost the part to Daniela Bianchi.

Hélène Chanel's first appearance in a Bond-styled action film was in 1965's *Operation Counterspy* (a.k.a. *Asso di Picche: Operazione Controspionaggio*). In this film, Bond Callaghan, the seventh Lord of Moreston (Giorgio Ardisson), is the best secret agent in the ranks of the Secret Intelligence Service. Callaghan receives an assignment to stop a criminal organization in Istanbul that is after an atomic scientist and his powerful weapons technology. Chanel recalled the film to authors Manlio Gomarsca and Davide Pulici in their book *99 Donne*: "We shot in Istanbul and I played an Eastern European spy camouflaged as a belly dancer. I took belly-dancing lessons for fifteen days, and when I saw the film I didn't recognize myself.... I became so popular, people stopped me in the street."

A role as a doomed woman in the obscure espionage thriller *Ring Around the World* (a.k.a. *Duello Nel Mondo*, 1966) followed. In that film, an insurance company investigates the deaths of clients. American actor Richard Harrison played the special agent. Following this film, she appeared in an eerie, melodramatic Italian thriller titled *The Night of Violence* (a.k.a. *Le Notti della Violenza*, 1966).

Chanel's next spy outing was in the low-budget film *Secret Agent 777: Invitation to Murder* (a.k.a. *Agente Segreto 777 Invito ad Uccidere*, 1967). In this spy movie, secret agent 777, Louis Jordan (played by Lewis Jordan), investigates the kidnapping of a nuclear scientist and finds that double agents are involved.

Her next feature, *The Courageous, the Merciless and the Traitor* (a.k.a. *Il Coraggioso, lo Spietato, il Traditore*, a.k.a. *The Brave, the Ruthless and the Traitor* (1967), is a spy thriller about a military train loaded with new weapons that is attacked, and secret documents are stolen. The spies battle it out in South America (where much of the film was shot) to retrieve them. Chanel commented (to the authors of *99 Donne*), "That film was shot in Caracas and the director was Edoardo Mulargia, the other name [assigned the director credit], Xiol Marchal, had probably had his name put on the credits for co-production reasons.

The dark stare of Hélène Chanel captivated many agents.

About the lead actor, Robert Anthony, whose real name was Espartaco Santoni, he was a Venezuelan actor, very popular in his home country."

A number of roles in westerns followed, and then she starred in a violent tale of police corruption and criminal gangs called *Gangster's Law* (a.k.a. *La Legge dei Gangsters*, 1969). The next year Chanel appeared in *Death Knocks Twice* (a.k.a. *La Morte Bussa Due Volte*, 1969), which was an Italian–West German thriller about a psychopathic murderer and criminal gangs, and featured Anita Ekberg in the cast.

Chanel started appearing in fewer and fewer films during the seventies, but one movie she made, the experimental film *Il Bocconcino* (1976), which consisted of chiefly close-up footage of the actors, was deemed unreleasable by its producers and ended up on the porno circuit with hardcore sexual footage inserted.

Nowadays Chanel is retired from acting, but with her husband has a thriving tourist business in Italy and is considering re-entering the film business on the production end.

Other films include: *Cjamango* (1967), *Killer Calibro 32* (1967), *Edipeon* (1970) and *Labbra di lurido blu* (1975).

Greta Chi

Half Chinese, half German Greta Chi was a college graduate with a degree in commerce living in Switzerland when she was encouraged by a family friend, actor Mel Ferrer, to pursue her dream of acting. She studied at the La Jolla Playhouse in California, and with drama coaches Jeff Corey and Martin Landau, before making her film debut in *Five Gates to Hell* (1959). Chi was hot for awhile and was a top contender for the lead role in *The World of Susie Wong* (1961), and for a supporting part in *Tender Is the Night* (1961). After failing to get cast in either film, Chi played the original spy girl Mata Hari in the obscure Spanish World War II thriller *La Reina del Chantecler* (1962). Returning to Hollywood, she was relegated to television, making appearances on a number of series, including *Bewitched* and *The Rogues*.

After guest starring as Ming Soon, with France Nuyen, in "The Prisoners of Mr. Sin" (10/27/65) on *Amos Burke, Secret Agent*, Greta Chi was cast in a supporting role in *Fathom* (1967) as the mysterious Jo-May. In this spy spoof, Raquel Welch plays a skydiver/dental hygienist named Fathom Harvil, who is tricked into retrieving the "Fire Dragon"—believing it is a failsafe device that could trigger a hydrogen bomb, when it is actually a stolen relic from the Ming Dynasty. Fathom is introduced to Jo-May via surveillance film provided by Colonel Campbell (Ronald Fraser). He informs Fathom that Jo-May is a major in the Mongolian KGB and describes her as "a tasty fortune cookie." Jo-May encounters Fathom holding a murder weapon and kneeling over a dead body in the villa of her partner, Peter Merriweather (Tony Franciosa). She accuses Fathom of killing the young man while Peter snaps photographs of her. When Peter believes Fathom's story of being a skydiver blown off course,

Greta Chi as the mysterious Jo-May, with her co-conspirators Reg Lye (Mr. Trivers) and Tony Franciosa (Peter Merriweather), in *Fathom* (20th Century–Fox, 1967).

Jo-May becomes indignant. She then secretly trails Fathom throughout Malaga. After Fathom shoots her caretaker, Mrs. Trivers, Jo-May and Peter chase Fathom into a bullring. Jo-May then disappears from the screen until the very end of the film. While making a wish, as Jo-May is about to blow out her birthday candles, Fathom flies by and drops the "Fire Dragon" into her cake. Jo-May turns out to be the only honest person who really wanted to return the object to its rightful owners.

Being that this was a Raquel Welch movie, Chi (or any other actress for that matter) doesn't get a chance to shine. She may have had acting talent, but she doesn't get the opportunity to display it much in *Fathom*. However, the exotic looking Chi had a wholesome look to her too, which made it hard to guess the true motives of her character.

Though the *Fathom* pressbook over-hyped Chi as the next big thing—"the 22-year-old Greta is emerging as one of the favorites for a top spot among international motion picture 'newcomers'"—this was her last film appearance. She re-surfaced in 1976 as the narrator for the made-for-TV movie *Farewell to Manzanar* and then disappeared from the Hollywood scene again.

Other films include: *Lisette* (1962) and *The Coffin from Hong Kong* (1964).

Tsai Chin

Tsai Chin was born in Shanghai, China, in 1937, the daughter of renowned Peking opera actor, Zhou Xinfang. The dark-haired, lithesome beauty adopted the Anglicized name of Irene Chow when she first appeared on British and U.S. shores, but she retained her birth name for her film roles. Settling in England, she was first seen onscreen in the film *The Yangtse Incident* (a.k.a. *Battle Hell*, 1957), and followed that with the role of a young woman named Primrose in a school plagued by a gun-toting juvenile delinquent (David McCallum) in *Violent Playground* (1958). But she gained fame starring in *The World of Susie Wong* in the West End.

Back on the big screen, Chin played one of her first hard-edged roles in the obscure co-production *The Treasure of San Teresa* (a.k.a. *Hot Money Girls*, 1959). In this film, expatriate American actor-singer Eddie Constantine (who usually played secret agents and private detectives in many French films during this period) stars as a former OSS agent named Larry Brennan who seeks Nazi gold hidden in a Czech convent.

Tsai Chin was hardly seen on the big screen for a number of years, and she may have appeared in a variety of roles for UK television programs seeking Asian actors for minority parts. But she struck gold in *The Face of Fu Manchu* (1965). In this, the first of a new series of films about the insidious Oriental mastermind villain Fu Manchu (Christopher Lee), Tsai Chin played his alluring but devilish daughter, Lin Tang. Somewhere between an old-fashioned pulp mystery and the obvious influence of the Bond films, the Fu Manchu series of the mid-to-late sixties was filled with cool gadgets, nefarious torture devices and a bevy of scantily clad women waiting to be rescued. The always demure but deadly Lin Tang would often assist her father in his world domination plans and was not above sacrificing an often disrobed female (or male) prisoner to show the forceful power of her father's dominion. What kept the modern Fu Manchu films from any kind of major cult status was a continuing lack of interesting heroes (and actors in these roles) used to combat the always interesting and show-stopping rants of British character actor Christopher Lee. But none of the heroes in these films approached the swaggering intensity of a Sean Connery, or those who followed in his footsteps. In this first entry, set in 1920s London, super detective Nayland Smith (Nigel Green) is assisted by a German adventurer (Joachim Fuchsberger) when Fu Manchu kidnaps a brilliant scientist (Walter Rilla) and his daughter (Karin Dor).

The following year, after an uncredited appearance in Michelangelo Antonioni's celebrated film *Blow-Up* (1966), Tsai Chin returned in the role of Lin Tang in the first Fu Manchu sequel, *The Brides of Fu Manchu*. In this entry, Nayland Smith (Douglas Wilmer) vows to stop Fu Manchu (Christopher Lee) from using a new weapon, a powerful ray gun. Lin Tang stands by her father, closely, as he uses a bevy of beauties as bait to lure the ever-vigilant Smith to his hidden lair. Chin then appeared in the low-budget but effective British film *Invasion* (1966) as one of a pair of female (but obviously Asian) interplanetary travelers that are mistaken for an advance invasion force come to Earth. Yoko Tani played the other female space alien.

Tsai Chin, as double agent Ling, beds Sean Connery (James Bond) in *You Only Live Twice* (United Artists, 1967).

Chin's work as Lin Tang, daughter of Fu Manchu, must have gotten her hired for the part of Ling in the official James Bond film *You Only Live Twice* (1967). In the film's prologue Chin is seen as Ling, who beds secret agent 007, James Bond (Sean Connery), in her Hong Kong apartment. She exclaims, "I give you the very best duck" in a wily play on Asian cuisine—or a randy line inserted by a screenwriter as a racial slur on the Asian community who for years in films were depicted as mispronouncing their English.

In any event, Ling's onscreen time is limited to kissing Bond then pushing a hidden button that propels the bed into the wall, signaling two machine gun–toting thugs to enter and smatter the now upright bed with hundreds of bullets, killing our hero (before the credits)! This is all a ruse by the British government to publicly keep 007 out of the way while he secretly undertakes a special mission in the Orient, one that involves his arch nemesis S.P.E.C.T.R.E.; Ling is, in actuality, an agent as well.

Chin returned as the evil Lin Tang, daughter of Fu Manchu (Christopher Lee), in Jess Franco's *The Blood of Fu Manchu* (a.k.a. *Against All Odds*, a.k.a. *Kiss and Kill*, 1968). In this entry the insidious master villain challenges the deductive powers of British detective (and hero) Nayland Smith (Richard Greene) by poisoning ten beautiful women and then sending them to inflict the kiss of death upon ten specially selected men. In Franco's direct sequel, *The Castle of Fu Manchu* (1969), the last film in the series to feature Chin, Fu Manchu is ensconced in a Turkish hideaway experimenting with more deadly potions while the hero Nayland Smith (Richard Greene) spends much of the film journeying to the lair.

Chin then appeared in a thinly veiled anti-war film about British soldiers recruited to a Singapore outpost. Today the comedy-drama *The Virgin Soldiers* (1969) is chiefly remembered due to an early acting appearance by the singer David Bowie. The sex comedy *Rentadick* (1972), wherein Tsai Chin appeared as Madam Greenfly, followed. In the '70s she joined the theater company the Cambridge Ensemble. Located in Boston, the drama company performed many classics, including *The Scarlet Letter*.

Chin went on to receive her Masters degree in dramatic literature and returned to China. There she was invited to teach drama at the Chinese Cultural Department in Beijing. Chin also performed in several theatrical productions and, it is rumored, appeared in the Chinese films *Qingmei Zhuma* (a.k.a. *Taipei Story*, 1985) and *Deiha Tsing* (a.k.a. *Dixia Ging*, a.k.a. *Love Unto Waste*, 1986). In 1988 Chin published her autobiography, *Daughter of Shanghai*, which told of her adventures beginning in China, then abroad, and then back. As well, she hinted at love affairs with Marlon Brando, Albert Finney, Cary Grant and Danny Kaye. In 1993 she had a prominent role in the American film *The Joy Luck Club* as Lindo, one of four women who have survived insurmountable odds while growing up in China, who now has to deal with the life of her Americanized daughter. Chin remains very active in Hollywood and became a Bond Girl again playing Madame Wu in *Casino Royale* (2006) starring Daniel Craig in his first outing as 007.

Other films include: *The Vengeance of Fu Manchu* (1967), *The West Side Waltz* (1995—TV), *Red Corner* (1997) and *Gold Cup* (2000).

Joan Collins

Joan Collins was born on May 23, 1933, in London, England. The shapely actress started her career by appearing as live set decoration in a number of minor films, before being rewarded with leading roles. In the seventies she became "Queen of the B-Movies" with appearances in a number of British and American horror films, and then hit cult status supreme with her role as Alexis Carrington on the *Dynasty* television series in America. Since the cancellation of that show in 1989, the former starlet has been more noticeable for her books (both fictional and autobiographical) and her emergence as a living legend by doing little more than showing up at haute couture gatherings and being seen with the rich and famous.

At nine years of age, being the daughter of a London theatrical agent, Collins made her entertainment world debut in a production of *A Doll's House* in a male role. Collins teetered on the edge of show business for a number of years in minor roles until she grew into a glamorous young woman with dark hair and a vary shapely frame. Like many other British actresses, her first film role, a supporting one, was in an Italian production, titled *Decameron Nights* (1953). The Hugo Fregonese production starred Louis Jourdan as Boccaccio, the famed lover, and within a series of three stories (all featuring Jourdan and female star Joan Fontaine) the tribulations of love and romance are put forth in a slightly risqué and comical fashion. Collins appears as Pampinea in one of the tales (and it is rumored that her role called for brief nudity not seen in English language export versions).

Another small role, as a beauty contestant, in *Lady Godiva Rides Again* (1953) followed, and then came her big break in the American-produced and European-lensed *Land of the Pharaohs* in 1955. But the dramatic film detailing the love of a man (Jack Hawkins) for an Egyptian Princess (Collins) was deemed too much for most audiences, who watched with snickering faces as the new British star ate up the screen in a hammy performance. As Princess Nellifer, she entombed her husband and then watched with glee as the slaves built a new empire. Collins followed this role by replacing Marilyn Monroe in *The Girl in the Red Velvet Swing* (1955), which documented the real-life turbulent love affair between turn-of-the-century wealthy New York scions Stanford White (Ray Milland) and Harry K. Thaw (Stewart Granger), with Collins in the middle as showgirl Evelyn Nesbit who was the cause for Thaw murdering White, one of the country's foremost architects, in cold blood. However, the film failed to find an audience and disappeared from screens not long afterwards, and is seldom seen today. Collins was back in historical garb in the Raoul Walsh–Mario Bava co-directed *Esther and the King* (a.k.a. *Esther e il Rei*, 1960), an Italian production about a beautiful woman who joins forces with a Persian king in the fourth century to combat his enemies. Court intrigue, romantic interludes and other attractive women (including Rosalba Neri) round out the movie. That same year Collins appeared in *Seven Thieves*, an enjoyable caper film remembered today for its unique cast (Edward G. Robinson, Rod Steiger, Eli Wallach and Collins) and comical misadventures.

Joan Collins' first espionage film was

The Road to Hong Kong in 1962. Co-starring Bob Hope and Bing Crosby, the movie, the last in the "road" series, featured Chester (Hope) and Harry (Crosby), two aging, failed vaudeville stars, ending up with Diane (Collins), a spy looking for a secret formula that will power a new kind of rocket, which enemy agents hope will send men to the moon, allowing them to rule the planet. Sometimes forced, the last pairing of Hope and Crosby in a feature is good for a few laughs, and Collins gets to play a femme fatale and sultry spy all in the same movie. The American-British co-production also features a number of interesting cameos (Peter Sellers, Robert Morley and David Niven) but ends on a bizarre note when Dorothy Lamour makes an appearance, and Dean Martin and Frank Sinatra appear (out of the blue) as astronauts to fly her and Collins away into their space boudoir.

Collins spent the next few years surfacing on magazine covers in the U.S. and in England, and made the occasional appearance on television shows that specialized in espionage. In *The Man from U.N.C.L.E.* episode "The Galatea Affair" (9/30/66) she played dual roles. Collins shined as the Baroness Bibi De Chasseur, a THRUSH agent, and plain old Rosy Shlagenheimer in this episode that recreated *My Fair Lady* within a comical spy spoof milieu. U.N.C.L.E. agents Illya Kuryakin (David McCallum) and Mark Slate (Noel Harrison) train a Bronx-born entertainer named Rosy to impersonate THRUSH agent Countess De Chasseur.

During the sixties Collins also made an appearance on the science fiction show *Star Trek*. In fact, if it weren't for her role as Edith Keeler in the *Star Trek* episode "City on the Edge of Forever" (4/16/67), she may have been stuck as a perennial starlet, already slightly forgotten by the mid-sixties. In this program her character must die as it is foretold in history; otherwise the Earth will be hurtled through cataclysmic events. Unable to stop his love from dying in order to save a planet is a hardship for star pilot James T. Kirk (William Shatner). Written by acclaimed science fiction writer Harlan Ellison, this *Star Trek* episode garnered accolades for its writing, performances (including Collins) and originality.

The next year Joan Collins returned to England to co-star in *Subterfuge* (1968), a spy film starring Gene Barry as CIA agent Donovan. Barry is sent to England on a secret mission to discover an international ring of enemy agents aided by British double agents. Undercover, he falls in love with Collins, as the wife of one particular suspected double agent (Tom Addams). Unfortunately, the film becomes mired in a series of confusing suspects and double talk. Collins admirers will do better than to run to locate this film, which features her in a different gown or dress in nearly every scene rather than fretting over the kidnapping of her young son by traitorous secret agents.

Surely an early nadir of Collins' career is the mistake of appearing (in the role of Polyester Poontang) in then-husband Anthony Newley's macabre X-rated comedy-musical-softcore sex extravaganza *Can Hieronymus Merkin Ever Forget Mercy Humppe and Find True Happiness?* (1969). That same year, in the *Mission: Impossible* episode "Nicole" (3/30/69), she had the distinction of being one of the few female characters whom the stoic IMF leader Jim Phelps (Peter Graves) allows himself to love. In an out-of-character episode, Phelps falls for the comely (and seemingly innocent) Nicole (Collins) during an IMF mission to infiltrate a foreign country to steal a priceless document containing a list of suspected double agents. However, Phelps is seriously wounded and allows Nicole to take him as far as the border in an elaborate ruse (by the enemy, for a change) to have the IMF steal the document, prove its

Joan Collins as Nicole with Peter Graves (IMF agent Jim Phelps) in the episode entitled "Nicole" on *Mission: Impossible* (Paramount Television, 1969).

value and keep it for their own nefarious use. Collins plays a mean femme fatale when, by the end of the episode, she reveals her true allegiances.

In feature films Joan Collins managed to survive the *Hieronymus Merkin* debacle and appeared in the spy thriller *The Executioner* (1970). In this film George Peppard stars as John Shay, a British secret agent assigned to ferret out double agents in his area. Suspecting many of his colleagues of being in collusion with enemy foreign powers, Shay spends much of the movie romancing the female cast (including Collins and Judy Geeson) before putting bullets into his enemies. The film coasts on an easygoing performance by Peppard, but the static direction by actor Sam Wanamaker makes the movie feel much slower paced than it actually is.

In 1971, Joan Collins co-starred in *Revenge* (a.k.a. *Inn of the Frightened People*), a movie about a group of people who all suspect a member of the household of being a child murderer. Then, in the quasi-science fiction fable film *Quest for Love*, she was the romantic interest for star Roger Moore (whom she reunited with in his post–*The Saint* UK television show, *The Persuaders*, in which he co-starred with Tony Curtis as one of two wealthy playboys who become mercenaries and adventurers). Collins appeared in the episode entitled "Five Miles to Midnight" (2/16/72) as Sidonie, a photographer who insists on helping the duo smuggle a Mafia informant (Robert Hutton) out of Italy.

In 1972 Collins began appearing in British horror films, which led to her being dubbed "The Queen of B-Movies" for a brief spell. During this period (which lasted until 1977) she starred in: *Tales from the Crypt* (1972), *Tales That Witness Madness* (1973), *Dark Places* (1973), *The Devil Within Her* (1975) and *Empire of the Ants* (1977). Alongside these sometimes affectionately regarded thrillers, Joan Collins also began starring in bawdy, risqué British sex comedies, showing more than a small amount of skin: *Alfie, Darling* (1975), *The Bawdy Adventures of Tom Jones* (1976), *The Bitch* (1978) and *The Stud* (1978). It was in the last two films (inspired by the like-titled books written by her sister, novelist Jackie Collins) that Joan Collins found new fame as a dress dropping, full figured queen of British sex movies.

These roles may have helped her win the part of supreme bitch Alexis Carrington in the long running and influential nighttime American soap opera *Dynasty* in 1981 (she was nominated for an Emmy Award for her performance in the show, in the 1983/1984 season). As Collins told fans on an *Oprah Winfrey Show* appearance in the winter of 1991, "You have to be a very nice woman to play a bitch, or it doesn't work." Since *Dynasty* has left the airwaves, Joan Collins has appeared in a reunion show, *Dynasty: The Reunion* (1991), and, more recently, in *The Flintstones in Viva Rock Vegas* (2000) and *These Old Broads* (2001—TV).

Finally, Joan Collins made international headlines when she sued her book publisher, Random House, for non-payment of money owed to her, and they, in turn, countersued. Apparently, Collins, who had written *Past Imperfect* and *Prime Time*, among other novels and autobiographies, had a $4 million contract with the publishing house, promising them two more novels. However, the publishers decreed the book unpublishable, to the extent of calling in star witness "editors" who called the work "drivel" and "ridiculous" during the court trial. Siding with the actress, the jury awarded her the money she was seeking, claiming that regardless of the judgment of the publisher, she did hand in a completed work called *A Ruling Passion*.

Other films include: *The Virgin Queen* (1955), *Rally 'Round the Flag, Boys!* (1959), *The Big Sleep* (1978), *Fearless* (1978), *Nutcracker* (1982), *The Making of a Male Model* (1983—TV), *Sins* (1985—TV), *In the Bleak Midwinter* (1995) and *Joseph and the Amazing Technicolor Dreamcoat* (1999).

Yvonne Craig

Though best remembered for her one-season appearance as Batgirl on the hit TV series *Batman* during the 1967-68 season, sultry Yvonne Craig had a prolific career before landing that star-making role. She was born Yvonne Joyce Craig on May 16, 1937, in Taylorville, Illinois. From the age of ten she knew she wanted to be a ballerina. When her family relocated to Dallas, Craig began training with Edith James, a former member of the Ruth St. Denis and Ted Shawn company. She became the protégée of Alexandra Danilova when the esteemed dancer came to Craig's school as a guest teacher. It was through Danilova that Craig won a scholarship to the School of American Ballet in New York. She eventually auditioned and was accepted into the Ballet Russe de Monte Carlo. While on tour she was spotted by producer Edmund Chevie in Los Angeles but turned down his offer of a role in the film *Rock, Pretty Baby* (1956).

Yvonne Craig returned to Hollywood in 1957 to study with another ballet teacher. While dining with Chevie she was introduced to John Ford's son Patrick, who was producing the western *The Young Land* (1959). Craig won the female lead as a Mexican, but before filming began she played a supporting role in the teenage exploitation film *Eighteen and Anxious* (1958). More film roles followed—a beach girl in *Gidget* (1959), a teen temptress who vamped Sal Mineo in *The Gene Krupa Story* (1959) and the town tramp who tries to snare rich playboy George Hamilton in *By Love Possessed* (1961).

Craig's big-screen persona softened during the mid-sixties as she was romanced by Elvis Presley in *It Happened at the World's Fair* (1963) and *Kissin' Cousins* (1964). She even joined the *Beach Party* gang for a Sun Valley frolic in *Ski Party* (1965). Craig never gave a really superlative performance (to be fair, she never really had good material to begin with), but she could always be counted on to be pert, perky and vibrant. Being a gorgeous brunette with big green eyes, she was a knockout wearing anything from skimpy bikinis to low-cut mini-dresses, and many a teenage girl copied her bob haircut in 1963, which she introduced during her first Elvis Presley movie.

Craig's first foray into the spy arena was an appearance on *The Man from U.N.C.L.E.* in the episode entitled "The Brain Killer Affair" (3/8/65). Though one of the earliest episodes filmed, it didn't air until more than half way through the first season. Craig played Cecille Bergstrom, a young woman who joins U.N.C.L.E. agent Napoleon Solo (Robert Vaughn) as he searches for missing U.N.C.L.E. chief Mr. Waverly (Leo G. Carroll), who is the prisoner of Dr. Agnes Dabree (Elsa Lanchester), a THRUSH agent who has created a mind-altering machine whose rays render the captive ineffectual. Cecille's brother is also a victim of her deadly experiment. Craig's screaming ability deserves special mention in this episode. As does her fiery performance on *The Wild Wild West* as Miss Ectascy La Joie, a seductive assassin whose every attempt to kill a Middle-Eastern despot is foiled by agent James West (Robert Conrad) in "The Night of the Grand Emir" (1/28/66).

For marquee name value (she was very popular with the Clearasil set), Yvonne Craig appeared in added scenes in two theatrically released *Man from U.N.C.L.E.* features. She was not in the original televised episodes. *One Spy Too Many* (1966) was the theatrical version of "The Alexander the Greater Affair" (9/17 and 9/24/65), which aired only once on NBC. It was never rerun or part of the syndication package. Craig portrayed Mr. Waverly's niece and secretary Maude, who keeps reminding Napoleon Solo throughout the film of their scheduled dates. The joke is that Solo doesn't remember asking her out, doesn't know her name or that she is related to Waverly. To spice up the film for European audiences, in one scene Maude is lying topless on her stomach in a bikini tanning under a sun lamp while she checks an airliner passenger list for Solo. At the end she reveals to Solo that he never made any such dates, and that it was her uncle's idea for him to keep his energy centered on her alone and not any other women so the rest of his time could be focused on the Alexander Affair.

Craig was also added to the theatrical version of "The Bridge of Lions Affair," retitled *One of Our Spies Is Missing* (1966) for the big screen. As agent Wanda (played on TV by a revolving door of actresses), Craig is Napoleon Solo's contact person at U.N.C.L.E. headquarters. She is onscreen by herself and has no interaction with any of the other actors as she informs Solo, via radio transmission, pertinent information regarding his mission. By this time the box office receipts for the *U.N.C.L.E.* films had waned in the U.S., so this and all subsequent films only were released abroad.

After starring as a mini-skirted scientist opposite Tommy Kirk in the cult

Yvonne Craig, as U.N.C.L.E. agent Maude, tries to get romantic with Robert Vaughn (Napoleon Solo) in *One Spy Too Many* (MGM, 1966).

cheapie *Mars Needs Women* (1966), Craig landed a smaller but higher profile role as Natasha, the Russian dancer cum spy, in *In Like Flint* (1967). Derek Flint (James Coburn) dances with her during one of her stage performances in Moscow. Afterwards they rendezvous in "the usual place" where Natasha trades in her tutu and classical music for some mod duds and rock 'n' roll. As Flint begins to charm some information about lady cosmonauts from her, she tries to drug him with a tainted cigarette. Flint then makes the connection between the rolling paper (also used to drug his boss Kramden), the Virgin Islands and the spa Fabulous Face. As the KGB closes in, Flint bids Natasha adieu with a kiss before pirouetting out of the window.

Doing the dance sequences in this film turned out to be very difficult for Yvonne Craig. Writing in her 2000 autobiography, entitled *From Ballet to the Batcave and Beyond*, she recalls that "...in the first lift, my partner felt me slipping out of his hands so he dug his thumb between my ribs to keep from dropping me. In the process he broke two of my ribs. I actually didn't know this at the time." Craig persevered and completed the scene but, to her disappointment, "the ballet sequences ... were shot at such a distance that it could have been *anybody* (including a robot) doing the dancing." Recalling Natasha's love scene with Derek Flint, Yvonne Craig writes, "James Coburn kisses better than any actor I've ever worked with, including Elvis!"

After a year's run as TV's Batgirl, Craig made her last spy appearance in "The Bill Is in Committee" (10/8/68) on *It Takes a Thief*, which also featured guest star Jocelyn Lane. She played Roxanne, the old flame of a magician who is being impersonated by Robert Wagner's Al Mundy. Her final feature film role was in the Don Knotts comedy *How to Frame a Figg* (1971). But Craig remained active during the seventies, guest starring on television. When the parts stopped being offered later in the decade, she segued into a successful career in real estate.

Renewed interest in Yvonne Craig surfaced at the time it was announced that Michael Keaton would don the mask of one half of the Dynamic Duo in *Batman* in 1989. Consequently, after making a number of talk show appearances with Adam West, Burt Ward and other former cast members, Craig co-starred in the direct-to-video film *Digging Up Business* (1990). Yvonne Craig passed away on August 17, 2015 from breast cancer. She was survived by her second husband Ken.

Other films include: *High Time* (1960), *Seven Women from Hell* (1961), *Advance to the Rear* (1964) and *Quick, Before It Melts* (1965).

Doris Day

Filmdom's eternal virgin, Doris Day (born Doris Mary Ann Von Kappelhoff on April 13, 1924, in Cincinnati, Ohio) began her career as a singer performing in clubs and on radio. By the mid-forties she was singing with Bob Crosby and Les Brown's bands. In 1948 she made her film debut in *Romance on the High Seas*. Typed as the girl-next-door, she played in a string of light-hearted musicals. Day was able to shine as *Calamity Jane* (1953) and went on to show her dramatic capabilities in *Love Me or Leave Me* (1955) and *The Man Who Knew Too Much* (1956). But her image as the perpetual chaste career woman in a series of comedies would dominate the rest of her career.

Beginning in 1959 with *Pillow Talk*, for which she received an Academy Award nomination for Best Actress, Day starred opposite such virile actors as Rock Hudson, Cary Grant, and James Garner in a series of extremely popular bedroom farces—*Lover Come Back* (1961), *The Thrill of It All* (1963), *Send Me No Flowers* (1964), etc. In each film the audience knew her character's virtue would remain intact no matter how much her leading man schemed to get her into bed. She was number one at the box office from 1960 through 1963. However, by 1966 Doris Day's screen popularity was waning. To counter, she hopped on the spy spoof band wagon with the funny *The Glass Bottom Boat* (1966) as a tour guide mistaken for a Russian spy by scientist Rod Taylor and the more '60s mod *Caprice* (1967) whose tag line proclaimed, "*Caprice* is a whim ... with a wham!"

Caprice, as directed by Frank Tashlin, succeeded best as a zany take-off on the glamorous cosmetics industry, with Doris Day as "the spy who came in from the cold cream." However, the film veers off into a confusing drug smuggling tale and loses its

Agents Doris Day (Pat Fowler) and Richard Harris (Christopher White) soak up the sun in *Caprice* (20th Century–Fox, 1967). (*Courtesy of Michael Monahan*)

punch. Day portrayed industrial spy Pat Fowler, daughter of a murdered Interpol agent. Richard Harris was cast as her romantic interest, Christopher White, an agent who may or may not be working for Interpol. To make her character more in tune with the times, it is suggested that Pat has had sex. As White tries to seduce her, she says, "Christopher, you are rushing me. I always wait at least an hour after eating." Femina Cosmetics owner Sir Jason Fox (Edward Mulhare) concocts a plan where Pat, ostensibly working for the company, is arrested for trying to sell Femina's new deodorant formula to a rival firm owned by Matt Cutter (Jack Kruschen) as a way to win Cutter's trust. The scheme works and Pat is hired by Cutter, but she is there to steal the secret formula developed by Dr. Stuart Clancy (Ray Walston) for a hairspray that prevents hair from getting wet—even when under water. Also involved in the espionage is Irene Tsu as a model who holds the key to the secret formula. Unbeknownst to Pat, Jason and Clancy are in cahoots to smuggle narcotics in a face powder the innocent Cutter produces. When Pat learns that Clancy's mother-in-law Madame Piasco (Lilia Skala), formulates the powder in Switzerland, she travels there and steals a vial from her shop. While she skis the same slopes where her father was killed, enemy agents attack Pat, who is rescued by White. They gather evidence against the two men, but a menacing scrubwoman (Clancy in disguise) traps Pat. After Clancy meets his own death, Pat is taken hostage by Jason and whisked off in his helicopter. White once again comes to Pat's rescue, shooting Jason and leaving a terrified Pat to land the helicopter on the Eiffel Tower.

The critics skewered *Caprice* in 1967.

If the film had stuck to spoofing the mod world of the cosmetics industry it would have been a delightful diversion from the typical spy movies of the time. Reviewer Norma Harrsion remarked, "Doris rushes about but the film's a loser." Joseph Gelmis, writing in *Newsday*, stated "The comedy is as stale as last year's High Camp." *Variety* was a bit more sympathetic (as it usually was) and remarked that, "*Caprice* is one of those occasional pictures about which it can be said fairly that it could have been better than it is." One of the film's major faults was in the casting of Day. This movie tried to shake her squeaky-clean, virginal image. Her Pat Fowler is a single secret agent who alludes to a sex life. Despite the hip attitude, false eyelashes, and mod hairstyles and clothes, the forty-ish Day just doesn't cut it as the female version of Derek Flint or Matt Helm. The film needed a Jane Fonda or an Ann-Margret to really pull it off. However, Doris Day didn't deserve the many nasty barbs written about her appearance. One critic, writing in the *Saturday Review*, was particularly mean-spirited and remarked that Day, "moves doggedly through the film from close-up to close-up that cruelly reveal the puckered skin around her lips, the tired lines about her eyes." It has been reported that Day never wanted to do *Caprice* in the first place. She had no interest in the character and felt the script was weak, but her husband, Marty Melcher, had contracted her for the role without her consent.

After turning down the role of Mrs. Robinson in *The Graduate* (1967), Day made three more unmemorable film appearances before retiring from the big screen in 1968. That same year she suffered a mental breakdown when she learned that her recently deceased husband had squandered and embezzled her $22 million fortune, leaving her penniless. Day persevered and returned to work, starring in the situation comedy *The Doris Day Show*, which lasted four seasons. In the eighties she hosted her own cable talk show entitled *Doris Day's Best Friends*. Today she lives quietly in Carmel, California, and is a champion of animal rights with the Doris Day Animal League.

Other films include: *Romance on the High Seas* (1948), *Tea for Two* (1950), *Young Man with a Horn* (1950), *The West Point Story* (1950), *On Moonlight Bay* (1951), *By the Light of the Silvery Moon* (1953), *Pajama Game* (1957), *Teacher's Pet* (1958), *Please Don't Eat the Daisies* (1960), *Midnight Lace* (1960), *Move Over, Darling* (1963), *The Glass Bottom Boat* (1966), *The Ballad of Josie* (1968), *Where Were You When the Lights Went Out?* (1968) and *Homeward Bound* (1994—TV) (as herself).

Lynda Day George

A beautiful willowy blonde with waif-like features, Lynda Day George was born Lynda Day on December 11, 1944, in San Marcos, Texas. Her father was an officer in the Air Force, so Day and her two brothers attended schools in various cities across the country. Her parents divorced when Day was a teenager and she settled in Phoenix, Arizona, with her mother and stepfather. She began modeling at age 15 to earn some money. After graduating high school, Day decided to move to New York to continue her modeling career, though she had a desire to attend medical school. At age 18 she married a man named Joseph Pantano. The acting bug bit her in New York and Day landed a role opposite the late, great Jason Robards, Jr., in the play *The Devils*. Day's first lead film role was in *The Gentle Rain* (1966) shot on location in Brazil in 1965. She played a frigid woman from New York City on vacation in Rio de Janiero who falls in love with a mute played by Christopher George (whom Day previously worked with on a photo shoot for a magazine). Life imitated art as Day and George became romantically involved.

In 1965 Lynda Day left her husband to be with George in Hollywood. After only a few days in town, Day landed a guest shot on *The Green Hornet*. Other roles followed on *The Fugitive*, *The F.B.I.*, *Hawk*, *Flipper*, *Felony Squad*, *The Invaders*, *The Virginian* and *Bonanza*. Her first spy role was in the episode entitled "A Matter of Royal Larceny" (4/23/68) on *It Takes a Thief*. Day got to demonstrate her comedic ability as a daffy beer heiress named Samantha Sutton who gets drunk and steals "The Royal Orb" from a high society bash in San Marco. It is up to government agent Al Mundy (Robert Wagner) to return the jewel before anyone notices it is missing, thus preventing an international incident.

Day continued doing guest shots and began appearing in TV movies. After returning to the big screen in the John Wayne western *Chisum* (1970), Day was hired as a regular in the TV series *The Silent Force*, which premiered on September 9, 1970. Day co-starred with Ed Nelson and Percy Rodriguez as agents assigned to work undercover to probe and obstruct the workings of the mob. Describing their duties to author Patrick J. White in *The Complete Mission: Impossible Dossier*, Day remarked, "We are sent into a town where organized crime—we often call it the syndicate—has taken over. We work undercover, probably for the federal government, although it isn't spelled out. The three of us rendezvous, plan the attack, capture the criminals, and turn them over to the local authorities." The critics abhorred *The Silent Force*; some described it as being a low-rent *Mission: Impossible*. "Bland and forgettable" was one of the nicer comments thrown this spy show's way. After only 13 weeks on the air preceeding *Monday Night Football*, ABC pulled the plug on this misfire.

Though dejected, Day's spirits immediately improved. She and Christopher George were married in late 1970 after both their divorces finally went through, and she was hired to replace Lesley Ann Warren on *Mission: Impossible*, now entering its sixth season. The producers were impressed with Day's cool blonde elegance and sophistication—traits Lesley Ann Warren lacked. Producer Bruce Lansbury told *TV Guide*, "We were looking for beauty, competence, and maturity; we found all these in her."

Though brought onto *Mission: Impossible* with much fanfare, Lynda Day George (as she was now billed) was the most underused and under appreciated of the series' leading ladies. *Variety* described her as being "pretty in a dancehall girl sort of way but lacks the necessary sophistication." It also did not help that during her second season on the show she became pregnant and was replaced by Barbara Anderson (of *Ironside* fame) for awhile. However, when she was afforded the opportunity, Day George played a variety of roles with real conviction. Among the roles her character of Casey had to play were, according to *The Complete Mission: Impossible Dossier*, "a murderess, showgirl, psychotic mental patient, amoral waitress, blackmailer and asthmatic socialite." Arguably her best performance was in "The Bride" (1/1/72), one of a handful of episodes that featured her most prominently. In "The Bride" Day George proved her versatility as an actress when

Publicity shot of Lynda Day George with her *Mission: Impossible* co-stars (*clockwise from upper left*) Peter Graves, Peter Lupus and Greg Morris (Paramount Television, ca. 1972).

Casey poses as the Irish mail order bride of Joe Corvin (James Gregory), an extortionist who has smuggled millions of underworld dollars out of the U.S. only to be reinvested in American businesses. His personal happiness with his bride is marred when it is revealed that she is a drug addict. When she "dies" from an overdose, he uses her coffin to smuggle out $8 million. However, the Syndicate discovers that the body in the coffin is a dummy and the money is missing. When they bring Corvin back to his apartment, Casey is there alive and well, with two tickets to Miami. She flees, leaving Corvin to meet a nasty end.

Commenting on her performance, author Patrick J. White remarked that Day George "displays an assortment of emotions, from sweetness to irritability to desperation. She also sports an Irish brogue.... In retrospect, 'The Bride' is one of the very few episodes to headline Lynda, making this show so much more watchable." Lynda Day George deservedly received a Golden Globe nomination in 1972 for "Best Actress in a Drama Series" for her performance, and the following year she was nominated for an Emmy.

After its seventh season, *Mission: Impossible* was cancelled in 1973. Leading roles in film should have come Day George's way, but she was relegated to mediocre TV movies and forgettable low-budget features. This is not too surprising since she remarked to *TV Guide*, "My marriage *is* my career. The other is my job.... I don't take roles if they interfere with my first obligation." But Day George did land important parts in two groundbreaking mini-series—*Rich Man, Poor Man* in 1976 and *Roots* in 1977—before being typecast as the damsel in distress. For example, in *It Happened at Lakewood Manor* (1977—TV) she is attacked by rampaging ants, and in *Cruise Into Terror* (1978—TV) she is terrorized by an evil spirit from an ancient sarcophagus. Believe it or not, things got even worse for Lynda Day George on the big screen. She starred, along with her husband, in low-budget horror movies such as *Pieces* (1981), about a college professor (Edmund Purdom) who kills women to collect their body parts for his human puzzle, and *Mortuary* (1984), featuring a killer who uses embalming tools on his victims.

In 1983 Lynda Day George was devastated by the death of her husband from heart failure. She purportedly went into seclusion for several years. She emerged to accept a guest role on *Murder, She Wrote* in 1985, and was out of the limelight again for a few years until she reprised her role of Casey in the episode entitled "Reprisal" on the new *Mission: Impossible* in 1989. Today she concentrates on her work in religious television, but did appear as herself in the documentary short *The Legend of Forrest Tucker* in 1997.

Other films include: *The Outsider* (1961), *Sound of Anger* (1968—TV), *Fear No Evil* (1969—TV), *Cannon* (1971—TV), *The Sheriff* (1971—TV), *She Cried Murder* (1973—TV), *Panic on the 5:22* (1974—TV), *The Trial of Chaplain Jensen* (1975—TV), *Barbary Coast* (1975—TV), *Mayday at 40,000 Feet!* (1976—TV), *Murder at the World Series* (1977—TV), *Racquet* (1979), *Casino* (1980—TV), *Beyond Evil* (1980), *Junkman* (1982) and *Young Warriors* (1983).

Danielle De Metz

Danielle De Metz was one of a number of European beauties who relocated to Hollywood and appeared in films and TV shows. The talented, auburn-haired beauty (born in Paris, France, in 1941) added an international flavor to several spy films and TV shows supposedly set around the world but actually filmed on the studio backlots. Being fluent in French, Italian, Swedish, Spanish and English, De Metz could be counted on to add spice to any part she essayed.

De Metz made her film debut at age ten in the French film *Andalousie* (1951). As an adult she played the girlfriend of experimenter Brett Halsey in *Return of the Fly* (1959) and a cave girl in *Valley of the Dragons* (1961). In *Gidget Goes to Rome* (1963) she was an Italian sexpot vying with Cindy Carol's surfing sweetheart for the affections of Moondoggie (James Darren). Danielle De Metz was also very active on television, guest starring on such series as *Thriller, Alfred Hitchcock Presents, The Rogues* and *Perry Mason*.

In 1966 De Metz made three guest appearances on small-screen spy shows. First up for her was the role of Raquel in the exciting episode "Bet Me a Dollar" (2/16/66) on *I Spy*. Agent Kelly (Robert Culp) bets his partner Scott (Bill Cosby) that he can disappear for a week and not be found. Just after he departs, Scott learns that Kelly has been infected by Anthrax and will die unless he is treated in 24 hours. *The Man from U.N.C.L.E.* took advantage of De Metz's wide-eyed innocence and employed her in two episodes. In one of the second season's lesser efforts, entitled "The Foreign Legion Affair" (2/18/66), she played a stewardess named Barbara who parachutes out of a plane with U.N.C.L.E. operative Illya Kuryakin (David McCallum) carrying a photo of a THRUSH secret code. They land in the desert and make their way to a Foreign Legion base manned by bungling Basil Calhoun (Howard Da Silva), and Kuryakin's partner Napoleon Solo (Robert Vaughn) must rush to their rescue before THRUSH finds them. And in "The Come with Me to the Casbah Affair" (11/11/66) she played Janine, the prize

Pierrot La Mouce (Pat Harrington, Jr.) wants from U.N.C.L.E. in return for turning over a rare book containing THRUSH secrets.

Danielle De Metz continued in the role of the innocent on *The Girl from U.N.C.L.E.* In "The Catacomb and Dogma Affair" (1/24/67) she played a young woman named Adriana Raffaelli who aids U.N.C.L.E. agents April Dancer (Stefanie Powers) and Mark Slate (Noel Harrison) in preventing THRUSH from plundering the Vatican treasury. More impressively, De Metz got to display her comedic talent in her third and final appearance on *The Man from U.N.C.L.E.*, as Yvonne in "The Five Daughters Affair" (3/31 and 4/7/67), which was edited into a feature film and released overseas as *The Karate Killers*. Kim Darby, as Sandy, accompanies Napoleon Solo and Illya Kuryalin around Europe to search for her half-sisters (Margo, Imogen and Yvonne) who may possess pieces of their murdered father's formula for turning sea water into gold. They find the fiery Yvonne at a ski resort in the Alps. She has just left her older lover Karl Von Kesser (Curt Jurgens) after he confesses that he is married. As the infuriated girl is checking out of the hotel, she is informed that THRUSH agent Randolph (Herbert Lom) paid her bill. When Randolph introduces himself to her,

A typically sixties mod look for Danielle De Metz, seen here in *The Party* (United Artists, 1968) with Peter Sellers and an unidentified actor.

Yvonne facetiously inquires, "Well, what are you? Santa Claus or old Nick in sheep's clothing?" Rudolph is after her suitcase containing a photograph with the missing piece to the formula. After a series of mishaps, Yvonne and Karl are reunited and the U.N.C.L.E. agents fend off THRUSH.

Danielle De Metz next appeared in the hard-to-find TV-movie *The Scorpio Letters* (1967), based on a novel by Victor Canning. This was a thrilling spy adventure starring Alex Cord, Shirley Eaton, Antoinette Bower and De Metz as Marie. It was one of the earliest made-for-TV movies filmed on location rather than on the studio backlot. An American agent (Cord) is reluctantly employed by the British secret service to smash an international blackmailing ring led by a person with the moniker of Scorpio. Though made for U.S. television, *The Scorpio Letters* was given a theatrical run overseas.

The Scorpio Letters was De Metz's last spy production. She went on to broadly play a bored Italian movie star who loves to eat in the Peter Sellers comedy *The Party* (1968), and played the seductive mistress of an Italian general in *Raid on Rommel* (1971) starring Richard Burton. Being the only female in the cast, this was a highly sought after role. Surprisingly, it was De Metz's last known feature film appearance. After doing a few more TV guest shots (*I Dream of Jeannie*, *Longstreet*), De Metz disappeared from Hollywood.

Other films include: *Black Invaders* (1960), *The Magic Sword* (1962), *Jessica* (1962), *Duel at the Rio Grande* (1963) and *Wake Me When It's Over* (1969—TV).

Mimi Dillard

Along with Judy Pace and Ena Hartman, Mimi Dillard was one of very few African-American actresses who could be considered a sixties starlet. As with her Caucasian contemporaries of the decade, this former Miss Ebony fashion model posed for cheesecake photos and had small roles in a few movies, including playing James Edwards' wife in *The Manchurian Candidate* (1962). A year later she starred with Horace Jackson and Maye Henderson in *Living Between Two Worlds* (1963), which featured an all-black cast. Dillard was also a staple of mid-sixties television, usually appearing as the lone African-American female on such TV shows as *The Dick Van Dyke Show*, *My Three Sons* and *Perry Mason*, and playing the recurring role of Molly on the short-lived sitcom *Valentine's Day* starring Tony Franciosa. And in 1965 Dillard (who was also a singer) became the first American performer to entertain in Prague, Czechoslovakia, as headliner of their "Christmas Festival."

Back on American TV, Mimi Dillard turned up in very minor roles in two spy adventures. "Memorandum for a Spy" (4/2 and 4/9/65), a two-part episode of *Bob Hope Presents the Chrysler Theater*, featured Robert Stack as an alcoholic, depressed agent committed to a mental hospital by the CIA to uncover a Russian spy. On *The*

Man from U.N.C.L.E. episode "The Re-Collector's Affair" (10/22/65), agents Napoleon Solo (Robert Vaughn) and Illya Kuryakin (David McCallum) investigate an organization purportedly hunting ex–Nazis to recover stolen works of art.

On the big screen, Dillard's appearance in *A Man Called Dagger* (1967) is fleeting but memorable. She may have been one of the first black actresses to play a spy during this period. Her character, an agent named Melissa, meets sexy secret agent Dirk Dagger (Paul Mantee) at the Los Angeles airport. Wearing black Capri pants and mod cat's eye sunglasses, Melissa's attire inspires Dagger to ask, "What do I call you—Kato?" They then drive off in her hot rod and give chase to ex–Nazi scientist Dr. Karl Rainer (Leonard Stone). They lose him only to be chased and shot at by the evil Rudolph Koffman's henchmen. When Dagger states he can't get a clear shot at them, Melissa declares confidently, "Don't worry about it. I'll show you how we do it at Le Mans." Dagger remarks quizzically, "Le Mans?" To which Melissa retorts, "Le Mans, Daytona, Sebring. A girl's got to do something with her weekends." She then hits the gas for a thrilling car chase through the Santa Monica Boulevard oil fields near the Los Angeles Airport. They make their escape by driving atop a rig. Melissa drives Dagger to the beach where he changes into his bathing suit to surf board out to his

Operative Mimi Dillard (Melissa) greets Paul Mantee as *The Man Called Dagger* (MGM, 1967).

contact—agent Harper Davis (Terry Moore). Later Melissa turns up briefly to help Dagger sneak into Koffman's headquarters, but her ruse is uncovered by Koffman and she is impaled on a meat hook.

Mimi Dillard's last film appearance was in the sex and spy comedy *The Man from O.R.G.Y.* (1970). As the tag line proclaimed, "Meet Steve Victor, a new breed of agent. He stands up for what he believes in ... SEX!" Robert Walker played Victor, a scientist/secret agent employed by the Organization for the Rational Guidance of Youth (O.R.G.Y.). His current research project is put on hold when he is assigned to locate three hookers (one of which is Dillard) who have just inherited $15 million from their former madam. The only clue Victor has to their identities is that each of them has a tattoo of a smiling gopher on their derrieres. Also hindering his search are two Mafia hit men, Luigi and Vito (Steve Rossi and Slappy White), who claim they are entitled to the fortune since they financed the brothel. Hooker number one, named Gina (Louisa Moritz), forfeits her share because she doesn't want her millionaire husband to know about her past. She provides Victor with leads on the other two girls, both of whom turn up dead, killed by the duplicitous Gina who actually wanted the fortune all for herself. She stabs Vito, who is about to kill Victor. As Gina is about to finish the agent off, Vito shoots her and she plunges out a window to her death.

Dillard continued acting through the early seventies doing guest shots on TV's *The Flying Nun*, *Julia*, *Felony Squad*, and *Tarzan*, among others, before retiring. She passed away on August 22, 2008.

Other films include: *My Six Loves* (1963), *Critic's Choice* (1963), *Seven Days in May* (1964), *The Strangler* (1964), *Looking for Love* (1964) and *The Cincinnati Kid* (1965).

Karin Dor

Born Katherose Derr on February 22, 1936, in Wiesbaden, Germany, the red-headed actress with arching eyebrows and piercing eyes began appearing in German films in 1954. Among her first movies were *The Big Test* (a.k.a. *Ihre Grosse Prufung*, 1954), *Rose Girl Resli* (a.k.a. *Rosen-Resli*) and *So Long as You Live* (a.k.a. *Solange Du Lebst*, 1955). Her first role of note was in the film *The Terrible People* (a.k.a. *Die Bande des Schreckens*, 1960). As Nora Sanders in this early German cinematic interpretation of a novel by the prolific British author Edgar Wallace, Karin Dor (her newly adopted stage and screen name) brought great attention to herself as an actress. She also appeared in other German film versions of acclaimed Edgar Wallace stories like *The Forger of London* (a.k.a. *Der Falscher von London*, 1961) as Jane Leith-Clifton and *The Green Archer* (a.k.a. *Der Grune Bogenschutze*, 1961) in the role of Valerie Howett. In 1962 Dor appeared in the sexy film *Mit Eva Fing die Sunde*, which was purchased by an enterprising American film producer and distributor. With new wraparound footage (directed by Francis Ford Coppola) added, it became the sex comedy *The Bellboy and the Playgirls* (1963).

That same year she appeared in her first European western *The Treasure of Silver Lake* (a.k.a. *Der Schatz im Silbersee*), as well as her first espionage film, *The Carpet of Cruelty* (a.k.a. *Der Teppich des Grauens*, a.k.a. *Carpet of Horror*). In this movie, Scotland Yard and Interpol investigate the theft of secret documents when a special agent is murdered. A crime syndicate may be the culprit. Although not officially based on an Edgar Wallace story, this film was released in Germany as part of the sixties Wallace resurgence and is often confused with the Wallace mysteries. Unlike Dor's roles in the previous Wallace adaptations she appeared in, her screen time here was minimal.

More of her can be seen in the delirious *The Invisible Dr. Mabuse* (a.k.a. *Die Unsichtbaren Krallen des Dr. Mabuse*, a.k.a. *The Invisible Claws of Dr. Mabuse*, 1962). In this science fiction–espionage melodrama inspired by the films of Fritz Lang, Dr. Mabuse, the criminal mastermind bent on world domination, plans to kidnap a scientist who has developed a machine that makes all matter invisible. Sent by Interpol, FBI agent Joe Como (Lex Barker) teams with the West German secret police, led by Gert Frobe. Dor co-stars as Liane Martin, wife of the scientist who has made himself invisible in order to elude Mabuse and his gang.

Dor would return to familiar Edgar Wallace territory as the imperiled lady in distress. During the next four years she appeared in the films *The Secret of the Black Widow* (a.k.a. *Das Geheimnis der Schwarzen Witwe*, 1962) in the role of Clarisse, *The White Spider* (a.k.a. *Der Weiss Spinne*, 1962) in the role of Muriel, *The Strangler of Blackmoor Castle* (a.k.a. *Der Wurger von Schloss Blackmoor*, 1962) in the role of Claridge Dorsett, *Room 13* (a.k.a. *Zimmer 13*, 1964) in the role of Denise, *Hotel der Toten Gaste* (1965) as Gilly Powell and *The Sinister Monk* (a.k.a. *Der Unheimliche Monch*, 1965) in the role of Gwendoline. She also teamed with Stewart Granger for the European westerns *The Last of the Renegades* (a.k.a. *Winnetou II*, 1964) and *The Last Tomahawk* (a.k.a. *Der Lezte Mohikaner*, 1965). Unfortunately, many of these films, while quite entertaining, were not afforded much of a theatrical release in English speaking countries (save for *Die Unsichtbaren Krallen des Dr. Mabuse*, which was released in the United States as *The Invisible Horror*).

Karin Dor's first taste of international success was in the role of Maria Muller Janssen in the British–West German co-production *The Face of Fu Manchu* (1965). As the daughter of a brilliant scientist, played by Walter Rilla, she (along with her father) is imperiled by the Oriental villain Dr. Fu Manchu (Christopher Lee). Coming to her aid after she is kidnapped and held in Fu Manchu's secret dungeon, are Scotland Yard inspector Nayland Smith (Nigel Green) and her beau (Joachim Fuchsberger, a veteran of many German-produced Edgar Wallace features). In *Upperseven: The Man to Kill* (a.k.a. *Der Mann mit den 1000 Masken*, a.k.a. *The Man with the 1000 Masks*, 1965), Dor really got a starring role befitting her voluptuous frame and strong facial features—as an FBI agent named Helen. In this film a Secret Service agent named Paul Finney (Paul Hubschmid), who is also a master of disguises capable of using his skills with latex and make-up to change his face with speed and skill, is known to all of his enemies as "Upperseven." Kobras (Nando Gazzolo), a master criminal who heads an international organization of murderers, is involved with Red Chinese agents who plan to steal millions in South African diamonds and rob the entire country of Sweden's bank money supply in order to fund a secret missile base in Africa, where they plot world domination with a sterilization ray. Finney/Upperseven is joined by Helen (Dor), and together they battle Kobras and his organization. Filled with many elaborately choreographed fistfights and cool Bondian gadgets, and filmed in a variety of countries, the movie copies the well worn Bond formula exactly, but tall leading man Hubschmid, while a dashing figure in action sequences, cannot carry a love scene realistically, making one such sequence (in which he shoots enemy agent Rosalba Neri dead after bedding her) both bittersweet and sublimely ridiculous.

In *Target for a Killing* (a.k.a. *Das Geheimnis der Gelben Monche*, a.k.a. *The Secret of the Yellow Monks*, 1966) Dor got to act alongside her western co-star Stewart Granger in another violent espionage film. Agent James Vine (Granger) is assigned to investigate a crime syndicate that attempts to assassinate an heiress (Dor) to a vast fortune, and to avenge the death of a fellow agent. Curt Jurgens is the main villain. She fared less successfully in the confused and confusing anthology of spy stories *Spy Against the World* (a.k.a. *Gern Habich die Frauen Gekillt*, a.k.a. *Killer's Carnival*, 1966). Dor appears in the role of Denise in this anthology of (three) spy stories starring Stewart Granger, Lex Barker and Pierre Brice, and set in Austria, Italy and America. Three international directors, Alberto Cardone, Robert Lynn and Sheldon Reynolds, helmed the film.

Karin Dor next appeared in an epic medieval fantasy released only to German theaters and television. She played the unlucky Brunhilde in *Nibelungen, Teil 1: Siegfried* and *Nibelungen, Teil 2: Kriemhilds Rache* (both 1966). She also co-starred with Lex Barker in the fondly recalled horror film *The Torture Chamber of Baron Sadism* (a.k.a. *Die Schlangengrube und das Pendel*, a.k.a. *The Snake Pit and the Pendulum*, 1967) directed by her then-husband, Harald Reinl. As the Baroness Lilian Von Brabant, Dor becomes embroiled in a centuries old revenge scheme concocted by a living dead Count (Christopher Lee). Colorful and eerie, the film was ahead of its time with depictions of cruelty and sadism.

Roles in European spy films that copied the Bond formula must have done her some good, for Dor was finally in a real Bond movie, specifically *You Only Live Twice* (1967). In this, the fifth entry in the series that starred Sean Connery, she played Helga Brandt, Agent No. 11 for S.P.E.C.T.R.E. On specific orders from criminal mastermind Ernst Stavros Blofeld (Donald Pleasance), she has been assigned to Japanese businessman Osato for a number of duties, including the extermination of British agent Bond. After fumbling Bond's assassination in a plane, Dor is rewarded by Blofeld with a nasty death via Piranhas. Bringing the series the type of shapely bad girl that hadn't been seen since Honor Blackman's Pussy Galore in *Goldfinger*, Dor was never given the opportunity to make her a truly memorable Bond girl (that role in this film was split between Japanese actresses Akiko Wakabayashi and Mie Hama, as Aki and Kissy respectively); instead she became a fleetingly memorable Bond villain, dead onscreen way before the film's thrilling climax inside a live volcano.

For a number of actors, the unlucky thing about appearing in a James Bond film is the curse of obscurity that seems to plague most of them afterward, especially those that have played villainous parts. For Karin Dor this seemed to be the case. In the odd import *Assignment Terror* (a.k.a. *El Hombre quel Vine del'Uomo*, a.k.a. *Dracula vs. Frankenstein*, 1969) she played Maleva Kerstein, an alien from outer space in humanoid form who took pity on Spanish actor Paul Naschy's werewolf, who had been revived by head alien Michael Rennie in an elaborate plan to resurrect real monsters to destroy the world. Dor's "human" qualities put her at odds with her masters and help to save the day—and the world. That same year she was afforded a nasty death scene in Alfred Hitchcock's feeble spy film *Topaz*.

After the weak critical reception of *Topaz*, Karin Dor seemed to have disappeared from the movies altogether and showed up on American television in the espionage themed series *It Takes a Thief* in "The Three Virgins of Rome" episode (11/6/69). She played Angela Styler, who meets S.I.A. operative Al Mundy (Robert Wagner), sent to Rome to guard three valuable paintings from possible theft.

Prisoner in the Middle (a.k.a. *Warhead*, 1974) may have been developed as a showcase for Dor's return to international feature films, but instead the film languished in the vaults years after its completion; with added footage, possibly from another feature, edited in, the resultant mess debuted on home video in the eighties. This is a ba- ing spy film with David Janssen, Christopher Stone and Dor (as an Israeli agent/soldier named Illora) all searching for a stolen atomic weapon that could endanger Israeli-Arab relations. The film seems to have been reconstructed from the remains of at least two unfinished films. The still quite attractive German star does seem at a loss, however, portraying a machine gun–toting Israeli agent.

After this film her roles became more infrequent, although she reappeared on-

Karin Dor brandishes a deadly weapon in this promotional pose for *You Only Live Twice* (United Artists, 1967).

screen in the German film *Johann Strauss: The King Without a Crown* (a.k.a. *Johann Strauss–Der Konig Ohne Crone*) in 1986, and was seen in such German television programs as *Die Grosse Freiheit* (1990), *Mein Freund, der Lippizanner* (1993) and *Der Preis der Liebe* (1997).

Other films include: *Frauenstation* (1976) and *Rosamunde Pilcher–Ruf der Vergangenheit* (2000—German TV).

Andrea Dromm

Lithesome blue-eyed blonde Andrea Dromm was born on February 18, 1945, on Long Island. She grew up in the upper middle class town of Manhasset. At age six she began modeling and progressed from department store catalogues to the cover of *True Confessions*. Modeling took a back seat to her education for awhile until she returned to New York City. She immediately became one of the most in-demand models, and was earning close to $75,000 a year before graduating from print ads to TV commercials. Her most memorable ad was for National Airlines. Dressed as a stewardess, she asked the TV viewer, "Is this any way to run an airline? You bet it is!"

The acting offers came rolling in, but Dromm was resistant at first. One of the earliest roles she accepted was that of Yeoman Smith in the second *Star Trek* pilot, entitled "Where No Man Has Gone Before." When the pilot was picked up as a series, Dromm passed on it to do movies. In 1988 she commented to *US* magazine, "Who would have known that *Star Trek* was going to take off like it did?"

Soon after, director Norman Jewison cast her in the role of Alison Palmer in the Oscar nominated comedy *The Russians Are Coming, the Russians Are Coming!* (1966), starring Alan Arkin. Dromm played the babysitter and neighbor to the children who discover the Soviet submarine that has run aground in their small coastal New England town. The film was a hit with both the critics and moviegoers. It was the fifth highest grossing film of 1966, with a box office intake of $8 million.

Dromm was handed the lead in her next film, *Come Spy with Me* (1967), co-starring fading matinee idol Troy Donahue. Since the film's tag line proclaimed, "They Frug in the water... Swim on the floor... And blow up the Caribbean... Come blow your mind... Come Spy with Me," it's no surprise the movie opens with a number of go-go boys and girls dancing in silhouette to the title track written and sung by Smokey Robinson. As secret agent Jill Parsons ("I'm an agent not a spy!"), Dromm is sent to Jamaica to solve the murders of two Americans just before a big meeting of the world's leaders aboard an aircraft carrier in the island's waters. Financier Walter Ludecker (Albert Dekker) has been laying bombs throughout the ocean floor to destroy the cruiser and create an international incident. Parsons masquerades as a skin diver contestant in a competition

Andrea Dromm as agent Jill Parsons is unaware of the lurking assassin Louis Edmonds (Gunther Stiller) in *Come Spy with Me* (20th Century–Fox, 1967).

hosted by swinging ex-surfer Pete Barker (Donahue) on his boat. She goes diving, does the new dance craze "the Shark" at a local discotheque and lounges by the pool. Oh, and she also finds time to locate Barker's kidnapped friend Samantha (played by Donahue's then-wife Valerie Allen—under 20 pounds of eye makeup), uncover Ludecker's plot and defuse the bombs.

Regarding the underwater scenes in *Come Spy with Me*, Andrea Dromm commented to *Look* magazine in 1967, "I had to look cool and marvelous. It helped that I used to go to Esther Williams movies."

Come Spy with Me was Dromm's second and final film. She was not impressed with Hollywood or filmmaking. She confessed to *Look*, "[Hollywood] is no place to learn acting. In the movies, you don't have to be a great actress: you're just a type. They expect you to do sexy things, like seduce people with your eyes. I felt susceptible and trapped." True to her word, Andrea Dromm returned to New York and never appeared in a film again.

Shirley Eaton

Shirley Eaton was born on January 12, 1937, in London, England. She was a child actress who had spent her early years in the British cinema in minor roles until she stunt doubled (horse riding primarily) for American actress Janet Leigh in the 1954 film *Prince Valiant*. She quickly began appearing in larger roles, predominantly in British comedies like *Doctor in the House* (1954), *Panic in the Parlor* (a.k.a. *Sailor Beware*, 1956), *Doctor at Large* (1957), *Further Up the Creek* (1958) and *The Naked Truth* (a.k.a. *Your Past Is Showing*, 1958). Eaton's stunning looks, blonde hair and bosomy figure soon had film producers clamoring to cast her in their next movie. Suddenly, from child actress to stunt extra to window dressing to a sexy supporting player, Eaton had begun to find herself in great demand, especially in risqué comedies that showcased her body.

In *Carry On Nurse* (1959), the first of the *Carry On* films in which she appeared in a supporting role (this time as Nurse Dorothy Denton), Eaton found a welcome home for her physical attributes, being an alluring tease for series stars Kenneth Connor, Sid James and Kenneth Williams. She would return in other entries in the long running series: *Carry On Sergeant* (1959) and *Carry On Constable* (1960). Similar roles in other competitive (to the *Carry On* series) sexy comedies were in *Get on with It!* (a.k.a. *Dentist on the Job*, 1962) and *Nearly a Nasty Accident* (1962). That same year she also appeared (along with future *Avengers* star Diana Rigg) in *Our Man in the Caribbean* (1962). This compilation of reedited episodes from the British espionage television series *The Sentimental Spy* was about a lovable rogue spy named Carlos Borella (Carlos Thompson) who becomes a willing victim in a million dollar swindle. Eaton followed this film with a resplendently hilarious and sexy performance in the Old Dark House spoof *What a Carve-Up!* (a.k.a. *No Place Like Homicide*, 1962), featuring *Carry On* series regulars Kenneth

Shirley Eaton, the golden girl of *Goldfinger* (United Artists, 1964).

Connor and Sid James (as well as future *You Only Live Twice* villain Donald Pleasance).

On the small screen Shirley Eaton could be seen in *The Saint* in the episodes "The Talented Husband" (10/14/62) and "The Effete Angler" (11/9/62), all originally telecast in Britain in 1962 but shown on American television in later years. In "The Talented Husband" Simon Templar (Roger Moore) investigates who is threatening the wife (Eaton) of a wealthy man. In "The Effete Angler" Templar becomes involved with a dangerous woman (Eaton) while on a fishing trip to Miami, Florida. Years later she returned to the show in another episode, "Invitation to Danger" (2/17/68).

In 1963, Eaton found herself in the hard-boiled espionage feature *The Girl Hunters* (1963) in the role of Laura Knapp. This British produced film, written by and starring Mike Hammer creator Mickey Spillane as his own literary private eye, was a violent affair in which Hammer's secretary Velma, who (unknown to him) was also an undercover international espionage agent, is killed by enemy agents. Driven to alcohol by Velma's death, Mike destroys an international spy network in the process of finding her killers and meets with the alluring and deadly femme fatale Laura Knapp (Eaton), a man-eater who attempts to plant big shotgun holes in our hero before getting her face blown off in the visceral finale.

Eaton's most celebrated role in the cinema was to follow. As Jill Masterson in the third James Bond film *Goldfinger* (1964), she is introduced to the audience, clad only in black bra and panties, lying on a chaise lounge on the balcony of villain Goldfinger's (Gert Frobe) hotel suite with a pair of binoculars in hand speaking into an advanced audio device attached to Goldfinger's hearing aid. Spying on a game of cards between her mentor and another man, and transmitting to him what cards his companion is holding, she is spotted by British agent James Bond (Sean Connery), who sneaks into her room and turns off the hearing aid device. When she whirls around and questions, "Who are you?" he answers in the now typical Bondian identification phrase, "Bond. James Bond." The agent beds the woman, but before he does he phones American agent and contact Felix Leiter to say that he would be unable to keep his appointment with the fellow spy because "Something big's come up," interpolating one of the series' earliest obvious uses of a risqué double entendre. In the morning, as he is retrieving a bottle of champagne from a refrigerator in the suite, he is attacked and rendered unconscious by Oddjob (Harold Sakata), one of Goldfinger's henchman. Regaining consciousness, Bond finds the dead body of Jill Masterson nude, face down on the bed, entirely painted in gold. In her autobiography *Golden Girl*, published in England in 1999, Eaton recalled being painted in gold and admitted that she was actually wearing a G-string for the scene, leaving a small patch of skin on her stomach exposed so she would not suffocate from the paint and die.

The role only allowed Shirley Eaton seven minutes of screen time, but it quickly became (and remained) one of the sexiest images from the entire Bond series—a woman lying on her stomach, seemingly nude, painted in gold. Such was her success in the film that she was even featured on the cover of *Life* magazine in 1964, painted in gold. Also mentioned in Eaton's *Golden Girl* autobiography is the battle she had with the film's producers over the promise that, as a recognized star, she would receive equal billing with fellow *Goldfinger* actress Honor Blackman (who portrayed Pussy Galore in the film); but Eaton did not. After the release of the film she settled out of court for an undisclosed sum; but Bond producers got the last laugh, as they decided to dub her voice for much of her performance, leaving only one ad-libbed line, "not too early," in her original voice.

Nevertheless, Eaton parlayed the attention and success of the film and her role into supporting parts in *Rhino!* (1964), *Around the World Under the Sea* (1965), as Dr. Maggie Handford, and the entertaining Agatha Christie thriller *Ten Little Indians* (1965), in the role of Ann Clyde.

Three years after *Goldfinger* Eaton was the titled villain (wearing a black wig) in the adventuresome, pop art influenced and titillating action film *The Million Eyes of Su Muru* (1967). In this film two secret agents (George Nader and Frankie Avalon) investigate a series of murders and discover that a secret society of Amazons are plotting to rule the world; their leader, Su Muru (Eaton), plans to use her all-female army (including *Beach Party* cast-offs Salli Sachse and Patti Chandler) to infiltrate the governments of all nations and major financial circles. That same year Eaton also appeared on American television in the little seen espionage thriller *The Scorpio Letters* (1967) as Phoebe Stewart.

In 1968, Eaton appeared in *Rio '70* (a.k.a. *La Ciudad sin Hombres*, a.k.a. *Women Without Men*, 1968), a sequel to *The Million Eyes of Su Muru*. In this crazy-quilt adventure film directed by the prolific Spanish filmmaker Jesus Franco, she seems much more of a nasty villain than in the first Su Muru film and even tortures a number of male and female prisoners (a frequent occurrence in Franco films of this period). In the movie a politician's daughter is kidnapped by the denizens of a secret society of women from the Amazon, and a secret agent (Richard Wyler) is sent to locate the young woman and find out more about the all-female criminal organization led by Su Muru (Eaton). Shirley Eaton also appeared in the same director's Fu Manchu film *The Blood of Fu Manchu* (a.k.a. *Against All Odds*, a.k.a. *Kiss and Kill*, 1968) as the deadly "Black Widow," but nowadays she maintains that much of her brief screen time in this film was either out-takes from *Rio '70* or footage from an unfinished third Su Muru feature planned by Franco.

In 1969 Shirley Eaton quit the acting business and settled into a quiet life with her husband Colin Lenton-Rowe. They had two children and lived a life outside of the glaring spotlight. With the new interest in the Bond phenomena bolstered by the recent Pierce Brosnan films and the DVD releases of the classic James Bond titles (including, of course, *Goldfinger*), Eaton came out of retirement of sorts in 1999 to join other actresses in a photo shoot for *Vanity Fair* magazine's November 1999 tribute to the Women of James Bond, to promote the release of her autobiography *Golden Girl*, to make several British television talk show appearances, to contribute commentary to the DVD documentary *Behind the Scenes: Goldfinger* (2000) and to make several appearances at conventions in the United States to meet and greet her fans who cherished her seven minutes of *Goldfinger* fame.

Other films include: *The Love Match* (1955), *Life Is a Circus* (1958), *In the Wake of a Stranger* (1958), *Nearly a Nasty Accident* (1961), *A Weekend with Lulu* (1962), *The Naked Brigade* (1965) and *Eight on the Lam* (1967).

Rossella Falk

Born Antonia Falzacoppa, this redheaded Italian actress with wide-set hazel eyes and high cheekbones comes from a royal family of sorts. One of her forebears was a cardinal in the Catholic Church; later on there reportedly was a saint in her family, Santa Lucia Fillipini, who was a nun in the 19th century. Her father was a general in both world wars, and the family wealth made her a countess when she was still in her twenties. Using the family name and riches, Falk shortened her name to the partially anglicized Rossella Falk and started her own theater company in the sixties, which she used to cast herself in important roles. She said to a UPI newsman in 1967, "Sometimes I think there has been a little madness in our family in recent generations. One of my great uncles was an enormously wealthy man who left his fortune to the Dante Poetry Foundation."

Having her own theater company meant that Falk never lacked for work and was never unemployed. Her first film role of note was in Fellini's celebrated film *8½* (1963), but most cinema audiences remember her villainous turn in Joseph Losey's *Modesty Blaise* in 1966. In this psychedelic pop art–live action comic book adventure, a sexy, super secret agent named Modesty Blaise (Monica Vitti) becomes involved in all kinds of intrigue and espionage. Falk portrays the deadly and seductive assistant to the film's villain, Gabriel (Dirk Bogarde), coming across the screen as one of the deadlier, psychotic female villains in spydom. Falk's role was that of a vicious killer named Mrs. Fothergill, providing a decidedly bisexual cast to her screen time with heroine Modesty Blaise. One of Falk's *Modesty Blaise* highlights is a sequence where she confronts a mime on the precipice of a cliff and proceeds to kill him by squeezing his head between her thighs, then throwing the lifeless body into the water.

Falk followed this role with a minor supporting one in the bizarre Robert Aldrich film *The Legend of Lylah Clare* (1968) about a slumming movie director (Peter Finch) modeling a starlet (Kim Novak) upon the visage of his late wife, a deceased Hollywood star. Better still for Falk were roles in popular Italian thrillers like *The

Fifth Cord (a.k.a. *Giornata Nera Per L'Ariete*, 1971), *The Black Belly of the Tarantula* (a.k.a. *La Tarantola dal Ventre Nero*, 1971) and *The Killer Is on the Telephone* (a.k.a. *L'Assassino ... E al Telefono*, 1972). Besides appearing in the above films, she spent much of the late sixties and early seventies dubbing English language vocal tracks onto Italian films meant for other countries. In 2001 she appeared in Dario Argento's *Non Ho Sonno* (a.k.a. *Sleepless*). She died on May 5, 2013.

Other films include: *Venuto del Sud* (a.k.a. *South Wind*, 1959), *Made in Italy* (segment "La Famiglia," 1966), *Alba Pagana* (1969), *Wandering Stars* (a.k.a. *Stelle Emigranti*, documentary, 1983), *I Giorni del Commissario Ambrosio* (1989) and *Storia d'Amore con I Crampi* (a.k.a. *Love Story with Cramps*, 1995).

Rossella Falk as the psychotic killer in *Modesty Blaise* (20th Century–Fox, 1966).

Sharon Farrell

Pretty blonde Sharon Farrell was born Sharon Fortham on December 24, 1946, in Santa Monica, California. She began ballet training at an early age, and as a teenager she was accepted into the American Ballet Company. Her theatrical stage debut was in a road company production of *Oklahoma*. Farrell moved to New York and began modeling, which led to more acting roles. She made her film debut in a small role in *Kiss Her Goodbye* (1959) but really got noticed in her role as Polly opposite Nick Adams in his second television series, *Saints and Sinners*, in 1962. When that show was cancelled after only 18 episodes, Farrell began getting steady work as a guest star on close to 100 series during the sixties. Farrell graced such varied TV fare as *Wagon Train*, *Gunsmoke*, *The Beverly Hillbillies*, *The Fugitive*, *I Dream of Jeannie*,

Sharon Farrell as wistful stewardess Sandy Wister greets Robert Vaughn (Napoleon Solo), unaware that he is a THRUSH imposter, in *The Spy with My Face* (MGM, 1965).

My Three Sons and *The Alfred Hitchcock Hour*, among others.

The Man from U.N.C.L.E. took advantage of Farrell's comedic ability and cast her as the harried girlfriend of U.N.C.L.E. agent Napoleon Solo (Robert Vaughn) in "The Double Affair" (11/17/64), released theatrically as *The Spy with My Face*. The original televised episode is much different from the theatrical version due to director

Joseph Cavelli's additional scenes, including the more adult ones between Farrell and Robert Vaughn. When the viewer first sees stewardess Sandy Wister, the forlorn lass is alone in her home all dolled up and tipsy—stood up by her boyfriend Napoleon Solo. He arrives at her apartment late and, though Sandy tries to resist his charms, she forgives him and they tumble into bed. The next night at a swanky restaurant Sandy confesses that she thinks Napoleon will desert her again. After vehemently denying it, Solo leaves Sandy to rendezvous with beautiful THRUSH agent Serena (Senta Berger). Sandy dumps her dinner on him and calmly walks out. Later she purposely spills a cup of coffee on him when he ignores her on a flight to Europe, unaware that it is not Solo but a THRUSH look-alike. Running into the faux Solo with Serena at a hotel in Austria, she agrees to go on an outing with them, unaware that they plan to kill her and the real Solo. After a series of car chases and fistfights, Serena kills the THRUSH double and Napoleon is reunited with Sandy, who kisses him to prove he is the real one. Farrell gives an amusing performance as Sandy and steals scenes from the other actors. *Variety*'s reviewer commented, "Femme honors go to Sharon Farrell as a cute sexpot."

Sharon Farrell was so good in *The Spy with My Face* that the U.N.C.L.E. producers invited her back for two additional episodes. In "The Minus X Affair" (4/8/66) Farrell played Leslie, the estranged daughter of Professor Lillian Semmler (Eve Arden), who has invented the drugs Plus-X (which "heightens all the human senses") and Minus-X (which temporarily causes adults to regress to children). U.N.C.L.E. is assigned to protect Lillian from THRUSH, unaware that she is a THRUSH agent. When Lillian decides to cooperate with the good guys, THRUSH operative Rollo (Theo Marcuse) kidnaps Leslie, forcing Lillian to give Plus-X to agents who will attack a government plutonium plant.

Farrell is once again the innocent on *The Man from U.N.C.L.E.* in "The Pieces of Fate Affair" (2/24/67), written by Harlan Ellison and Yale Edoff. This time she is Jacqueline Midcult, the author of *The Pieces of Fate*, which seems to be based on a series of missing THRUSH diaries. Two THRUSH agents, played by Theo Marcuse and Grayson Hall, are sent to kidnap her. Their attempt fails, but Jacqueline is injured in the struggle and develops amnesia. The U.N.C.L.E. agents take her back to her hometown in hopes of reviving her memory. The episode's finale occurs as U.N.C.L.E. and THRUSH converge on the attic of her uncle's home, where the diaries are hidden. Though one of the third season's best episodes, this was never aired in syndication due to the fact that co-writer Ellison used his friends' names as character names. One of them sued, tying up this episode in litigation for years. It finally was rerun during the mid-eighties.

Continuing to play kooky characters, Sharon Farrell gives a superlative performance as saloon girl Cloris Colton, desperate to be accepted by high society, in "The Night of the Amnesiac" on *The Wild Wild West*. While agent James West (Robert Conrad) is escorting a shipment of the small pox vaccine for the entire western states, he is grazed in the head by a bullet and wanders into the nearest town. Wounded and suffering from amnesia, the bare-chested West saves Cloris from a drunken cowpoke. She takes him home after he collapses, but when he awakens he accidentally destroys her prize Cassandra Mums. When West offers to buy her more, an upset Cloris wails, "You can't buy Cassandras! You have to grow them! Just like you can't make rich old biddies let me into their flower show." West uses his macho bravado to persuade Cloris to help him regain his memory.

Feature films belatedly took note of Farrell and she gave two standout performances in 1969. *Marlowe* cast her as Orfamay Quest, who hires James Garner's gumshoe to find her missing brother; and in *The Reivers*, starring Steve McQueen, she played Corrie, a whore-with-a-heart-of-gold who befriends an 11-year-old boy. After winning rave reviews and being voted a "Star of Tomorrow" in 1970, Farrell disappeared from the limelight after suffering an embolism that almost killed her and her unborn baby in 1971. Her son, Chance Boyer, was born prematurely but healthy. Farrell suffered brain damage, experienced memory loss and had to learn to read and write all over again. Following the advice of close friend Steve McQueen, Farrell kept her condition a secret from Hollywood.

By 1974 Sharon Farrell had recovered enough to return to work. However, her husband John Boyer left her in the process. She appeared in a few horror and made-for-TV movies (she met her current husband, writer Dale Trevillion, on the set of *The Premonition* in 1976) before being signed for the role of Lori Wilson during the last season of *Hawaii Five-O* in 1979. In 1981 she appeared in the Oscar nominated film *The Stunt Man* starring Peter O'Toole. Farrell quickly morphed into a character actress and played a variety of parts—big and small. Her most recognizable role is that of Florence Webster on the hit daytime drama *The Young and the Restless*. Slated to play the role for five episodes only in 1991, she was signed to a three-year contract and is still making recurring appearances on the soap.

Other films include: *A Lovely Way to Die* (1968), *The Love Machine* (1971), *The Eyes of Charles Sand* (1972—TV), *It's Alive* (1974), *The Last Ride of the Dalton Gang* (1979—TV), *The Fifth Floor* (1980), *Sweet Sixteen* (1981), *Lone Wolf McQuade* (1983), *Night of the Comet* (1984), *Can't Buy Me Love* (1987), *Lonely Hearts* (1991), *A Gift from Heaven* (1994), *Timeless Obsession* (1997) and *Last Chance Love* (1997).

Barbara Feldon

Considered one of the *ultimate* spy girls of the sixties, *Get Smart*'s sleek brunette Barbara Feldon was born Barbara Hall on March 12, 1941, in Pittsburgh, Pennsylvania. As a child she immersed herself in books and studied ballet. After graduating high school she entered Carnegie Mellon and became a Shakespearean scholar. With her degree in hand, Feldon moved to New York and got a job in the chorus of a Ziegfeld Follies revival. She made her TV debut as a contestant on *The $64,000 Question* and won the show's top prize, with Shakespeare as her subject. In 1958 she put her acting career on hold when she married photographer Lucien Verdoux Feldon. They opened an art gallery together, and after Feldon shed 30 pounds she became a very sought after fashion model. Commercials naturally followed, and she is best remembered for her sultry turn as the spokeswoman for Top Brass cologne ("I want a word with all you tigers... Grr") during the early sixties.

Regarding her tremendous success as a model, Feldon told columnist Earl Wilson in 1965 that, "The agencies all said, 'She can't do commercials ... she will not sell.' I was not fashion magazine chic. But soft sell was about ready to happen! I was so soft sell, I just kind of whispered. And I was tongue-in-cheek. It was right-time-at-the-right-place. I was suddenly in vogue."

So in vogue that naturally Hollywood came a-calling. Before she was cast as Agent 99 (on *Get Smart*), Feldon appeared in what many consider one of the all-time best episodes of *The Man from U.N.C.L.E.* "The Never-Never Affair" (3/22/65) was skillfully directed by Joseph Sargent and written by Dean Hargrove. Feldon gives an amusing performance as Mandy Stevenson, an U.N.C.L.E. translator who yearns for excitement ("I'm dying of acute dullness"). She is sent out on a fictitious mission as a courier to pick up tobacco ("special blend Eye of Dogs number 22") for U.N.C.L.E. chief Mr. Waverly (Leo G. Carroll), but she is mistaken by THRUSH as the courier assigned to transport a microdot listing U.N.C.L.E.'s 12 undercover agents.

As Feldon described herself to *TV Guide* in 1966 ("I'm Pop Art on camera"), she was the perfect choice to play the beautiful, intelligent, leggy Agent 99 on *Get Smart*. Created by Mel Brooks and Buck Henry, the series premiered in September 1965 and poked fun at the entire spy genre. Working for CONTROL, 99 (whose real name was never revealed) is partnered with Agent 86, Maxwell Smart (Don Adams), to foil KAOS' various far-out plans to take over the world. Each week the agents try to foil the diabolical plot of some mad man or woman. In the course of each episode, *Get Smart* spoofed everything from the gadgets used by the agents to the work of spying itself as just a nine-to-five job. But *Get Smart*'s popularity was mostly due to Adams' dedicated but ba· ed, clumsy and oblivious Maxwell Smart, a polar opposite of such suave secret agents as James Bond and Napoleon Solo, who were extremely popular at that time. His catchphrases, such as "Would you believe...?" "Sorry about that, Chief!" and "Missed it by *that* much!" became regular anticipated jokes. Smart was always getting himself and 99 into threatening situations, with 99 suggesting the plan of how to extricate themselves from their predicament. The self-absorbed Smart, a mixed-up little boy at heart, brought out the mothering in 99, who was completely infatuated with the bungler. Though he would take credit for her ideas, take advantage of her devotion and his seniority as a CONTROL agent, and make a snide comment or two (he once remarked, "You're too statuesque, 99!"), 99 endearingly followed him through adventure after adventure. Some of her offbeat undercover assignments included posing as an art dealer ("Kisses for KAOS"), manicurist ("Maxwell Smart, Alias Jimmy Ballantine"), harem girl ("The Man from YENTA"), the wife of a German rocket scientist ("Pussycats Galore"), a flamenco dancer ("Viva Smart"), a hippie biker chick ("The Mild Ones"), gangster Connie Barker ("The Secet of San Vittorio"), a Mexican singer ("Tequila Mockingbird") and a maid ("How Green Was My Valet"). In *Get Smart*'s last season 99 faced her biggest challenge by saying yes to Max's marriage proposal. Later she gave birth to twins.

When the series first began it was the writing and especially Don Adams' performances that wowed the critics. *Variety* declared that she "was okay with a light chore." As the series progressed, Feldon more than held her own against Adams' superlative clowning, and she was nominated for two Emmy awards for "Outstanding Actress in a Comedy Series" in 1968 and 1969.

Regarding the making of *Get Smart*, Barbara Feldon told *People* magazine in 1983 that, "We were always laughing." And she commented about her character to author Joey Green in *The Get Smart Handbook* that, "At first 99 was very trepidatious vis-à-vis Max: afraid to say the wrong thing, very, very careful of his ego, extremely adoring, almost embarrassed about her ability to figure things out that he couldn't figure out. It was kind of pre-feminist ... it never radically changed from that, although she got cheekier as the years went by." She also remarked, "A lot of women have said 99 was a role model for them. Because she was smart and always got the right answer. And that was one of the first roles on television that showed women that way."

Barbara Feldon made one more sojourn into the world of spies with a guest shot as Kate on the short-lived series *Search*. Feldon's episode, entitled "In Search of Midas" (11/8/72), featured Doug McClure's playboy operative Christopher R. Grover investigating the disappearance of a millionaire.

Post–*Get Smart*, Feldon's career has been terribly disappointing, as Hollywood once again misused a very talented actress. Her most memorable role was as a fanatical beauty pageant organizer in the underrated *Smile* (1975), directed by Michael Ritchie. Other than that, Feldon has been mired in forgettable TV movies. Beginning in 1982 she hosted her own cable TV talk show called *The '80s Woman*, which ran for a few years. Though Feldon was noticeably absent from the *Get Smart* feature film *The Nude Bomb* (1981), she did get to reprise her role as Agent 99 in the reunion movie *Get Smart, Again!* (1989—TV) and in the failed return series for FOX in 1995. This new *Get Smart* centered on Max and 99's son Zach Smart, played by Andy Dick. 99 was no longer with CONTROL and instead

Don Adams and Barbara Feldon, as agents Maxwell Smart and 99, find themselves in another precarious situation on *Get Smart* (NBC-TV, ca. 1965).

was working as a Congresswoman. Feldon also made appearances on the TV comedy series *Cheers* and *Mad About You* during the nineties.

Barbara Feldon currently resides in New York City and has concentrated on stage and voiceover work (most notably as the narrator of the PBS series *The Dinosaurs!* in 1992, and more recently as the narrator for *CNN Presents*). In 1996 she staged her one-woman show "Love! For Better and Verse" in which she sang the novelty song "99," which was originally released during *Get Smart*'s heyday.

Other films include: *Fitzwilly* (1967), *Getting Away from It All* (1971—TV), *Playmates*

(1972—TV), *What Are Best Friends For?* (1973—TV), *Let's Switch!* (1975—TV), *No Deposit, No Return* (1976), *A Guide for the Married Woman* (1978—TV), *Sooner or Later* (1979—TV), *Children of Divorce* (1980—TV), *Secrets* (1986—TV) and *The last Request* (2002).

Anne Francis

Anne Francis (born on September 16, 1930, in Ossining, New York) had a long career before she starred as TV's first female private detective cum secret agent, Honey West. She began as a child model and soon progressed to appearing on Broadway and in a number of radio soap operas. In the late forties Hollywood beckoned, but after appearing in a few minor roles Francis returned to New York. She appeared in a number of live television productions and hosted the NBC series *Versatile Varieties* from 1949 through 1950. Darryl Zanuck took notice of her and signed her to a contract with 20th Century–Fox. After three years she left Fox and signed with MGM, where she starred in some of her most memorable films, including *Bad Day at Black Rock* (1954), *Battle Cry* (1955), *Blackboard Jungle* (1955) and *Forbidden Planet* (1956). Francis went freelance in the late fifties, and after appearing in a few films, including *Girl of the Night* (1960) and *The Crowded Sky* (1960), she concentrated on television, which included an appearance in "Jess-Belle," one of the best episodes of *The Twilight Zone.*

Before Anne Francis became the law abiding Honey West, she played the evil THRUSH operative Gervaise Ravel in two early episodes of *The Man from U.N.C.L.E.* In "The Quadripartite Affair" (10/6/64) she and her THRUSH partner Harold Buffington (John Van Dreelen) use a fear gas to try to topple various Eastern European governments. And in "The Giuco Piano Affair" (11/10/64) Ravel returns and is chased by U.N.C.L.E. through the Andes mountains. Both of these episodes also featured Jill Ireland as Marion Raven, the innocent who is enlisted by U.N.C.L.E. to help stop Ravel.

Francis' journey to being cast as Honey West began at a famous restaurant. Writing in her autobiography, entitled *Voices from Home: An Inner Journey,* Anne Francis stated, "One day I had lunch with my agent at the Brown Derby. Although he knew I had not wanted to be tied down to a series ... what kind of project might I find interesting? I presented the idea of a kind of female Amos Burke with lots of action, glamour and a comedic flair." The next day Francis' agent received a phone call from producer Aaron Spelling, who had seen her at the restaurant and thought she would be perfect for the role of Honey West. Francis was first introduced as the slinky detective in the *Burke's Law* episode "Who Killed the Jackpot?" (4/21/65), as West and Amos Burke (Gene Barry) find themselves investigating the same murder.

Honey West began as a regular TV series that September. It was based on the popular series of novels by Gloria and Forest G. "Skip" Fickling, beginning with *This Girl for Hire* in 1957 and ending with *Honey* on Her Tail in 1971. However, the pulp Honey was always losing her clothes and being rescued in the nick of time by her loyal and virtuous boyfriend Sam Bolt. The series kept the boyfriend (played by John Ericson), but the TV Honey had no problems keeping her exotic wardrobe on. It was one of the first continuing drama series to star an actress in the lead role. Honey West was a private eye who relied first on "smiles, sweet talk and flapping eyelashes" to outwit the bad guys. But if things got rough or out of hand she was an expert in karate. (Francis trained with Hawaiian instructor Gordon Doversola to look authentic in the close-up shots.) If things got really desperate, Honey would reach into her black alligator attaché case and pull out a pearl-handled derringer or a fountain pen that sprays tear gas or exploding earrings or even a walkie-talkie concealed in a jeweled compact. And Honey could rest assured that her adoring boyfriend/partner was always nearby. No expense was spared in outfitting Honey. She drove a Cobra sports car equipped with a telephone, and $50,000 was budgeted for her wardrobe, which included "a tiger-skin bathing suit with matching cape, an all-black ensemble consisting of leotards, boots, turtle-neck shirt, belt and gloves, and a billowing ball gown that converts into culottes for chase sequences." And Honey also owned a man-hating ocelot named Bruce Biteabit, which she had tied to a silver leash.

Produced by Aaron Spelling, Honey West first aired on September 17, 1965, on ABC opposite Gomer Pyle, USMC on CBS and the second half of The Sammy Davis, Jr., Show on NBC. The premiere episode, entitled "The Swingin' Mrs. Jones," had Honey going undercover in high society to bust up a blackmail ring. More of a private eye than spy, Honey investigated such standard crimes as arson, kidnappings and robberies. In most cases Honey would masquerade as someone to uncover the culprit. In "The Princess and the Paupers" (10/29/65) Honey grooves with the record business crowd to locate a kidnapped rock 'n' roll singer (Bobby Sherman). "A Nice Little Till to Tap" (12/31/65) features Honey as a bank teller who is being wooed by a suave thief (Anthony Eisley) for inside information. The 2/11/66 episode featured Francis in a dual role as Honey and as her look-a-like, Pandora Fox, a thief who sets Honey up for a heist of missing furs.

Honey West received mostly fair reviews during its run, while Anne Francis received relatively good reviews for her performances. For example, Variety noted that, "the good meat of this little half hour continues to be on the fine bones of star Anne Francis rather than the scripts." One exception was Cleveland Amory, writing in TV Guide, who nicknamed her character "Jane Blonde" and commented, "The very casting—or miscasting—of Miss Francis to begin with should set your mind at ease: Her unsuitability for the role is proof it's a spoof." Most critics disagreed and Francis went on to win the Golden Globe Award for "Best Actress in a Drama Series." She was also nominated for an Emmy award but lost to Barbara Stanwyck in The Big Valley.

Despite excellent ratings, ABC cancelled Honey West after only one season. According to Anne Francis, "They [ABC] were able to buy The Avengers from England for less than it cost to produce our show." The popularity that Honey West brought Francis may have helped her to be cast in the high profile role of Georgia James in Funny Girl (1968), starring Barbra Streisand. But this golden opportunity turned into a nightmare as most of her scenes were literally deleted from the movie before they were even filmed. Though her publicist blamed the prima donna attitude of Streisand, Francis felt it was director William Wyler's decision alone because he may not have wanted the character in the film.

Undeterred, Francis continued to

Anne Francis as the shapely detective *Honey West* (Four Star Productions, 1965).

work and made three more excursions into the spy genre. First up was *Mission: Impossible*. During the series fourth season, Francis was just one of a number of actresses hired to fill the void left by Barbara Bain's departure. In "The Double Circle" (12/7/69) Francis played IMF agent Gillian Colbee, who tempts art collector Victor Laszlo (James Patterson) with a priceless artifact in order to induce him to sell a stolen fuel formula to the Americans and not to the United Peoples' Republic as his partner Ray Dunson (Jason Evers) wants to. This episode is memorable because the IMF team constructs a penthouse suite, which is a complete duplicate of Laszlo's, one floor below his in their elaborate plan to make Dunson think Laszlo will betray him.

Francis played Aline Masterson in an episode of *Assignment: Vienna*, one of three series (the other two being *The Delphi Bureau* and *Jigsaw*) that rotated under the umbrella title *The Men* during the 1972-73 season. The series, actually shot on location in Europe, starred Robert Conrad as American expatriate Jake Webster, who uses his restaurant called Jake's Bar & Grill as cover for his work as a spy for the United States government. Webster, who had a dark, mysterious past, is given assignments by Major Caldwell (Charles Cioffi), who kept him from being thrown in jail. In Francis' episode, entitled "Queen's Gambit" (11/9/72), also guest starring Joby Baker and Robert Lyons, Webster goes on the search for stolen crown jewels. Francis' final role in the spy genre was that of Beth Parker in "Countdown to Panic" (2/7/73) on *Search*. This episode featured Hugh O'Brian as Probe agent Hugh Lockwood who searches for a man infected with a deadly virus before he begins an epidemic.

Francis remained quite active and worked steadily through the early nineties in TV movies and guest shots. In the eighties she had recurring roles as Altovise Cooper on *Dallas* in 1981, and Mama Jo on *Riptide* in 1984. She produced, directed and wrote a short film entitled *Gemini Rising*, which played film festivals and aired on PBS. Anne Francis spent her final years in Santa Barbara until her passing from lung cancer on January 2, 2011.

Other films include: *Summer Holiday* (1948), *Lydia Bailey* (1952), *Susan Slept Here* (1954), *Rogue Cop* (1954), *Don't Go Near the Water* (1957), *The Satan Bug* (1965), *Brainstorm* (1965), *Hook, Line & Sinker* (1969), *The Love God?* (1969), *Mongo's Back in Town* (1971—TV), *Fireball Forward* (1972—TV), *Pancho Villa* (1972), *Cry Panic* (1974—TV), *The Last Survivors* (1975—TV), *A Girl Named Sooner* (1975—TV), *Agatha* (1979), *Detour to Terror* (1980—TV), *Laguna Heat* (1987—TV), *Poor Little Rich Girl: The Barbara Hutton Story* (1987—TV), *Little Vegas* (1990), *The Double O Kid* (1993), *Have You Seen My Son?* (1996—TV) and *Lover's Knot* (1996).

Eunice Gayson

Born March 17, 1931, in Surrey, England, Eunice Gayson has a place in the James Bond canon as the only woman to appear as the same character in more than one Bond film (aside from the actresses who have appeared as Miss Moneypenny). Beginning her career on the British stage, Gayson's first film role was in *Melody in the*

Eunice Gayson as Sylvia Trench attempts to dissuade Sean Connery (James Bond) from beginning his next mission in *From Russia with Love* (United Artists, 1963).

Dark (1948). She followed this with a succession of film appearances, including *Down Among the Z Men* (1952), which is about a band of criminals (including Peter Sellers) who visit a small town to steal a professor's scientific formula; the adventure film *Zarak* (1956), set in Britain's India colonies, and the Hammer Film production *The Revenge of Frankenstein* (1958).

Zarak director Terence Young remembered Eunice from that film and cast her as Sylvia Trench in *Dr. No* (1962), the first of the James Bond films with Sean Connery. The character of Miss Trench is a wealthy society woman whom Bond meets in the casino "Les Ambassadeurs" in London, near the opening of *Dr. No*. Fascinated by her ability to play the card game with skill and determination, even when losing, as well as her alluring figure, Bond asks of her, "I admire your courage, Miss?" She replies: "Trench. Sylvia Trench. I admire your luck, Mister...?" Bond answers (cigarette dangling from his mouth): "Bond. James Bond." He beds her after finding her playing golf in his suite, naked but for one of his own shirts that she uses to adorn her body. In the second Bond film, *From Russia with Love* (1963), Gayson returned as Sylvia Trench, seen having a quick tryst with the agent in a rowboat by a lake before he is sent on a mission to Istanbul. Bond asks Sylvia to wait for him, but it is never made quite clear if he indeed does return to her after completing his mission.

Gayson's friendship with Terence Young, the director of these two Bond films, had gone back to 1956 at least; and it seemed that with Young on board leading the Bond films as director, that she would be around as Sylvia Trench for a number of them. But Young left *Goldfinger* in pre-production and new director Guy Hamilton took over the film, making changes in the story line, and Gayson was never again seen as Sylvia Trench.

However, espionage aficionados could take comfort as Gayson popped up in such popular British television shows as *Danger Man* (a.k.a. *Secret Agent*), in the episode "A Man to Be Trusted" (1964), and *The Avengers*, in the episode "The Quick-Quick Slow Death" (1965, telecast in the U.S. on 2/5/66), where she played the character Lucille Banks. She also appeared in "The Invisible Millionaire" (2/13/64) and "The Saint Bids Diamonds" (1965) on *The Saint*, and she played Countess Marie in "Thrust and Counter Thrust" (9/29/72) in *The Adventurer*, a Gene Barry espionage program. This is her last known film or television credit. Gayson later had a successful run on the UK stage in *The Sound of Music* and stayed a thespian, concentrating on live comedies, dramas and musicals for much of her career.

Other films include: *My Brother Jonathan* (1948), *To Have and to Hold* (1950), *Miss Robin Hood* (1952), *One Just Man* (1954), *Dance Little Lady* (1955) and *The Last Man to Hang* (1956).

Gila Golan

Gila (pronounced Jeelah) Golan's exact birth date is unknown. She claimed that she was found, a seemingly abandoned baby, on the streets of Krakow, Poland, during World War II in 1943 or 1944. She told an Associated Press journalist in 1965, "My first memory in life ... it was in a village in Poland. A man came and picked me up and carried me on his shoulder down a dark street."

With her true parents not known, she was named Zoshia Zavatski by her adopted parents and raised for a time by a Catholic family before she ended up in a Jewish home for "lost" children. In 1948 she was sent to France for schooling, and by 1951 she was living in Israel, her name changed to Mara (and later Miriam, then Mera) Goldenburg. Within a few short years she had joined a Kibbutz and was studying to be a teacher.

Years later, Zavatski/Goldenberg won the "Miss Israel" beauty contest and competed in London, England, in the "Miss World" beauty contest; she was a runner-up in the finals. Returning to Israel, she resumed her studies to become a teacher until she was sent (along with other promising models) to the 1961 World Trade Fair in the U.S. The now fully-grown woman was sporting a 36-23-36 frame, a height of 5'7" and a weight of 118 pounds. She decided to stay in this country and changed her name to Gila Golan. (In 1966 she remarked to columnist Sidney Skolsky, "Gila means joy. Golan is the name of a beautiful mountain in Israel.") She studied the English language, as well as acting, with coach Herbert Berghof, and her first film role was as the young girl in *Ship of Fools* (1965). "When I met Mr. [Stanley] Kramer, he told me I was supposed to play the part

Gila Golan brandishes a six-shooter and an alluring outfit in this promotional pose from *Our Man Flint* (20th Century–Fox, 1966). (*Courtesy of Michael Monahan*)

of a sixteen-year-old ugly duckling. I was desperate; I knew I must have been at least twenty-one at the time." That same year she won reams of publicity as "Miss Golden Globes," which culminated as hostess of their annual awards ceremony. Golan, along with Jocelyn Lane, Mia Farrow, Rosemary Forsyth and Raquel Welch, was also featured in a *Life Magazine* article praising the end of the Great Girl Drought in Hollywood.

Gila Golan's main claim to fame is as the female lead in the spy spoof *Our Man Flint* (1966). As the sinister and deadly female companion (named Gila) to Edward Mulhare's megalomaniac character, she entices and makes life hell for super secret agent Derek Flint (James Coburn), who is the man from Z.O.W.I.E. and a special agent for the President of the United States himself. Featuring a heretofore unseen brand of martial arts (Coburn was at the time a real-life student of Bruce Lee), Flint's seemingly limitless array of gadgets and gizmos, and his amazing way with women, the film took in millions at the box office and spawned a less successful sequel (*In Like Flint* in 1967). Golan recalled for the AP columnist, "20th Century–Fox had me read with Mr. Coburn. They had me do a scene from Thomas Wolfe's *The Web and the Rock*. There were pages and pages of speeches. It [the book] was about a woman trying to save the man she loves from destroying himself ... then he [the director] tested me in a bikini, I was so embarrassed. Anyway, I got the part. *Our Man Flint* is a James Bond type movie and I play the villainess who tries to outwit James Coburn. Why I was tested with the Thomas Wolfe story for that part, I'll never know."

When *Our Man Flint* became a huge box-office sensation, Gila Golan was touted as the next big female superstar. Alas, it was not to be. She went on to play a co-starring role as an unstable, man-hating patient of psychiatrist Janet Leigh in the Jerry Lewis comedy *Three on a Couch* (1966) and made her final film appearance in the Ray Harryhausen special effects–laden western adventure *Valley of Gwangi* (1969), starring James Franciscus. She retired from acting that same year after marrying Marty Rosenhaus, a member of the Columbia Pictures Board of Directors. After his death in 1980 Golan remarried and now resides in Florida and New York.

Other films include: *Catch as Catch Can* (1968).

Shelby Grant

The spy spoofs *Our Man Flint* (1966) and *In Like Flint* (1967) were huge box-office hits and made actor James Coburn a star. But none of the actresses who played the Flint girls were so lucky, which is not surprising because these films didn't give them much to do. Sort of a combination of James Bond's Miss Moneypenny and Matt Helm's Lovey Kraveszit, Flint's assistants helped him keep his international playboy life in gear. Of the seven actresses to play these roles in the two films, the one who showed the most promise was Shelby Grant. Though not the most beautiful of the Flint girls (her eyes are a bit wide apart and she has a Romanesque nose), she projected a lively animation that made her stand out.

Shelby Grant was born Brenda Thompson on October 19, 1940, in Orlando, Oklahoma. After graduating college she became a schoolteacher but left the profession when she was discovered by a 20th Century–Fox talent scout and put under contract. Needing a more original name, she told columnist Hedda Hopper that she "drew Shelby Grant out of a hat." Her first roles at Fox were bit roles playing a party guest in *The Pleasure Seekers* (1964) and a nurse in *Fantastic Voyage* (1966). Nevertheless, Grant got noticed, and due to her poise, offbeat beauty and talent she was voted a Hollywood Deb Star for 1966.

The classic spy spoof *Our Man Flint* (1966) stars James Coburn as Derek Flint, a hip, high-living secret agent sharing his luxurious New York penthouse with four luscious international beauties—Leslie (Grant), Anna (Sigrid Valdis), Gina (Gianna Serra) and Sakito (Helen Funai). Their ideal living arrangement is interrupted by Lloyd Cramden (Lee J. Cobb), the head of ZOWIE, when a computer picks Flint as the most qualified agent to stop an organization called GALAXY from controlling the world through its weather. As the shapely French cutie, Shelby Grant first appears onscreen shaving Flint—to the

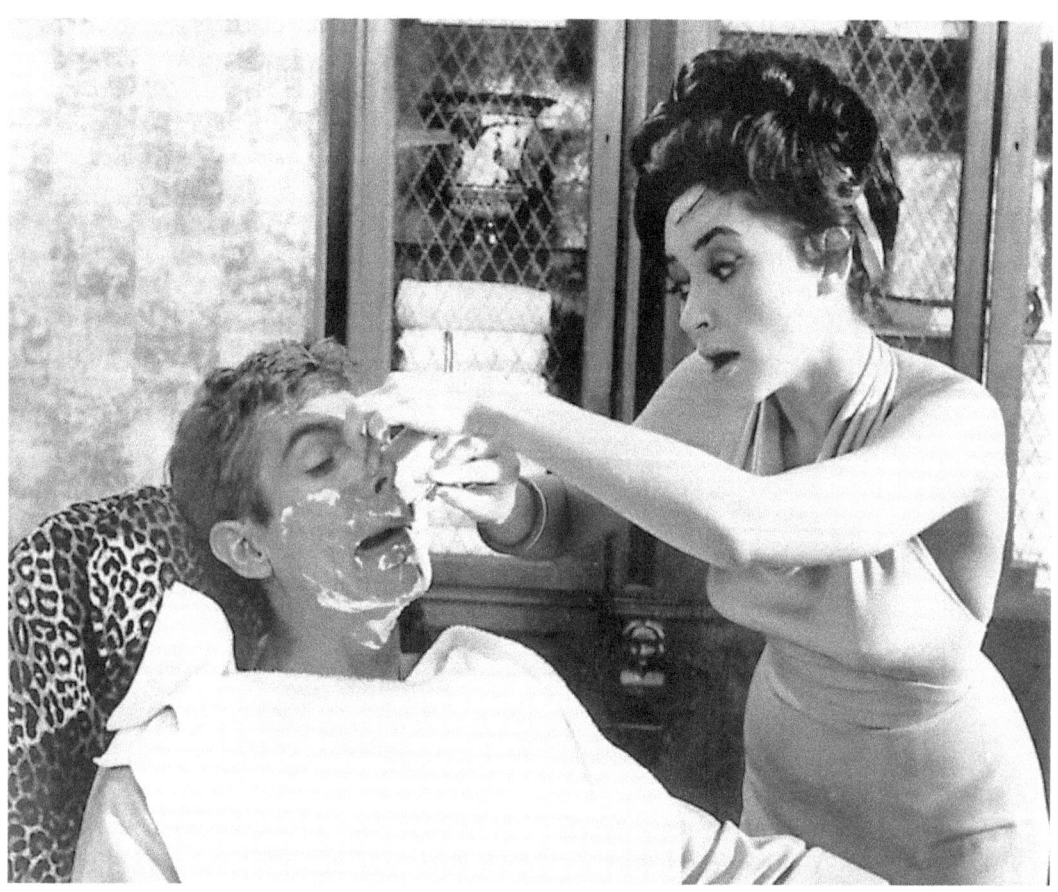

Shelby Grant, as Leslie, caters to James Coburn (super spy Derek Flint) in *Our Man Flint* (20th Century–Fox, 1966).

consternation of Cramden, who has come to personally plead with Flint to accept his assignment. After Flint refuses, he accompanies his lady friends (in beautifully designed futuristic evening gowns by Ray Aghayan) to one of New York's most fashionable restaurants. As Flint is dancing with Sakito, one of GALAXY's assassins, Gila (Gila Golan), thrusts a poison dart at Flint. It misses him but instead hits Cramden. The murder attempt forces Flint to change his mind and flush out GALAXY. He bids his women adieu and heads to France when he learns that three of GALAXY's top agents are operating out of Marseilles. Flint is seized and taken to a remote volcanic island off of Italy where he learns his lovely roommates have been programmed into pleasure units. Flint finds Leslie and the rest of the girls in the "reward rooms." He de-programs them ("You are not a pleasure unit") and sabotages GALAXY's weather controlling machine. As the island paradise blows up, Flint gets his girls out of danger by putting them in barrels and floating them to safety.

As with the other actresses, Grant plays her part enthusiastically. She commented to Hedda Hopper, "I had some good action, a chic wardrobe and featured billing." However, most of the time Grant and the other girls are there to just fawn over Coburn's Flint. They are forever kissing him or looking adoringly into his eyes.

So it is a bit surprising—or maybe not—that by the film's end they heartily accept Gila into their circle. Most of Grant's reviews were like those of *Variety*, which found she and the others "nice to look at," or Leo Mishkin of the *Morning Telegraph* who wrote, "Gila Golan, Gianna Serra and all the others decorate the scenery most attractively." In the film's sequel the number of girls is reduced from four to three, with none of the actresses from *Our Man Flint* reprising their roles.

After marrying Chad Everett in 1966, Shelby Grant was dropped from Fox and her focus shifted from her acting career to raising a family. In 1969 she made an ill-advised decision by choosing the horror film *The Witchmaker* (1969), directed by *Green Acres* actor Alvy Moore, as her big-screen comeback. Her co-stars included spy gal Thordis Brandt, Moore, Anthony Eisley and a bevy of *Playboy* centerfolds. Needless to say, Grant never made a film again. After making intermittent television appearances in the early seventies on *Marcus Welby, MD* and three episodes on her husband's hugely popular series *Medical Center*, Grant faded from the acting profession and became a writer. She and Everett were happily married until Grant's passing on June 25, 2011.

Other films include: *Come Blow Your Horn* (1963), *A Global Affair* (1964) and *John Goldfarb, Please Come Home* (1964).

Alizia Gur

Dark-haired and exotic, Alizia Gur (sometimes billed as Aliza Gur and Alicia Gur) was born Aliza Gross in Israel. Her parents had fled Germany during World War II and settled in the new country, where Gur became "Miss Israel" in 1960.

Alizia Gur as Vida, the battling Gypsy girl from *From Russia with Love* (United Artists, 1963), attempts to vamp Sean Connery (James Bond).

That same year she placed first runner-up in the "Miss Universe" pageant, which led to a career in acting. She was cast in the small but memorable role of Vida in *From Russia with Love* (1963), the second James Bond adventure starring Sean Connery. Gur and Martine Beswicke are remembered for their fight scene, one of the cinema's most ferocious catfights. Vida, the tall brunette with wild eyes, fights with fellow gypsy girl Zora (Beswicke) for the love of a man. When enemy agents interrupt the scantily clad fracas, resulting in a stormy gun battle, Bond (Connery) asks the Gypsy camp leader to have the girls stop fighting. Instead, he offers both battling hellions to Bond for the night as payback for the way the British agent fought and aided the rebels against the attackers.

In 1964 Gur married Sy Schulman, director of Hollywood's Cedars of Lebanon Hospital. Now living in Los Angeles, the foreign beauty was cast in a number of TV spy shows to add international glamour. In the *Amos Burke, Secret Agent* episode entitled "Deadlier Than the Male" (11/17/65), she played Carmen. This installment of the short-lived series was set in Spain, as agent-for-hire Amos Burke (Gene Barry) must stop a deposed South American dictator (Arnold Moss) from returning to power.

Alizia Gur was again hired for decorative purposes (along with Barbara Bouchet and Donna Michelle) in the low-budget espionage film *Agent for H.A.R.M.* (1966). Peter Mark Richman stars as Adam Chance, a spy assigned to protect a defecting Eastern European scientist from enemy agents and his own super weapon, which destroys flesh. Gur played his covert Mideastern contact, who teaches him a couple of moves to protect himself and who is dejected when he rebuffs her advances.

Returning to England for a short period of time, Gur appeared in two films. After playing a small role as beauty pageant entrant Miss Peru, in *Contest Girl* (a.k.a. *The Beauty Jungle*, 1966), she starred in the creepy horror film *The Beast of Morocco* (a.k.a. *The Hand of Night*, 1966), as a mysterious, evil woman who turns out to be a vampire.

Back on the small screen in the U.S., Gur guest starred on three spy programs. In "The J for Judas Affair" (9/25/67) on the last season of *The Man from U.N.C.L.E.*, Chad Everett played the duplicitous THRUSH operative Adam Tenza, who has his rich industrialist father (Broderick Crawford) assassinated. Failing to protect the elder Tenza, U.N.C.L.E. agents Napoleon Solo (Robert Vaughn) and Illya Kuryakin (David McCallum) are sent to locate Tenza's missing brother, James. Gur next played it for laughs in the *Get Smart* episode "Absorb the Greek" (2/8/69) as the fiery Gina Paponickolini, who is purposely matched up with the Chief (Edward Platt) at a computer dating service to learn the secret formula for eternal youth, passed on to him by her husband. Finally, in "The Night of the Cossacks" (3/21/69) on *The Wild Wild West*, Gur portrayed Marie, a servant to the ruling family of the mythical country Karovnia, who is having a secret romantic relationship with Prince Gregor (Dean Stockwell), heir to the throne, which is being challenged by the villainous Count Balkovitch (John Van Dreelen).

Alizia Gur's final film appearance was in *Tarzan and the Jungle Boy* (1968), starring Mike Henry. She made a few more TV appearances before giving up her acting career. Purportedly, after Gur's divorce from Shulman, she was married for a time to Sheldon Shrager, but that too ended in divorce.

Other films include: *Night Train to Paris* (1964) and *To Kill a Dragon* (1967).

Jean Hale

Jean Hale was born on December 27 in Salt Lake City, Utah. Always dreaming of becoming an actress, she attended two years of college to appease her disapproving father. Hale eventually made it to New York and began studying at the Neighborhood Playhouse, where she met actor Dabney Coleman, whom she married. Her first shot at movie stardom came when Sandra Dee's agent arranged for her to meet with executives from MGM. So impressed were they by the beautiful strawberry blonde with the big blue eyes that they had Delbert Mann write in a special role for her in *Butterfield 8* (1960), starring Elizabeth Taylor. Astonishingly, Hale turned it down to remain with Coleman in New York, and she returned to the stage.

Jean Hale's first film was the never-released *Felicia* (1963), shot on location in Puerto Rico. Her official film debut was as a coed stalked by a maniac in Del Tenney's Connecticut-lensed horror film *Psychomania* (1963). Shortly thereafter, a pregnant Hale and Coleman relocated to Hollywood. After her first daughter was born, Hale was cast as a man-hungry lieutenant in *McHale's Navy Joins the Air Force* (1964) and dyed her hair a golden whitish-blonde to play a ruthless Hollywood actress in *The Oscar* (1966). She also made numerous guest appearances on television, including episodes of *The Alfred Hitchcock Hour*, *Bob Hope Presents the Chrysler Theatre* and *McHale's Navy*, among many others.

Hale also donned western garb for "The Night the Terror Stalked the Town" on *The Wild Wild West*, which aired on 11/19/65. This episode is memorable for featuring Michael Dunn in his second appearance as Dr. Miguelito Loveless. Hale played Marie, a beautiful woman who kidnaps agent James West (Robert Conrad) by allowing him to pick her up at an expensive restaurant. When he enters her coach, West is rendered unconscious by knockout gas. Marie then delivers him to Dr. Loveless, who is hiding out in a ghost town. There Loveless, with his seven-foot-tall assistant Voltaire (Richard Kiel), performs an operation changing the face of his henchman Janus (Chuck O'Brien) to an exact duplicate of West's. Loveless then sends the fake West back to infiltrate the Secret Service. The only way the real James West can prove his identity is by kissing the smitten Marie, who helps him escape from the clutches of Dr. Loveless (who flees to return again).

Recalling the show, Jean Hale comments, "Ross Martin was just wonderful to work with while Robert Conrad was very private. Michael Dunn was a fascinating actor and quite the ladies man. I had to keep reminding him that I was married."

In 1967 Jean Hale landed one of that year's most sought-after roles. Due to the success of the previous year's *Our Man Flint*, the role of Lisa, opposite James Coburn's high-living Derek Flint, in *In Like Flint* was very high profile. It was rumored that Dick Zanuck, the head of 20th Century–Fox, wanted Catherine Deneuve for the part. Hale tested and became the favorite of producer Saul David, who convinced Zanuck to offer her the role. Though *In Like Flint* didn't gross as much as the original, it still made a very respectable $5 million and was the eighteenth highest grossing film of 1967.

In Like Flint was released with the tag line: "Flint's back. In action... In danger...

In the Virgin Islands... Where the bad guys... *Are girls!*" Flint, who is still reporting to Lloyd Cramden (Lee J. Cobb), the head of ZOWIE, must thwart a secret society of women who are plotting to take over the world. Led by Lisa Norton (Hale) and the world's three top female fashion leaders (Anna Lee, Hanna Landy and Totty Ames), they operate from a lavish spa in the Virgin Islands called Fabulous Face. Their plan is to take over a space station that controls nuclear weapons. To reach their goal, they disguise two of their women as golf caddies and kidnap the President of the U.S. and replace him with imposter Trent (Andrew Duggan). They also lure Flint's three new attendants (Mary Michael, Diane Bond and Jacki Ray) to the island where they and the paying clientele get "brain and hair washing at the same time" as a way to get the rest of the female population to support their nefarious plot. When Trent turns on the women with the help of General Carter (Steve Ihnat), the females join forces with Flint to stop Carter. Lisa rounds up her Amazonian staff (including Thordis Brandt, Marilyn Hanold and Eve Bruce) and initiates "Operation Smooch," whereby they distract Carter's men by kissing and caressing them. Flint ends up on a rocket with Carter and prevents him from destroying the world. As the end credits roll, two female astronauts rescue Flint and they float in space as "Your Zowie Face" plays on the soundtrack.

In Like Flint opens memorably with an erotic, red tinted montage of women being pampered at a spa. As the title credits roll, the tint dissipates and the camera focuses on the stunning Jean Hale, dressed in a white midriff, wordlessly making her way through the resort to the accompaniment of Jerry Goldsmith's catchy theme. Director Gordon Douglas uses Hale's beauty and physical attributes to grab and hold the audience's attention from the beginning. "The opening is very exciting but I was ner-

Jean Hale as the alluring femme fatale Lisa in *In Like Flint* (20th Century–Fox, 1967).

vous about doing it," admits Hale. "The models in the scene were really nude. This was daring for 1967. But Gordon shot it tastefully and I think made a beautiful artistic statement."

Though spy fans find *In Like Flint* inferior to its predecessor, the screenplay by Hal Fimberg contains some very clever lines. For instance, when Flint learns of the imposter posing as president, he says incredulously, "An actor—*as president?*" Fimberg wrote this as a joke, never expecting that years later it would come true. His script also addressed the issue of oppression of women.

As for Hale, she makes a lovely though not very villainous femme fatale. (*Film Daily* commented that she "is altogether fetching as the power-yearning cutie.") Her Lisa is a cool blonde who remains very icy throughout most of the film. However, after only one kiss from Derek Flint, she immediately falls for him and realizes the errors of her ways. Hale's best moments occur towards the beginning of the movie when her character disguises herself as straight-laced schoolteacher Norma Benson from Roanoke, Virginia, to set up Cobb's character Cramden on an indiscretion charge. She gets herself seated next to him at his favorite restaurant and starts up a conversation. Before he knows it, Cramden is out cold and in bed with Lisa. Photos circulate and Kramden is forced to resign. The idea for the disguise was Hale's.

Commenting on the film overall, Jean Hale says, "*In Like Flint* was a hard picture to do. Since it was shot on location, there were a lot of special camera set-ups. But Gordon Douglas made everything easy for us. He was great. I remember he had so much trouble coordinating the scene with those funny boats we use to get to the other island near the end of the film. Everything that could go wrong did. First the water was choppy. Then the boats didn't go fast enough and kept bumping into each other. The stunt coordinators had a hard time with this scene." As for the cast, Jean responds, "James Coburn is adorable and easy, yet challenging to work with. He is a very sweet gentleman. Anna Lee is a marvelous woman. My parents bought the house she owned in Connecticut when I was eight years old. I spoke with her briefly and told her that I wanted to become an actress. Then almost twenty years later we were co-starring in a film together. It was a very unusual coincidence."

When Jean Hale won the role of Lisa in *In Like Flint* she also nabbed a lucrative contract with 20th Century–Fox. But her next film role, that of George Segal's feisty gun moll in *The St. Valentine's Day Massacre* (1967), was her last. Things at Fox quickly turned sour for Hale who passed on the role of the ill-fated Jennifer in *Valley of the Dolls* (1967) and could not tour internationally to promote *In Like Flint* due to family commitments, and became pregnant for the second time.

Hale's last spy appearance was in the short-lived series *The Silent Force*, featuring Lynda Day George. Though Hale turned down *Valley of the Dolls*, she got her chance to play a woman who does herself in with an overdose of pills in the episode entitled "The Deadly Game of Love" (10/5/70), also guest starring Peter Mark Richman and Joan Van Ark. In the episode the Syndicate blackmails Hale's character, Corrine, into becoming a high-class prostitute. Ashamed of what she has become, she commits suicide. The Silent Force infiltrates the luxury Washington spa that the Syndicate is operating from to expose them.

Hale made a few more intermittent TV appearances (*Hawaii Five-0*, *The Mod Squad*, *Cannon*, etc.) but gave up her career in the mid-seventies to devote more time to her family, which included child number three. Hollywood lost a very capable actress who never really got the chance to prove that she was more than a Marilyn Monroe clone. Hale's devotion to her family was so strong that at one point she had to turn down esteemed director George Cukor's offer to study with him in England for a year.

The Colemans' marriage sadly came to an end in the early eighties. Jean Hale briefly returned to acting in 1987 but found being involved in production more to her liking. Today she is a proud grandmother and is partners with writer/director Michael Tobias in a production company.

Other films include: *Taggart* (1964), *Pals* (1987—TV), *Thanksgiving Day* (1990—TV) and *Lies Before Kisses* (1991—TV).

Mie Hama

Mie (pronounced Me-ah, meaning beautiful twig) Hama was born on November 20, 1943, in Tokyo, Japan. After graduating from high school, Hama's first job was as a bus conductor on a route in a suburb of Japan. One day she found herself walking around a local movie studio and was approached by a film director and his producer to become an actress. She said that she would let them know after first asking her mother for permission, but when she returned, she learned it was only for one film. But the movie business, being a place of steady employment, Hama soon found that she was away from her bus conducting day job so much that she was fired for her absences. When she pleaded with them that she was stuck acting in film roles, they relented and, instead of a harsh dismissal, released her from the contract, leaving her free for movie stardom.

Mie Hama's first film role was in the Japanese movie *Gen-O and Prince Fudomyo* (a.k.a. *Gen to Fudomyo*, a.k.a. *The Youth and His Amulet*, 1961), a historical costume melodrama. She followed this film appearance with the crime melodrama *Fangs of the Underworld* (a.k.a. *Anokugai No Kiba*, 1962) and then began a career playing heroines and villains in elaborate fantasy films and Kaiju Gaiga (Japanese Monster Movies) like *King Kong vs. Godzilla* (a.k.a. *Kingukongu Tai Gojira*, 1962); as Fumiko Sakurai, *Samurai Pirate* (a.k.a. *Daitozoku*, a.k.a. *The Lost World of Sinbad*, 1963) as The Princess; *Dagora, the Space Monster* (a.k.a. *Uchu Daikaiju Dogora*, 1964), as an unnamed female bank robber; and *Frankenstein Conquers the World* (a.k.a. *Furankenshutain Tai Chitei Kaiju Baragon*, 1965), as the aptly named "Screaming Lady."

Mie Hama's career then began to shift back towards more dramatic leading roles, similar to the one in the crime film *100 Shot, 100 Killed* (a.k.a. *Hyappastsu Hyakuchu*, a.k.a. *Ironfinger*, 1965), but received worldwide attention in the espionage caper movie *What's Up, Tiger Lily?* (1966), which was little more than an altered, re-edited, English-dubbed (all masterminded by Woody Allen) Americanization of the 1964 film *International Secret Police: Key of Keys* (a.k.a. *Kokusai Himitsu Keisatsu: Kagi No Kagi*), in which she was originally billed as "Mystery Moll #2." She followed these roles with a major villain turn in *King Kong Escapes* (a.k.a. *Kingukongu No Gyakushu*, 1967) as Madame Piranha.

Then came her appearance in the James Bond film *You Only Live Twice*, which was also her first English-speaking role in a film. Hama was a bit healthier than the average Japanese girl, with her exquisite features, beckoning eyes and 35-23-35 frame, making her a natural addition to the Bond canon of voluptuous leading ladies. She told a *New York Daily News* reporter in the fall of 1967 that she was shipped off to England and was scared, not knowing much English at the time. She almost returned to her native Japan but impressed Bond producers by studying the language intensively for six weeks to get ready for the role, with a little assistance from Bond star Sean Connery, who made her feel at ease in the film. "I like Connery," she said. "I don't like [the character of] James Bond. Bond is always a playboy with many playgirls. Connery is a warm heart."

Her character, Kissy Suzuki, in the fifth James Bond adventure *You Only Live Twice* (1967) became known as the first woman in the series to marry the globe-

The seductive Mie Hama shows why she was selected to co-star as Kitty in *You Only Live Twice* (United Artists, 1967).

and Bond follow the trail of two dead islanders to the coast of a volcanic island and are met with a lethal gas. Once inside, Hama's Kissy character lets her fighting fists fly with the best of the secret agents as she and Bond attempt to affect the rescue of the crews of the rocket ships kidnapped by Blofeld's S.P.E.C.T.R.E. agency of deadly criminal assassins.

One little-known real-life tragedy befell Mie Hama during the film's shoot. When she arrived in Japan with the film crew to shoot the underwater scenes for the movie, the weeks of learning English and preparation had taken their toll, and on the set she was stricken with heat prostration. As a favor, Sean Connery's then-wife, Diane Cilento, donned a black wig and, with the assistance of the make-up crew, turned herself into a passable double for Hama. Cilento did the underwater swimming sequence in Hama's stead until she recovered, since the Connerys had by then become very familiar and friendly with Hama. As a side note, author Raymond Benson, when he was assigned by the Ian Fleming estate to write all new 007 adventures in the '90s, briefly revived the character of Kissy Suzuki in his short story *Blast from the Past*, published in *Playboy* magazine in January 1997. Mie Hama continued her acting career until 1968, when she shifted her attention towards television. In 1973 she became a popular talk show hostess in Japan, and her career on television thrived well into the eighties.

trotting secret agent. But this marriage, a faked one, was an arrangement between the British Secret Service and the Japanese S.I.S., headed by Tiger Tanaka (Tetsuro Tamba). It was an effort to use the mock ceremony (done on a Japanese island named Ama, populated with pearl diving men and their spouses) as cover for the mission of the British agent (his face altered via minor plastic surgery to become Oriental in basic features) who is investigating the disappearance of U.S. and Russian spaceships and their crews. Hama proved herself an adept newly recruited S.I.S. agent when she

Other films include: *Futari no musuko* (a.k.a. *Different Sons*, 1962), *Sunano Kaori* (a.k.a. *The Night of the Seagull*, 1968).

Susan Hart

Dark haired and sultry, Susan Hart's film career consisted of mostly "bikinis and monsters." She was fetching and had talent, but her big-screen efforts limited her to either shaking her scantily clad figure on the beach or fleeing from some hideous creature. At a time during the mid-sixties when actresses were often touted as the next reigning sex symbol, Hart's measurements (usually stated as 37-23-36) always received mention in press releases.

Susan Hart was born on June 2, 1941, in Palm Springs, California. She appeared in a number of school plays as a child and teenager. After graduating from high school she spent some time in Hawaii. There she was spotted by a talent scout who gave her his card. Returning to California, she contacted him and he signed her as a client. Soon after, Hart made her professional acting debut on an episode of *The Joey Bishop Show* and her feature debut in the low-budget horror film *The Slime People* (1963). The following year she appeared in a trio of beach movies. Set in Hawaii, *Ride the Wild Surf* (1964) was the best of the three, as she played a local girl smitten with surfer Tab Hunter, much to her mother's chagrin. Noticed by AIP co-founder and future husband James Nicholson, Hart was given a part in *Pajama Party* (1964). Though all she did was wiggle her shapely body, she did it with panache and was a standout as Gilda, landing a contract at AIP.

The sexy brunette's first lead role for AIP was in the sci-fi film *War-Gods of the Deep* (1965), co-starring Vincent Price and Tab Hunter. Her next move, *Dr. Goldfoot and the Bikini Machine* (1965), a goofy take-off on the James Bond film *Goldfinger*, featured her as a bikini-clad robot. Surprisingly, this spy spoof was quite amusing and grossed $2.5 million, a smash hit for AIP standards. *Dr. Goldfoot and the Bikini Machine* (1965) was filmed on location in San Francisco by director Norman Taurog. The script was by Elwood Ullman and Robert Kaufman, based on a story by James Hartford. The film stars Vincent Price as mad scientist Dr. Goldfoot (named for his wearing of gold slippers) who plans on capturing the fortunes of the world's richest men with the aid of his invention. As lights blink, dials wiggle, horns blow and the machine vibrates, manufactured bikini-clad robots (Patti Chandler, Salli Sachse, Deanna Lund, China Lee and Marianne Gaba among them) are produced one by one. Hart played Goldfoot's most prized robot, No. 11, named Diane, who is sent out to entrap playboy millionaire Todd Armstrong (Dwayne Hickman) but is hampered by the bumbling of inept Secret Agent 00.5, Craig Gamble (Frankie Avalon).

Hart showed a lot of promise in her role as Diane and handled the physical comedy aspects of the role excellently. As Diane is programmed to speak many different languages, Hart used an array of accents (including Southern, French, British, etc.) to good reviews. *Variety*, in particular, raved, "Susan Hart is very good in a role which demands several dialects, human warmth, and robot inanimity, often in rapid sequence." Hart credits her well-received performance to director Norman Taurog, who treated her kindly and gave her confidence.

Budgeted at $1.4 million, *Dr. Goldfoot and the Bikini Machine* is quite elaborate for an American International production.

In *Dr. Goldfoot and the Bikini Machine* (AIP, 1965) Susan Hart is a sexy robot named Diane programmed to kill, and Frankie Avalon is the inept agent 00.5, Craig Gamble, sent to stop her. (*Courtesy of Michael Monahan*)

According to the press notes, more than $150,000 was spent on creating "a haunted palace, a pit and a pendulum, and an electronic device that manufactures a dozen beauties in bikinis." And if you watch closely you can spot cameos from AIP stars Annette Funicello, Deborah Walley, Harvey Lembeck and Aron Kincaid. The film also has an interesting pre-release history. It was to be originally titled *Dr. Goldfoot and the Sex Machine*. And it was conceived as a musical along the lines of the *Beach Party* movies. The first to go was the title, which was a bit too risqué for 1965. The film was shot with only one musical number in place (in which Price's Dr. Goldfoot sings about the bikini machine), but it was excised prior to the film's release. Purportedly, the producers thought that Price came across as too fey.

To promote the film, an hour special, entitled *The Wild World of Dr. Goldfoot*, aired in place of *Shindig* on 11/18/65. It featured Price, Kincaid, Hart and some of the bikini girls. Hart also accompanied Avalon, Chandler, Hughes and Bobbi Shaw on a $40,000 world tour to promote the movie. Their itinerary included London, Amsterdam, Rome, Madrid, Singapore, Sydney, New Dehli, Cairo, Hong Kong, Tokyo, Manila and Honolulu.

Dr. Goldfoot and the Bikini Machine received good notices from critics around the world. It is a pleasant, campy take-off on the whole James Bond phenomenon. The film was such a hit that AIP commissioned a sequel, to be called *Dr. Goldfoot and the S Bombs*, with Price and Hart. The inept sequel was re-titled *Dr. Goldfoot and the Girl*

Bombs (1966) and filmed in Italy by director Mario Bava, with only Price reprising his role. But perhaps the highest compliment paid to *Dr. Goldfoot and the Bikini Machine* is that 25 years later Mike Myers cribbed bits and pieces of this film for *Austin Powers: International Man of Mystery*.

After donning a blonde wig as *The Ghost in the Invisible Bikini* (1966), Hart made her final appearance in the spy genre in "The Night of the Fugitives" (11/8/68) on *The Wild Wild West*. Hart (resembling and sounding a lot like actress Yvonne Craig) played Rhoda, the glamorous double-crossing owner of the Diamond Horseshoe Saloon ("When a girl, um, does a favor she should get a favor; like they always say, quid pro quo") who is searching, along with everybody else, for bookkeeper Norbert Plank's syndicate records. But this episode is more notorious for the almost fatal head injury suffered by series star Robert Conrad while doing one of his own stunts on a landing above a saloon.

Susan Hart stopped acting in the late sixties to raise her son. She pursued a singing career and cut a number of singles for MGM Records, but none became hits. Sadly, in 1972 her husband passed away. Susan Hart has since remarried and currently resides in Palm Springs. She is a champion precision figure skater and is still involved on the fringes of show business. She holds the rights to and handles the licensing of at least ten early AIP films (including *I Was a Teenage Werewolf*), and she recently appeared in a documentary on the history of AIP entitled *It Conquered Hollywood!*, which aired on the American Movie Channel in 2001.

Other films include: *A Global Affair* (1964) and *For Those Who Think Young* (1964).

Gloria Hendry

Gloria Hendry was born in 1949 in Jacksonville, Florida, and then raised in Newark, New Jersey. The svelte but shapely and attractive black actress worked for a time as an assistant to the legal secretary of the NAACP. She then tried her hand at modeling before she auditioned for the position of a "bunny" at a Playboy Club, which at the time was enjoying the height of its namesake publication's fame as an upscale men's club located in several major cities in the U.S.

Turning her interest to acting, Hendry's first film role was a small part in *For the Love of Ivy* (1968). She then found equally small, but interesting, roles in then-controversial socio-political films like the comedy-drama *The Landlord* (1970) and the violent action movie *Across 110th Street* (1972). She appeared in the Larry Cohen–directed film *Black Caesar* that same year (opposite star Fred Williamson, as his amour, Helen) and returned in the direct sequel *Hell Up in Harlem* (1972). As the so-called Blaxploitation film genre began to rake in monies at the domestic U.S. box office, Hendry's roles in these last three films were seen by many an urban and suburban film audience. A role in another such action movie, *Slaughter's Big Rip-Off*

(1973), cemented her place as a fierce, take-no-prisoners kind of woman who could hold her own against former real-life football jocks turned actors Williamson and Jim Brown in movies where the violence was stylized but brutal and the message was win at all costs against society.

Hendry commented, "I was chosen for these particular roles, like *Black Belt Jones*, because I had the athletic body. I was trained by Chuck Norris' stunt team to enable me to get me ready for that particular movie. One thing that I was aware of while doing these particular movies, my part in the script, being a female, not being the victim, but being the tough woman. I feel that now I can look back. But, during the time, what had come my way, I was making the best of it. And I did exactly that. I'm not proud of everything. But my persona was affecting, where people saw me as a certain way."

Obviously, the appearance of a sexy but strong woman appealed to the producers of the James Bond films as they were casting the first of the Roger Moore Bond movies titled *Live and Let Die*. "My manager called me from New York," recalls Hendry. "He asked me to come back to New York for an audition. I went to see Harry Saltzman and I put on my best outfit. I walked in through the door, I sat down and he said, 'Madam, how soon can you fly?' and I said, 'This evening,' and off I went. They put me onto the next flight and they sent me out to meet with [the director] Guy Hamilton and Roger Moore in New Orleans. We just talked; there was no script reading or anything like that. A week later my manager called me and said I got the part."

In *Live and Let Die* (1973), British secret agent James Bond (Roger Moore) is pitted against the mysterious Dr. Kananga (Yaphet Kotto), a prime minister of a Caribbean island who is also a voodoo king, and who is also known as Mr. Big, a U.S. gangster who plans on flooding the world's drug market with of mix of tainted uncut heroin and voodoo. Hendry appears as Rosie Carver, an American operative working with the British government stationed on the same island on which Bond is investigating Mr. Big/Dr. Kananga, and who happens to introduce herself as "Mrs. Bond." Hendry recalled of the sultry scenes she filmed with then-new Bond Roger Moore, "I didn't know Roger personally, but it was a wonderful environment that he created, because when you are one to one with your acting partner there is nothing else. It was wonderful. He wanted everything to work, so did I. He was very giving."

Even more surprising was the interracial bed scene that Bond filmmakers scripted into the movie between Rosie and Bond. "We were never thinking one way or the other, as another human being to another, and as I'm lying on top of him doing the scene and it's a closed set. I'll tell you a story, I had eaten garlic the night before and I'm bending over Roger and he said, 'You didn't!' and I said, 'Yeah, I had garlic last night.' He said, 'You're lucky, I'm married to an Italian woman,' and as I'm kissing him we're not going through a turmoil of feelings about kissing one another. It was filmed in Jamaica. ... Up in the hills down there, I believed we passed Ian Fleming's home on our way on a boat ride, that was pointed out to me ... Ochas Rijos."

Gloria Hendry even recalls a very funny real-life occurrence that made it easier lying in bed with a famous matinee idol and television star in a multi-million dollar movie. "When I was flipped over, at the beginning, when I meet Bond, when I'm in his room and my wig was not supposed to have fallen off. I don't exactly remember but I think that there was a length of something that got caught on to the wig and it fell off. That was both embarrassing and hysterical." However, much of America was

As an American agent sent to assist Roger Moore (James Bond) on a dangerous mission in *Live and Let Die* (United Artists, 1973), Gloria Hendry was one of the few women in the James Bond cinematic canon to be called "Mrs. Bond."

not yet ready for interracial love scenes between a white man and a black woman, even in 1973, supposedly one year after the unofficial end of the turbulent sixties. In many U.S. markets Hendry's name suddenly disappeared from advertising, as well as her likeness. She explains, "My name was pulled in various places. I no longer saw that my name was being mentioned in the movie. As opposed to how it was in the beginning when I saw my picture on the cover of different magazines about 'Mrs. Bond,' which I was. But after the immediate publicity blew off, all of a sudden you didn't see me anymore. I didn't get invited to anything, or being aware of anything. All of a sudden it's a Bond movie where even if you rented the video, it's as if I didn't exist.

There were cuts in the movie that I learned about later on. I was surprised. It hurt, it majorly hurt—just the point of it—the point of whoever had that kind of control. I was very disappointed in the inhumanity, just in the creative process.... As I'm talking about it now ... creatively, it affected me."

In *Live and Let Die*, after Hendry's character is killed, it leaves the rest of the film to Moore to woo, make love to, then save Jane Seymour before Kananga and his henchmen can exact final vengeance on Bond for deflowering the virginal British psychic Seymour. In the eighth James Bond film and the first with Roger Moore in the leading role, the Bond producers had come far from the Sean Connery films, but not very far from the Ian Fleming novels that inspired the whole series, because, like *From Russia with Love* and portions of *Goldfinger*, this film also had a sadistic streak that would make Fleming proud.

After *Live and Let Die*, Gloria Hendry appeared in *Savage Sisters* (a.k.a. *Ebony, Ivory and Jade*, 1974) and *Black Belt Jones* (1974), where she co-starred with real-life martial artist and former Bruce Lee co-star from *Enter the Dragon* (1973) Jim Kelly. Regarding her career up to that point, Hendry remarked, "Out of the roles that were given me for what they were, I liked doing *Black Caesar*, because it had a nice story line, *Live and Let Die* and *Black Belt Jones*."

Nowadays Hendry is active in theater, cabaret, singing in clubs and working on her autobiography, "I'm directing and I'm singing. I'm a jazz singer, I've been singing over the years anyway. I love performing; I've just finished doing a play called *The Waiting Room*, where I played Billie Holiday. I did some performances of that as a one-woman show, and as for what's coming up? I think I'm going to be doing a play in California and I'm writing a book ... it's called *Gloria*." Her last film role was in *South Bureau Homicide* (1996) as Mrs. Cummings, a school principal.

Other films include: *Seeds of Tragedy* (1991—TV), *Pumpkinhead II: Blood Wings* (1994) and *Lookin' Italian* (1994).

Sharyn Hillyer

The sultry Sharyn Hillyer was one of a number of sexy starlets who graced the television landscape during the sixties. Though she made the occasional film, her talent was never fully tapped and she was restricted to decorative roles in sitcoms and drama series. As a teenager she was discovered by Ozzie Nelson and had numerous bit roles on his family sitcom, *The Adventures of Ozzie and Harriet* beginning in 1960. During the 1962-63 season she progressed to a recurring role as coed Sally Taft. After leaving the Nelson nest, Hillyer had small roles in *Hud* (1963), and on television in *Burke's Law* (she appeared on the cover of *TV Guide* with star Gene Barry), *The Rounders* and *The Man from U.N.C.L.E.*

Sharyn Hillyer's first brush with *The Man from U.N.C.L.E.* was in 1963 when she essayed a small role as a stewardess in the pilot episode, entitled "The Vulcan Affair" (9/22/64). When the pilot was picked up as a series, she was called in to discuss an on-going role, but things did not work out. "The producer I spoke with propositioned me—there was a condition to the part," says Hillyer. "I turned him down and as long as he was on the show I didn't work on it. When he left they called me and I came back in and started doing it on a fairly regular basis." With Hillyer out, a handful of actresses (including Linda Ho, Dodie Marshall, Yvonne Craig and Leigh Chapman) played helpful U.N.C.L.E. secretaries and receptionists (usually named Wanda) who were seen scurrying around the New York headquarters during *The Man from U.N.C.L.E.*'s first two seasons. All young, beautiful and curvaceous, they usually were limited to bringing U.N.C.L.E. chief Mr.

Waverly (Leo G. Carroll) news of agents Napoleon Solo or Illya Kuryakin's whereabouts, or producing dossiers on THRUSH agents. With the show's original producer gone by season two, Hillyer played Wanda in two later episodes, "The Project Deephole Affair" (3/18/66) and "The Indian Affairs Affair" (4/15/66).

Perhaps tired of the rotating cast of actresses, producer Boris Ingster invited Sharyn Hillyer back to play the recurring role of Wanda exclusively during the show's third season. "What they would do is, whenever that role would show up they would contact me, and if I was available they would call the character Wanda," remarks Hillyer. "If I was not available they'd put a different name on the character and bring in someone else." For example, actress Kay Michaels was used as U.N.C.L.E. agent Sarah in "The Take Me to Your Leader Affair" during this period.

A communications officer, Wanda had nothing more to do than look good, feign concern for a missing Illya or Napoleon, or fight off Solo's advances. Hillyer though, handled her role with style. For instance, in "The Pop Art Affair" (10/21/66) Solo (Robert Vaughn) tries to entice the coy Wanda to go out with him just as his partner Illya (David McCallum) calls in from a Greenwich Village coffee house. ("He has such perfect timing," says Solo sarcastically.) Later she helps Solo try to lo-

Sharyn Hillyer (left) with Arlene Charles, Robert Vaughn, David McCallum and Victoria Carroll in an early publicity still promoting *The Man from U.N.C.L.E.* (MGM-TV, ca. 1964). (Billy Rose Theatre Collection, The New York Public Library for the Performing Arts, Astor, Lenox and Tilden Foundations)

cate a missing Illya. And in "The Five Daughters Affair, Pt. 2" (4/17/67) she runs into Mr. Waverly's office when she receives word that an U.N.C.L.E. plane "was hijacked in Austria. THRUSH got away with Mr. Solo, Mr. Kuryakin and the girl [Kim Darby, as Sandy]." Sharyn Hillyer remembers, "There was always this flirtation between Wanda and Solo. I was usually in a huff because he would go off and get involved with other women. I was left back at headquarters, so there were always scenes of me steaming. I remember one episode ["The My Friend the Gorilla Affair" (12/16/66)] where Vaughn's character was going to Africa and I got to give him his inoculations before he went. And so Wanda kind of got even with him for always running off and flirting with women all over the world. She got to give him a number of shots with a big needle." Among Hillyer's other episodes were "The Sort of Do-It-Yourself Dreadful Affair" (9/23/66), "The Concrete Overcoat Affair" (11/25 and 12/2/66) and "The Pieces of Fate Affair" (2/24/67).

As for the show's stars, Hillyer comments, "Robert Vaughn was nice and friendly enough, but he kept to himself. He was professional but he wasn't much fun. He wouldn't hang out, whereas David McCallum would. David was playful and would have lunch with me. I don't remember a lot about Leo G. Carroll. He didn't hang around much between scenes. He was very nice and always courteous to me. He was also very generous as far as time and working with someone, but he was sometimes a bit forgetful." Sharyn Hillyer was dropped by the new producer, Anthony Spinner, the following year ("I never knew why") and replaced by Barbara Moore as Lisa. However, the show wasn't around for long, as The Man from U.N.C.L.E. was cancelled halfway through its fourth season due to low ratings.

Hillyer made one more sojourn into spydom, as "the Girl" in the Get Smart episode entitled "Snoopy Smart vs. the Red Baron" (9/28/68). Max, 99 and the Chief travel to 99's hometown in Idaho to prevent KAOS from unleashing a bacterium that would destroy the state's potato crops. Hillyer's other TV guest shots include episodes of Please Don't Eat the Daisies, Mannix and Star Trek. In 1969 Hillyer traveled to Southeast Asia to entertain the GIs as part of a handshaking tour for the USO. Journeying to remote outposts throughout South Vietnam, she experienced the horrors of war first hand. She never returned to acting, settling for domesticity with her second husband instead. She resurfaced in 1990, along with other Vietnam veterans, appearing as herself reminiscing about her experiences in Vietnam in special episodes of China Beach, including the Emmy-nominated "Vets." Today Sharyn Hillyer is a well-respected psychotherapist (she has appeared on numerous TV discussion shows) and resides in Los Angeles.

Other films include: A Guide for the Married Man (1967) and Doctor, You've Got to Be Kidding! (1968).

Jill Ireland

Pretty blonde Jill Ireland was born on April 24, 1936, in London, England. After a stint as a dancer she signed a contract with the Rank Organization and made her film debut in *Oh, Rosalinda!* (1956) as a ballerina. The following year she married actor David McCallum. Between 1958 and 1963 she appeared in over ten forgettable British films, the most notable being *Carry On Nurse* (1959). Ireland came to Hollywood in 1964 with her husband after he landed a co-starring role as Illya Kuryakin in *The Man from U.N.C.L.E.* Perhaps due to their relationship, she holds the record for most appearances as "the innocent" on that series, with four episodes, including the two-parter "The Five Daughters Affair." Nepotism aside, Ireland is in top form in each episode.

Ireland made two first season appearances on *The Man from U.N.C.L.E.*—in "The Quadripartite Affair" (10/6/64) and "The Giuco Piano Affair" (11/10/64), playing the innocent Marion Raven. In the first episode Marion is recruited by U.N.C.L.E. to help foil the evil plans of THRUSH operative Gervaise Ravel (Anne Francis), who they believe is connected to the murder of a UN scientist in Yugoslavia. The second episode has U.N.C.L.E. agent Napoleon Solo (Robert Vaughn) using Marion as bait to entrap the power-hungry beauty who escaped.

"The Tigers Are Coming Affair" aired on November 5, 1965, during *The Man from U.N.C.L.E.*'s second season. In this episode Ireland played Suzanne de Serre, a French botanist and chemist who travels to India accompanied by U.N.C.L.E. agents Napoleon Solo (Robert Vaughn) and Illya Kuryakin (David McCallum) masquerading as, respectively, a magazine writer and photographer. She gets entangled with Prince Panat (Lee Bergere), who is using chemicals to destroy the jungle and is forcing his people to work in the diamond mines.

Commenting on making "The Tigers Are Coming Affair" to *TV Guide* in 1966, Jill Ireland said, "In the last *U.N.C.L.E.* all the love scenes were between Robert Vaughn and me, with both of us ignoring David completely. But I found I couldn't kiss Bob—it would make me laugh."

Ireland proved she had a flair for light comedy in her fourth and final appearance on *The Man from U.N.C.L.E.* "The Five Daughters Affair" aired in two parts on 1/11 and 1/17/67 and was released theatrically overseas as *The Karate Killers* (1967). Jill Ireland portrayed wacky, free-spirited Imogen, one of murdered Dr. True's five daughters holding a key piece of information that will lead U.N.C.L.E. to the whereabouts of the dead scientist's formula for turning common seawater into gold. True's daughter Sandy (Kim Darby) is found at the home and accompanies the agents to Europe to find her half-sisters. As Napoleon, Illya and Sandy arrive in London to find her, Imogen is arrested for indecent exposure by a constable (Terry-Thomas). A go-go dancer, Imogen removes her trench coat at her hearing and shocks the court because all she is wearing is a skimpy bikini. The agents accompany Imogen back to the discotheque to look for anything that her father may have sent her. As the singing group Every Mother's Son perform their hit song "Come on Down to My Boat Baby," Imogen tries to get the agents to loosen up and dance. In her dressing room, THRUSH agents attack Solo and Illya. As

Jill Ireland (Marion) with then-husband David McCallum (Illya Kuryakin) during the filming of "The Quadripartite Affair" on *The Man from U.N.C.L.E.* (MGM-TV, 1964).

they fight throughout the disco, Sandy finds the second photograph. As the police come to break things up, the THRUSH agents flee and the constable is united with Imogen once again.

In between *U.N.C.L.E.* appearances, Ireland starred as Marion Starett in the short-lived TV western series *Shane*, with David Carradine, in 1966. When *The Man from U.N.C.L.E.* came to an end in 1967 so did Ireland's marriage to McCallum. After her divorce was final, Ireland married actor Charles Bronson the following year. Beginning with *Rider on the Rain* in 1970, Ireland was usually seen on the big screen playing the love interest of her husband, distracting him for a fleeting moment from whatever adventure he was involved with. Among her more varied roles were that of a prostitute in *The Mechanic* (1972), the wife of an unjustly imprisoned man (Robert Duvall) in *Breakout* (1975), the marked girlfriend of a crime boss in *Love and Bullets* (1979) and the endangered wife of the president in *Assassination* (1987).

Jill Ireland received her best reviews for the underrated western and box office flop *From Noon to Three* (1976). As lonely Amanda Starbuck, she has a three hour romantic tryst with outlaw Graham Dorsey (Charles Bronson), who is reportedly killed a short time later. Amanda turns him into a folk hero only to have him re-surface alive and well. In 1984 Ireland went through a bout of breast cancer and wrote about her ordeal in the 1987 book *Life Wish*. She became the chairperson for the National Cancer Society. And she also found time to co-produce two of Bronson's movies—*The Evil That Men Do* (1984) and *Murphy's Law* (1986). In 1989 she wrote a second book, entitled *Life Lines*, detailing her efforts in saving her adopted son Jason McCallum from a life dependency on drugs. Sadly, he died of a drug overdose shortly after the book was published, and Jill Ireland succumbed to cancer on May 18, 1990, at the age of 54. She purportedly was working on her third book, to be titled *Life Times*, when she passed away.

Other films include: *The Big Money* (1956), *Hell Drivers* (1958), *So Evil So Young* (1961), *Twice Around the Daffodils* (1962), *Villa Rides* (1968), *The Family* (1970), *Chato's Land* (1971), *The Valachi Papers* (1972), *Hard Times* (1975), *Breakheart Pass* (1976), *Death Wish 2* (1982), *Count* (1987) and *Hollywood and Horses* (1989—documentary).

Karen Jensen

Kittenish blonde Karen Jensen was born on August 18 in San Francisco, California. Her mother encouraged her beautiful but very shy teenaged daughter to enter a local beauty pageant to gain confidence. Karen was the youngest contestant to ever win the Miss San Carlos pageant. More contests followed, and then Jensen began modeling. Her face appeared on billboards across the country for Granny Goose Potato Chips. During the Miss California pageant she was spotted by a talent scout from William Morris and brought to the attention of Jack Warner. After completing a screen test, she was signed to a contract at Warner Bros.

Jensen made her acting debut on the George Burns–Connie Stevens sitcom *Wendy and Me* in 1965. After appearing on a few more TV shows she left Warner Bros. and signed with Universal. She made her film debut in *Out of Sight* (1966), the third beach film from Lennie Weinrib, who also directed *Beach Ball* and *Wild Wild Winter*. To pump new life into the beach formula, the spy angle was added to appeal to a more varied audience. Shot on location at Zuma Beach, the movie features Karen Jensen as Sandra, a beach beauty who overhears madman Big D (John Lawrence) of the crime syndicate F.L.U.S.H. plotting with his cohorts Mousie (Jimmy Murphy) and Huh! (Norman Grabowski) to sabotage an upcoming rock and roll fair. Big D abhors rock music and, with a destructive ray, plans to wipe out "the big stars from England" Freddy & the Dreamers. Throughout the film other rock acts, such as Gary Lewis & the Playboys (who impress the most with the rockin' opening number "Malibu Run"), the Turtles, the Astronauts, and the Knickerbockers, pop up to audition for entrance into the festival. Sandra tells her boy-crazy friend Marvin (Carole Shelyne) of Big D's dastardly plan, and they decide to contact secret agent John Stamp for help. However, Sandra mistakes butler Homer (Jonathan Daly) for Stamp. Wishing to be an agent himself, Homer accepts the case without revealing who he really is. Big D learns of Stamp's/Homer's involvement and sends three curvaceous female assassins. The bungling Homer eludes them and the mysterious Girl from F.L.U.S.H. (Rena Horten), as well as the advances of man-hungry Marvin. In the end, Homer prevents Big D from ruining the concert, and the Girl from F.L.U.S.H. turns out to be a disguised John Stamp (John Lodge), angry that Homer has taken his hot rod without permission.

Though the fetching bikini-clad Karen Jensen is simply charming as the sweet Sandra, the film is stolen by the automobile ZZR, which was designed by George Barris specifically for the movie at a cost of $22,000 and received more attention than the cast or rock acts. Inspired by the Aston Martin from *Goldfinger*, the ZZR featured twin eight-cylinder engines, flamethrowers in each fender, a parachute that disconnected to envelope chasing cars, and a tar and feather feature.

Jensen continued at Universal, appearing in movies (including the Doris Day western *The Ballad of Josie*) and on TV (in such series as *Run for Your Life*, *The Virginian*, *Bob Hope Presents the Chrysler Theatre* and *Dragnet*). Her lone guest shot on a spy TV series was "The Night of the Legion of Death" episode on *The Wild Wild West* (11/24/67). This episode dealt with a

Karen Jensen as Sandra made a fetching beach bunny in the spy spoof *Out of Sight* (Universal, 1966).

ditioned for a number of leads in films but landed the role of grasping starlet Rachel Holt on the TV series *Bracken's World*, beginning in September 1969. Though the show was only a modest hit (it was cancelled in January 1971), the showy role of Rachel brought Jensen reams of publicity as she received numerous invitations for print interviews and game and talk show appearances.

After *Bracken's World* ended, Karen Jensen returned to the spy genre in *The Salzburg Connection* (1973), which was based on a novel by Helen MacInnes. Barry Newman played Bill Mathison, an attorney representing a New York publisher, sent to Salzburg to meet with photographer Richard Bryant (Patrick Jordan) regarding a book of Austrian lake photographs. Bryant (who, while diving in Lake Finstersee, recovered a chest containing a list of Nazi collaborators) turns up dead, and Mathison gets entangled in a complicated web of international intrigue as agents from various countries descend on Salzburg to retrieve the chest. Jensen tries valiantly but isn't convincing as double agent Elissa Lang, who is working for the Russians and Red Chinese. Masquerading as a student, Elissa befriends Mathison at his hotel. Later she bugs his room and follows him to Bryant's photo shop. While he is busy with Bryant's widow (Anna Karina), Elissa ransacks the place. As she is leaving, another agent chases her into a nearby building. In an amazing feat of derring-do, the desperate Elissa flings herself at his body and he is killed as they fall down a large flight of stairs. Elissa dies shortly thereafter in a botched car explosion rigged by herself.

figurehead-like governor named Winston Brubaker (Kent Smith) who rules his territory like a dictator; but it is his secretary, Deke Montgomery (Anthony Zerbe), who is the real force. Karen Jensen played Caroline Kitterridge, who helps secret service agents James West (Robert Conrad) and Artemus Gordon (Ross Martin) bring Brubaker down when he makes a run for president. They then discover that it is Montgomery and a secret band of followers named "Black Legion" who are really in control. Montgomery wants to rule the country, but when Brubaker does not show up at a rally, the townspeople walk out on the defeated secretary.

In 1968 Jensen signed with a more aggressive agent who felt that Universal was holding her back. After balking at playing a small role in another episode of *Dragnet*, Jensen walked out on her contract. She au-

Critics weren't kind to *The Salzburg Connection*, and rightly so. Though beautifully shot on European locations, it is a confusing mess, despite some interesting camera techniques by director Lee H. Katzin. *Variety* called it "an inept drama," while *Cue* remarked that it was "disconnected espionage so bungled that it doesn't even rate a junior G-man badge."

During the seventies Jensen (much to her chagrin) found herself typecast in sexpot roles. In 1975 she took a break from acting when she and her then-husband, actor John Neilson, moved to Northern California. When she returned to Hollywood two years later, the only work she was able to get was a guest appearance on *Happy Days*. She left the business in the early eighties to concentrate on painting and writing. Soon after, she divorced Neilson, and in 1990 she married actor Michael Stroka of *Dark Shadows* fame. Her first manuscript was turned into a Canadian movie titled *Primo Baby*, but her happiness was marred by the death of Stroka from cancer. Karen Jensen recently wed actor Brendon Boone of *Garrison's Gorillas* fame, and they have a Civil War film titled *Preacher and Co.* in production.

Other films include: *Sullivan's Empire* (1967), *Prelude* (1968—short), *Congratulations, It's a Boy!* (1971—TV), *The Snoop Sisters* (1972—TV), *I Love a Mystery* (1973—TV) and *Louis Armstrong–Chicago Style* (1976—TV).

Kathy Kersh

Former Miss Rheingold of 1962, Kathy Kersh was a sexy, shapely blonde who was destined for stardom. She had talent but like a number of her contemporaries (either due to bad luck, poor management or personal distractions—Kersh was wed famously to Vince Edwards and Burt Ward) never made it to the top. Her acting career began with a bit part on *77 Sunset Strip*. After playing a recurring role as Jethro's love interest caterer Marian Billington on *The Beverly Hillbillies* during its third season, Kersh could be seen in *My Favorite Martian*, *Burke's Law*, *Ben Casey* and *Wendy and Me*. Her contribution to the spy genre was in the small but memorable role of a THRUSH girl who beats up Robert Vaughn in *The Man from U.N.C.L.E.* She continued with the bad girl roles as the Joker's alluring girlfriend Cornelia on *Batman* in "The Impractical Joker" and "The Joker's Provoker." During the seventies, Kersh and former *Lost in Space* star Marta Kristen shocked their fans with their seminude love making scene in *The Gemini Affair* (1974).

Kathy Kersh began working as a model for print ads at the tender age of eight. She graduated to commercials four years later. Modeling led to the prestigious Miss Rheingold contest where she made it to the finals in 1962 and won. ("They told me that it was unusual in that I got twice as many votes than the runner-up who got twice as many votes as the person who came in third. It had never happened before.") When Kersh returned to Hollywood following a year's reign as Miss Rheingold she was the first actress put under contract to Filmways by producer Martin Ransohoff. Soon after another sexy blonde—Sharon Tate—joined her. "I adored Sharon Tate," exclaims Kersh. "We were rivals in a way but it didn't matter—we were both nice people. Physically, Sharon was one of the most beautiful women I had ever seen in my life. And in that business you see *everyone* without make-up. She was a gorgeous, stunning woman. She was not a great actress but she didn't have to be. We stayed good friends and she even fixed me up with Jay Sebring."

Kersh's only foray onto the big screen during the sixties was in the small role of James Coburn's girlfriend in the 1964 feature The Americanization of Emily ("I spent the whole day in bed with James Coburn—nothing lewd! He was very nice and hysterical to work with."). She did lots of television including a Ben Casey directed by its leading man and Kersh's then-husband Vince Edwards, who went on to star in the spy film Hammerhead. "I've always said that it was the one time we really got along because I *had* to do what he told me to do," remarks Kersh with a laugh. "Vince was volatile but when it came to directing he quieted right down and got to work. And he worked hard at it." Kersh followed this with her memorable turn as THRUSH girl Bambi in the episode "The Girls from Nazarone Affair" on The Man from U.N.C.L.E. In this episode Solo and Illya tangle with a bevy of superwomen on the Riveria who have in their possession a serum that provides great strength. A schoolteacher (Kipp Hamilton) on vacation abroad helps them defeat the nefarious THRUSH girls.

A fetishist's delight, "The Girls from Nazarone" (4/12/65) is infamous for the number of times Robert Vaughn's Napoleon Solo gets beat up by beautiful blonde women. First Danica d'Hondt as Lucia Nazarone manhandles Solo then her flaxen-haired helpers played by Kersh and Sharon Tate take turns throttling the U.N.C.L.E. agent. "I had so much fun playing a bad girl," exclaims Kersh. "I hardly ever got to play anyone bad. When you are blonde and you are pretty you get typecast. They didn't write intelligent pretty blondes at the time. They were often stupid and I think I had a mental block against that. I'm not stupid and I went to get a degree in Business with a specialization in finance graduating Magna cum laude. So I did not play dumb blondes very well and often enough I did not get those roles. It was great to play a bad guy. And I remember thinking at the time that 'I didn't have to smile through that whole show!' And I got to beat up people—that was a first for me."

Coincidentally, both of Sharon Tate's excursions into the spy genre involved her use of fisticuffs. In "The Girls of Nazarone Affair" on The Man from U.N.C.L.E., Tate and Kersh play THRUSH girls who team up against Robert Vaughn's Napoleon Solo. In The Wrecking Crew, Tate has a martial-arts fight scene with co-star Nancy Kwan, which Bruce Lee advised on. According to fellow Filmways contract player Kathy Kersh, "Sharon and I had never done a fight scene before. The stunt people choreographed it."

Being novices concerning fight scenes, Kersh and Tate rehearsed with Robert Vaughn ("I respected him very much as an actor but he was rather pompous and a bit full of himself") and the stunt men who choreographed this scene. "At one point, Sharon was supposed to hold his arms back and I was supposed to hit him in the stomach," recalls Kersh. "In the rehearsal, I didn't hit him very hard. I didn't have a lot of experience doing this so he stopped the scene and said, 'Now look, you can hit me as hard as you want. Hit me as hard as you can.' He was holding in his stomach tight. So I hit him and he said, 'See, you can't hurt me.' He was a little annoying the way he carried on and on.

"Before we actually went before the cameras, I said to Sharon, 'When you grab his arms from behind rather than just grabbing him—I want you to grab his arms and snap him back. And then quickly stick your knee right in the small of his back. I'll hit him in the stomach.' Sharon was very athletic and she thought that it was a great

A publicity photo from *The Man from U.N.C.L.E.* (MGM-TV, 1965) with (left to right) Danica d'Hondt (Lucia Nazarone), Sharon Tate (THRUSH girl), David McCallum (Illya Kuryakin) and Kathy Kersh (Sophie).

idea. And that's what we did. Sharon snapped him back, which he totally did not expect and I punched him good in the tummy. He doubled over. We really didn't hurt him—that wasn't the point—but it was his pride that was injured. I remember some of the cast and crew turning away so as not to laugh in front of him. After he got up he said something like 'Maybe you shouldn't do it like that.' Sharon and I had a good laugh."

Kersh continued acting on television and had another memorable role as Cornelia the Joker's narcissistic girlfriend in two episodes of Batman. Though she wound up marrying the Boy Wonder, Burt Ward, (the marriage was short-lived) it is Cesar Romero whom Kersh has the most praise for ("He was such a doll and such a gentleman."). Soon after Kersh quit the business and began taking college courses. She had a daughter with Vince Edwards whom she needed to support. However, she was coaxed by director Matt Cimber to star opposite Marta Kristen in The Gemini Affair (1974), whose tag line proclaimed, "A different kind of love story." Seeking fame in Hollywood but only finding rejection, two beautiful women slowly begin to fall in love. Though doing the nude scenes was an issue for her, Kersh agreed to star because of the character's crying and drunken scenes. "I had never cried on camera before," says Kathy incredulously. "I had been so typecast and was so frustrated for so many years I thought this was a chance to show more of what I was capable of doing."

Kersh never acted again after The Gemini Affair. After receiving a degree in business, she had a very successful career in commercial real estate and currently resides in the San Fernando Valley.

Sylva Koscina

Born August 22, 1933, in Zagreb, Croatia (Yugoslavia), Sylva Koscina became an Italian resident from the age of 12 when her family moved to Italy. Her full-figured body, pouty lips, multi-colored eyes (they were described in 1967 as containing shades of blue, gray, green and gold) and wild mane of blonde hair immediately caught the notice of enterprising fashion cognoscenti after she left Naples University (where she majored in the study of physics and mathematics), and she began her career as a model.

Sylva Koscina's first film was *Siamo Uomini o Caporali?* in 1955. Minor roles followed, and then she co-starred with Steve Reeves in *Hercules* (a.k.a. *Le Fatiche di Ercole*, a.k.a. *The Labors of Hercules*, 1957) in the role of Iole, his love interest. The following year she returned in the same role for the sequel *Hercules Unchained* (a.k.a. *Ercole e la Regina di Lidia*, a.k.a. *Hercules and the Queen of Lydia*).

Similar parts in other costume epics the likes of *Herod the Great* (a.k.a. *Erode di Grande*, 1958), *The Siege of Syracuse* (a.k.a. *L'Assedio di Siracus*, 1960), *The Iron Mask* (a.k.a. *Le Masque de Fer*, 1962) and *The Swordsman of Sienna* (a.k.a. *Lo Spadaccino di Sienna*, 1962), kept her in a variety of attractive but confining costumes, and in the background as mostly a romantic foil for a succession of leading men more interested in derring-do than their attractive co-star (save for the film's finale when they return to romancing). Koscina also showed great comedic talents in the comedies *Toto in Paris* (a.k.a. *Toto a Parigi*, 1958), *Toto in the Moon* (a.k.a. *Toto Nelle Luna*, 1958) and in the Christopher Lee–starring vampire satire *Hard Times for a Vampire* (a.k.a. *Tempi Duri Per I Vampiri*, a.k.a. *Uncle Was a Vampire*, 1959), in the role of Carla.

After exhibiting a brief but impressive dramatic turn in French director Georges Franju's *Judex* (1963), she made her first espionage film, *Agent 8¾* (a.k.a. *Hot Enough for June*, 1964). In this delightful comedic romp set in Eastern Europe, a Czech-speaking British writer (Dirk Bogarde) is made a junior executive in a glassware company and sent to Prague on business. In reality, he is set up to be a pawn in a deadly espionage game. A British Secret Service agency wants him to steal a secret formula, but he falls for the sexy daughter (Koscina) of the head of the Eastern European counterespionage outfit.

The next year, she was back in the arms of an agent in the obscure, but exciting *Baraka X-77* (a.k.a. *Baraka Sur X 13*, 1965). In this film a French scientist has invented a poison gas that a criminal gang intends to use to conquer the world. The scientist is captured and incarcerated in a hospital where the movie's villains plot to have him reveal the secret formula needed to produce the deadly gas. Secret agent X-77 (Gerard Barray), with the aid of a nurse (Koscina), finds where the scientist is being held and plans his rescue.

Another small but spirited role in Federico Fellini's *Juliet of the Spirits* (a.k.a. *Giulietta degli Spiriti*, 1965) prepared Koscina for her next adventure film, co-starring with European hunk Horst Buchholz in *That Man from Istanbul* (a.k.a. *L'Homme d'Istambul*, 1965). In this delightful film an American club owner (Buchholz) is conned into becoming a spy for an international network by a beautiful operative (Koscina) in an attempt by U.S. authorities to ensure the safe return of a kidnapped scientist.

Even more obscure was *Four Queens for an Ace* (a.k.a. *Carre de Dames Pour un As*, 1966), where Interpol agent Dan Layton (Roger Hanin) chases an escaped international criminal in Spain who has killed five men and changed his identity via plastic surgery. As the European spy film craze heightened, Koscina became in-demand with filmmakers from other countries outside of the French and Italian features that she was making at the time, and her next role, as Penelope in *Deadlier Than the Male* (1967), was her biggest hit, with international recognition awaiting her. In *Deadlier Than the Male* the former private eye and special agent Bulldog Drummond (Richard Johnson), now working as a freelance insurance agent, soldier of fortune and spy for hire, investigates murders committed by two female assassins named Penelope and Erma (Koscina and Elke Sommer). Their ultimate target is a Middle Eastern King in a plot devised by a madman named Peterson (Nigel Green). That same year Koscina reunited with *That Man from Istanbul* co-star Buchholz in the seldom seen spy caper *Johnny Banco* (1967), in the role of Laureen Moore.

Making worldwide news, Koscina barely escaped death in the late sixties when her trusted caretaker at her Italian villa went berserk and shot three people to death in her home. Luckily the actress was on a film shoot in South Africa at the time and was not around when the killer went on his rampage. Another news item of note from March 1969 detailed a horrible brawl between the actress and actor Laurence Harvey on the set of a film. Apparently, the actor punched Koscina so hard in the jaw during a scene that he severely injured the

As the sexy and deadly Penelope, Sylva Koscina (right) was paired with the equally stunning Elke Sommer (Erma) as assassins who murdered for fun and profit in the British film *Deadlier Than the Male* (Universal, 1966).

starlet, bringing the shooting to a halt. However, the always-working Koscina had no dearth of film roles and quickly jumped into another movie after she recovered.

The actress explained to syndicated American columnist Earl Wilson in 1967 how she felt about her busy work schedule in the late sixties: "I made one picture after another just to make money, I didn't care about the role. Now after eight years I can say, 'Sylva, you were crazy.'" While Koscina managed to parlay her international recognition into a small number of roles in major Hollywood films, such as *The Secret War of Harry Frigg* (1968) with Paul Newman and *Hornet's Nest* (1970) with Rock Hudson, she seemed to have retreated slightly and spent the rest of her career in Italian genre movies.

Sylva Koscina made few films in the seventies and eighties, and briefly retired from acting in 1987 after an appearance in the all-star Italian sex comedy *Rimini, Rimini* (1987). She returned to acting in 1993 with dramatic roles in *Ricky and Barrabas* and *Kim Novak Is on the Telephone* (a.k.a. *Ce Kim Novak al Telefono*, 1994), but she died, the result of a long illness, on December 26, 1994. Today she is remembered as one of the truly beautiful stars of the European cinema, who had made quite an impression on male audience members through the roles that she enlivened on the screen.

A melancholy postscript to her career is ten minutes of recently unearthed out-takes from Mario Bava's *Lisa and the Devil* (a.k.a. *Lisa e iL Diavolo*, a.k.a. *The House of Exorcism*) from 1972 featuring the actress in a decidedly overzealous and nearly pornographic lovemaking scene with co-star Gabriele Tinti, footage that was shot and then left out of the finished film, as it seemed to have been decided upon that maybe the sequence contained a bit too much realism. A hot one, that cute Sylva Koscina.

Other films include: *Three Bites of the Apple* (1968), *A Lovely Way to Die* (1968), *Carla and Lola* (a.k.a. *Nel Buio del Terrore*, 1971), *Manhunt: The Italian Connection* (a.k.a. *La Mala Ordina*, 1972), *The Crimes of the Black Cat* (a.k.a. *Sette Scialli di Sete Gialli*, 1972), *Delitto d'Autore* (1974), *Casanova and Company* (a.k.a. *Sex on the Run* (1976), *Asso* (a.k.a. *Ace*, 1981) and *Mani di Fata* (1983).

Nancy Kovack

Bewitching Nancy Kovack (born on March 11, 1935, in Flint, Michigan) was a sometimes blonde, sometimes brunette actress who played leads in B-movies and supporting roles in major films during the sixties. Due to her ability to play drama and comedy to good effect, she was never typed, and her roles ranged from the girl next door to neurotics and venomous vixens. However, talented as she was, Kovack never reached superstardom.

While attending the University of Michigan, Nancy Kovack won a number of local beauty titles. After graduation she headed for New York. In 1958 she made her Broadway debut in *Disenchanted* and became a regular on Dave Garroway's *Today Show* and *Beat the Clock*. In 1959 Kovack was spotted by talent scouts from Columbia Pictures who immediately signed her to a contract. Her film debut was as a tipsy housewife in *Strangers When We Meet* (1960). Other early film roles included Medea in *Jason and the Argonauts* (1963), Odette in *Diary of a Madman* (1963), with Vincent Price, and Annie Oakley opposite The Three Stooges in *The Outlaws Is Coming* (1965). On television Kovack became one of the sixties' busiest actresses. Among her many, many guest appearances were episodes of *Burke's Law*, *Perry Mason*, *Bewitched* and *Twelve O'Clock High*. She usually so impressed the producers of these shows that she was invited back to appear in additional episodes.

Kovack's first role in the spy genre was as Miss Flostone, a THRUSH agent and assistant to the diabolical Dr. Agnes Dabree (Elsa Lanchester), who has invented a deadly brain-altering machine, in "The Brain Killer Affair" (3/8/65) on *The Man from U.N.C.L.E.* "The King of Diamonds Affair" (3/11/66) gave her more to do as Victoria Pogue, whose pudding is used by British mobsters led by Blodgett (Larry D. Mann) to smuggle diamonds into the U.S. On *Honey West* she played Nicole, an actress whose jewel collection is stolen while she is being interviewed on TV, in "The Gray Lady" (12/10/65). With her alluring features, Nancy Kovack was better suited for the bad girl roles. In "Apollo" (11/20/67) on *I Spy* Kovack, as sinister Bronwyn, played second fiddle to Pippa Scott's more menacing agent Bobbie intent on sabotaging the U.S. space program, and the Apollo project in particular. On the lighter side, Nancy Kovack guest starred on *The Double Life of Henry Phyfe* in "The Reluctant Lover" (2/10/66), playing the married Chou Chou who has a severe crush on Agent U-31 (Red Buttons) and holds in her possession a list of enemy agents.

On the big screen Nancy Kovack (remarkably resembling Honor Blackman in *Goldfinger*) played a small but pivotal role in *The Silencers* (1966). Her alluring though treacherous character Barbara appears at the beginning of the film and is the catalyst that returns retired agent Matt Helm (Dean Martin) to espionage. When Helm enters his home he discovers a trail of women's clothes and underclothes ("Treasure hunt!") leading to his bedroom, where he finds the curvaceous Barbara clad only in one of his shirts. When Helm asks what he should be doing with her discarded clothes, Barbara responds, "Just throw them anywhere. I won't be needing them till morning." As Matt is about to succumb to her charms, he mistakenly assumes that she was sent by his former boss from ICE to entice him back to the agency. In actuality, she is an enemy agent working for madman Tung-Tze. Helm shrugs off her advances, but the persistent Barbara won't take no for an answer. As they are in an embrace Barbara pulls out a dagger to stab him. However, before she can plunge it into his neck, she is shot twice in the back. Helm looks up to see his former partner in spying, Tina Batori (Daliah Lavi), who says, "It's been a long while. Sorry for the interruption—but she likes to scratch."

Later in the decade Kovack played Jaimie McQue in "One Night in Soledad" (9/24/68) on *It Takes a Thief*. In the second season opener, thief-turned-SIA agent Al Mundy (Robert Wagner) is sent to a Latin America country to steal a dead body—the son of the country's dictator—to block a political uprising. Her second guest shot on the series was as Penny Colbert in "38-23-36" (4/8/69). Mundy, masquerading as a fashion photographer, has to figure out which of the contestants of the Miss United Nations Beauty Pageant stole a microdot containing information about a secret anti-missile system and killed an agent. All he has to go on is the agent's dying words, "38-23-36." Nancy Kovack's final spy role was as KAOS agent Sonja, who runs a Knight's Stamp Redemption Center that is a front for a KAOS munitions depot, in "The Day They Raided the Knights" (1/11/69) on *Get Smart*. Sonja tangles with Agent 99 (Barbara Feldon), who takes a part-time job there when she is laid off by a computer from Control.

During the late sixties Nancy Kovack continued making small screen appearances on such hit series as *Star Trek*, *The*

The first Matt Helm feature, *The Silencers* (Columbia, 1966), featured Nancy Kovack as the deadly assassin Barbara.

F.B.I., *Family Affair* and *Hawaii Five-O*. She even received an Emmy nomination for "Best Supporting Actress in a Drama Series" in 1969 for her riveting performance in "The Girl Who Came in from the Tide" on *Mannix*. Her film roles included Miss B. in the Carl Reiner comedy *Enter Laughing* (1967) and the worried wife of stranded astronaut James Franciscus in the Oscar-winning *Marooned* (1969).

Kovack's acting career trailed off after she married conductor Zubin Mehta in the early seventies. Her final TV appearance was in a 1975 episode of *Ellery Queen*, starring Jim Hutton. Kovack was out of the spotlight for years but remained highly influential in New York and Los Angeles music circles. In 1986 she came out of retirement to play George Sand in *Chopin, Liszt and Their Literary Ladies*, the final concert of the *Concerts Plus* series at Merkin Hall. Most recently, Kovack's name was in the press as she filed embezzlement charges against her bookkeeper and personal assistant, Susan McDougal (the wife of Jim McDougal, who was involved in the Whitewater scandal), for fraudulent credit card expenses and forged checks totaling $150,000. A Santa Monica jury later found McDougal not guilty. Nancy Kovack currently resides in Munich, Germany, where her husband is now the Music Director of the Bavarian State Opera.

Other films include: *Cry for Happy* (1961), *The Wild Westerners* (1962), *Diary of a Madman* (1963), *Sylvia* (1965), *The Great Sioux Massacre* (1965), and *Tarzan and the Valley of Gold* (1966).

Nancy Kwan

Nancy Kwan was born in Hong Kong on May 19, 1939, to a Chinese father and British mother. The lithe Kwan, standing 5'3", with slightly Eurasian features, jet black hair and fair skin, soon followed her heart and studied, at age 18, to be a ballet dancer. At England's famed Royal Ballet School she danced for four hours a day and also studied a variety of related arts, like stage make-up, all this while still completing her high school subjects for eventual graduation. Her school's affiliation with local theater companies soon led Kwan to minor roles (including one as a "spear carrier" in a stage production of *Aida*). After she finished her scholastic studies she vacationed in France, Italy and Switzerland before returning to her native Hong Kong. There she auditioned for stage producer Ray Stark and eventually screen tested for a role in the proposed film *The World of Susie Wong*, which at the time was enjoying a successful run on the Broadway stage.

Kwan told a journalist for the Internet magazine *Goldsea Asian Americans*, "They didn't know about my acting because I had never acted before, but they offered to start me at $300 a week on a seven year contract. It was a lot of money to me then." Kwan was sent to America and lived in a dormitory for young actresses coming from overseas. She went to acting school in Hollywood before going to New York. Finally, Stark cast her as a bar girl when *The World of Susie Wong* went on the road. Besides the minor part, Kwan also understudied the lead, France Nuyen, whose success onstage landed her the title role in the movie about the comely Chinese prostitute who has a love affair with an American. With Nuyen off to England to act in the movie, Kwan graduated to the official lead in the stage production and was touring in Toronto, Canada, when she heard from Stark. Apparently, there were some problems with or between Nuyen and producer Stark, and

Kwan was asked to screen test again for the movie. With a new director and star (Nancy Kwan), filming began all over again in England. As her appearance was slightly Eurasian, the movie's make-up people were forced to make Kwan appear more Chinese.

The World of Susie Wong (1960) became a box-office sensation. Nancy Kwan was hailed for her performance and shared the Golden Globe for the "Most Promising Newcomer–Female" with Ina Balin and Hayley Mills in 1960, and was voted a "Star of Tomorrow" in 1961. She followed this part with a similar role as one of the female leads in *Flower Drum Song* (1961), another film based on a stage production (a hit Rodgers and Hammerstein show). But this musical also retains prestige as being the first big-budget American film with an all–Chinese cast. By this time, certain unpleasantries surrounding the release of *The World of Susie Wong* appeared. It seemed that the Chinese and Chinese-American community were distraught by the representation of Asian womanhood in the film, particularly in the manner in which Kwan's character was depicted, being a loose-moraled woman in love with an American (William Holden) who loved her, despite her hidden "other life." This attention brought to the film may have led to *Flower Drum Song* being rushed into production to offset all the negative press.

However, prominent roles in a succession of American-produced comedies, including *Arrividerci, Baby* (1966) and *Lt. Robin Crusoe, U.S.N.* (1966), did little to advance her career as a dramatic actress, and by the mid-sixties Nancy Kwan journeyed to Europe to co-star in the spy film *The Corrupt Ones* (a.k.a. *Die Holle von Macao*, a.k.a. *The Peking Medallion*, 1966), an international co-production co-directed by the German Frank Winterstein and the British James Hill (from a script co-authored by *The Avengers* co-creator Brian Clemens). The movie starred Robert Stack, Elke Sommer and Kwan in the role of Tina, the head of the villainous Red Chinese agents after American adventurer Stack who possesses (after being given the item by a secret agent following a fierce battle) the "Peking Medallion," a key to an ancient Chinese treasure. The film was little seen then, and today remains an obscurity. Filled with hyperkinetic fistfights and wild chases, the movie, had it been more properly marketed, would have been a terrifically violent capper to the usually moribund action movies made at the time.

Kwan co-starred (as Wen Yu-Rang) in the last of the Dean Martin Matt Helm films, *The Wrecking Crew* (1969), which, like

As the inscrutable and seductive Chinese agent Yu-Rang, Nancy Kwan assisted the dangerous Count Contini (Nigel Green) in *The Wrecking Crew* (Columbia, 1969). (*Courtesy of Michael Monahan*)

all the films before it in the series (*The Silencers* [1966], *Murderer's Row* [1966] and *The Ambushers* [1967]), was less about the noirish, violent hero of the Donald Hamilton books on which they were based and more similar to the James Bond spoofs like *Our Man Flint* (1966). Unfortunately, Kwan's inscrutably exotic Chinese agent in cahoots with evil villain Count Massimo Contini (Nigel Green) became set dressing for a film populated by top-heavy starlets (Tina Louise as Lola the stripper and Elke Sommer as Linka Karensky) and a seemingly boozed-up star. However, the inclusion of one of the series' largest budgets and fight choreography by Bruce Lee and Chuck Norris (who has a tiny role) also makes it one of the most intriguing of the Helm films.

In 1969 Kwan also appeared in the Canadian film *The Girl Who Knew Too Much*, as Revel Drue, a woman involved with the star, Adam (Batman) West, who is a former agent investigating intrigue. This tepid thriller was followed by the equally low-budget and lackadaisically directed *That Lady from Peking* (1970), where, as Sue Ten Chan, Kwan becomes a woman after star Carl Betz (fresh off his TV hit *Judd for the Defense*), who plays a writer involved in an international intrigue as he is on the hunt for the secret diary belonging to a Russian diplomat. The film reveals its boob tube origins and may have been designed as a television movie (former American TV teen idol Bobby Rydell is also in the cast), but the inclusion of some violent scenes and sexually suggestive imagery doomed it immediately to B-movie status. But even then, it seems to have been barely released.

Nancy Kwan moved back to Hong Kong, and in 1972 she married Austrian hotelier David Giler. Afterwards she began to appear in a number of low-budget films shot in Indonesia and the Philippines. Among these, *Wonder Women* (a.k.a. *The Deadly and the Beautiful*) was the best. As Dr. Tsu, Kwan was the atypical mad scientist. She was beautiful, as well as hard and dedicated to her mission, creating a small army of female Filipino warriors who are usually clad only in skimpy bra and panties while doing their kung fu kicks or toting guns. The film has gained quite a formidable cult status for lovers of quirky Philippine movies. However, Kwan probably wished she had her old Hollywood career back rather than be remembered for a Manila-set movie in which the highlight is a number of scenes involving near naked chicks beating down the male cast members (including bovine agent Ross Hagen).

Another interesting entry in Kwan's filmography is the Indonesian horror film *Night Creature* (1977), in which she co-starred (as Leslie) with veteran British horror movie veteran Donald Pleasance in a story about a big-game hunter (Pleasance) and a quasi-supernatural killer leopard. She came back to the United States in 1979 and appeared in the film *Project: Kill* (1980), which, like the films before it, was another cheap, low-budget production shot in the Philippines. Leslie Nielsen (*Naked Gun* series) stars as Jonathan Trevor, a former secret agent and martial arts expert who, weary of his profession, which has always dogged him, is chased by killer fellow agent Gary Lockwood. That Kwan's performance in the film can barely be remembered is a testament to the movie's lack of distribution and seemingly incoherent story line (several plots meander throughout).

In recent years Nancy Kwan has appeared in *Walking the Edge* (1983), a film about a woman who avenges the death of her mob-related family by seeking the assistance of a taxi driver (Robert Forster), and she appeared as Ms. Yang, a restaurateur, in *Dragon: The Bruce Lee Story* (1993). In the eighties and early nineties, Kwan was seen on late night infomercials selling "Oriental Pearl Cream" to housewives seeking the "secret of youth." Her career as an actress seems to primarily remain in the past.

Her son, Bernie Pock, has taken on the Kwan entertainment tradition and is now an actor and stunt coordinator who uses his knowledge of the martial arts to arrange fight scenes for numerous television shows.

Other films include: *The Main Attraction* (1962), *Tamahine* (1963), *Honeymoon Hotel* (1964), *Fate Is the Hunter* (1964), *Nobody's Perfect* (1968), *Hawaii Five-O* (1968—TV), *The McMasters* (1970), *Angkor: Cambodian Express* (1981), *Blade in Hong Kong* (1985—TV) and *Miracle Landing* (1990—TV).

Jocelyn Lane

Beautiful Jocelyn Lane was born Jackie Lane on May 16, 1937, in Vienna, Austria. The younger sister of international model Mara Lane, Jackie followed her sister into modeling and also became a very popular cover girl, being dubbed "the British Bardot." Purportedly, Cecil Landau, the man who brought Audrey Hepburn to Hollywood, discovered Lane in a British TV play entitled "Afternoon of a Nymph." He built a revue around her but she had to drop out due to illness. After relocating to Hollywood in the early sixties she changed her name.

The newly named Jocelyn Lane made her American film debut opposite Elvis Presley in *Tickle Me* (1965) and wowed the critics with her beauty rather than her acting talent. As with Mary Ann Mobley in *Harum Scarum* (1965), Lane too played an Arabian princess in that same year's *The Sword of Ali Baba*. Both actresses had screen presence and were voted "Stars of Tomorrow" in 1965 by theater owners in *The Motion Picture Herald*. Unbelievably, Mobley and Lane placed higher in the poll than Julie Christie! Lane's stunning looks and icy screen persona made her ripe for the spy genre, though she was limited to small-screen ventures.

Lane's first two excursions into the spy arena did not give her much to do. In "The Re-Collector's Affair" (10/22/65) on *The Man from U.N.C.L.E.* she played Lisa Donato, the innocent who aides U.N.C.L.E. agents Napoleon Solo (Robert Vaughn) and Illya Kuryakin (David McCallum) in ending the reign of the Re-Collectors. They were a renegade group who execute ex-Nazis and take priceless art work, which they stole during the war, to sell back to the original owners. Lane was then cast as Angelina in "Whatever Happened to Adriana, and Why Won't She Stay Dead?" (12/1/65) on *Amos Burke, Secret Agent*. In this episode, Gene Barry as Burke tangles with an enemy agent (Albert Paulsen) suspected of smuggling missiles into a Latin American country.

In the United Nations sponsored TV-movie *The Poppy Is Also a Flower* (1966), Jocelyn Lane was just one of many international stars (including Senta Berger, Marcello Mastroianni, Omar Sharif, etc.) who made cameo appearances in this spy adventure. Adapted from an original story penned by Ian Fleming, the plot focused on two agents (Trevor Howard and E. G. Marshall) sent to Iran to investigate the murder of an associate (Stephen Boyd). To put an end to the organized crime ring that distributes drugs to the West, the agents lace opium with radioactive tracers so that they can track its path as it is disbursed throughout Europe. Lane played a society photographer working at a nightclub in Monte Carlo who takes some pictures for Howard of suspected drug trafficker and murderer Serge Marco. The shoddy film had a very strong anti-drug message—too potent for some critics.

Arguably, Jocelyn Lane gives one of her best performances as the vicious vixen Dominque O'Shaunessy in "The Night of the Watery Death" (11/11/66) on *The Wild Wild West*. In this episode, Marquis Philippe (John Van Dreelen) plans to create an underwater city in the Pacific to control the world's shipping. His consort, Dominque, first appears as a Mermaid in the Mermaid Bar, who uses a blow-dart to render secret service agent James West (Robert Conrad) unconscious. Her later antics include teasing West with a series of kisses as he lay bound to a bed, and gassing Artemus Gordon (Ross Martin), his partner. On *It Takes a Thief*, Lane played the mini-skirted Michelle in "The Bill Is in Committee" (10/8/68) as SIA agent Al Mundy (Robert Wagner) goes undercover as a magician to prove a despot of a tiny country is bribing a Congressman to keep aid coming.

Though she appeared semi-nude in the pages of *Playboy* magazine in September of 1966, the big screen found Jocelyn Lane cast as traditional western women rather

Jocelyn Lane (left), modly attired in a scene from the Italian comedy *How to Seduce a Playboy* (Chevron, 1966), with Peter Alexander, an unidentified actress and Renato Salvatori (in background).

than the glamorous sexpot, à la Brigitte Bardot, who she strongly resembled. However, two roles stand out. In the violent motorcycle movie *Hell's Belles* (1969) Lane essayed the role of a tough leather miniskirted biker chick who is deserted by her vicious boyfriend, Adam Roarke, when he steals Jeremy Slate's prize motorcycle. Slate takes Lane along as he tracks down the gang to exact his revenge. And in her last feature, *A Bullet for Pretty Boy* (1970), she played the thrill-seeking girlfriend of the notorious gangster, played by Fabian Forte.

Jocelyn Lane retired from the acting profession in the 1970s when she purportedly married into Spanish royalty. Today she is rumored to be divorced and living on the French Riviera. But there have also been reports that she is living back in her native England doing voiceovers.

Other films include: *Incident at Phantom Hill* (1966), *How to Seduce a Playboy* (1966) and *Land Raiders* (1969).

Sue Ane Langdon

With curves galore to match her perky personality, Sue Ane Langdon (born on March 8, 1936, in New Jersey) played a variety of kooks and goofy dames throughout the sixties. After the death of her father when she was only two years old, Langdon's mother, a former opera singer, began teaching voice lessons at local colleges around the country. After attending North Texas State and the University of Idaho, Sue Ane went to New York where she found work as a singer at Radio City Music Hall and was a performer on Broadway. She relocated to Hollywood in the late fifties and landed a recurring role as Kitty Marsh on the comedy series *Bachelor Father* in 1959. She left the show in 1961 and appeared on a number of TV shows, including *Surfside 6*, *77 Sunset Strip*, *Perry Mason*, *Bonanza*, *The Andy Griffith Show*, *Gunsmoke* and *The Dick Van Dyke Show*, among many others. Appearing on the cover of *Life* magazine led her to a short stint as Alice Kramden opposite Jackie Gleason on his variety series *American Scene Magazine* in 1962.

On the TV spy front, Langdon turned up in the fourth episode of *The Man from U.N.C.L.E.*, entitled "The Shark Affair" (10/13/64), as the klutzy Elsa. Her husband, Harry Barnman (Herbert Anderson), is the latest craftsman to be abducted by a modern day pirate, Captain Shark (Robert Culp), who is obsessed with the belief of imminent nuclear devastation. The show's running gag is that Elsa keeps slamming doors into helpful U.N.C.L.E. agent Illya Kuryakin (David McCallum).

"I had met Robert Vaughn previously before doing this," says Sue Ane Langdon. "He has the same atmosphere about himself as Napoleon Solo in the show—a very tongue-in-cheek polish and too, too suave! Bob Culp played the villain and didn't hang around the set that much. He was not unfriendly but we didn't have much opportunity to talk to each other. I also think he immersed himself in his character on and off screen. I saw him years later and he was much looser, with a great sense of humor. That didn't come out when we worked together."

In "The Night of the Steel Assassin" (1/17/66) on *The Wild Wild West* Langdon (in a change of pace role) brought an innocent sexiness to the part of Nina Gilbert, a prim young doctoral student whose uncle, R.L. Gilbert (John Pickard), is murdered by an assassin nicknamed "Iron Man." When Nina produces a photograph of eight officers in her uncle's regiment during the Civil War, secret service agent James West (Robert Conrad) identifies President Grant as one of the two surviving men. Torres (John Dehner) is the other, and Nina goes to warn him that his life is in danger, unaware that he is the killer. Torres hypnotizes Nina to "seize the day ... and laugh." Later West finds the scantily clad Nina working as a showgirl at the local saloon where she dances and whoops it up with the town's cowboys.

On the big screen Sue Ane Langdon's roles ranged from a fortuneteller lusting after Elvis Presley in *Roustabout* (1964), to an office secretary who can't resist the charms of a carpet cleaner (Sean Connery) in *A Fine Madness* (1966), to an adulterous housewife in *A Guide for the Married Man* (1967). She even created quite a stir during the mid-sixties by baring her shapely derriere first at the close of *The Rounders* (1965) and then in the pages of *Playboy*. So it was not too surprising that she played a scantily clad bad girl in the spy film *A Man Called Dagger* (1967), directed by Richard Rush (whom Langdon describes as being, "very nice. Considering the low budget, I think he did the best he could."). Saddled with doing an accent, Langdon makes a sexy and duplicitous femme fatale. (*Independent Film Journal* commented that Langdon "plays with flair, employing a suspiciously Gabor-like accent.")

Her scenes begin when Paul Mantee, as agent Dirk Dagger, pretends to be an insurance investigator and pays a call to her health spa under the pretense of finding a missing Swedish girl. The self-centered Ingrid only wants to talk about her healthy regimen. She then asks, "Mr. Dagger, do you fence?" He doesn't but accepts her challenge to try to get information out of her. She ends the match by ripping off her top and throwing it on Dagger's sword, prompting him to comment, "Touché." After exercising and lunching, where she reveals that she is a friend of meat packing tycoon Rudolph Koffman (Jan Murray), Ingrid seductively invites Dagger to join her in a nap: "You've become part of my daily routine, Mr. Dagger." Dirk willingly obliges. Unbeknownst to them, they are spied on by Koffman. Later he congratulates Ingrid for feeding information to Dagger as he ordered, but he slaps her for "taking three hours to tell him."

After the death of fellow agent Melissa, Dagger pays another visit to Ingrid, who is taking a steam bath. He locks her in and keeps raising the temperature until she tells him how to get into Koffman's office. Ingrid refuses but Dagger is insistent. She pleads for her life ("*Dagger, please, please let me out. Dagger, I'll do anything—anything.*"). Ingrid finally gives him the information so Dagger turns on the cold water and dryly quips, "Just play it cool."

Being the owner of a health farm, the character of Ingrid was scantily clad throughout the film. Langdon is seen wearing a towel, a short fencing shirt, a halter-top with sweat pants, and nothing at all (to the audience's imagination anyway) in a steam bath. "I don't remember what I wore in that shower scene," remarks Sue Ane Langdon. "Of course I had frosted glass in front of me but I can't recall if I had anything on in back of there. But I do remember that fencing outfit. It was kind of pinned together. If you notice there is no opening on it. I don't even remember who

Sue Ane Langdon, as Ingrid, playfully fences with Paul Mantee's virile agent Dirk Dagger in *A Man Called Dagger* (MGM, 1967).

the costume designer was. I also did my own fencing. My husband Jack studied fencing in New York, and he was hired to help with that scene. He coached Paul and I, but you really didn't see us fence too much. He taught us the positions, so I was doing it relatively legitimately."

Langdon also recalls a couple of scenes that did not make it into the final print. "There was a scene on a massage table with my dog sitting beside me. My hair in this film was all different colors. The dog was a white West Highland Terrier and they used vegetable dye on it to match all the streaks in my hair. I did a promo tour for the film with my dog 'of many colors.' While in New York City people would walk up to me and say, 'Oh, the poor thing,' as if the colors were hurting her ... for gosh sake, it washed right out! But you don't see the dog much in the final version of the film. There was another shot of people hanging on meat hooks like Jan Murray was at the end. That didn't make the final cut either. "

Not that Langdon felt any of these shots would have helped the film. The budget seemed to be the major hindrance. "That watch of Dagger's did an awful lot of stuff. And the walls of the corridors of the meatpacking plant where made of tinfoil on pieces of plywood frame. It was obvious that the walls weren't very thick or heavy. All expense was spared on this epic! I think if we could have had a little better direction or a little better budget or a little better script, any of that might have helped the film. I recently ran into Eileen O'Neill at an autograph convention and she told me that *A Man Called Dagger* has built up a cult following. I was taken aback, but I am glad the fans are enjoying the film!"

The seventies found Sue Ane Langdon concentrating on television over film. The sixties sexpot morphed into a dutiful housewife in the sitcom *Arnie*, beginning in 1970, and she won a Golden Globe Award as "Best Supporting Actress in a Series" for her performance. After the show was cancelled in 1972, Langdon could be seen in a number of TV movies and in guest stints on such series as *Love, American Style*, *Police Story* and *Banacek*. She was also a regular on the series *Grandpa Goes to Washington* during the 1978-79 season. Her last film appearance was playing Weird Al Yankovic's aunt in the comedy *UHF* (1989). Married since the mid-sixties, Langdon is still active in the Hollywood community. She makes the occasional appearance at conventions and film festivals, where she is always warmly welcomed.

Other films include: *Strangers When We Meet* (1960), *The Great Imposter* (1961), *The New Interns* (1964), *When the Boys Meet the Girls* (1965), *Frankie and Johnny* (1966), *The Cheyenne Social Club* (1970), *The Evictors* (1979), *Without Warning* (1980), *Zapped!* (1982), *The Vals* (1985), *Hawkin's Breed* (1987) and *Zapped Again* (1989).

Daliah Lavi

Born Daliah Levenbuch on October 12, 1942, in the kibbutz of Shavei-Zion, just north of Haifa, Israel, Daliah Lavi became a fiercely independent young woman at a time when Israel was consolidating its freedom and frontiers. Her Russian father, Reuben, and her German mother, Ruth, went to Israel as refugees in the 1930s and stayed in the newly adopted homeland. At a young age Daliah helped her father work the family farm while her mother, armed with a rifle, stood by, watching for marauding Arabs. Lavi was ten years old when she decided that she wanted to become a ballet dancer.

In 1952 Kirk Douglas was filming *The Juggler* in Israel, near to where Lavi lived, and nearly every day the young girl would go down and dance for the film crew. Douglas became enamored of the young talented girl and helped to arrange for her to attend ballet school with distant Levenbuch relatives in Sweden. She danced with the Stockholm Opera Company and was apparently well received by audiences, but as she turned 16 years of age, her body started to grow out of the typical ballet student rail-thinness and into more womanly, voluptuous curves. She made her film debut in a little-known Swedish movie, *Hemsoborna*, in 1955, but then returned to Israel at age 16. Upon her return Lavi served in the Israeli army from 1955 to 1960, putting her career choices on hold.

Conversant in several languages and nearing the age of 20, she was now a stunning, olive-skinned beauty, with a height of 5'7", lustrous black hair and doe-like brown eyes. After making her Israeli film debut in the 1960 action movie *Brennender Sands* (a.k.a. *Blazing Sands*, a West German co-production), she then appeared in a number of French productions, beginning with *Candide ou L'Optimisme au Xxe Siecle* in 1961.

Within the year, news of Daliah Lavi's sexy looks and talent as an actress garnered her roles in many European productions, like the West German–produced *The Return of Dr. Mabuse* (a.k.a. *Im Stahlnetz des Dr. Mabuse*, 1961), where she appeared as Maria Sabrehm. In this thriller with espionage overtones, the criminal mastermind Dr. Mabuse continues to strive for world domination with his criminal organization. An FBI agent (Lex Barker) in league with a West German Police Inspector (Gert Froebe) is sent by Interpol to wreak havoc on the evil empire. Lavi appeared on the fringes of the story as a woman in distress, but the film was released worldwide, enlarging her audience.

Still in her early twenties she reunited with her former benefactor Kirk Douglas as his co-star in the film *Two Weeks in Another Town* (1962). Her performance in this film was noticed by the critics, and she received a Golden Globe nomination for "Most Promising Newcomer—Female." She said at the time to a Columbia Pictures press agent that Douglas had remarked that, "I had grown a lot since he last saw me."

A frightening role as a possessed woman in Brunello Rondi's powerful Italian horror film *Il Demonio* (1963) bought the actress acting accolades. She followed this movie with a co-starring part (opposite Christopher Lee) in Mario Bava's *The Whip and the Body* (a.k.a. *La Frusta e il Corpo*, 1963), where she appeared as Novenka Menliff, a woman who is hauntingly devoted to her dead lover in quite an unhealthy manner. Lavi also appeared in European westerns like *Apache's Last Battle* (a.k.a. *Old Shatterhand*, 1963), but her first proper role in a spy movie was in *Spy Hunt in Vienna* (a.k.a. *Schusse im Dreivierteltakt*, a.k.a. *Shots in ¾ Time*, 1964), an Austrian thriller about a secret agent (Pierre Brice) who travels all over Eastern Europe to track down a stolen device for a missile guidance system. Unfortunately, Lavi was lost in a cast filled with numerous co-stars, including the equally sensuous Senta Berger. Lavi also appeared in the German film *DM Killer* (1965), of which little is known, and was then cast by American director Richard Brooks for his epic tale *Lord Jim* (1965), in the featured role of "The Girl." As Ilona Bergen, a pretentious film actress, she became one of the victims in the all-star mystery thriller *Ten Little Indians* (1965), but her big break came in 1966 when she was cast as the incredibly sexy femme fatale Tina Batori in *The Silencers*, one of the very popular Matt Helm films with Dean Martin. In this sly, sexy spoof of the Bond films, Lavi (as a former partner of the agent from ICE) prevents Martin's Helm character from meeting his end (via a long dagger) at the hands of Nancy Kovack's seductive enemy agent, who is embracing him while raising her arm high in the air (to plunge the knife into his back). Like a woman scorned, Lavi comments to Helm, "Sorry for the interruption..." as she kills the tempting enemy agent and saves Helm. Lavi gives a fierce performance as the seductive agent who turns against Helm, but she was unjustly overlooked by the critics, who lavished all praise on Stella Stevens' klutzy heroine.

Lavi garnered a more prominent role (as Princess Natasha Romanova) in *The Spy with the Cold Nose* (1966). This satire of the James Bond films is about an innocent veterinarian (Laurence Harvey) who is drafted into becoming a spy for competing countries. In the goofy movie, a search for a secret transmitter device placed on a dog collar leads to numerous sight gags. As a side note, the film was nominated for two Golden Globe awards in 1967 for "Best Foreign Language Film (English language)," and Lionel Jeffries received a nod for "Best Performance by an Actor in a Motion Picture Comedy or Musical."

Probably one of Daliah Lavi's most well remembered roles was as Lady James

Bond, a.k.a. "The Detainer," in the all-star *Casino Royale* in 1967. In the film, Lavi is the sultry seductress spy who gives Dr. Noah (Woody Allen) the dangerous bomb pill that explodes, killing the entire cast (including the movie's numerous James Bond characters, played by men and women alike).

The same year she appeared in the science fiction satire *Those Fantastic Flying Fools* (a.k.a. *Blast-Off*, 1967), but made an impression in one of her most dramatic roles as Maria Cholon in the Australian film *The High Commissioner* (a.k.a. *Nobody Runs Forever*, 1968). In this movie, an Australian policeman (Rod Taylor) journeys to London to arrest his country's most powerful politician on a 25-year-old murder charge. He is persuaded to delay the arrest because of a peace conference that the politician is attending, uncovers a plot to kill the "High Commissioner" by foreign spies, and reluctantly is forced to protect him and destroy the spy ring. Lavi inhabits the film as a dangerous woman who seduces the hero in an attempt to keep him from his mission.

In 1969 Lavi appeared as Helga in *Some Girls Do* (1969), the sexier and much more risqué sequel to the 1967 Bulldog Drummond–secret agent movie *Deadlier Than the Male* (1967). In this film Drummond (Richard Johnson) battles a deadly army of female robots and faces the return of his arch nemesis, the sinister megalomaniac Carl Peterson (James Villiers), who is again bent on world domination, this time by destroying planes with a deadly ray.

In the British spy spoof *Some Girls Do* (United Artists, 1969), Daliah Lavi's Helga seduces Richard Johnson (insurance agent Bulldog Drummond) before attempting to murder him. (*Courtesy of Michael Monahan*)

Lavi's role is modeled on Elke Sommer's Erma character from *Deadlier Than the Male*, the prequel. Like that movie, in which Ms. Sommer was paired with Sylva Koscina as Penelope, the more seductive and sex-minded of the two killers, in *Some Girls Do* Lavi is paired with Beba Loncar (as Pandora). Daliah Lavi returned to Israel to appear in the European co-production western (and her last feature) *Catlow* (1971) in the role of Rosita, alongside star Yul Brynner.

In 1969 Lavi was contracted to sing some Hebrew songs in a BBC variety program, resulting in a contract with the Polydor label in 1970. She then decided to concentrate on a singing career and gave up acting. Her first single, "Liebeslied Jener Sommernacht," became a hit, and she continued to chart other hit songs into the early seventies, becoming one of Germany's most successful female singers. With her beautiful alto voice, Lavi sings in many languages (including English, French, German and Hebrew). In 1991 German television viewers got the pleasure of seeing Lavi return to the screen in the TV movie *Mrs. Harris und der Heiratsschwindler*, and a few years later in the series *Duell Zu Dritt* (1997). She also returned to the German concert stage in 1993 sporting undyed gray hair, but she was as beautiful as ever. Now retired from performing, she resides in the southeastern United States with her husband.

Other films include: *Un Soir le Plage* (1961), *Das Schwarz-Weiss-Rote Himmelbett* (1962) and *Das Grosse Liebesspiel* (1963).

Margaret Lee

Purportedly born on August 4, 1943, in England, Margaret Lee has, as an actress, become very recognizable to a generation of movie fans that grew up watching her perform in numerous European films in the sixties and seventies. While her early life previous to her film career is nearly impossible to document due to a lack of biographical information, the actress appeared on Italian screens in her first film, *The Three Avengers* (a.k.a. *I Tre Nemici*, 1962), in a minor role. Within a short time, with her full mane of flowing blonde tresses and being tall of stature, Lee found herself cast as a "Glamour Girl" in a number of small roles in Italian films, including *Due Samurai per Centro Geisha* (1962) starring the popular Italian comedians Franco Franchi and Ciccio Ingrassia.

In 1963 she appeared in the muscleman movie *Samson and the Sea Beast* (a.k.a. *Sansone Contro I Pirati*, a.k.a. *Samson Against the Pirates*). The following three years saw appearances in numerous Italian comedies and the odd drama, with all of her roles being of a minor stature. Her first science fiction film credit was *The Twelve-Handed Men of Mars* (a.k.a. *I Marziani Hanno Dodici Mani*, 1964), and she followed this role with an appearance in the Lucio Fulci–directed anthology film *The Maniacs* (a.k.a. *I, Maniaci*, 1964), in which she appeared alongside Barbara Steele.

When Italian film producers jumped on the phenomenal James Bond bandwagon in the mid-sixties and began to churn out dozens of films influenced by the popular literary and film character, Lee became a familiar face in a number of these movies. Her first role in such a picture was in *Fury in Istanbul* (a.k.a. *Agente 077 Dall'Orient Con Furore*, a.k.a. *Agent 077: From the East with Fury*, 1965). In this Italian-French-Spanish co-production she became the chief love interest for (American) star Ken Clark's muscular secret agent 077, a.k.a. Dick Mallory. In the tale, which involved the agent being assigned to investigate the kidnapping of a nuclear scientist by a criminal organization bent on world domination, Lee could do little but appear on the sidelines waiting to be rescued, a true "Bond Girl" imitation. She then appeared in *Secret Agent Superdragon* (a.k.a. *New York Chiama Superdrago*, a.k.a. *New York Calling Superdragon*, 1965), an Italian-French-West German co-production featuring another American actor (Ray Danton) as a naval intelligence agent sent to battle the sinister international criminal organization The Black Wolves, who are intent on using their drug "Syncron 2" to control the minds of United States students in order to rule America and then the world. In this film Lee appeared as a seductive femme fatale. The production *Our Agent Tiger* (a.k.a. *Le Tigre se Parfume à la Dynamite*, a.k.a. *The Tiger Sprays Himself with Dynamite*, 1965), starring French actor Roger Hanin as debonair Interpol agent Louis Rapire (a.k.a. "The Tiger"), saw Lee appearing as a malicious enemy agent who becomes one of the (brief) love interests for our hero. The Tiger tangles with foreign spies on a Caribbean island as a hunt ensues for valuable uranium deposits amidst a revolution.

The next year saw Lee appear alongside the comic American actor Tony Randall in the espionage adventure *Bang! Bang! You're Dead!* (a.k.a. *Our Man in Marrakech*, 1966). In this film Randall portrays an American innocent on a vacation abroad who becomes involved in a case of mistaken identity and is chased by a potpourri of agents (including Senta Berger and seductive enemy agent Lee). As chief villain Herbert Lom's lover and sinister murderess, Lee manages to look at once sexy and deadly.

Margaret Lee next appeared in the confusing *The Spy Against the World* (a.k.a. *Gern Habich die Frauen Gekillt*, a.k.a. *Killer's Carnival*, 1966). Rumored to have been intended as an anthology film that would be sold to television stations worldwide, the movie was too violent and incoherent for the few theatrical audiences who saw it in Italian, Austrian and French theaters before it fell into obscurity. Stewart Granger, Lex Barker and Pierre Brice star in the three individual episodes that are connected by a thin interlocking theme. Lee appears (briefly) in one of the episodes as a mysterious woman.

She had a much better (and larger) role in *The Great Diamond Robbery* (a.k.a. *Colpo Maestro Al Servico di Sua Maesta Britannica*, a.k.a. *Master Stroke in the Service of Her Britannic Majesty*, 1966). In this film Lee appears in the strong role of a woman working for enemy agents who is coerced to fall in love with a designated victim and then actually does. An actor in Spaghetti Westerns (Richard Harrison) is forced to join a band of criminals to pull off several heists in Europe. Eventually, it is all proven to be a ruse, as the criminal gang was, in reality, none other than an international secret service organization working with Scotland Yard to smoke out a diamond robbery ring. However, this too is a smokescreen, as it turns out that a rogue Scotland Yard inspector (Adolfo Celli) heads his own criminal organization and has plans for the diamonds (including using them to build a deadly laser ray device). After winning the heart of a traitorous damsel in distress whom he is instructed to woo (Lee), the actor succeeds in winning out over the villains and is asked to join the secret service.

Lee also appeared in the obscure *Dick*

Margaret Lee, as the sexy but deadly Samia Voss, listens intently to Herbert Lom (Mr. Casimir) as Klaus Kinski (Jonquil) looks on in Bang! Bang! You're Dead! (a.k.a. *Our Man in Marrakech*, AIP, 1966).

Smart 2.007 (1966), a spoof of Bond movies and the popular "Flint" films starring James Coburn, thereby becoming a spoof of a spoof. American actor Richard Wyler stars as secret agent Dick Smart, who battles the sinister "Lady Lister Organization" as it seeks to rule the world through the use of a deadly diamond-powered ray. Finally becoming a chief villain in a spy-oriented film, Lee has the role of the beautiful but deadly Lady Lister. However, the listless direction by Franco Prosperi (of *Mondo Cane* fame) and the obvious low budget (spare sets, monotonous camera set-ups) saw the film relegated to late-night viewings on Italian television, and there is no record of a U.S. or British theatrical release, even in the sixties.

Returning to the "Glamour Girl" image that fueled her career in its infancy, Lee appeared alongside a bevy of stunning actresses in the film *Kiss the Girls and Make Them Die* (a.k.a. *Se Tutte le Donne del Mondo*, 1966). A CIA agent (Michael Connors) learns that a megalomaniacal industrialist (Raf Vallone) is involved with Chinese agents in an attempt to sterilize the world and keep a select group of women (including Lee, Beverly Adams, etc.) for himself. Beautifully shot on Brazilian locations by director Dino Mauri (assisted by Henry Levin), the film remains a colorful and, at times, comedic spoof.

The international success of director Mario Bava's Dino De Laurentiis–produced *Diabolik* (a.k.a. *Danger: Diabolik*, 1967) led to the production of Stefano Vanzina's own *Here Comes Dorellik* (a.k.a. *Arriva Dorellik*). This film showcased Italian comedian and singer Johnny Dorelli as Dorellik, a Diabolik clone who is a bumbler and ordinary person outside his elaborate costume; but once inside his outfit he gains confidence and becomes a master thief and womanizer, as well as a murderer. The unsure direction of the film careens all over the place, with the movie often taking on the tone of an espionage thriller when all of the secret service organizations of the world are called upon to assist in the capture of Dorellik. But the film does provide a highlight in Lee's heroine role as Dorellik's love interest (a part similar to that of Marisa Mell in the original *Diabolik*). Also in 1967, Lee appeared in the obscure *Coplan Saves His Skin* (a.k.a. *Coplan Sauve Sa Peau*), a French film starring Claudio Brook as the famed French agent originally created by author Paul Kenny, who wrote the same-titled novel upon which this movie is based.

Five Golden Dragons (1968), a British co-production with several European countries, was a failed attempt to make former American television comedy star Robert Cummings into a suave super agent hero. Although Lee tops the cast as the main female star, she and Cummings seem to have difficulty with the film's apparent interest in showcasing many of the international "stars," like Christopher Lee, Klaus Kinski, George Raft, Brian Donlevy and Maria Perschy. As a result, this hampers the flow of the story from moving within a progressive pattern.

As Lee matured as an actress she yearned for better roles in films. However, as fate would have it, the European cycle of spy movies was nearing an end, and one of her last productions featuring an espionage theme also happened to contain one of her best performances in this genre. *OSS 117 Murder for Sale* (a.k.a. *Pas De Roses pour OSS 117*, a.k.a. *No Roses for OSS 117*, 1968) is an enjoyable and involving film that appears much more serious than the bulk of the Italian and French productions in the genre that preceded it. American actor John Gavin acquits himself well in the film as the French secret agent, and although Italian actress Luciana Paluzzi has a more prominent (but brief) role (as Gavin's chief love interest), she disappears from the film. Lee's brief but important scenes midway through the film motivates the hero from that point onward. That same year she appeared in *A Candidate for the Killing* (a.k.a. *Un Sudario a la Medida*, 1968), a tale of a wandering adventurer named Nick Warfield (John Richardson) who hitchhikes his way across the South of France. He is tricked into becoming involved with an assassination attempt when he discovers that he is the exact physical double of the real killer. He seeks the aid of Interpol.

The turning point in Lee's career came when she accepted the role of a woman named Olga, a lesbian fashion designer who had been involved with a murdered girl named Wanda, in Jesus Franco's *Venus in Furs* (1968). The film is about James Darren's Jimmy Logan character, a jazz trumpeter in Istanbul who could be recovering from a bad acid trip, may be stuck in the midst of one, or might, in fact, be dead. *Venus in Furs* begins with Darren's Logan finding the dead body of a woman (Maria Rohm) washed ashore on a lonely beach. She had been killed by a number of people (at an orgy). The film, via a series of flashbacks, shows what happened to the woman named Wanda. When Jimmy begins playing the jazz clubs, Wanda reappears as Venus (also Rohm), who is back from the dead to avenge her murder. Lee's role as Olga is certainly different from anything she had done onscreen before, and it paved the way for a more sensationalist attitude in her acting roles.

She next appeared as a woman persecuted as a witch and burned at the stake in

Jesus Franco's *The Bloody Judge* (a.k.a. *Night of the Blood Monster*, 1969). In this West German, Spanish and Italian co-production (based on actual events in the life of the real-life title character who lived 1648–1702), Christopher Lee starred as Lord George Jeffreys, a ruthless Chief Justice who pursues, prosecutes and tortures enemies of the British crown by accusing them of witchcraft. Margaret Lee had a role as one such unfortunate who is burned at the stake. Her death sets the events of the film in motion as it centers on Maria Schell (playing her sister), who is wooed by one of the film's heroes, as well as "noticed" by Judge Jeffreys. Later on that same year Lee had extensive nude scenes with German actress Christiane Kruger and Annabella Incontrera in Italian director Riccardo Freda's *Double Face* (a.k.a. *A Doppia Faccia*, 1969), a thriller wherein Klaus Kinski starred as a harried police inspector suspected of the possible murder of his wife Helen (Lee), who, it is revealed through flashbacks and a serious of revelations, was a swinging girl involved in a number of scandalous relationships (some with other women), porno films and the underworld.

Despite her busy movie schedule, Margaret Lee found time to appear in the British spy series *The Protectors*, starring Robert Vaughn, Nyree Dawn Porter and Tony Anholt as three of the world's top agents. In Lee's episode, entitled "The Numbers Game" (12/29/72), she played Susan Crediton, the wayward daughter of British nobility who finds herself entangled in a heroin smuggling operation.

In Vincenzo Rigo's sexploitative thriller *The Killers Are Our Guests* (a.k.a. *Gli Assassino Sonmo Nostri Ospiti*, 1974) Margaret Lee appeared in numerous scenes as the (often) undraped sexual plaything to a number of suspects, each of them a possible murderer. After this film she seemed to disappear from the entertainment world for nearly two decades before returning in the Italian police thriller *Neapolitan Sting* (a.k.a. *Stangata Napoletana*) in 1982, of which little is known. However, she did have a featured role in director Dino Risi's 1983 film *Sex with a Will* (a.k.a. *Sesso E Volentieri*), in which she reunited with former *Dorellik* co-star Johnny Dorelli. She was favorably seen in the company of a number of Italian sex symbols of the seventies, such as Laura Antonelli and Gloria Guida.

Other films include: *Circus of Fear* (a.k.a. *Das Ratsel des Silbernen Dreiecks*, 1966), *Questi Fantasmi* (1968), *Cinque per L'Inferno* (1968), *Banditi a Milano* (1968), *Slaughter Hotel* (a.k.a. *La Bestia Uccide a Sangre Freddo*, a.k.a. *The Beast Kills in Cold Blood*, 1971), *Papestan, Papestan Aleppe* (1974) and *Stangata Napoletana* (1984).

Suzanna Leigh

Blonde ingenue Suzanna Leigh was born Suzanna Smyth on July 26, 1945, in Cavisham, Berkshire, England. Her father was a professional gambler who died when his daughter was six years old. Her mother is a millionaire property developer, but mother and daughter have been estranged for years. Before her father passed away he encouraged Suzanna's dreams of acting and told her that her godmother was actress

Vivien Leigh. When the inquisitive girl was 11 years old she sought out the elder Leigh, who lived nearby. She told Hester Lacy, writing in *The Independent on Sunday (London)*, in 1999, "She [Vivien Leigh] said that she had known my father... It was about 15 years after she'd done *Gone with the Wind* and she was stunning, beautiful and slender with dark hair. She said she didn't mind if I used her name."

The newly named Suzanna Leigh enrolled in drama school as a teenager but dropped out after only two terms. She came into the acting field via appearances on British television shows, including episodes of *The Saint* ("The Wonderful Liar," 1964) and *The Sentimental Agent* before landing the lead in the French TV series, *Trois étoiles*. Stardom came by way of a phone call from her agent—film producer Hal Wallis was in London looking for a new Shirley MacLaine. Leigh bolted from her Paris set, got on the first plane back to England, and banged on Wallis' hotel door saying, "I'm the one you're looking for." Impressed, Wallis offered Leigh a screen test, and before she knew it she was whisked off to Hollywood, cast as one of the romantic leads (as a stewardess) in the Wallis-produced film *Boeing, Boeing* (1965) alongside co-stars Tony Curtis and Jerry Lewis. Leigh followed up this role with an appearance in the Elvis Presley movie *Paradise, Hawaiian Style* (1966). "I was thrilled when the offer came to go to Hollywood but I think I was ready for it.... They spent a lot of money on this one. Usually they shoot the Presley pictures in three weeks, this one took three months."

Leigh was signed for another Presley picture, but the Screen Actors' Guild prohibited it, reportedly in retaliation for British Equity refusing Charlton Heston's request to work on a film in England. Impatient to work, Suzanna Leigh found herself back in the UK co-starring in the dreary horror movie *The Deadly Bees* (1967).

Her first role in an espionage film was in the risqué British adventure *Deadlier Than the Male* (1967) as one of many beautiful actresses who attempt to seduce aging agent Bulldog Drummond (Richard Johnson). Overshadowed by fellow cast members Elke Sommer and Sylva Koscina (as a deadly pair of sexy psycho assassins), Leigh ultimately leaves little impression in the film, her role reduced to a mere cameo. In *Subterfuge* (68), another British-produced espionage movie, she had a much larger role. The film, about an American agent (Gene Barry) who is on holiday in England and becomes involved in murder and is kidnapped and tortured, did little business at worldwide box offices due to its harsh noir-ish atmosphere, but Leigh does perform well as a femme fatale alongside scene stealer Joan Collins.

If it was stardom that Leigh was after, it still eluded her when she was cast in the Hammer Film production *The Lost Continent* (1968). As the escaping wife of a terrorist, she joins other troubled passengers on an old freighter bound for a South American port. Overloaded with a deadly cargo of munitions, the ship is blown off course by a terrible storm into a forgotten land with a ghostly ship's graveyard and peopled by descendants of the Spanish Inquisition. While the movie was ahead of its time in terms of Leigh's risqué behavior with a number of the male passengers (including an attempted rape scene), the movie proved too horrific for most audiences, especially at its grim climax. She returned to Hammer Films to appear in the lesbian vampire movie *Lust for a Vampire* (a.k.a. *To Love a Vampire*, 1971) and made an appearance on the television series *The Persuaders*, starring Roger Moore and Tony Curtis, in the episode "Chain of Events" (11/26/71).

Regarding her decision to abandon Hollywood and the second Elvis Presley film, Leigh remarked to *The Independent*,

In the spy thriller *Subterfuge* (Commonwealth United, 1968), Suzanna Leigh as Donetta (left) matches wits with the equally tantalizing Joan Collins (Anne). (*Courtesy of Michael Monahan*)

"With hindsight I should have just stuck it out. I was supposed to do all these other pictures. It would have meant being out of work just sitting there. But when you're 20 and you're getting so many offers from Europe—I really couldn't believe that between Hal Wallis and Elvis they wouldn't have been able to sort it out. My agent had died. So I went back to England."

Leigh's final big-screen appearance was in the disastrous *Son of Dracula* (1974), starring Ringo Starr (of The Beatles) and Harry Nillson. Afterwards she became a regular on the British TV program *The Chippy Kids* (1976–1980). In 1972 Leigh began a ten-year relationship with Tim Hue-Williams. He deserted her in 1982 when she was four months pregnant. Their daughter Natalia was born that year, though, despite positive DNA testing, Hue-Williams denies paternity.

In recent years, to support herself and her daughter, Suzanna Leigh worked as an interior designer, gave etiquette lessons and sold the *Encyclopædia Britannica* at Heathrow Airport. Leigh's wish is to return to the U.S. and restart her acting career. She has become a regular at autograph shows and has written her autobiography, entitled *Paradise, Suzanna Style*. Her last words to *The Independent* were, "I should have stayed in Hollywood. But you don't know what's going to happen."

Other films include: *The Pleasure Girls* (1966), *Docteur Caraibe* (1970) and *Beware My Brethren* (a.k.a. *The Fiend*, 1971).

Helga Line

Helga Line was born Helga Lina Stern on July 14, 1932, in Berlin, Germany. As World War II started, Line, her brother and her mother immigrated to Portugal. Growing up in the sunny climate of this new land, she studied hard and excelled at ballet and gymnastic classes. The family name changed to Line (with an emphasis on the "e") and she joined a local circus as a contortionist and ballerina.

In 1947 Line changed career directions and began to pursue modeling. That same year, after winning a beauty contest, she was offered a role in a film production titled *La Mantilla de Beatriz*, to be shot in Lisbon. A few years afterward she moved to Spain where her experience as a dancer garnered her small roles in a number of musical comedies (at that time, that country's chief cinematic output). As Line grew into adulthood, so did the features of her face change accordingly. The cheekbones were high and the lips full, displaying their European heritage, while her skin darkened from the hot sun of her newly adopted homeland. Her eyes, wide, expressive and almond shaped, were offset by the striking full-headed mane of red hair.

One of her first major roles was in the Spanish-Italian co-production *The Sign of Zorro* (a.k.a. *Il Segno di Zorro*, 1963), which was clearly an attempt to emulate the successful peplums or sword and sandal films, then popular in Italy. Her next big role came with *Horror* (a.k.a. *The Blancheville Monster*, 1963), where she played a cruel governess who plots to drive a young heiress insane. The Gothic black and white atmosphere so effectively used in similar Italian productions of this period was well drawn, and with this film Line became a possible contender for the same kind of roles offered to femme fatales and heroines of the caliber of Barbara Steele. However, Line also had an eclectic personality and chose to appear only in productions based in her homeland (at least for the moment). She appeared in a number of Italian sword and sandal films that were shot on Spanish soil, with titles like *The Spartan Gladiators* (a.k.a. *La Rivolta dei Sette*, 1964) and *The Triumph of the Ten Gladiators* (a.k.a. *Il Trionfo dei Dieci Gladiatori*, 1964).

Two years after appearing in *Horror*, Line got her chance to upstage Barbara Steele by acting alongside her in Mario Caiano's *Nightmare Castle* (a.k.a. *L'Amante d'Oltretomba*, a.k.a. *The Night of the Doomed*, 1965), another Gothic horror film in which Line had a dual role (as both a possibly treacherous maid and a recently revived jealous mistress who has returned from beyond the grave ... maybe).

Helga Line's first espionage film was *Mission Bloody Mary* (a.k.a. *Agente 077 Missione Bloody Mary*, 1965), in which she played Dr. Freeman. The story has the Chinese, in a bid for world domination, steal an atomic bomb; secret agent Malloy (Ken Clark) is assigned to retrieve it. In the enjoyable but hackneyed romp *Operation: Poker* (a.k.a. *Operazione Poker*, 1965), a secret agent named Glen Foster (Roger Browne), a.k.a. Agent OS 14 of the CIA, investigates a fellow agent who is a gambler and a possible double agent, then goes on a hunt for a missing diplomat and battles Soviet spies. In the Spanish, French and Italian co-production *Cifrato Speciale* (a.k.a. *Message Chiffre*, 1966), Line appeared alongside Lang Jeffries, who starred as a special agent for the intelligence agency C.U.R.D.;

Helga Line, star of many European espionage and horror films.

Jeffries is sent to Istanbul to discover who has stolen a secret anti-gravity formula developed by scientists working with enemy agents. She reunited with Horror director Alberto De Martino for the kinetic Bond-type film *Special Mission Lady Chaplin* (a.k.a. *Missione Speciale Lady Chaplin*, 1966). In this elaborately designed espionage film, secret agent Dick Malloy (Ken Clark) investigates the disappearance of an atomic submarine and a secret organization that uses a deadly liquid. The film also featured Daniela Bianchi (of *From Russia with Love* fame).

In Europe the popularity of the adult comic strip (called "Fumetti" in Italy, the country where it was most popular), which featured nudity and violence, beget a whole subgenre of films featuring masked super villains. To make the theme more palatable to cinema audiences, moviemakers often added a dollop of goodness to these sinister, costumed anti-heroes. Line's first such film was *Mister X* (a.k.a. *Avenger X*, 1966), where the seemingly retired masked adventurer-soldier of fortune-sometime criminal named Mister X (Norman Clark, whose real name was Pier Paolo Capponi) is framed for the murder of a wealthy industrialist. Coming out of semi-retirement, Mister X must defeat the criminal gang responsible, which also happens to traffic in illegal drugs and weapons.

A much more prominent role awaited Helga Line in Sergio Grieco's *Password: Kill Agent Gordon* (a.k.a. *Password: Uccidere Agente Gordon*, 1967), a violent and nihilistic espionage film. An American agent (Roger Browne) investigates the murder of a spy informant, which leads to a criminal ring involved in smuggling drugs and weapons to third world countries. In the obscure Spanish spy film *Master Stroke in the Service of the Sifar* (a.k.a. *Colpo Sensazionale al Servizio del Sifar*, 1968) she appears in a minor role alongside the hero, played by Stan Cooper (whose real name is Stelvio Rossi).

With the popularity of the Italian thriller, Line made the big step and appeared, along with Carroll Baker and Erika Blanc, in Umberto Lenzi's *So Sweet, So Perverse* (a.k.a. *Cosi Dolce ... Cosi Perversa*, 1970) and had small roles in *My Dear Killer* (a.k.a. *Mio Cara Assassino*, 1971), and *House of Insane Women* (a.k.a. *Exorcism's Daughter*, 1971). A more prominent, though still minor, role was in *Horror Express* (a.k.a. *Panico en el Transiberio*, 1972), where she appeared alongside terror film screen icons Christopher Lee and Peter Cushing as a stowaway aboard a train harboring a bizarre alien creature.

Suddenly, out of the blue, Line seemed to have become a Spanish horror film queen and began to appear in a number of graphic horror movies. Among her horror credits are *The Mummy's Vengeance* (a.k.a. *La Venganza de la Momia*, 1973), in which she appeared as an Egyptologist. She had a cameo role as a high priestess in former Bond director Terence Young's *War Goddess* (a.k.a. *La Guerriere dal Seno Nudo–Le Ammazzoni*, a.k.a. *The Amazons*, 1974), a film in which the Amazons were depicted as nude fighting women. In recent years Helga Line teamed with former Italian screen beauty Karin Schubert in the erotic film *Black Venus* (a.k.a. *Venus Negra*, 1983). She then had a brief career revival, buoyed by her appearance in two films by the acclaimed Spanish filmmaker Pedro Almodovar, *Laberinto de Pasiones* in 1982 and *La Ley del Deseo* in 1986.

Other films include: *Kriminal* (1966), *Il Marchio di Kriminal* (1967), *I Leopardi di Churchill* (1970), *Buen Funeral, Amigos, Paga Sartana* (1970), *The Saga of the Draculas* (a.k.a. *La Saga de los Draculas*, 1972), *El Espanto Surge de los Tumbas* (a.k.a. *Horror Rises from the Tomb*, 1973), *The Vampire's Night Orgy* (a.k.a. *La Orgia Nocturna de los Vampiros*, a.k.a. *Orgy of the Vampires*, 1973), *Santo vs. Dr. Death* (a.k.a. *Santo Contra el Doctor Muerte*, a.k.a. *Masked Man Strikes Again*, 1973), *Asesino de Munecas* (1975), *China 9, Liberty 37* (1978), *Estigma* (1979), *Black Candles* (a.k.a. *Los Ritos Sexuales del Diablo*, 1980), *Madame Olga's Pupils* (a.k.a. *Las Alumnas de Madame Olga*, 1980) and *El Aliento del Diablo* (1993).

Sue Lloyd

Born in Aldenburgh, Suffolk, England, on August 7, 1939, lovely Sue Lloyd began acting at an early age with appearances (uncredited) on British television programs. One of her first films is the movie *Seven Ways from Sundown* (1960). The lithe, blonde actress appeared in a variety of roles during the next several years, from playing the damsel in distress in the Hammer Film production *Hysteria* (1964) to a guest appearance in two unrelated episodes of the popular British espionage program *The Avengers* ("The Murder Market" and "A Surfeit of H20," both 1965).

After appearing in number of episodes of British television programs, including "The Height of Fashion" (1963) on *The Sentimental Agent* and three appearances on *The Saint*, starring Roger Moore as agent Simon Templar—"Luella" (1/23/64), "The High Fence" (2/20/64), playing a gorgeous movie star who dates Templar, and "The Revolution Racket" (11/5/64)— Lloyd gained recognition (as a brunette) in the classic spy film *The Ipcress File* (1965). In this thriller, a British intelligence agent, Harry Palmer (Michael Caine), who was also a former black marketeer and opportunist during the war, is pressed into service when a fellow agent is killed and the scientist he had been guarding is kidnapped and brainwashed. Palmer is directed to track down the murderous double agent (Nigel Green) responsible. In *The Ipcress File* Lloyd makes her first appearance in a Palmer film as a secretary/agent who shares his bed briefly. In the obscure *The Return of Mr. Moto* (1965), a low-budget British espionage film with Henry Silva as Mr. Moto, Lloyd appears as an attractive cipher when the Oriental Interpol policeman investigates insurance fraud and possible enemy agent tampering in the destruction of valuable oil fields.

On television Lloyd appeared in episodes of the series *The Baron* (as Cordelia Winfield), assisting art dealer, adventurer and Scotland Yard operative John Mannering (Steve Forrest, Dana Andrews' younger brother) in his adventures. The

In *The Ipcress File* (Universal, 1965) Sue Lloyd played Jean Courtney, the resourceful secretary/ agent who bedded agent Harry Palmer.

show lasted only one year (1966–1967) but racked up 30 episodes in its brief run. In one feature film version of the series, titled *Mystery Island* (1966), Mannering discovers enemy plans to steal a U.S. space capsule by foreign agents. Another feature film version of the series (like *Mystery Island*, also taken from a two-part episode of the show and then marketed to American theaters and television), *The Man in the Looking Glass*

(1968), has Mannering (Forrest) masquerading as a gangster in order to thwart the theft of Britain's crown jewels by yet more foreign agents. Novelist John Creasy, using a pseudonym, created the main character of The Baron.

In 1968 Sue Lloyd co-starred with horror film veteran Peter Cushing in the brutal *Corruption*, the tale of a mild-mannered surgeon who, tortured by guilt, sinks into murder and madness in an attempt to restore the ruined face of his bitter fiancée. She followed this role with an appearance in Mick Jagger's film debut, *Ned Kelly* (1970), about the Australian outlaw. A minor role followed in *Percy* (1971), the now nearly forgotten British film about a man who has the world's first penile transplant (it's a big one, hence all the women, including Lloyd, chase after him for the length of the movie).

Though she was very active in British films, Lloyd still found time to grace the small screen. She continued her string of guest shots begun in 1964 on *The Saint* in "The Man Who Liked Lions" (11/18/66), "Simon and Delilah" (3/24/67), "Island of Chance" (4/7/67) and "The Time to Die" (11/10/68). Other credits include "Black Out" (4/27/69) on *Department S* and "Take Seven" (10/1/71) on *The Persuaders* where Danny Wilde (Tony Curtis) and Lord Brett Sinclair (Roger Moore) investigate the reappearance of a young woman's supposedly dead brother who has sole claim on his parents' estate. Also in 1971, Sue Lloyd (performing the role of Hannah Wild) debuted in a (short-lived) stage play entitled *The Avengers*, based on the popular television program of the same name. Actor Simon Oates played the role of John Steed (Oates had appeared in at least four episodes of the original program upon which this production was based).

A more reserved role awaited Lloyd in the serious espionage drama *Innocent Bystanders* (1973), a film about a Russian scientist who escapes from a Soviet prison camp and the British, Russian and U.S. agents seeking him out before his former comrades order his death. The British agent (Stanley Baker) is a shaky senior operative who was tortured on a recent assignment but seeks reinstatement with all honors, so he tackles the case and involves a seemingly innocent bystander (Geraldine Chaplin) into the spy game.

Lloyd seemed to have disappeared from feature films for a few years but returned in director Lindsay Shonteff's adult-themed James Bond spoof *Number One of the Secret Service* (1977). The next year she appeared in *The Revenge of the Pink Panther* (1978), the weakest of Blake Edward's Inspector Clouseau films starring Peter Sellers.

In the early nineties Sue Lloyd reunited with *Ipcress File* co-star Michael Caine for two more additions to the series. She returned to her original role as Harry Palmer's amour briefly in the 1995 Canadian TV movie *Bullet to Beijing* (a.k.a. *Len Deighton's Bullet to Beijing*). Her memoir *It Seemed Like a Good Idea at the Time* was released in 1998. She passed away on October 20, 2011.

Other films include: *Attack on the Iron Coast* (1968), *That Riviera Touch* (1968), *That's Your Funeral* (1974), *The Stud* (1978), *Rough Cut* (1980), *Eat the Rich* (1987) and *UFO* (1994).

Beba Loncar

Beba Loncar was born in Belgrade, Yugoslavia, on April 28, 1943. The buxom blonde actress appeared in local Slav productions beginning with *The Ninth Circle* (a.k.a. *Deviti Krug*), her first film role, in 1960.

Loncar made several more Yugoslavian films before she landed a co-starring role in the American big-budget adventure movie *The Long Ships* (1964). In that film, two Viking brothers (Richard Widmark and Russ Tamblyn) steal a Norse king's funeral ship and kidnap his daughter (Loncar) to head off in search of the "Mother of Voices," a huge solid-gold bell. Along the way the Vikings have to contend with a Moor prince (Sidney Poitier). In this violent and sadistic adventure film, Loncar came across as a beauty onscreen. However, her acting took a back seat to the testosterone performances of the chiefly all-male cast.

In 1965 Beba Loncar appeared in *Slalom*. In the role of Helen, she co-starred with former Bond girl Daniela Bianchi in this tale about a newlywed (Vittorio Gassman) and his friend (Adolfo Celli) who become involved with a gang of deadly counterfeiters intent on flooding the U.S. economy with phony cash. Gassman, Celli and Bianchi travel the globe, from ski resorts to the Egyptian desert, in this adventure comedy that sometimes spoofs the Bond films. In *The Fuller Report* (a.k.a. *Rapporto Fuller, Base Stoccolma*, 1966) she starred as a Russian ballerina (named Svetlana) who becomes embroiled in an intended assassination plot of the President of the U.S., who is about to attend a World Health Organization meeting in Stockholm. Former secret agent (and racecar driver) Dick Worth (Ken Clark) saves the day—and the life of Loncar's gorgeous dancer.

In the tongue-in-cheek spy romp *Lucky, the Inscrutable* (a.k.a. *Lucky, el Intrepido*, 1967), Loncar co-stars along with the Italian beauty Rosalba Neri. Spanish director Jess Franco's film stars Ray Danton as "Lucky the Inscrutable," a James Bond–style secret agent assigned the task of locating a counterfeiting factory. During the course of the film, "Lucky" battles nefarious enemy agents and encounters a bevy of beautiful women, all seeking to seduce him.

Some Girls Do (1969) was the second British film in the late sixties to feature the Bulldog Drummond character (as played by Richard Johnson). In this sequel to *Deadlier Than the Male* (1966), Drummond once again confronts super villain Carl Peterson (James Villiers in this film, and Nigel Greene in the prequel) who this time is sabotaging new modernized aircraft. Drummond, as always, finds much time to romance the lovely ladies in the cast, including Daliah Lavi and Loncar as the deadly and voluptuous duo Helga and Pandora, two femme assassins who delight in seducing then murdering their male victims. Loncar's Pandora seems to be the less vicious of the two female killers but delights in sexually enticing her intended victims with her (usually scantily-clad) body and a strange-looking camera that hypnotizes its victims with a bright flash. Once the men have been incapacitated, Helga and Pandora go to work.

Beba Loncar spent much of the seventies and early eighties acting in Italian sex comedies, dramas and the occasional thriller. Her last role of note was in *Don't*

Beba Loncar (right) as the giddy, deadly assassin Pandora in *Some Girls Do* (United Artists, 1969), with Daliah Lavi (Helga) and Richard Johnson (Bulldog Drummond). (*Courtesy of Michael Monahan*)

Look in the Attic (a.k.a. *La Ville delle Anime Maldette*, 1981), an Italian horror thriller where, as Elisa, the female cousin of two strange brothers, she inherits a supposedly haunted mansion only to learn that she has been chosen to bear the child of an unholy incubus.

Other films include: *Massacre in the Black Forrest* (1965), *Interrabang* (1969), *Who Killed the Prosecutor and Why?* (a.k.a. *Terza Ipotesi Su un Caso di Perfetto Strategia Crimianle*, 1972), *The Last Decameron* (a.k.a. *Decameron No. 3*, 1972), *La Polizia Ordina: Sparate Ha Vista* (1976) and *Sunday Lovers* (1981).

Tina Louise

Slinky redhead Tina Louise was born Tina Blacker on February 11, 1934, in New York City. Her parents were divorced when Louise was very young, and she attended private boarding schools after her mother's remarriage. She was already an accomplished singer and nightclub performer (with the revue *Musical Comedy with a Latin Beat*) before she became a star on Broadway as Appasionata Von Climax in *Lil' Abner*. Hollywood soon beckoned and she made her film debut in the much sought after role of Griselda in the film version of Erskine Caldwell's *God's Little Acre* (1958). Louise wowed the critics as the earthy farm nymph and shared the Golden Globe Award for "Most Promising Newcomer—Female" with Linda Cristal and Susan Kohner. Dramatic roles followed in *The Trap* (1959), *Day of the Outlaw* (1959) and *The Hangman* (1959), but none of these films were major hits.

Feeling stifled by Hollywood typecasting, Tina Louise fled to Europe in 1960. She settled in Italy and, after being cast as a reporter based on George Sand, a French journalist who dressed as a man, in Roberto Rossellini's *Viva L'Italia* (1960), she toiled in less than spectacular Italian epics, including *The Siege of Syracuse* (1960). Her first spy role was as Alexandra Bastegar, a Nazi operative who infiltrates a U.S. army troop stationed in the Vosge Mountains, in *Armored Command* (1961), co-starring Howard Keel and Burt Reynolds (in his feature movie debut). Louise returned to the U.S. in 1963 and was accepted as a member of the Actor's Studio, studying with Lee Strasberg.

She was again cast as a sexy spy in *Fanfare for a Death Scene* (1964), which was originally produced as an episode of *Kraft Suspense Theatre* but never aired. Instead, it was released theatrically overseas. An intended pilot, this was an ass-kicking, violent and intelligent spy drama (highlighted by a great jazzy score by Al Hirt) that was deemed too graphic for television. Richard Egan starred as a secret agent searching for a missing scientist who invented a secret formula sought after by enemy factions. Also featured were Burgess Meredith, Ed Asner and Telly Savalas.

While appearing on Broadway in the musical *Fade Out, Fade In*, with Carol Burnett, Louise got the call to co-star in the farcical comedy series *Gilligan's Island* in 1964. The idea of a show revolving around seven shipwrecked castaways on an island seemed limited, but Louise accepted it for the money, hoping it would last only 13 weeks. However, the show surprised all the pundits and was a smash (with the audience, but not the critics). *Gilligan's Island* made Tina Louise a household name, and the part of the sexy but dumb movie star Ginger Grant was a role she would forever be identified with, much to her chagrin.

After the cancellation of *Gilligan's Island* in the summer of 1967, Louise set about getting varied roles with vigor. Among her TV guest shots from this period were episodes of *Bonanza*, *Love, American Style*, *Ironside* and an early appearance as Anna Martine on *It Takes a Thief* in "Totally by Design" (2/20/68). In this episode agent Al Mundy (Robert Wagner) masquerades as a couturier in the palace of a Middle Eastern president to try to gain access to the president's Swiss bank account to remove the money before he can use it for aggression against his neighboring countries.

In 1969 Tina Louise co-starred on the big screen in the last Matt Helm adventure, *The Wrecking Crew*. As the exotic Lola Medina, Louise is onscreen for a short amount of time but definitely leaves an impression. (*Variety* remarked that Louise "appears briefly but effectively.") Lola is the jilted ex-lover of Count Massimo Contini (Nigel Green), who has hijacked a billion dollars of gold intended for the British economy. She "accidentally" bumps into Dean Martin's Matt Helm in his hotel's lobby as he is checking in and whispers to him to meet later at her apartment. Unbeknownst to Lola, Contini's new girlfriend, played by Elke Sommer, watches her. At her apartment, between the romantic banter with

A determined-looking Tina Louise as the Mata Hari–like spy in *Armored Command* (Allied Artists, 1960).

Helm, Lola agrees to give him information about Operation Rainbow, but in return she demands "Massimo Contini destroyed and one million dollars." Before Helm can answer, Lola is killed opening a bomb-rigged bottle of Scotch.

Tina Louise also appeared in the made-for-TV film *Call to Danger* (1973), a *Mission: Impossible* clone. That series' former star, Peter Graves, played a federal agent who enlists "ordinary" people to help find an underworld informer who has been kidnapped. Louise played a mobster's mistress whom Graves romances to get information. Directed by Tom Gries, the cast also included Michael Ansara, Ina Balin, Clu Gulager and Diana Muldaur.

While most of her fellow *Gilligan's Island* castaway's careers slowed during the seventies, Tina Louise kept right on working. Her acting skills were stretched playing an eclectic range of roles, including a "perfect" wife in *The Stepford Wives* (1975), a lesbian in *Death Scream* (1975—TV) and a tough Southern prison guard in *Nightmare in Badham County* (1975—TV).

During the eighties she got the opportunity to work with esteemed director Robert Altman in O.C. and Stiggs (1985), but the film was not a hit. During the nineties Louise authored the book *Sunday*, published by Golden Books, in which she recounted her childhood experiences growing up in a boarding school. Though she continues to write and act, most of Tina Louise's time is spent as a volunteer schoolteacher instructing children to read in New York City, where she currently resides.

Other films include: *The Warrior Empress* (1960), *For Those Who Think Young* (1964), *The Good Guys and the Bad Guys* (1969), *The Happy Ending* (1969), *How to Commit Marriage* (1969), *Mean Dog Blues* (1978), *Friendships, Secrets and Lies* (1979—TV), *The Day the Women Got Even* (1980—TV), *Dog Day* (1984), *Evils of the Night* (1985), *Johnny Suede* (1991), *Welcome to Woop Woop* (1997), *Little Pieces* (2000) and *Growing Down in Brooklyn* (2000).

Joanna Lumley

Joanna Lumley was born in Srinagar, Kashmir, India, on May 1, 1946. The daughter of a military career soldier, she lived her early childhood years in a variety of Asian and Middle Eastern countries before the family settled in England. Like many an aspiring actress, an early first love was ballet, but the lithesome blonde's attempt to enter the esteemed Royal Academy of Dramatic Arts was stalled when she failed to pass an audition.

Becoming a photographic, then fashion, model, Lumley soon graced many a magazine, her big break being a layout in *Queen* magazine. Shortly thereafter she studied acting more earnestly and never looked back. Her first role (uncredited) in a film was a bit part in the sexy spy movie *Some Girls Do* (1969), alongside stars Daliah Lavi, Beba Loncar and Richard Johnson. Lumley's first role of note (and credited this time) was in the James Bond film *On Her Majesty's Secret Service* (1969) as the English girl whom Bond (George Lazenby) beds in an attempt to seduce the women who are under the spell of his arch-rival, Blofeld (Telly Savalas).

Joanna Lumley appeared in many British television programs, among them *Are You Being Served?* and *The Morecambe and Wise Show*, but could be seen to better advantage in the sex comedy *Don't Just Lie There, Say Something* (1973). She also had a featured role in *The Satanic Rites of Dracula* (1973), in which she played Jessica Van Helsing, granddaughter of Professor Van Helsing (Peter Cushing), the esteemed vampire hunter who is still stalking his rival, Count Dracula (Christopher Lee), in the twentieth century.

In 1976 Lumley joined Patrick Macnee and Gareth Hunt in *The New Avengers*, a British, French and Canadian-produced series that attempted to rejuvenate the classic *Avengers* formula for the seventies. As Purdy, the glamorous agent who assists agents John Steed (Macnee) and Mike Gambit (Hunt) on a variety of missions, Lumley was certainly eye candy for the television audiences. Sadly, before the show could find its proper rhythm, it was canceled due to a lack of interest from CBS network programmers in the U.S. who con-

Joanna Lumley as Purdy in *The New Avengers* (TF1, 1976).

sidered it too violent (it debuted on late night television two years later).

Four years later she appeared on *Sapphire and Steel* (1979), one of the most bewildering, strange and perplexing fantasy series ever produced for television. Although extremely popular with British audiences upon its first transmission, the show never really caught on and was quickly canceled after it lost viewers. It didn't find a mass audience due to the Rubik's cube plotting of many of the episodes, which played around with the ideas of time continuums and fantasy, all within a detective and espionage show milieu.

Appearing in two *Pink Panther* films (after the death of series star Peter Sellers), *The Trail of the Pink Panther* (1983) and *The Curse of the Pink Panther* (1983), she failed to find a niche as a leading lady. But she found a number of good supporting roles in films such as *Shirley Valentine* (1988), *Cold Comfort Farm* (1995) and *James and the Giant Peach* (1996). Contemporary television audiences recall Joanna Lumley from her role as Patsy Stone, the aging, foul-mouthed, boozy former glamour girl from the very popular show *Absolutely Fabulous* (1992), which lasted several seasons, including a number of reunion specials and a feature film released in 2016.

Other credits include: *Tam Lin* (1969) *Games That Lovers Play* (1971), *Lady Chatterly vs. Fanny Hill* (1980), *The Weather in the Streets* (1983), *Prince Valiant* (1998), *Mad Cows* (1998), *A Rather English Marriage* (1998), *Maybe Baby* (2000) and *The Cat's Meow* (2001).

BarBara Luna

Actress BarBara Luna's career spans a staggering 52 years. Of Italian, Hungarian-Jewish, Spanish, Portuguese and Filipino descent, Luna (born on March 2, 1939, in New York City) has played a wide variety of Hispanic, Asian, Italian and other exotic roles on stage and screen. She made her Broadway debut in 1949, playing one of Ezio Pinza's French-speaking children in Rodgers and Hammerstein's *South Pacific*. After appearing in the Broadway stage productions of *The King and I* and *Teahouse of the August Moon*, Luna relocated to Hollywood in 1957. She made her film debut in *Tank Battalion* (1958), but garnered fine notices as the blind South Sea island girl Camille in *The Devil at Four O'Clock* (1961), starring Spencer Tracy and Frank Sinatra.

Luna's contribution to the spy genre was limited to the small screen, beginning with an early episode of *The Wild Wild West* entitled "The Night of the Deadly Bed" (9/24/65). While investigating the death of his contact, secret service agent James West (Robert Conrad) sees a beautiful Mexican woman (Luna) dancing the Flamenco. When she tells West her name is Gatita he says, "A little pussycat." Gatita retorts, "I promise I won't scratch." But she does. They share a shot of tequila up in her room, but Gatita has drugged the salt put on the rim of West's glass. He awakens just in time to escape from a descending bed of nails lowering to crush him. It turns out that Gatita is just one of many prisoners of Monsieur Flory (J. D. Cannon), an expatriate of France. He has concocted a wild scheme to take over Mexico while keeping the United States from interfering by destroying "with an engine of destruction" the main railroad lines, preventing troop movement.

Luna gives a fiery, though compassionate, performance in "The Night of the Deadly Bed" as a woman who will do anything to help her fellow villagers. It also afforded her an opportunity to display her dancing prowess. Robert Conrad gives an earnest performance, but he is best in the action and fighting scenes, and when disrobing to display his amazing muscled torso—all of which became staples of the series. BarBara Luna remembers that "Bob Conrad was adorable—very macho and very cute. We laughed a lot. I was married to Doug McClure at the time. I think because we were all buddies it made a big difference. In fact, he used to date Doug's first wife, who is one of my closest friends. I really liked Ross Martin too. He was a very caring human being. When he said, 'Good morning. How are you?' you knew he really meant it."

Luna guest starred in the role of Consuela, with Ed Asner and Nico Minardos, in the *Amos Burke, Secret Agent* episode "Nightmare in the Sun" (10/20/65). Gene Barry's Amos Burke gets himself thrown into prison to discover who masterminded the attempted assassination of a key political figure. Recalling this shoot, Luna states, "Gene Barry was a prima donna. He is the only actor that I had to get into a little snit about. I had a lot of dialog and business and he was sort of clowning around. I said to the director, 'When he's ready to work call me. I'll be in my trailer.' I had never done that in my life, and until this day it was the *only* time. I never knew what his reaction was and I didn't care. They eventually came and got me and we shot the scene. Today I am very friendly with Gene and his wife Ann. They are dear people."

Robert Conrad (James West) questions BarBara Luna (as the fiery Gatita) in "The Night of the Deadly Bed" episode on *The Wild Wild West* (Paramount Television, 1965).

The spy series *Mission: Impossible* cast BarBara Luna as an agent in two episodes. The first was "Elena," airing on 12/10/66 during the show's first season, which starred Steven Hill as IMF commander Dan Briggs. Luna played Elena Del Barra, assigned to stop enemy spies planning to infiltrate and take control of her country. Her masquerade is uncovered and she is brainwashed by the enemy. Her behavior shows signs of severe emotional disturbance. The IMF mission is to investigate and deprogram Elena. In this episode Luna gives a tour-de-force performance as Elena. However, personally she was disappointed in the episode "because it was too much of me. It was before they had the format of focusing on the team as a whole." As for interacting with the cast, Luna remarks, "Steven Hill was becoming a Rabbi at that time so it was hard because he couldn't work on Fridays because of his faith. But most of my scenes were with Martin Landau [Rollin Hand] who I loved working with. He is so funny—he's Mel Brooks. I am friendly with him to this day and I tell him that all of the time."

Luna's role as Marnya was mere window dressing in one of the best and last episodes of *The Man from U.N.C.L.E.* In "The Man from Thrush Affair" (12/4/67) Robert Vaughn gives one of his best performances as Napoleon Solo, who travels (solo, as David McCallum's Illya is nowhere to be found) to the island of Irbos to squelch THRUSH's $3 billion earthquake making machine. "When I saw this episode recently it looked like I was walking through it," remarks Luna. "I was very boring in it. I thought Robert Vaughn was very good though. As for acting with him, he is not unpleasant to work with, just aloof. When I see him at conventions, he still is very aloof, but I like him anyway."

Luna's final guest star turn in the spy genre was a second appearance on *Mission: Impossible*. She again played an IMF agent in the episode "Time Bomb" (12/21/69) during the series' fourth season. Luna was one of a number of actresses hired to fill the void left by Barbara Bain's departure. ("If I was a candidate to permanently replace Barbara Bain I didn't know it," says Luna.) As agent Wai Lee, she helped the IMF team stop scientist Anton Malek (Morgan Sterne) from turning a nuclear reactor into an atomic bomb to wipe out the capital of the Federated People's Republic and starting a war.

Luna remained very active during the seventies, appearing on such popular series as *Cannon*, *Kung Fu*, *The Six Million Dollar Man*, *ChiPs* and *Hawaii Five-0*. As in the sixties, Luna found her film roles scarce, but she chewed the scenery when cast as Cat, a hot-tempered convict, in *The Concrete Jungle* (1982). Luna stole the film from star Jill St. John and walked away with acting honors via a truly entertaining performance. She continued in the villainess mode on daytime television playing Inga on *Search for Tomorrow* (1984) and the evil Maria Roberts on *One Life to Live* (1986–1987).

Today BarBara Luna looks better than ever and is still a very sexy lady. Warm and friendly, she is a favorite at sci-fi and autograph conventions (due to her performance as Marlene Moreau in *Star Trek*'s classic episode "Mirror, Mirror"), making the most intimidated fans feel comfortable enough to talk with her. She continues to act and was most recently seen as Sydney Jacobs on the soap *Sunset Beach*, and in the Showtime original movie *Noreiga: God's Favorite* (2000).

Other films include: *Elmer Gantry* (1960), *Five Weeks in a Balloon* (1962), *Dime with a Halo* (1963), *Mail Order Bride* (1964), *Ship of Fools* (1965), *Synanon* (1965), *Firecreek* (1968), *The Gatling Gun* (1972), *Brenda Starr* (1976—TV), *Woman in the Rain* (1976), *Lady Against the Odds* (1992—TV) and *Fools Paradise* (1997).

Deanna Lund

Sexy blonde Deanna Lund is best remembered by sixties fans for her fiery redheaded turn as Valerie Scott in the hit sci-fi TV series *Land of the Giants*. As the mini-skirted jet setter, Lund left an indelible impression, especially on male viewers, as her conniving but endearing character is menaced by everything from giant people to giant cats and gorillas. In feature films Lund excelled at playing the bad girl. Never the ingenue, she could always be counted on to give convincing performances as a callous young girl.

Lund was born on May 30, 1937, in Oak Park, Illinois. Her family moved to Florida when Lund was a child. Being very introverted, Lund was convinced by her dad to take a drama course in college. Soon she was starring in a number of university plays, including *Bus Stop* and *The Crucible*. Her acting career was put on hold after she married a rodeo rider. Though the marriage was short-lived, Lund became the mother of two children. After her divorce she relocated to Miami to get away from her ex-husband. Work as a weather girl led to film roles as the "other woman" in *Run for Your Wife* (1965) and *Johnny Tiger* (1966).

Arriving in Hollywood in 1965, Deanna Lund's sojourn into the world of suave secret agents began with *Dr. Goldfoot and the Bikini Machine* (1965). Vincent Price played the mad doctor who plans on taking over the world by having his army of female robots seduce rich and powerful men. Frankie Avalon is the inept secret agent who stumbles onto the plot as robot Susan Hart is sent after millionaire Dwayne Hickman. Lund was one of Dr. Goldfoot's bikini-clad robots. She played No. 8, who was assigned to marry and eliminate a rich Italian diplomat. "Frankie Avalon and Susan Hart were very sweet," remarks Lund. "Norman Taurog was a fine director. However, I wasn't very happy standing around in a gold bikini for six weeks, but I needed the money. I got to know Vincent Price better while attending various sci-fi conventions with him years later. He was a very pleasant man."

Lund had another small role (as Miss Sweet, a lab assistant) in the spy film *Dimension 5* (1966), starring Jeffrey Hunter and France Nuyen. Lund's character works with the scientist who creates the time-travel belts allowing secret agents Justin Power (Hunter) and Kitty (Nuyen) to go a few weeks into the future to save Los Angeles from an A-bomb attack. During this period Lund played bit roles in many films. So it is no surprise that she cannot recall anything particular about *Dimension 5*. However, she found herself in a humiliating situation years later. "I saw France Nuyen at a sci-fi convention and was so embarrassed because I didn't remember working with her. I remembered Jeffrey Hunter, who was such a nice guy, but France was a blank." In the *Amos Burke, Secret Agent* episode entitled "Peace, It's a Gasser" (11/3/65), Lund portrayed a WAC assigned to an Air Force Base where Gene Barry's Burke suspects a terrorist group will attack.

The spy film *Out of Sight* (1966) featured Deanna Lund in a more prominent role. ("This was fun and I didn't have to wear a bikini!" exclaims Lund.) As one of the "Out of Sight Girls" she was the secret weapon of Big D (John Lawrence) and his last resort to eliminate agent John Stamp, who is being impersonated by his bungling butler, Homer (Jonathan Daly). With flaming red hair and clad in a black leotard under a see-through dress, Lund is a knockout as the seductive Tuff Bod. After being released from her holding tank, she says, "Gee, it's nice to be out again." When she is told her assignment is to kill special agent John Stamp, she remarks, "Groovy! I've always wondered—now I'll find out." Big D asks, "What is that?" Tuff Bod replies, "What makes him so special." Snooping around Big D's, Homer stumbles across Tuff Bod "selling Girl Scout cookies." While Homer trades witty repartee with Tuff Bod, Big D's henchman Huh! (Norman Grabowski) sneaks up behind Homer and knocks him unconscious. He awakens shackled to a perpetual tape deck that plays the same song over and over, driving him to lose his sanity. Big D leaves Tuff Bod to watch over Homer as a horrible 1920s tune plays incessantly. She tires of the song and puts on a groovier tune to dance to. When she releases Homer to do the Frug with her, he tricks her, straps her to Big D's device, and escapes.

Lund continued playing supporting parts until her role as a lesbian stripper in the Frank Sinatra detective drama *Tony*

Deanna Lund, as Tuff Bod (left), tries to block out the sound from a 1920s record as Jonathan Daly (center, agent John Stamp) is tortured by (from left) Jimmy Murphy (Mousie), Norman Grabowski (Huh!) and John Lawrence (Big D) in *Out of Sight* (Universal, 1966).

Rome (1967) brought her to the attention of producer Irwin Allen. Without even meeting with her, Allen signed Lund to play intergalactic castaway Valerie Scott in his fourth series, *Land of the Giants*. Starring Gary Conway, Don Matheson (who became husband number two), Kurt Kaszner and Don Marshall, *Land of the Giants* premiered in September of 1969 and ran for two seasons. Budgeted at $250,000 per episode, at that time it was the most expensive TV show on the air. Due to its high costs in creating elaborate special effects, ABC-TV passed on a third season.

After *Land of the Giants* was cancelled, Deanna Lund was purportedly almost signed for the spy series *Search* in the role of Gloria Harding, a telemetry specialist, in 1972. However, a "misunderstanding" with one of the show's producers led to Angel Tompkins being cast instead. Undeterred, Lund continued acting throughout the seventies and eighties. However, she deserved better roles than what were offered. Among the highlights were playing a cave girl who invents the first kiss on a very funny episode of *Love, American Style*, and bad girl Peggy Lowell on the daytime soap *General Hospital*. Later she was able to display her comedic talents opposite Jerry Lewis in the comedy *Hardly Working* (1981).

Today Deanna Lund is as gorgeous as ever and should be getting many more acting offers than she does. To keep busy between roles she is a world traveler, an author (*Valerie in Giantland*), a songwriter and a fan favorite at autograph shows and science fiction conventions across the country. She can also be seen on the Home Shopping Network plugging Forever Spring, and she has a very active fan club, called Friends of Deanna Lund, Inc., which promotes the star and her non-profit organization Victims of Violence No More.

Other films include: *Once Upon a Coffee House* (1965), *Sting of Death* (1966), *Paradise, Hawaiian Style* (1966), *Panic in the City* (1968), *Hustle* (1975), *Hanging by a Thread* (1979—TV), *Stick* (1985), *Witch Story* (1989), *Elves* (1989), *Red Wind* (1991—TV), *Roots of Evil* (1992) and *Obsession* (1992—TV).

Carol Lynley

With her blonde hair, blue eyes and porcelain complexion, Carol Lynley was one of the early sixties' most popular actresses. She was born Carole Jones on February 13, 1942, in New York City. At age seven she began ballet training and by ten she was modeling, quickly becoming one of the highest paid pre-teen models in the world. Her first professional acting gig was at age 12 in the touring company of *Anniversary Waltz*. Work on many live television productions followed before she made her Broadway debut in *The Potting Shed*, for which she won a 1957 Theatre World Award for her performance. She made her film debut in Walt Disney's *The Light in the Forest* (1958), for which her performance earned her a Golden Globe nomination for "Most Promising Newcomer—Female." Soon after, Carol Lynley returned to New York to play a pregnant unwed teen who undergoes an abortion in the revered Broadway play *Blue Denim*, and she repeated her stage role in the watered down film version (she is "saved" before she can go through with the "dirty" deed). *Blue Denim* (1959) was a major hit, and Lynley won kudos (including a second Golden Globe nomination) for her poignant performance. In 1961 she scored another box-office bullseye starring as Allison McKenzie in *Return to Peyton Place*, for which she was voted a "Star of Tomorrow."

After a brief hiatus from acting (Lynley had a short-lived marriage to Fox public relations manager Mike Selsman beginning in 1960), Lynley returned to the big screen, most notably in *Under the Yum Yum Tree* (1963) with Jack Lemmon, *The Cardinal* (1963) and Otto Preminger's cult mystery *Bunny Lake Is Missing* (1965).

In 1966 Carol Lynley relocated to England to remain close to boyfriend David Frost (their on-and-off relationship lasted for 18 years). While in Great Britain she appeared in *Danger Route* (1968), starring Richard Johnson and Barbara Bouchet. Johnson played Jonas Wilde, a karate expert and British secret service agent ("He is a weapon," the tag line proclaimed) licensed to kill who wants to resign, with Lynley as his beautiful girlfriend Jocelyn, a market researcher. Wilde's superior, Canning (Harry Andrews), assigns him to one last mission—eliminate a Czech defector being held by the Americans. Wilde completes his assignment, but CIA agent Lucinda (Sam Wanamaker) captures him and

Carol Lynley, as the double-crossing Jocelyn, is about to meet her maker at the hands of Richard Johnson (agent Jonas Salk) in *Danger Route* (United Artists, 1968).

informs him that someone is eliminating British agents. When Canning turns up missing, Wilde journeys to the Channel Islands. Perplexed how the enemy knew his every move throughout his mission, Wilde comes to the realization that Jocelyn is an informant. When he returns home she serves him a deadly cocktail, but Wilde dispatches her with a karate chop to the neck. The missing Canning turns up alive and convinces Wilde to remain an agent.

Danger Route was an intriguing and

serious spy thriller in the vein of *The Quiller Memorandum*. *Film Daily* called it a "toned-down James Bond yarn." Director Seth Holt does a deft job of keeping the action moving, though the plot becomes a bit confusing after awhile. Costumed in mod mini-skirts and hairstyles, Carol Lynley looked gorgeous. Though second-billed, she is missing throughout the middle of the film, with only two scenes of her at a wild party talking on the phone with Johnson. Nevertheless, Leonard Maltin, writing in *Leonard Maltin's Movie and Video Guide*, remarked, "Appearance (in both senses of the word) of Lynley and Bouchet give a little boost to typical secret agent tale with several plot twists."

Carol Lynley switched sides for *The Helicopter Spies* (1968), which was the feature film version of *The Man from U.N.C.L.E.* two-part episode "The Prince of Darkness Affair" (10/2 and 10/9/67), written by Dean Hargrove. THRUSH is after a ray generator called the Thermal Prism, and Waverly recruits master criminal Luther Sebastian (Bradford Dillman) to aid agents Solo and Illya in retrieving it. But Sebastian (the leader of a religious sect called The Third Way) plans to snatch the Prism to control the balance of power in the world. Lynley plays the episode's innocent, Annie, who stumbles into the plot determined to get Napoleon to lead her to Sebastian because "my fiancé Hugh Winslow of the Bakersfield Winslows is in a Turkish prison because Sebastian framed him for a murder *he committed*. I've spent a whole year collecting evidence. I must free my poor Hugh from that awful prison." The episode's running gag is that the brothers (each played by H. M. Wynant) of Hugh's cellmate (also framed by Sebastian) accompany her, and as one is killed off another takes his place. The U.N.C.L.E. agents are forced to bring Annie along, but she becomes more of a thorn-in-the-side with her interference. Lynley looks fantastic in this role and gives a delightful performance as the misguided Annie. Her performance is truly a standout.

Lynley also guest starred on *It Takes a Thief* in the episode titled "Boom at the Top" (2/25/69). At a lavish high-fashion gala, SIA operative Al Mundy (Robert Wagner) must flush out a small-time thief who has inadvertently stolen a microdot. The question for Mundy is which thief (Carol Lynley, Roddy McDowall or Barry Sullivan) has the object. Mundy also has to break the fail-safe mechanism of an armed briefcase, shackled to a fellow agent, containing plans for a Polaris missile. The exquisite gowns and furs worn by Lynley were designed by Luis Estevez, who makes a cameo as himself.

Carol Lynley is best remembered for her effective performance as terrified pop singer Nonnie Parry in the granddaddy of all disaster movies, *The Poseidon Adventure* (1972). Despite her fear of heights, she did all her own stunts and even warbled the Oscar-winning song "The Morning After." Unfortunately, the SS *Poseidon* wasn't the only thing that sank into the ocean. Undeservedly, Lynley's film career went with it. She never appeared in a major studio production again, and she was relegated to low-budget features, made-for-TV films and episodic television (she holds the dubious record for most guest stints on *Fantasy Island*). Lynley had better luck on stage, receiving some of her finest notices when she replaced Sandy Dennis in the hit 1975 Broadway comedy *Absurd Person Singular*, co-starring Geraldine Page.

During this period the most memorable film performance Carol Lynley gave (which took advantage of her flair for light comedy) was as Annabelle West in Radley Metzger's remake of *The Cat and the Canary* (1978), also starring Michael Callan, Honor Blackman and Wendy Hiller. Unfortunately, major distribution problems prevented this surprisingly entertaining film from being released in the U.S. until 1982.

In the eighties and nineties Carol Lynley popped up now and again in direct-to-video drivel such as *Dark Tower* (1988), with Michael Moriarty, and *Spirits* (1993), with Erik Estrada. Undaunted, the hardworking Lynley keeps persevering and recently played the tired manager of a motel in the feature *Drowning on Dry Land* (2000), starring Barbara Hershey. She currently lives in Malibu, has participated in a number of AIDS benefits and is a regular at autograph conventions throughout the country.

Other films include: *Hound-Dog Man* (1959), *The Last Sunset* (1961), *The Stripper* (1963), *The Pleasure Seekers* (1964), *The Shuttered Room* (1968), *The Maltese Bippy* (1969), *Once You Kiss a Stranger* (1969), *The Immortal* (1969—TV), *Norwood* (1970), *The Night Stalker* (1972—TV), *The Four Deuces* (1975), *Bad Georgia Road* (1977), *Fantasy Island* (1977—TV), *Vigilante* (1983), *Blackout* (1988), *Neon Signs* (1997) and *A Light in the Forest* (2002).

Arlene Martel

A graduate of the High School of the Performing Arts, Arlene Martel (born Arline Sax on April 14, 1936, in New York City) is one beauty whose talent was never fully appreciated by Hollywood. Despite winning her school's highest acting honor, Martel was relegated to the small screen upon her arrival in Tinseltown. Undeterred, she gave her acting all in standout episodes of some of the sixties' most beloved fantasy programs, including *The Outer Limits*, *Star Trek* and *Bewitched*. Dubbed "the Chameleon" by honchos at Universal Studios due to her expertise with foreign dialects, Martel had a special quality also perfect for television's spy programs, where her roles ranged from helpful secret agents to murderous terrorists.

Arlene Martel had a number of television credits behind her under her real name (including *The Twilight Zone*, *The Untouchables* and *Route 66*) before she changed her name and landed a supporting role as the glamorous Gemma Lusso in "The King of Knaves Affair" (12/22/64) during the first season of *The Man from U.N.C.L.E.* This episode featured Paul Stevens as Fasik el Pasad, a deposed ruler of an unidentified country who is constructing an army of notable crime figures to help him regain power. Robert Vaughn and David McCallum, as U.N.C.L.E. agents Napoleon Solo and Illya Kuryakin, are assigned to infiltrate Pasad's operation and stop him. "What I remember most about David McCallum was his hair," says Martel with a laugh. "It was very silky and blonde and I wished that mine looked like that! He seemed very preoccupied in doing the job well."

Additional roles followed for Martel on *The Wild Wild West* and *It Takes a Thief*. In "The Night of the Circus of Death" (11/3/67) on *The Wild Wild West*, Martel played Erika, a lion tamer. ("I remember I had to wear a very abbreviated costume. But I was cast in many things in that way. I guess my figure must have been pretty good in those days.") Erika is entangled in a counterfeit money operation also involving the director of the Denver Mint's wife, his assistant, a circus performer and a fashion designer. West and Gordon are as-

Publicity of Arlene Martel.

signed to track down the source before they undermine the U.S. economy. In "Guess Who's Coming to Rio?" (1/7/69) on *It Takes a Thief*, she played a beautiful Russian named Katrina Malenski. ("I wore a slinky black lace slip in this role and had a lot of running scenes in the rain. In fact, in most of the spy TV shows that I did I had a lot of running scenes.") Katrina ruins agent Al Mundy's (Robert Wagner) Rio vacation with Contessa del Mundo (Dana Wynter) when she asks Mundy to help her defect. "Robert Wagner was a darling man to work with," remarks Martel. "He was very generous and kind. Alejandro Rey was also very pleasant. I remember that he had an intriguing accent and I would listen intently to him speak, in case I was cast in another Hispanic role."

Martel also had a knack for comedy and wasn't restricted to doing drama. She made guest appearances on such TV sitcoms as *I Dream of Jeannie*, *The Flying Nun* and *The Monkees* (playing a Russian agent in "The Spy Who Came in from the Cool"), and she had a recurring role as helpful Allied spy Tiger on *Hogan's Heroes*. Her most memorable roles during this period were the evil witch Malvina on *Bewitched* and T'Pring, Spock's intended on *Star Trek*. With her exotic looks, the big screen never knew what to do with her, as her only major film role during the sixties was a biker chick in *Angels from Hell* (1968).

Arlene Martel returned to the spy genre playing a fanatical revolutionary named Atheda in "Terror" (2/15/70) on *Mission: Impossible*. Atheda was the girlfriend of ruthless terrorist Ismet El Kabir (Michael Tolan), condemned to death for mass murder in the Middle Eastern country of Suroq. However, he is about to be pardoned by Ahned Vassier (David Opatoshu), a high ranking official and secret supporter of Kabir's. The IMF's mission is to see that Kabir is never released. To do that they begin playing Atheda, Kabir and Vassier against one another in an elaborate web of lies and deceit. Though she was playing a tough, determined woman, Martel says, laughing, "Every time I had to fire my gun I jumped about twelve feet in the air. I thought, 'This is not going to look authentic.' I had to try to find a way to control my reaction to the sound of the gun. I guess I mastered it because the director, Marvin Chomsky, seemed pleased. Marvin was quite wonderful. He really allowed me to "explore the moment" to the degree that I could. Not many TV directors were concerned about the actor's performance. But Marvin was very supportive."

Her final spy appearance was in an episode of *The Delphi Bureau*, which, along with the spy show *Assignment: Vienna*, was one of the three rotating series under the umbrella title *The Men*. Laurence Luckinbill starred in *The Delphi Bureau* as Glenn

Garth Gregory, one of the secret agency's top agents who reports directly to the president and whose only contact is Anne Jeffreys as Sybil Van Loween, an agent posing as a Washington society matron. In Martel's episode, entitled "The Terror Broker Project" (3/17/73), also guest starring William Windom and Sharon Acker, a government agent named Quick (Dean Jagger) plants Gregory into a group of executioners nicknamed the "Four White Camellias" to uncover the name of their next intended target.

Martel continued acting steadily through the early eighties—from making three appearances on *Columbo*, starring Peter Falk, to playing an INTERPOL agent on *The Six Million-Dollar Man* to playing an Irish convict named Adulteress on *Battlestar Galactica*. She also appeared in a few TV movies and had the dubious honor of appearing in the off-the-wall musical *Chatterbox* (1977) about a talking vagina. A few years later she took a hiatus from her career to devote herself to her family. Now that her children are all grown and have "left the nest," in 2001, Arlene Martel began acting again (the video *Star Trek: Of Gods and Men*) and writing too co-authoring the screenplay *Whisper Into My Good Ear* with Joseph Brutsman. She passed away on August 12, 2014.

Other films include: *The James Dean Story* (1957—documentary), *The Glass Cage* (1964), *Adventures of Nick Carter* (1972—TV), *Indict and Convict* (1973—TV), *Conspiracy of Terror* (1975—TV), *Dracula's Dog* (1978) and *The Day the Loving Stopped* (1981—TV).

Marlyn Mason

Perky Marlyn Mason could sing and dance, but, unfortunately, she came to Hollywood at a time when the musical was a dying breed. This didn't stop this talented brunette, however, from getting work in varied roles. Mason was born on August 7, 1940, in San Fernando, California. At age nine she was enrolled in singing and dancing classes, and later was accepted into the children's wing of the Players Ring Theatre. Before her eighteenth birthday she was appearing on stage in such shows as *Cinderella*, *Heidi* and *Tom Sawyer*. During this time, Mason also began to land acting roles on television's *Matinee Theater*. After graduating high school in 1958, Mason worked as a dancer for Harold Minsky at the Dunes in Las Vegas, where she met her first husband. After her marriage dissolved, she returned to Los Angeles in 1962 to join *The Billy Barnes Revue*. She won raves for her "Pink Pussycat" routine, and the nonstop television offers came rolling in.

With her great mod sixties look and lively personality, Marlyn Mason was ripe for the spy genre. Appearing in over 100 television programs during the sixties, including *Dr. Kildare*, *Bonanza*, *The Rogues*, *Ben Casey* and *The Fugitive*, it is understandable that Mason cannot remember much about her first guest shot on *The Man from U.N.C.L.E.* in "The Fiddlesticks Affair" (1/18/65). As the naïve innocent, Susan Callaway, Mason is recruited by U.N.C.L.E.

to help safecracker Marcel Rudolph (Dan O'Herlihy) break into a THRUSH vault and destroy its contents. Her second appearance was in "The Deadly Quest Affair" (10/30/67). She played heiress Sheila Van Tillson, a struggling modern artist living in a ten-block condemned area of Manhattan. Claiming to have rejected her father's wealth, she still sports an emerald necklace around her neck. U.N.C.L.E. agent Napoleon Solo (Robert Vaughn) is surprised to find Sheila there as he is searching for his partner Illya Kuryakin (David McCallum) who is being held prisoner by vengeful enemy Viktor Karmak (Darren McGavin). Discovering Solo with the girl, Karmak gives them until dawn to save Illya from being poisoned while hunting them through the deserted streets with his prized jaguar by his side.

Though Mason found Darren McGavin to be "terrific to work with" and just adored David McCallum, she had a bit of a problem with Robert Vaughn. "We had to do a kissing scene," recalls Mason. "In those days when people kissed on television and in movies it was all very tame stuff. There was no slurping and nobody was eating anybody's face like you see nowadays. So we do this scene and Vaughn just *jams* his tongue down my throat. Of course the actress in me just kept on acting, but I was not responsive. I was trying to keep my mouth shut. I was so stunned, and I decided that I was just not going to say anything. We did this in one take but I thought, 'There is no way that they are going to see this in the dailies and pass it. We're going to have to do this again.' Sure enough, the next day the director came and told us we had to do the scene over again. I was watching out of the corner of my eye as the director took Robert Vaughn aside and told him, 'You can't kiss her like that.' We did it a second time and he made a half-ass attempt to do it again. But my mouth was tightly shut."

In the *I Spy* episode "The Weight of the World" (12/1/65), Mason's character, named Vicki, joins agents Alexander Scott (Bill Cosby) and Kelly Robinson (Robert Culp) as they try to retrieve a vial containing the bubonic plaque virus developed by the Red Chinese before it is released on the people of Japan. "Bill Cosby and Robert Culp were snappy young actors," remarks Mason. "Because they had their own dialog thing going between them, you had to go in, leave your ego off to the side and jump in with both feet. You had to really keep up with the pace they set and just work hard. They kept you on your toes. Both of them were very nice, but Robert Culp was not very approachable. It was not that he was stuck up or anything, but actors have their own way of working. If they didn't want to socialize I would just stay to myself or talk with somebody else."

Marlyn Mason's last foray into the spy milieu was playing IMF agent Sandy in "Crack Up" (12/9/72) on *Mission: Impossible*. During the show's final season, star Lynda Day George became pregnant and took a leave from the series. Each week there was a different actress playing an IMF agent. In Mason's episode, Sandy is recruited to get contract killer Peter Cordel (Alex Cord) to reveal the Syndicate employer he works for. Usually cast as the girl next door, this role gave Mason the chance to act sexy and alluring ("The change of pace roles were the best—the bitches were the most fun") as she charmed Cordel into thinking his boss wants him dead and gets him to join a competing mob faction. Recalling the cast, Mason comments, "Peter Graves was great fun to work with. We previously starred in a western pilot with [the singing duo] Chad and Jeremy. And I had known Alex Cord for years. I was friendly with him and his then-wife Joanna Pettet. I was even in their home. Alex was a character. I always had the feeling that he just loved himself, [but] I liked him anyway."

In between spy roles Marlyn Mason had the opportunity to demonstrate her vocal and dancing abilities in the musical television specials *Carousel* and *Brigadoon*, both starring Robert Goulet, and on Broadway in *How Now Dow Jones*. Though Mason had a prolific career on television during the sixties, Hollywood did not make use of her on the big screen until 1969 when she copped a lead role as a feisty entertainer opposite Elvis Presley in the period piece *The Trouble with Girls*. In 1971 Mason did a much heralded nude scene as the bored wife of a gym teacher who seduces one of his students (Kristoffer Tabori) in *Making It*. Back on the small screen Mason played Nikki Bell, the assistant to James Franciscus' blind private eye, in *Longstreet* during the 1971-72 TV season. And she also appeared in a number of made-for-TV movies, including the Emmy-winning *A Storm in Summer* (1970) with Peter Ustinov, and *That Certain Summer* (1972) with Hal Holbrook. The remainder of the seventies and eighties found Mason, like so many actresses of her generation, being underutilized, doing television guest shots (i.e., *Marcus Welby, M.D.*, *Barnaby Jones*, *Dynasty*, *Charles in Charge*, etc.) and mediocre made-for-TV movies.

Today Marlyn Mason resides in a beautiful town in Oregon. Though she has left the rat race of Los Angeles behind her, she still has not given up on her acting career and most recently played an energetic grandmother in the made-for-TV movie *Fifteen and Pregnant* (1998).

Publicity shot of Marlyn Mason (Vicki) and Robert Culp (Kelly Robinson) in "The Weight of the World" on *I Spy* (Paramount Television, 1965).

Other films include: *Harpy* (1970—TV), *Escape* (1971—TV), *Outrage* (1973—TV), *Christina* (1974), *Attack on Terror: The FBI vs. the Ku Klux Klan* (1975—TV), *The New Adventures of Heidi* (1978—TV), *My Wicked, Wicked Ways ... The Legend of Errol Flynn* (1985—TV), *Lonely Hearts* (1991—TV) and *Miles from Nowhere* (1992—TV).

Lois Maxwell

Lois Maxwell was born Lois Hooker on February 14, 1927, in Canada. She began acting at an early age, with one of her first film roles in the 1947 screen comedy *That Hagen Girl*, for which she received a Golden Globe Award for "Most Promising Newcomer—Female." Despite the auspicious start, her journey in Hollywood was one fraught with minor roles in B programmers like *Crime Doctor's Diary* (1949). Lois Maxwell moved to Italy, where she made an impressive showing in the film *Tomorrow Is Too Late* (a.k.a. *Domani e Troppo Tardi*, 1949) in the role of Anna, one of two schoolteachers who conducts classes for underprivileged youths and finds herself in a quandary when the sex education seems to go too far. Maxwell then moved to England where she appeared in a number of mysteries and drama films like *Lady in the Fog* (1952) and *Woman in Hiding* (1953). She returned to Italy in 1954 to appear in *La Grande Speranza* (a.k.a. *Submarine Attack*) as a British nurse named Lily, who is rescued (along with other survivors of a submarine attack) by the Italian sailors who sunk their ship. By the film's end, Maxwell's Lily falls in love with the handsome submarine commander (Renato Baldini), and he with her, revealing warmth and daring seldom shown in post-war films of the era.

Back in England, Lois Maxwell appeared in a number of films, most notably the thrillers *The Unstoppable Man* (1959) and *Face of Fire* (1959). In 1960 Maxwell appeared in an episode of *Danger Man* (the British show that would become *Secret Agent* in the U.S.) titled "Positions of Trust." Afterwards she appeared in "The Little Wonders" (1/11/64) episode of *The Avengers*. In 1962 Maxwell was hired to portray Miss Moneypenny, the secretary to M (Bernard Lee), the head of the British secret service, and the woman who hands James Bond his assignments in 14 films in the Bond series, all of them made between 1962 and 1985. As Miss Moneypenny, Maxwell gave the series its anchor, often grounding each episode with touches of affection and realism via brief, sometimes witty, repartee between her character and the actor playing James Bond (Sean Connery in six films, George Lazenby in one and Roger Moore in seven).

In nearly all of her appearances as Miss Moneypenny, Maxwell always treated the Bond character as the "man who got away" or "the unobtainable man." As the series progressed, so did the risqué elements in the brief conversations between the Bond and Moneypenny characters, to the point of containing obvious double entendres. By no means a starlet by the time she made her first Bond film, *Dr. No*, in 1962, Maxwell imbibed her character with a touch of humanism not often seen in the series until the nineties' version of the Bond movies (with Pierce Brosnan as Bond and Samantha Bond as Moneypenny) brought the Moneypenny character more in line with contemporary characterizations and feminism. This was something that the older films, as they were scripted, rarely did. The other Bond films that Lois Maxwell appeared in were *From Russia with Love* (1963), *Goldfinger* (1964), *Thunderball* (1965), *You Only Live Twice* (1967), *On Her Majesty's Secret Service* (1969), *Diamonds Are Forever* (1971), *Live and Let Die* (1973), *The Man with the Golden Gun* (1974), *The Spy Who Loved Me* (1977), *Moonraker* (1979), *For Your Eyes Only* (1981),

As the original Miss Moneypenny, Lois Maxwell appeared in more James Bond films than any other actress. She is pictured here with frequent co-star Sean Connery (James Bond).

as *The Baron* (in "Something for a Rainy Day," 1965), *The Saint* (in "Interlude in Venice" and "Simon and Delilah," 3/24/67), *Department S* (in "The Ghost of Mary Burnham," 2/18/70) and *The Persuaders* (in "Someone Is Waiting," 2/25/72). Her only other non–James Bond spy film was *Operation: Kid Brother* (a.k.a. *O.K. Connery*, 1967), an offbeat action movie produced in Italy where Neil Connery, Sean Connery's real-life brother, portrayed the brother of James Bond, murdered at the movie's offset. As the character of Max, Maxwell got to brandish firearms and battle villains, while supporting player Bernard Lee (M in many of the official Bond movies) had a brief role as Commander Cunningham, a spoof of the M character.

In 1970 Maxwell appeared as the co-star in the Canadian television series *Adventures in Rainbow County*. In 1973 she made the little-known film *Peep*, a Canadian thriller about a professor who takes in a male and female boarder and then sexually experiments with each person, aggravating his already psychotic wife (Maxwell), ending in a disturbing climax. An unusual role for an actress that most audiences recall seeing as a happy-go-lucky, but seemingly unfulfilled lady-in-waiting.

Octopussy (1983) and *A View to a Kill* (1985).

"Strangely enough [my favorite Bond movie is] *On Her Majesty's Secret Service*," commented Maxwell to a journalist for *MSNBC News* in 2000. "If it were just a movie standing alone, instead of part of the series, it was beautifully constructed and the dialog was there, the excitement was there, and Diana Rigg was there. It is a terrific movie. George [Lazenby] is a nice person, but he was very badly advised, in my opinion. He wouldn't sign a five-picture contract, and he could have. He was offered it."

Besides, her appearances as Miss Moneypenny in the James Bond films, Lois Maxwell appeared in such espionage series

Lois Maxwell's later works include the television film *Martha, Ruth and Edie* (1988) and *Lady in the Corner* (1989). As for who made the best James Bond, Maxwell says (according to her *MSNBC* interview): "Oh, Sean Connery. But then, he didn't have to follow anyone." She died on September 29, 2007.

Other films include: *The Dark Past* (1949), *Lolita* (1962), *Come Fly with Me* (1963), *The Haunting* (1963), *The Adventurers* (1970), *Age of Innocence* (1977), *Eternal Evil* (1987) and *Rescue Me* (1988).

Diane McBain

A Warner Bros. talent scout discovered sleek blonde Diane McBain (born on May 18, 1941, in Cleveland, Ohio) while she was still in high school during the late fifties. At the time, she was a successful model and a member of a community theater in Glendale, California. After appearing in a number of Warner Bros.–produced television series, McBain made her film debut in *Ice Palace* (1960), starring Richard Burton and Robert Ryan. Her excellent performance earned her a seven-year contract with the studio. With her cherubic face, blue eyes and flaxen blonde hair, McBain was part of a group of young actresses, including Connie Stevens, Carol Lynley and Yvette Mimieux, who were popular at that time in Hollywood. However, whereas these actresses usually embodied the ingenue, McBain was typecast as the bad girl who always lost the leading man.

In Diane McBain's second feature, *Parrish* (1961), she played a spoiled heiress who rejects poor Troy Donahue in favor of the rich Hampton Fancher. Marrying for money rather than love, she turns to booze to drown her sorrows. McBain made such an impression in this film that she became typecast as the bitch. In *Claudelle Inglish* (1961) she perhaps gives her finest performance as Erskine Caldwell's town tramp who uses so many men that she meets a tragic end. After two seasons as kooky socialite Daphne Dutton on *Surfside 6* (1960–62), McBain appeared in three hit films in 1963, most memorably playing a sympathetic nurse in *The Caretakers* (1963), starring Robert Stack and Joan Crawford. That year exhibitors voting in *The Motion Picture Herald* named her a "Star of Tomorrow."

After leaving Warner Bros. in 1964, McBain went freelance, and her journey into the spy genre began. She made two appearances on *The Wild Wild West*, portraying the bad girl both times. In "The Night of a Thousand Eyes" (10/22/65), briskly directed by Richard Sarafian (who also helmed the pilot), McBain played assassin Jennifer Wingate, who is hired to terminate agent James West (Robert Conrad), investigating the looting of riverboats sailing the Mississippi River. While kissing, Jennifer attempts to kill West but fails. ("I'm afraid I singed your bulletproof vest," admits Jennifer.) Succumbing to his charms, Jennifer tells West all she knows of the riverboat scam.

During the filming of this episode, Diane McBain (as with many actresses) had to put up with Robert Conrad's insecurity about his height. But her problem with him was more to do with his image of himself. "Robert Conrad was short," says McBain matter-of-factly. "He also wore a huge ego so that no one would ever accuse him of being short. I had to stand in a hole, which the crew dug for me every time I had to be next to Conrad during our love scenes. Then they'd put him on a box. Not very romantic, I'm afraid, but true."

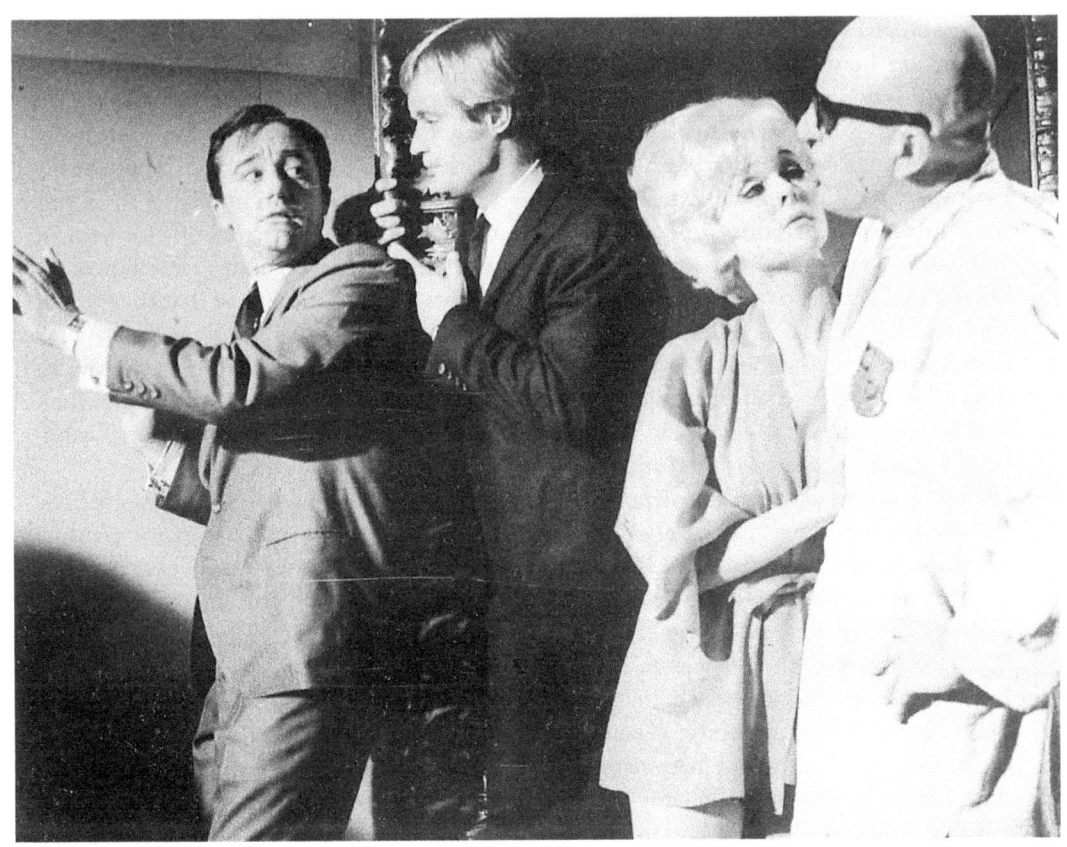

Diane McBain and Telly Savalas as the battling DeContinis with Robert Vaughn (Napoleon Solo) and David McCallum (Illya Kuryakin) in *The Man from U.N.C.L.E.* episode "The Five Daughters Affair," which was released theatrically as *The Karate Killers* (MGM, 1967).

McBain's second *Wild Wild West* episode, entitled "The Night of the Vicious Valentine" (2/10/67), is memorable due to the Emmy-winning performance of Agnes Moorehead as Emma Valentine, a charming matchmaker who marries off her young employees to rich powerful men and then has them murdered to collect their wealth. McBain played Elaine, one of Emma's minions.

In the comedic episode "The Deadly Toys Affair" (11/12/65) on *The Man from U.N.C.L.E.*, Diane McBain played likeable rich girl Joanna Lydecker. The brazen blonde accidentally gets involved with her flamboyant friend Elfie Von Donck (Angela Lansbury), and U.N.C.L.E. agents Napoleon Solo (Robert Vaughn) and Illya Kuriyakin's (David McCallum) efforts to rescue Elfie's genius nephew (Jay North) from the clutches of THRUSH.

Diane McBain had another comedic role on *The Man from U.N.C.L.E.* in "The Five Daughters Affair" (1/11 and 1/17/67), which was released theatrically overseas as *The Karate Killers* (1967). She played Margo, one of murdered Amanda True's (Joan Crawford) five stepdaughters U.N.C.L.E. is searching for. Each daughter holds a key piece of information that will lead U.N.C.L.E. to the whereabouts of Dr. True's formula for turning common seawater into gold. U.N.C.L.E. agents discover Margo without a stitch of clothes on. After

Napoleon gives her his jacket, Margo rants on and on how her husband, Count de Fanzini (Telly Savalas), is broke and has sold off everything (including her clothes) to keep his mansion. They sneak down into his study to look for her mail, where de Fanzini confronts them. Soon after, THRUSH ambushes them. A fight ensues, which is broken up by the arrival of the fire department, called by Margo's stepsister Sandy (Kim Darby). During the melee Sandy gets trapped in a secret room that holds the de Fanzini fortune. As the agents are about to depart Rome, the newly rich and reconciled de Fanzinis arrive at the airport with the first piece of the puzzle—a photograph of Dr. True, which he mailed to Margo.

As the battling but loving de Fanzinis, McBain and Savalas are extremely amusing. Though they yell and scream at each other and are only interested in money (one of Margo's first questions to Napoleon is, "Are you rich?"), the love between them shows through. Describing what it was like to work with Telly Savalas, McBain reveals, "Telly Savalas was such a sexy man, very virile, as was David McCallum. Telly was the kind of man who could go up to any woman, sweep her into his arms and take her right there, no matter where. Not that he did that to me—I only imagined it. But, I'd bet a bundle he could. David McCallum wouldn't have had any trouble doing the same thing, either. It may not be true, but I imagined these men had endless women crawling in and out of their dressing rooms at all hours. When you work with actors in that milieu, especially on a set with limited contact, it is difficult to get to know them all that well. Telly seemed to keep to himself unless it had something to do with business. Then, he was always available. But he was, on every relevant occasion, very pleasant to be around and to work with."

"The Five Daughters Affair" features one of McBain's sexiest roles. When the audience first encounters Margo she is naked and you see her bare back. Throughout the rest of her time onscreen, McBain is draped in a man's sport coat and then a very sheer mini-robe. Regarding her risqué scenes, McBain comments, "There really was not all that much nudity. If there was more than the briefest second of skin, it was someone else's body. They taped my breasts over the nipples so that they would not show, and I was mostly with my back to the camera. But they do have ways to make it look like you're totally nude when all you've done is the most minimal exposure."

In 1966 McBain starred opposite Elvis Presley in *Spinout*, her last major production. With her exquisite cheekbones and flaxen hair, McBain was subsequently typecast as a sort of bitchy prom queen from hell beginning in a series of exploitation movies for American International Pictures. Her last spy film was *The Delta Factor* (1970), based on a novel by Mickey Spillane. Christopher George starred as an international adventurer framed for a $40 million theft. To prove his innocence he accepts the CIA's offer to pose as agent Yvette Mimieux's husband and to impersonate a drug dealer to rescue a scientist from a Caribbean fortress. McBain accepted the role of a beautiful informant named Lisa Gordot, though she was chagrined to play second fiddle to Mimieux, whom she was always compared to at the beginning of her career.

As she entered her thirties, Diane McBain was finally able to shake the hellion roles. She continued acting in films (of the barely released kind) and on television (i.e. *Mannix*, *Marcus Welby, M.D.*, *Charlie's Angels*, etc.) throughout the seventies, taking a few years off to spend time with her son. During the eighties she had recurring roles on *Days of Our Lives* as Foxy Humdinger and *General Hospital* as Claire Howard.

Today Diane McBain is as lovely as

ever and continues to act, taking young grandmother-type roles. Most recently she appeared in *The Christmas Path* (1999—TV) and in the hit gay movie *The Broken Hearts Club: A Romantic Comedy* (2000), starring Dean Cain.

Other films include: *Black Gold* (1963), *Mary, Mary* (1963), *Thunder Alley* (1967), *Maryjane* (1968), *The Mini-Skirt Mob* (1968), *Wicked, Wicked* (1973), *Deathhead Virgin* (1974), *Donner Pass: The Road to Survival* (1978—TV), *The Red Fury* (1984), *Fly from the Hawk* (1986) and *Invisible Mom II* (1999).

Marisa Mell

Marisa Mell was born Marlies Theres Moitzi on February 25, 1939, in Vienna, Austria. Throughout her life she always seemed to have invited, caused or been on the receiving end of trouble. Possessed of a face that seemed brought to life from an ancient Greek or Roman statue (despite her Austrian heritage), Mell possessed a full, wide mouth, a noble nose and wide, staring eyes, the kind that let few enter into her haunted soul.

Mell's first screen appearance was in the film *Das Licht der Liebe* in 1954 (billed as Maria Mell). Two more minor roles followed before she gave a terrific (and uncredited) performance as Liliane, a nightclub dancer, in the film *The Five Sinners* (a.k.a. *Das Nachtlokal Zum Silbermond*, 1959), a lurid tale of white slavery. In *The Brave Soldier Schwik* (a.k.a. *Der Brave Soldat Schwejk*, 1960), in which she also remained uncredited, Mell appeared as Oily, a woman of questionable morals who attempts to redeem the doomed lead, played by Heinz Ruhman. Years later Werner Herzog and Klaus Kinski remade it as *Woyzek*. After numerous minor roles, Mell finally found a decent one in the film *The Devil's Daffodil* (a.k.a. *Das Geheimnis der Gelben Narzissen*, 1961), where Scotland Yard investigates competing U.S. criminal gangs who fled the U.S., then years later continued their rivalry under the murderous hand of a mysterious third party. In this espionage tale about drug smuggling and murder, she appeared alongside Joachim Fuchsberger, Christopher Lee and Klaus Kinski.

Shortly after appearing in British director Ken Russell's first feature, *French Dressing* (1963), as a French starlet engaged to promote a sea resort, she was involved in a car wreck in France that slightly disfigured her. Plastic surgery restored her face, leaving a slight curl on her upper lip, adding more mysterious elements to her already haunted visage.

Mell co-starred as an undercover Interpol agent in the British-West German co-production *City of Fear* (1965), a tale about a Canadian newsman named Mike Foster (Paul Maxwell) who becomes involved in intrigue behind the Iron Curtain in Hungary. She is featured in the British espionage film *Masquerade* (a.k.a. *Operation Masquerade*, 1965) as Sophie. In this spy movie, a secret agent (Cliff Robertson) is called in when vital talks with a Middle Eastern state over oil concessions break down at the U.N. He becomes involved with foreign powers and spies in a conflict over custody of an heir to the throne of the same Middle Eastern country.

In Giorgio Ferroni's *Secret Agent SuperDragon* (a.k.a. *New York Chiama Superdrago*, a.k.a. *New York Calling Superdragon*, 1965), Mell appeared as Charity Farrel, a double agent. In this film, a CIA agent with the code name "Super Dragon" (Ray Danton) battles "the Black Wolves," a sinister organization involved in producing the drug, "Syncron 2," which is made to control U.S. students in a plan to rule the world and destroy American cities in the process. The film also featured Margaret Lee. In *Operation Doublecross* (a.k.a. *Train D'Enfer*, 1965) Mell played a seductive double agent named Frida, as a French agent (Jean Marais) chases a criminal gang led by a West German professor who wants to blow up a train a Middle Eastern King is riding on.

It was around this time that Marisa Mell chose to settle in Italy, making it her new home. Here she quickly became the subject of local gossip columns, and remained so for another ten years, for her romances (The Shah of Persia, Warren Beatty, Alain Delon, Stephen Boyd, Roman Polanski, etc.) and substance abuse arrests (alcohol to drugs). The long-stalled film version of the Italian comic strip (called "Fumetti" in its native country) *Diabolik* was finally entering a "Go" phase when film producer Dino De Laurentiis hired the Italian horror movie maestro Mario Bava to direct it. After settling on a re-written version of the film's already multi-written screenplay (downplaying much of the sex and violence that appeared in the popular strip), everyone settled on American actor John Philip Law as the lead character Diabolik and Catherine Deneuve as Eva Kent, his mistress and partner in crime. However, just as production began, Deneuve was gone and Marisa Mell took her place.

In the film *Diabolik* (1968), the master criminal spends most of his time robbing from the wealthy, the state and the entire country's money reserve whilst spending the rest of his time making love (to Mell's Eva Kent) and enjoying his wealth in his hidden lair (the size of a small city!). When the country enlists the aid of every possible criminal element to help catch Diabolik, things become much more complicated for our anti-hero. After *Diabolik*, Mell appeared in Lucio Fulci's underrated thriller *One on Top of the Other* (a.k.a. *Una Sull'Altra*, 1969) in the dual roles of Susan Du Murrier and Monica Weston. It seems that a man (Jean Sorel) has been accused of the murder of his wife. Did he really do it? Is she really dead? Or is there some sinister plot afoot?

Mell then appeared in two thrillers by the same director (Jose Antonio Nieves Conde), with both featuring the same leading man (Stephen Boyd). *Marta* (a.k.a. *Treason Story*, 1971) and *Carla and Lola* (a.k.a. *Nel Buio del Terrore*, 1971) are psychological terror films, neither one worthy of the talents of Marisa Mell or Boyd, who died a few years later in Europe without regaining his once prestigious Hollywood fame.

Umberto Lenzi's Edgar Wallace tribute *Seven Orchids Stained in Red* (a.k.a. *Sette Orchidee Macchiate di Rosso*, 1971) is a much better effort than Mell's previous thrillers, and in the role of Anna Sartori, one of the would-be victims of a maniacal killer, she shines briefly. While still garnering press in the Italian gossip columns, Mell's film career seemed to have stalled in a succession of B movies, where once it showed great promise.

Marisa Mell virtually disappeared from the screen and from public life between 1980 and 1990. When she reappeared she was disoriented and virtually penniless. Possibly the years of hard living, alcohol and drugs had finally taken their toll. Mell appeared in a hardcore pornographic men's magazine called *Men* (although she did not participate in any of the surrounding activities in the photos). Returning to the big screen, Mell played the role of Nephele in Italian director Aristede Mas-

Marisa Mell as Eva Kent stands by her man, John Phillip Law (Diabolik), in the film *Diabolik* (a.k.a. *Danger: Diabolik*, Paramount, 1968).

saccesi's (a.k.a. Joe D'Amato) fantasy action film *Quest for the Mighty Sword* (a.k.a. *Ator L'Invincible*, 1990) and then returned to Austria. Subsisting on welfare and barely making ends meet by doing poetry readings and appearing in the odd, locally produced film like *I Love Vienna* (1991), Mell was then diagnosed with thyroid cancer. After months of unsuccessful treatments and therapy, Marisa Mell died on May 15, 1992, in Vienna, Austria, at the age of 53.

Other films include: *The Secret of the Red Orchid* (a.k.a. *Das Ratsel der Roten Orchidee*, a.k.a. *The Puzzle of the Red Orchid*, 1962), *Pena de Muerte* (1973), *Mahogany* (1975), *Casanova and Co.* (a.k.a. *Sex on the Run*, 1976), *L'Ultima Volta* (1976), *Mad Dog Killer* (a.k.a. *La Belva Con Mitra*, a.k.a. *Wild Beasts with Machine Guns*, 1977), *The Obscene Desires* (a.k.a. *L'Osceno Desiderio*, 1977), *Ring of Darkness* (a.k.a. *Un' Ombra Nell'Ombra*, 1979), *Peccati a Venezia* (1980) and *Sensatione D'Amore* (1990).

Donna Michelle

Buxom Donna Michelle (born on December 8, 1945, in Los Angeles) was *Playboy*'s "Miss December" in 1963 and was later voted "Playmate of the Year" for 1964. Resembling Brigitte Bardot, Michelle was quickly signed for films. She was usually cast for her physical attributes only, as none of these roles required much acting ability. She never had the chance to create any type of screen persona and was just another beautiful body from the pages of *Playboy* who flickered on the big and small screens for a few years before fizzling out.

After playing a bit part as a party guest in *Goodbye Charlie* (1964), Michelle played man-hungry Animal in *Beach Blanket Bingo* (1965). She also began doing television. Though Michelle was known from the pages of *Playboy* as a kittenish beauty with a mane of wild dirty blonde hair, her TV appearances seemed constraining. In "The Double Affair" (11/17/64) on *The Man from U.N.C.L.E.* (which was released theatrically as *The Spy with My Face* in 1965), Michelle (with her hair in a tight bun) played THRUSH girl Nina, a masseuse who doesn't say very much. She is assigned to guard U.N.C.L.E. agent Napoleon Solo (Robert Vaughn) as he is being held captive in Zurich while his THRUSH impersonator infiltrates U.N.C.L.E. When Solo makes an attempt to escape, she karate chops him in the neck, rendering him unconscious. Later, in a sensuous scene, she gives him a massage as he is chained to a bed, which leads to lovemaking.

In the following year's two-parter "The Alexander the Greater Affair" (9/17 and 9/24/65), which was released theatrically as *One Spy Too Many* (1966), Donna Michelle keeps popping up throughout the film, either exquisitely coiffured or half-naked. As the adulterous Princess Nicole, she is infatuated with the diabolical Alexander (Rip Torn), who idolizes his namesake, Alexander the Great. At an elegant soiree in her honor, she becomes his Queen in a human game of chess against Napoleon Solo, who defeats him—to his embarrassment. As she dances with the victor, her jealous husband, Prince Phanong (James Hong), threatens Solo's life. Later,

Donna Michelle as Princess Nicole tries to entice Robert Vaughn (Napoleon Solo) into her bath in *One Spy Too Many* (MGM, 1966).

Nicole makes love to Alexander and is caught by her husband. To spice up this scene for European audiences, a shot of them in bed, highlighting Michelle's naked back, was added. The insatiable Nicole also tries to lure Solo into her Jacuzzi as he searches for Alexander's missing wife Tracey (Dorothy Provine) at his salon.

In *Agent for H.A.R.M.* (1966) Michelle was back to a less glamorous role as the head of H.A.R.M.'s secretary, Marion. Following in the tradition set forth by Miss Moneypenny in the James Bond films, Marian has a romantic thing for secret agent Adam Chance (Peter Mark Richman). The shapely Michelle is wasted in this film, as she is only shown sitting behind her desk in a few scenes at the beginning of the movie and does not contribute to the plot at all. You know a Bond spoof is really bad when it takes a beautiful *Playboy* Playmate and doesn't exploit her body. Michelle wasn't used to good advantage either in "Lori" (9/21/66) on *I Spy*.

French filmmakers, however, knew what to do with Michelle's major attributes as she co-starred in the 1968 releases *La Nuit la Plus Chaude* (a.k.a. *The Night of the Three Lovers*) as a lesbian stripper, and in *Le Bal des Voyous* (a.k.a. *Playmate*) as a duplicitous fashion model. Donna Michelle retired from acting in the early seventies to work as a *Playboy* magazine photographer. She passed away on April 10, 2004.

Other films include: *Mickey One* (1965) and *A Company of Killers* (1970—TV).

Mary Ann Mobley

Pretty, brown-eyed Southern belle Mary Ann Mobley was born on February 17, 1939, in Biloxi, Mississippi. After graduating Brandon High School, Mobley received a four-year scholarship to the University of Mississippi. Though she lost the first beauty contest she entered, Mobley went on to win a string of local titles and then was tapped to represent Mississippi in the 1959 "Miss America" contest, winning the crown. After she completed her yearlong reign, Mobley moved to New York and used her scholarship money to further her music and drama studies. She joined the variety program *Be Our Guest* in 1960 as their female vocalist, but she was dropped from the show after only 13 weeks. The Broadway musical *Nowhere to Go but Up* followed, but it closed after only nine performances. Undaunted, she remained in New York, studying at the Actor's Workshop.

Mobley relocated to Hollywood in 1963 and began making frequent guest appearances on television in such shows as *Burke's Law* and *Perry Mason*. In 1964 she made the jump to feature films with a starring role in the teenage musical *Get Yourself a College Girl*. Her "sweet as apple pie persona" transferred to the big screen well enough to win her the Golden Globe Award for "Most Promising Newcomer—Female" (along with Mia Farrow and Celia Kaye), and she received a nomination from the American Cinema Editors for "Best Actress in a U.S. Film Debut." In 1965 the Hollywood Make-up Artists and Hairstylists voted her a "Deb Star of the Year." The enthusiasm for Mobley was so great that she was even voted one of the top ten "Stars of Tomorrow" in 1965, placing higher on the list than Julie Christie, Richard Johnson and Senta Berger. At bit too saccharine when playing the ingenue, Mary Ann Mobley was most effective when cast against type—the thrill-seeking girlfriend of John Dillinger (Nick Adams) in *Young Dillinger* (1965) and a Southern vamp opposite Elvis Presley in *Girl Happy* (1965).

Add to that list her performance as a neophyte agent in *The Man from U.N.C.L.E.* episode entitled "The Moonglow Affair" (2/25/66), which was the pilot for the spin-off series *The Girl from U.N.C.L.E.* In this episode, U.N.C.L.E. agents Napoleon Solo (Robert Vaughn) and Illya Kuryakin (David McCallum) are investigating the sabotaging of space launches when a quartzite radiation protector that is controlled by THRUSH agent Arthur Caresse (Kevin McCarthy) incapacitates them. Waverly brings in Section Two operative trainee April Dancer (Mobley) and pairs her with older agent Mark Slate (Norman Fell). They have 46 hours to retrieve the antidote to save Solo's life and find Illya.

Bedecked in designer gowns, Mary Ann Mobley was stunning as the glamorous April Dancer. Her Southern background added a vulnerability to the role that worked wonders, making her a very convincing agent. She was sweetly naïve with Norman Fell, and strong and more confident with McCarthy. As directed by Joseph Sargent and written by Dean Hargrove, "The Moonglow Affair" was one of the series' better episodes from the second season. With the ratings high, NBC was immediately sold on the series, but not on Mobley. The producers originally wanted Stefanie Powers for the series pilot, but she was unavailable, making a film. Dorothy Provine was also considered. When *The Girl from U.N.C.L.E.*

Mary Ann Mobley as the original Girl from U.N.C.L.E., April Dancer, with Norman Fell (agent Mark Slate) in "The Moonglow Affair" on *The Man from U.N.C.L.E.* (MGM-TV, 1966).

was ready to go into production, Powers was again offered the role, and this time she accepted. The powers-that-be deemed Mary Ann Mobley "too soft" and felt she didn't "have the necessary qualities audience-wise" to carry the role week after week. In hindsight, producer David Victor remarked to Jon Heitland, author of *The Man from U.N.C.L.E. Book*, "I thought that in order for *Girl from U.N.C.L.E.* to have a life of its own, it should have a more vulnerable, neophyte kind of lady who was supported in the beginning of her career. When Stefanie came in, she was so strong and so powerful in her own right, she became sort of an equal of the other agents, rather than the new girl on the team." His instincts proved right, as *The Girl from U.N.C.L.E.* never found an audience and lasted only one season.

In the two-part episode "Old Man Out" (10/8 and 10/15/66) on the first season of *Mission: Impossible*, Mobley played trapeze artist Crystal Walker. She is part of the IMF team posing as carnival performers to free Anton Cardinal Vossek (Cyril Delevanti), the leader of an Eastern European country's freedom movement, being held captive in Seravno Prison. The jail is adjacent to a park, where the carnival sets up its tents. To gain access to the prison, IMF agent Rollin Hand (Martin Landau) is caught pick-pocketing some patrons and sent to the prison. The devised plan to free the Cardinal goes awry when he is transferred to solitary confinement. After team director Briggs (Steven Hill) gets word to Rollin, a new plan is activated. Writing in *The Complete Mission: Impossible Dossier*, Peter J. White commented, "In this show more than any other, the IMF seems composed of human beings. The agents talk casually and joke with one another. ... It's a colorful, extremely visual show with lively performances, especially from Mary Ann Mobley who shines as Crystal." With such a performance, it's surprising that Mobley was never invited back to reprise her role, or was never considered as a permanent replacement for Barbara Bain when she left the series.

Istanbul Express (1968), directed by Richard Irving, is a made-for-TV movie reuniting *Burke's Law* star Gene Barry and frequent guest performer Mary Ann Mobley. In this slick thriller they played spies posing as art dealer David Lundon and his flighty girlfriend Peggy Coopersmith traveling on the Trans-Europa Express to Istanbul to bid for some valuable papers from a dead scientist. The highest bidder must pay in cash, and Barry is to rendezvous with fellow spies on the train who will each supply one number to the five-digit Swiss bank account. Also on the train is Senta Berger as their adversary and John Saxon as a French security agent.

Istanbul Express was Mary Ann Mobley's last film for a long stretch of time. She married actor Gary Collins in 1968, and their daughter Clancy was born the following year. Her last spy role was playing Lelia Moen in the episode "Short Circuit" (9/27/72) on the series *Search*. This episode featured Doug McClure as playboy Probe operative Christopher R. Grover, who searches for a madman before the villain can blow up Probe headquarters.

During the early seventies Mobley seemed to give up any ambitions to become a serious actress and became more of a "personality," working steadily on television during the next two decades. Among the wide variety of TV shows she appeared on were *Ironside, The Virginian, Love, American Style, Kraft Music Hall, The Sixth Sense, The Partridge Family, Fantastic Journey, The Love Boat, Fantasy Island*, plus all the major talk and game shows. In 1985 she replaced Dixie Carter as Conrad Bain's wife on *Diff'rent Strokes*. Later she made four guest appearances on *Falcon Crest* in 1988, playing a psychiatrist. She and her husband also appeared in documentaries for World

Vision, informing the world of the massive food shortages in Africa. Sadly, Mary Ann Mobley passed away from breast cancer on December 9, 2014.

Other films include: *Harum Scarum* (1965), *Three on a Couch* (1966), *King's Pirate* (1967), *For Singles Only* (1968), *The Girl on the Late, Late Show* (1974—TV), *Crazy Horse and Custer: The Untold Story* (1990) and *Bandit: Bandit Bandit* (1994—TV).

Terry Moore

Busty brunette Terry Moore (born Helen Koford on January 7, 1929, in Los Angeles) made only one excursion into the spy realm, starring as agent Harper Davis in the spy spoof *A Man Called Dagger* in 1967. This low-budget entry was a big step down for this fifties star, who had received an Academy Award nomination for her supporting role in *Come Back, Little Sheba* (1952).

Terry Moore made her film debut at age 11 in *Maryland* (1940) and went on to play a string of adolescent roles using a variety of stage names. Her breakout role was in the hit film *Mighty Joe Young* (1949). During the fifties the well-endowed actress was typed as the sexpot in such films as *Shack Out on 101* (1955) and *Peyton Place* (1957). Her film appearances became infrequent in the sixties as she was mostly relegated to B-westerns. Moore's private life usually overshadowed her career, especially when she disclosed that she secretly married billionaire Howard Hughes in 1947 and that they were never officially divorced.

In the spy spoof *A Man Called Dagger* (MGM, 1967), Moore portrayed Los Angeles based agent Harper Davis, who is assigned to work with Dirk Dagger (Paul Mantee) in foiling the plot of the nefarious Nazi Rudolph Koffman (Jan Murray). Though top-billed, Moore doesn't make her first appearance onscreen until almost 25 minutes into the film. When the audience first encounters Harper, the bikini-clad agent is observing Koffman's waterfront headquarters from a boat anchored offshore. She is joined by Dagger, who has paddled over on a surfboard. As the two lovers reminisce, the sexy Harper can't resist Dagger's charms. Lying on top of the bare-chested hunk, Harper backs off to tend to business ("I'm compulsive, Dagger—business before pleasure") just as Dagger pops open the champagne. As she fills Dagger in on Koffman, the villain orders one of his men to plant a bomb on board. Luckily, Dagger suspects foul play and he and Harper escape before the boat explodes. As Dagger goes to interrogate Koffman's girlfriend Ingrid (Sue Ane Langdon), Harper is left to watch over Koffman's place. She is captured by him and offered to Dagger as a trade for Erica (Eileen O'Neill), the woman Koffman had programmed to kill Dagger. After reuniting with Dagger, Harper pulls a gun on him. Dagger jumps out of the moving vehicle just as she opens fire. Harper chases him through a park but is overpowered and subdued by him. Dagger then realizes that, while in Koffman's captivity, Harper was implanted with a

Poster art for *A Man Called Dagger* (MGM, 1967), starring Paul Mantee and Terry Moore (pictured at right).

radio device to follow his commands. After feeding Dagger some cryptic information about Koffman, Harper passes out. She resurfaces at the end of the film to frolic with Dagger and Erica on the beach.

Terry Moore is not too convincing as a super agent in *A Man Called Dagger*. (Though *Independent Film Journal* remarked that she "does nicely by her tongue-in-cheek agent role.") Moore fills the physical requirements of the part but seems awkward handling the everyday aspects of being a spy, from employing a gun to stalking a suspect. Her lack of chemistry with star Paul Mantee is extremely evident, as compared to Mantee's scenes with his other co-stars, particularly Eileen O'Neill and Sue Ane Langdon.

Terry Moore took a respite from acting in the seventies and returned to the big screen during the eighties. She even wrote, produced and played a supporting role in the film *Beverly Hills Brats* (1989). Still looking terrific, she appeared semi-nude in the pages of *Playboy*. Recent credits include a small role in the remake of *Mighty Joe Young* (1998) and a cameo as herself in *Howard Hughes: His Women and His Movies* (2000—TV).

Other films include: *My Gal Sal* (1942), *Since You Went Away* (1944), *Son of Lassie* (1945), *Beneath the 12-Mile Reef* (1953), *Daddy Long Legs* (1955), *Between Heaven and Hell* (1956), *Bernadine* (1957), *A Private's Affair* (1959), *Town Tamer* (1965), *Waco* (1966), *My American Cousin* (1985), *Hellhole* (1985), *Death Blow* (1987), *Marilyn and Me* (1991—TV), *Second Chances* (1998) and *Stageghost* (2000).

Rosalba Neri

Rosalba Neri was born on June 19, 1940, in the small town of Forli in Romagna, Italy. Some sources list her year of birth as 1940, while others claim it's a few years earlier. Neri came from a quiet middle class family. In the mid-fifties she won a trip to Hollywood, California, via a talent contest. While in the U.S. she journeyed to well known American cities and briefly considered joining The Actor's Studio in New York before returning to Italy and enrolling in the C.S.C. (the Centro Sperimentale de Cinematografia). This was the technical and acting school for cinematic studies that was started by Mussolini during his Fascist regime due to his love of the cinema. Before graduating in 1959, the young Neri gained small roles in productions such as *I Pinguini Ci Guardino* (1955), *Due Sosia in Allegria* (1956), *Vivendo, Cantando Che Male Ti Fo?* (1957) and *Moglie Pericolose* (1958).

Rumored to be unhappy with the decorative but very minor roles that she was getting in films, Neri briefly considered abandoning her acting career when Mario Bava helped to cast her in the American-Italian co-production *Esther and the King* (a.k.a. *Esther e il Rei*, 1960), which was credited to the director Raoul Walsh. One of the reasons for her career revival might have been that Bava may have noticed the striking physical change that Neri had undergone as an adult. She then possessed a very unique appearance that contrasted with the glamour girl looks of most other performers of the period. She possessed a slim figure highlighted by a curvy frame, thick, straight jet-black hair, and eyes that seemed as big as saucers but were surrounded by brows that added to her countenance. Neri's most famous feature were her cheekbones, which when angular (during periods when she appeared to be gravely thin) gave her a look not unlike classic Greek or Roman statues. When her cheeks were full and apple-like (which was most of the time later on in her career), it gave her an appearance of conniving malevolence or of a scheming nature. Later in life the lines of her face added to a smile that spelled either exotica or doom.

Rosalba Neri's first role in an espionage film was in Giorgio Simonelli's *Two Mafiosi Against Goldginger* (a.k.a. *Due Mafiosi Contro Goldginger*, 1965). In this comedic romp, two foolish photographers (popular Italian comedians Franco Franchi and Ciccio Ingrassia) use their cameras to photograph people at a posh party. Unknowingly, one of the cameras contains a hidden gun and they accidentally assassinate a politician. The pair end up being stalked by the British secret service (and its best agent, played by George Hilton), then end up in the service of the CIA and become involved in the world domination plans of the evil Dr. Goldginger (Fernando Rey). A sexy female fatale, Agent 00024 (Neri), lends the inept pair a hand, but the actress chiefly appears on the fringes of the story as a curvaceous temptation for our inept heroes (her third appearance in a film with Franco and Ciccio). That same year she was back in a slinky, sheer dress in *James Tont: Operation Goldsinger* (a.k.a. *James Tont Operazione U.N.O.*, a.k.a. *The Wacky World of James Tont*, 1965) where a Secret Service agent named James Tont (Lando Buzzanca) investigates Goldsinger (George Wang), an Asian megalomaniac who plans to rule the world. Like the film before it, this was another obvious spoof of the James Bond films, complete with an unauthorized use of the *Goldfinger* villain (renamed in these films Goldginger and Goldsinger).

Neri got to sing a love song, after bedding the hero, in the above average *Upperseven: The Man to Kill* (a.k.a. *Der Mann mit den 1000 Masken*, a.k.a. *The Man with the 1000 Masks*, 1965). In this obscure, exciting entry into sixties spy cinema, Secret Service agent Paul Finney (German actor Paul Hubschmid) is a master of disguises capable of using his skills with latex and make-up to alter his face with speed and skill. Finney is known to all of his enemies as "Upperseven." Kobras (Nando Gazzolo), a master criminal who heads an international organization of murderers, is involved with Red Chinese agents who plan to steal millions in South African diamonds and rob the entire country of Sweden's bank supply in order to fund a secret missile base in Africa. There Kobras plots world domination with a sterilization ray. Finney/Upperseven is joined by Helen (Karin Dor), an FBI agent, and together they battle Kobras and his organization. After Neri's brief onscreen love song, she is revealed to be an agent for Kobras and is murdered by Upperseven, making her appearance a brief but memorable one.

After appearing in a number of westerns during this period, including *Arizona Colt* (a.k.a. *The Man from Nowhere*, 1966) and *Dynamite Jim* (1966), Neri turned her physical talents back towards the spy genre. In *Password: Kill Agent Gordon* (a.k.a. *Password: Uccidere Agente Gordon*, 1966), American agent Gordon (Roger Browne) investigates the murder of a spy informant, leading to a criminal ring involved in smuggling weapons to third world countries. Neri is featured in a minor role as a villainess in a film already overcrowded with bit parts played by familiar Italian character actors and actresses. *Superseven Calling Cairo* (a.k.a. *Superseven Chiama Cairo*, 1966), the tale of a British agent, "Superseven" (Roger Browne), assigned to find radioac-

Rosalba Neri (Elena) and Eddie Arent (Kaiser) in a scene from *Target: Frankie* (Germany, 1967).

tive material stolen from a British laboratory and taken to Cairo where he battles international spies, including a devilish neo–Nazi played by Massimo Serato, featured Neri in a memorable role of a woman who gains the trust of the hero but is really a double agent.

In the Italian-Spanish co-production, *Elektra One* (a.k.a. *Con la Muerte e el Espalda*, a.k.a. *With Death on Your Back*, 1967), Neri has another one of those "window dressing" roles as an attractive but potentially deadly seductress. In this film, a U.N. scientist working on a secret formula for releasing Man's aggressive instincts is murdered, and his assistant, a sexy blonde (Vivi Balch), is hunted by the criminal organization "Elektra." U.S., Chinese and Russian agents all seek to find her and the doctor's papers that detail the cure for Elektra's deadly narcotic drug, which they plan to use to turn people crazy and threaten the NATO military powers. George Martin plays the special agent on the case.

Neri then co-starred in the seldom seen *Target: Frankie* (a.k.a. *Feuer Frei auf Frankie*, 1967). When an American scientist (Joachim Fuchsberger) is killed in Europe, the CIA sends the deceased man's playboy lookalike brother (Fuchsberger), who has been recruited to become an agent, to escort the dead scientist's assistant (Neri) safely back to America. In Europe the agent encounters the sinister spy organization "the Rainbow." Neri then appeared in a minor role as "The Countess" in *OSS 117 Murder for Sale* (a.k.a. *Pas de Roses pour OSS 117*, a.k.a. *No Roses for OSS 117*, 1968). In this action-packed international co-production, secret agent OSS 117 (John Gavin) trades identities with an expert assassin to infiltrate the secret organization of killers led by a megalomaniac named "the Golem" (Curt Jurgens), who is hell bent on eventual world domination. This film also contains appearances by Luciana Paluzzi and Margaret Lee.

One of Neri's last roles in an espionage film was a fairly large part as Yaka, the head of the Albanian Secret Police, in Jesus Franco's *Lucky, the Inscrutable* (a.k.a. *Lucky El Intrepido*, a.k.a. *Lucky, the Intrepid*, 1967). In this wacky, wild and completely insane film (partly inspired by the Italian Fummeti comic books and partly by director Franco's always experimenting mind at the height of one of his creative peaks), a soldier of fortune, adventurer and agent for hire named Lucky (Ray Danton) is employed by a secret organization to investigate murders that lead to another, sinister, organization of counterfeiters.

As censorship in Europe began to relax, the amount of sexy, exploitative films being made in Italy began to rise. In *Top Sensation* (a.k.a. *The Seducers*, 1969) Neri appeared in two graphic Sapphic love scenes (one with Barbara Bouchet), and she again appeared in the nude in the thriller *Slaughter Hotel* (a.k.a. *La Bestia Uccide a Sangue Freddo*, a.k.a. *The Beast Kills in Cold Blood*, 1971). In this film, in which she performed in a number of seemingly uninhibited erotic couplings, Neri was to become the victim of a maniacal killer who stalks an asylum. In recent years a hardcore pornographic version of the film has surfaced in France containing sequences featuring the actress that seem like part of the original production (but might possibly be inserts filmed by foreign distributors).

Neri finally received a good leading role in actor-director Mel Welles' incredible film, *Lady Frankenstein* (a.k.a. *La Figlia di Frankenstein*, a.k.a. *The Daughter of Frankenstein*, 1971). As the daughter of the famous surgeon and experimenter Dr. Frankenstein (Joseph Cotten), she displayed an equal amount of the sinister (when cutting apart bodies) and the erotic (when coupling with her own creation, an extremely well endowed man). Another Italian horror film that has become a cult favorite is Paolo Solvay's *The Devil's Wedding Night* (a.k.a. *Il Plenilunio dell Vergine*, a.k.a. *The Full Moon of the Virgins*, 1973). In this lurid, blood and sex–soaked vampire film, Neri (billed in English language prints of the film as Sara Bay) stars as the Countess De Vries, one of the brides of Dracula. Throwing caution and personal morals to the wind, Neri appears nude for nearly the entirety of the film's running time (cementing her apparently unwanted reputation as primarily an erotic actress), alternately attempting to seduce the twin brother heroes (played by Mark Damon) and vamping the local nubile maidens.

As Neri's career began to wind down, she appeared in a small role in the violent gangster film *Big Guns* (a.k.a. *Tony Arzenta*, a.k.a. *No Way Out*, 1973) with Alain Delon, and in the thriller *Lo Strano Ricatto di Una Ragazza per Bene* (1974). Despite a brief return to the screen via the 1985 Italian television miniseries titled *Olga and Her Children* (a.k.a. *Olga e I Suo Figli*), Rosalba Neri has moved on to other pursuits in her life. She commented to authors Manlio Gomarasca and Davide Pulici for the book *99 Donne*: "I decided to give it up because I felt satisfied with what I had done, at least in quantity, if not in quality. When my husband-to-be proposed to me and offered a trip around the world, leaving everything [behind], I accepted. Before then, I was jumping on and off planes, traveling from one set to the next, inventing emotions. On our boat, I really lived those emotions, traveling across the ocean. We sailed on our boat to the Caribbean, the French Polynesian islands. I live in a wonderful house, a sixteenth century castle with thirty acres of land all around, we have horses and I go riding every day. I feel good here, absolutely. Now and then, my past pops up, either I meet someone or someone sees me on TV and remembers me ... so, I'm living my life as best I can."

Other films include: *Hercules in the Haunted World* (a.k.a. *Ercole al Centro della Terra*, a.k.a. *Hercules at the Center of the Earth*, 1961), *Hercules Against the Sons of the Sun* (a.k.a. *Ercole Contro I Figli del Sole*, 1964), *Kindar, the Invulnerable* (a.k.a. *Kindar L'Invulnerabile*, 1964), *The Lion of Thebes* (a.k.a. *Leone di Tebe*, 1964), *Hercules Against the Black Pirate* (a.k.a. *Sansone Contro il Corsaro Negro*, 1964), *Hercules of the Desert* (a.k.a. *La Valle dell'Eco Tonante*, 1964), *I Lunghi Giorni dell'Odio* (1967), *99 Women* (a.k.a. *99 Mujeres*, 1968), *Justine* (a.k.a. *Marquis De Sade's Justine*, a.k.a. *Deadly Sanctuary*, 1969), *Two Males for Alexa* (a.k.a. *Due Maschi per Alexa*, 1971), *Amuck* (a.k.a. *Alla Ricera del Piacere*, 1972), *L'Amante del Demonio* (1972), *Smile Before Death* (a.k.a. *Il Sorriso Della Iena*, a.k.a. *The Smiles of Gena*, 1972), *The Girl in Room 2A* (a.k.a. *La Casa della Paura*, a.k.a. *The House of Fear*, 1973), *The Arena* (a.k.a. *La Rivolta delle Gladiatrici*, a.k.a. *Naked Warriors*, 1973) and *Il Pomicione* (1976).

Rosemary Nicols

Rosemary Nicols co-starred as one of a trio of British agents working in the elite *Department S* in the television show of that same name. As Annabelle Hurst, she was the scientific brain of the outfit, studying cases via her computer lab printouts, using logic to help solve difficult ones, almost the "Scully" of her day (in reference to Gillian Anderson's *X-Files* role). Nicols held her own amongst a cast that included Joel Fabiani as Stewart Sullivan and Peter Wyngarde as the colorful Jason King.

Nicols was born Rosemary Claxton in 1942 in Bradford, England. She made her TV debut in the series *Badgers Bend* and attended the Central School of Speech and Drama. Roles in repertory followed before she appeared on stage with Topol in *Fiddler on the Roof* in the West End. She had a very minor role in *The Guns of Navarone* (1961) before landing a prominent part in *The Pleasure Girls* (1965), in which she, Francesca Annis, Suzanna Leigh and Annika Wills played four lovely lasses who discover the travails of womanhood while sharing a flat in swinging mid-sixties London. Returning to British TV, Nicols portrayed Anne Heriot, who joins forces with her

Rosemary Nicols as Annabelle in *Department S* (ITC, ca. 1969), the UK precursor to *The X-Files*.

brother-in-law Drew (Jeremy Wilkin) to prove alien forces have landed and are brainwashing humans in the British sci-fi series *Undermind* in 1965.

After appearing in a few more films and a 1967 episode of the espionage series *Man in a Suitcase* ("Against the Stream"), Nicols was cast in her second series, *Department S*, in 1969. The show was not atypical of the similar ITC-produced series of the day (like *The Champions*, which also sported a trio of agents), and the episodes on this program usually boasted intriguing plots, a good amount of action and a cast that worked well together. In every episode, *Department S*, the most elite of Interpol's satellite agencies, would inherit cases that their parent organization failed to solve. Jason King (Wyngarde) was the chief member, a dandified, hedonistic, part-time writer of crime novels who often projected himself into the character that he wrote about to become an "action man." Sullivan (Fabiani) was the down-to-earth member of the trio, leaving Annabelle (Nicols) to be the analyst and scientific member of the team. Often sparks flew between the Annabelle and King characters via their competing ways of solving unusual crimes. Twenty-eight episodes were produced before the series was canceled in 1970. This was much to the relief of Nicols who recently told a reporter that she did not get along with Wyngarde and felt that she was only there to add glamour to the show.

Rosemary Nicols seemed to have retired from acting a few years later, but she left an indelible mark by appearing in this show, as well as on the *Man in a Suitcase* episode "Against the Stream" and on *The Persuaders'* "Greensleeves", which aired on 10/8/71. Her last film appearance was in *Bridges to Heaven* (1975) with Hugh Griffith.

Other films include: *Breaking Point* (British-TV, 1966), *Brown Eye, Evil Eye* (1967) and *The Mini-Affair* (1967).

France Nuyen

The daughter of a Chinese father and French mother, actress France Nuyen was born France Nguyen Vannga on July 31, 1939, in Marseille, France. As a young girl she attended the L'Ecole des Beaux Arts School where she excelled in painting and sculpture. At the tender age of 14½ she accompanied some of her friends to the Cannes Film Festival in 1953. The strikingly beautiful Nuyen caught the eye of two esteemed photographers, and her portrait was seen throughout the world as "The Girl on the Beach at Cannes" in *Life*, *Look* and *The Saturday Evening Post*, among others. In January of 1957 Nuyen and her mother immigrated to New York City where she enrolled at the Canover Modeling Agency and began working in a bakery. Before landing a modeling job, the agency submitted Nuyen's photographs to producers at 20th Century–Fox who were seeking a girl to play the ingenue in Rodgers and Hammerstein's *South Pacific* (1958), to be directed by Joshua Logan. Before she knew it, the exquisite beauty, who only spoke French at the time, was offered a contract by 20th Century–Fox and was off to the South Seas. The film, starring Mitzi

Gaynor and Rossano Brazzi, was a tremendous success. Nuyen was simply enchanting as Liat, the daughter of Bloody Mary (Juanita Hall), who falls in love with the ill-fated lieutenant (John Kerr), and Nuyen received a Golden Globe nomination for "Most Promising Newcomer—Female."

Joshua Logan was so impressed with the neophyte actress with the exquisite features that he offered her the starring role in his new Broadway show entitled *The World of Susie Wong*. Despite her inexperience and lack of training, Nuyen was excellent as the call girl with a heart of gold who falls in love with an American artist (William Shatner) in Hong Kong, and she became the darling of the New York critics. Her performance earned her a Theatre World Award, and she appeared on the cover of all the major magazines of the time. After producer Ray Stark signed her to do the film version of *The World of Susie Wong* opposite William Holden, super stardom seemed inevitable. However, after filming for a month on location in England, the original director and Nuyen were let go. The press had a field day maliciously speculating why Nuyen was replaced.

Undaunted, France Nuyen returned to Hollywood. Columnists were sounding the death knell for Nuyen's acting career until producer-director Jack Webb and actor Robert Mitchum came to her rescue. They were about to begin filming the World War II service comedy *The Last Time I Saw Archie* (1961) and chose Nuyen for the second female lead. Set during the waning days of World War II, the film cast Mitchum as an army private who cons everyone into thinking he is a general. Webb portrayed his buddy, while Nuyen essayed the role of a suspected Japanese agent who was really a decoy to trap the real spy.

Due to her professionalism while making *The Last Time I Saw Archie* (reportedly Mitchum and Webb negated all the vicious press against her), Nuyen's career picked up steam. She appeared as a local Chinese girl raped by a Communist officer in director Leo McCarey's *Satan Never Sleeps* (1962), starring William Holden and Clifton Webb as priests who run a mission in 1949 China as the Communists are taking over. In *Diamond Head* (1963) Nuyen portrayed the mistress of a bigoted Hawaiian plantation owner (Charlton Heston). Most memorably, she was *A Girl Named Tamiko* (1962), who was the true love of a brash Eurasian photographer (Laurence Harvey) looking to marry a wealthy American girl (Martha Hyer) for citizenship.

Nuyen returned to the spy realm with *Dimension 5* (1966), which cast Jeffrey Hunter as agent Justin Power from Espionage, Inc. and Nuyen as his Hong Kong associate Kitty. They wear time travel belts and journey a few weeks into the future to stop a plot by Dragon, a Chinese Communist organization, from destroying Los Angeles with an A-bomb. They discover parts of the bomb hidden in a shipment of rice on an import company's freighter. Unfortunately, they are captured by Dragon's leader, Big Buddha (played by Harold Sakata, of *Goldfinger* fame). As they are about to be executed, they are saved by one of Dragon's agents (Linda Ho). Power and Kitty kill Big Buddha and save Los Angeles. At one point there was talk of a sequel, but Nuyen passed on reprising her role. The follow-up film was never produced.

On television, Nuyen continued in the spy genre. She guest starred as Zenie, with Michael Dunn, Greta Chi and Robert Cornthwaite, on *Amos Burke, Secret Agent*. In this episode, entitled "The Prisoners of Mr. Sin" (10/27/65), agent Amos Burke (Gene Barry) travels to an island paradise to locate a missing cryptographer (Cornthwaite) being held captive by the maniacal Mr. Sin (Dunn). In "The Cherry Blossom Affair" (11/19/65) on *The Man from U.N.C.L.E.*, Nuyen played Cricket Okasada, a film student who inadvertently joins

Publicity shot of France Nuyen (Cheng) and Robert Culp (Kelly Robinson) in the episode "An American Empress" on *I Spy* (Paramount Television, 1967).

U.N.C.L.E. agents Napoleon Solo (Robert Vaughn) and Illya Kuryakin (David McCallum) to battle THRUSH leaders Mr. Kutuzov (Woodrow Parfrey) and Harada (Jerry H. Fujikawa) in the Far East, who have acquired a volcano-activating device. One of the episode's highlights is when Cricket and the two agents are strung up like puppets and maneuvered to kill each other.

France Nuyen made four guest appearances on I Spy—in "The Tiger" (1/5/65), "Always Say Goodbye" (1/26/66), "Magic Mirror" (3/15/67) and "An American Empress" (12/25/67). In "The Tiger" she is very good as Sam, the daughter of an American physician (Lew Ayres), both of whom are being held captive by the Chinese Communists in the Southeast jungle. Kelly (Robert Culp) and Scott (Bill Cosby) are sent in to rescue them, but they are hampered by Kelly's fragile state of mind due to his closeness to Sam and his last failed mission in the China Seas. In "Magic Mirror" Nuyen reprises her role as Sam, now the lover of a deposed Spanish general (Ricardo Montalban) plotting to return to power. When Kelly learns that Sam is with General Vera through her own volition, he is ordered to find out her true motives and eliminate her if she has turned traitor. And in "An American Empress" Nuyen played Cheng, an unwitting tool masquerading as the Empress of China by Red Chinese agents as part of a conspiracy to return a Chinese monarchy to power. Regarding her performance, D. P. Cole comments on the web site entitled I Spy–the Definitive Site: "France Nuyen, once again, proves what a versatile actress she is…"

Despite her talent (she was excellent in "Elaan of Troyius" on Star Trek), the seventies found Nuyen, like most of her contemporaries, mired in mediocre features and made-for-TV movies. She played one of the passengers terrorized by a spectral druid in Horror at 37,000 Feet (1972—TV), a human mutant in Battle for the Planet of the Apes (1973) and a Hawaiian harridan in Deathmoon (1978—TV). She also appeared in the obscure spy film The Big Game (1972), directed by Robert Day. According to the Internet Movie Database, the plot centered on two soldiers of fortune who are hired by a professor to protect his invention that can control armies. Nuyen played Atanga. Also in the cast were Stephen Boyd, Ray Milland, Cameron Mitchell and Brendon Boone.

In the eighties, with her hair cropped short, France Nuyen emerged as a very smart and attractive leading lady. Her career got a major boost when she landed the role of Dr. Paulette Kiem on the acclaimed medical drama St. Elsewhere. In the nineties she was one of the stars of the hit film The Joy Luck Club (1993).

Currently sporting a nifty short blonde hairstyle, the elegant France Nuyen continues to act today—mostly recently in the 1999 episode "The Ripper" on The Outer Limits. She is a regular at celebrity autograph shows and science fiction conventions throughout the country.

Other films include: In Love and War (1958), Man in the Middle (1964), Black Water Gold (1969—TV), One More Train to Rob (1971), Code Name: Diamond Head (1977—TV), Return to Fantasy Island (1978—TV), Jealousy (1984—TV), Midas Valley (1985—TV), China Cry: A True Story (1990), A Passion to Kill (1994), OP Center (1995—TV), Angry Café (1995) and A Smile Like Yours (1997).

Eileen O'Neill

Radiant Eileen O'Neill was another talented sixties performer who worked steadily on the small screen throughout the decade but rarely got the chance to shine on the big screen. However, O'Neill proved what a talented actress she was by playing a variety of roles (often under a blonde wig) in comedy series, dramas and variety shows. She also appeared in a number of TV espionage shows, episodes of sitcoms spoofing the spy phenomenon, and the feature film *A Man Called Dagger* (1967).

Eileen O'Neill was born on July 3 in Philadelphia, Pennsylvania. As a teenager she enrolled in the Philadelphia School of Modeling and Charm and began appearing in local beauty contests, which led to a regular stint on a locally produced television program called *The Joe Pyne Show*. She left the program to try her luck in Hollywood. After landing a commercial her first week in town, O'Neill never returned home.

O'Neill made her film debut in a small role in *A Majority of One* (1960), starring Rosalind Russell. She next played a haughty teen vamp in the rock and roll exploitation film *Teenage Millionaire* (1961), starring Jimmy Clanton and Diane Jergens. But her big break came when she was cast as Sgt. Gloria Ames on the Aaron Spelling TV series *Burke's Law*, starring Gene Barry, beginning in 1963 for two seasons. O'Neill also turned up in the reformatted series *Amos Burke, Secret Agent* in the episode "Or No Tomorrow" (12/15/65), which was set in Ceylon (now called Sri Lanka, southeast of India). An Asian prince (Lee Bergere) threatens to use a deadly fungus to destroy his country's rice crop unless the U.S. government releases two political prisoners in its custody.

"The James Bond movies were such a hit, everybody was trying to emulate them," explains O'Neill. "That was the reason they changed *Burke's Law* to *Amos Burke, Secret Agent*. I played a double agent named Betty Hamilton in that *Amos Burke* episode. It was such a fun part to play. I was a brunette and a blonde in the episode. There were kooky things in the script, as well as some serious things. I liked the duality of this role. On *Burke's Law* I was one character on one level. In this episode I had a broader scope of character and a fabulous wardrobe."

Sitcoms began spoofing the spy genre during the mid-sixties, and O'Neill guest starred in four of them. In "The Private Eye" (10/6/65) on *The Beverly Hillbillies* she played bad girl "K," who, along with her partner "J" (Donald Curtis), try to trick secret agent Jethro Beaudine (Max Baer, Jr.) into drilling "an escape hatch" into the floor of his office, which sits right above the Commerce Bank's vault. Jethro ineptly tries to impress the duo, who he thinks are from 00 headquarters in London.

"Butterball" (2/13/66) on *My Favorite Martian* was less amusing but gave O'Neill more of a chance to display her comedic abilities. In a short blonde wig and black leather, she played Delilah, a telephone company employee working in their blueprint division who is drugged with Zombie juice by the evil mastermind Butterball (Larry D. Mann), an obvious take-off on Goldfinger. He kidnaps Tim (Bill Bixby), believing that he is an agent working for Topseek, which he plans to destroy with a series of bombs activated by a telephone call. For the first part of the show O'Neill's character is in a trance-like state ("Being an actress, it was very hard not to react to what was going on"). But once she comes out of it—via a kiss from Tim—her character turns out to be somewhat of a klutz. Recalling the shoot, Eileen O'Neill says, "Bill Bixby was very sweet. Ray Walston used a lot of cue cards. But he was a very nice man. Afterwards, he used to call me to see how my career was progressing."

Eileen O'Neill (again as a blonde) guest starred as Agent Shirley, with Murray Matheson as KAOS mastermind Cedric Devonshire, in the *Get Smart* episode titled "Smart, the Assassin" (2/11/66). Devonshire is an employee of the Regency Club where agent Maxwell Smart (Don Adams) and the Chief (Edward Platt) go to relax and play chess. He has Maxwell Smart kidnapped and programmed to kill the next person who says checkmate. However, the hypnosis ends at midnight and, unfortunately for KAOS, Max has picked that day to read up on his chess strategy. Each *Get Smart* episode was known for their way-out gadgets, and the one introduced in this episode is called the Cone of Silence—a cylinder of soundproof Plexiglas that lowers from the ceiling, preventing anyone outside of it from hearing the conversation between the two people inside.

In *The Double Life of Henry Phyfe*, O'Neill guest starred as Rita (described by O'Neill as being "somewhat of a kook") on the episode entitled "Visit to Washington" (3/24/66). The fumbling Phyfe (Red Buttons) needs to learn safe-cracking in order to successfully complete his assignment to break open a safe in Washington and stuff it with phony documents. Rita, an expert, comes to his aid and sneaks into the office with him to blow up the safe. Regarding her kissing scene with Buttons, O'Neill recalls, "After Rita and Phyfe have wired the room, I'm holding the detonator on my lap as we are crouched down behind this desk and decide I want one last kiss to remember my moment of greatness. Red had to lean over and kiss me with his eyes closed while hitting the detonator with his elbow. But the detonator was about the size of a nickel. Red's elbow was hitting every place but the detonator. We had to do that take a number of times because he kept missing the mark."

Spy spoofs were not limited to TV shows. Eileen O'Neill was featured in one of the most expensive commercials produced up to that point in 1966. ("Most commercials are shot in a few hours—we filmed for four nights.") She played a glamorous spy, clad in a trench coat and carrying a briefcase, who is on the run from enemy agents to help promote Max Factor's Sheer Genius with "005—five secret moisturizing agents." With the agents closing in on O'Neill's spy, she sits at a makeup mirror and applies Sheer Genius. As the commercial ends with O'Neill escaping in an Astin Martin (the same car James Bond drove), the announcer warns, "Don't get caught without Sheer Genius makeup."

On the big screen, O'Neill co-starred with Paul Mantee in *A Man Called Dagger* (1967). An absurd spy spoof made on the cheap, *A Man Called Dagger* owes its enjoyment to Paul Mantee's macho athletic hero who has a way with the ladies. O'Neill is also very good as Erica, a blonde newly arrived in California from Canada to work at a beauty farm run by the pampered Ingrid (Sue Ane Langdon). Ingrid's evil paramour, the wheelchair-bound Rudolph Koffman (Jan Murray), a former SS colonel who operates a meatpacking plant as a front for his neo–Nazi group, kidnaps Erica. He uses her as part of his plan to take over the world. She is brainwashed to follow Koffman's orders, transmitted via a small radio receiver drilled in her tooth. After Erica's friend Joy (Maureen Arthur) tips off Dagger regarding her disappearance, Erica turns up in Dagger's room. ("Dagger, how do you feel about girls who wake up in strange hotel rooms with strange men and

Eileen O'Neill as Erica braces for death as Paul Mantee (agent Dirk Dagger) saves her from being sliced in two in *A Man Called Dagger* (MGM, 1967).

no memory?") While Dagger consoles her, the programmed Erica unsuccessfully tries to kill him by stabbing him with a dagger-shaped hair band. Dagger returns Erica to Koffman in exchange for his kidnapped partner, Harper Davis (Terry Moore). After

Dagger forcefully persuades Ingrid to reveal the secret entrance to Koffman's hideout, he arrives just in time to rescue a tied-up Erica from a swinging scimitar. The climactic fight between Dagger and Koffman takes place in a meat locker with hundreds of hanging carcasses. The film ends with a bare-chested Dagger relaxing on a beach with Harper and Erica. As the bikini-clad women playfully tickle him, the last shot is of their derrieres with "The End" superimposed over them.

"There is one scene from *A Man Called Dagger* that still strikes me," recalls O'Neill. "It is when I'm drugged and I wake up in a strange bed after Paul Mantee rescues me the first time. Paul is sitting over me and I had to look at him and say, 'I hope it isn't inevitable. I don't think I could relax and enjoy it.' The line at that time tickled me and I think it was gutsy for its day. Paul is a very giving actor—what I call an actor's actor. I liked working with Terry Moore and Jan Murray also. Jan was a stand up comedian—the Borsht Belt and all of that. It is always fun when you are working with a comedian because they innately have to say funny things all the time. Even though he was playing the villain, he kept the set light and airy."

What *A Man Called Dagger* is most famous for is the scene where Dagger rescues Erica from a swinging scimitar. "In that scene, I was strapped vertically to a tiger skin on the wall," comments O'Neill with a laugh. "My dress was pulled up to reveal my legs. Of course, mandatory grunts and groans abounded." That scene, as staged by director Richard Rush, is the film's most exciting, enhanced by the sexual energy released by Mantee and O'Neill. In *Movies on TV, 1972-73 Edition*, critic Steven H. Scheuer describes O'Neill as, "pretty, and merits better."

The most confusing aspect of *A Man Called Dagger* is the billing. Though essentially the film's female lead, O'Neill is billed fifth in the advertisements and seventh in the film's credits. Although her name is correct in the ads, the second "L" of O'Neill is omitted in the film's credits. Terry Moore receives top billing, followed by Jan Murray, Sue Ane Langdon and Paul Mantee. "I would guess that since it was a low-budget film they needed some names to pull people into the theater," suggests O'Neill. "Paul was known in the industry but not to the public. I was known in television, not films. They needed recognizable names so I think it was just a marketing judgment."

Eileen O'Neill continued making TV appearances in the late sixties and was a regular on the variety show *Operation: Entertainment* in 1968. Her last theatrical feature was the comedy *Loving* (1970), starring George Segal, in which she had a supporting role. She retired from acting in the early seventies to work with her husband, attorney and real estate developer Richard Barich, who passed away a few years ago. Eileen O'Neill (now a permanent blonde) is as gorgeous as ever and is contemplating a return to show business. She currently has a new agent and can be seen making personal appearances at autograph shows.

Other films include: *Four for Texas* (1963), *Kiss Me, Stupid* (1964), *The Third Day* (1965) and *The Loved One* (1965).

Luciana Paluzzi

Born on June 11, 1931, in Rome, Italy, Luciana Paluzzi began her rise to stardom by modeling for Italian fashion magazines. She quickly attracted the attention of Italian film producers who were seeking a new rival for famed actresses Gina Lollobrigida and Sophia Loren. Although it is rumored that she appeared in *Three Coins in the Fountain* (1954) in a brief walk-on, her first proper celluloid credit would be the Italian comedy-drama *I Have Seven Daughters* (a.k.a. *I Sette Peccati di Papa*) in the role of Patricia, in 1954. Quickly garnering the attention of foreign producers, Paluzzi journeyed to France to appear in the film *Mademoiselle Striptease* (a.k.a. *En Effeuillant la Marguerite*, a.k.a. *Please, Mr. Balzac!*, 1956), an inconsequential film that was produced to exploit the popularity of "saucy" continental films.

During the next two years she appeared in a variety of roles in Italian and French productions, but her first genre film credit was a brief appearance as an Amazon character in Pietro Francisci's *Hercules* (a.k.a. *Le Fatiche di Ercole*, a.k.a. *The Labors of Hercules*), the first Steve Reeves–starring muscleman movie, filmed in 1957. Brought to the attention of British film producers, Paluzzi appeared in tiny roles in productions like *Sea Fury* and *Tank Force* (both 1958), but they did little to propel her career.

Paluzzi appeared in the short-lived British and American co-production television program *Five Fingers* in 1959, as the alluring and seductive Frenchwoman Simone Genet. Based on the popular 1952 film, also titled *Five Fingers*, that starred James Mason (and was allegedly based on a true life incident) as a British civil servant who had sold secret documents to foreign enemy agents, this espionage-oriented series met with little attention from the viewing audience. It folded after a brief run of 17 episodes.

Paluzzi then journeyed to Germany in 1959 to appear in a minor role in Fritz Lang's epic two-part adventure film *The Tiger of Eschanpur* (a.k.a. *Der Tiger von Eschnapur*) as the dark and sensual Baharani. She also appeared in this role in the film's second half (released separately and titled *The Indian Tomb*, a.k.a. *Das Indische Grabmal*). The American release of the film (combining both episodes and minus several hours of footage) appeared two years later as *Journey to the Lost City*.

Paluzzi seemed to flounder as an actress for a year as she was seeking better, more prominent roles. During this time she appeared in *The Reluctant Saint*, a U.S.–Italian co-production about a Franciscan monk in the 17th century. Although the film was released in 1962, she managed to get her first role (as Rafaela) in an American film proper in *Return to Peyton Place* (1961), acting alongside such performers as Carol Lynley, Jeff Chandler and Mary Astor.

Paluzzi apparently spent some time filling out her figure, for when she appeared onscreen again, in *Muscle Beach Party* (1964) as the shapely Julie, she now appeared more voluptuous and certainly a contender for the kind of Euro sexpot roles that American and British producers were seeking to fill with European actresses. Her big break finally came when British film producers Albert Broccoli and Harry Saltzman signed her for the fifth James Bond film, *Thunderball*, in 1965 as Fiona Volpe

Luciana Paluzzi gave quite a few men the jitters as the deadly and seductive killer Fiona Volpe in *Thunderball* (United Artists, 1965).

(after original choices Faye Dunaway and Julie Christie were considered). Paluzzi also screen tested for the role of the film's heroine, Domino, but Thunderball producers thought that she would make a better villain, and they were certainly right.

Cast alongside film series hero James Bond, played by Sean Connery, Paluzzi appeared as a female executioner who becomes Bond's chief nemesis while he is on assignment in the Bahamas. When we are first introduced to her shapely figure, Fiona is seen stalking the British agent and assigning one of her own henchmen to kill him. Over the course of the movie she is given the chance to drive incredibly expensive vehicles at speeds far exceeding the speed limits, murder with quickness and precision, and make love to her enemy (on her own terms) as if garnering a trophy. In the film, her demise is rather quick and abrupt, but that is because the lengthy movie also has two other chief villains to contend with (Adolfo Celli's Emilio Largo and the mostly-unseen Blofeld, master of the international criminal agency S.P.E.C.T.R.E.). As well, Paluzzi could not take too much attention away from former Miss Italy and Miss Europe Claudine Auger, who had the leading female role as the heroine, Domino. In hindsight, she did. The combination of her gutsy performance and attitude made viewers remember her far more than screen ingenue Auger, who seems to have been cast for appearance rather than talent. It would have been more interesting to see Paluzzi essay that role instead. Eighteen years later the film was remade as *Never Say Never Again* (1983), and her role in the original film was performed by Barbara Carrera, as the character of Fiona Volpe was re-named Fatima Blush.

The following year (1966) Paluzzi appeared on international theater screens in the first *The Man from U.N.C.L.E.* feature film, *To Trap a Spy*, which included extra footage of Paluzzi needed to pad the pilot episode "The Vulcan Affair." Her scenes shot for *To Trap a Spy* were then added to the episode "The Four-Steps Affair" (2/22/65). In *To Trap a Spy*, Paluzzi appeared in racy sequences with U.N.C.L.E. star David McCallum. In the same scenes shown in "The Four-Steps Affair" she is only shown disrobing in another room. In this early episode, the U.N.C.L.E. agents guard a visiting young prince whom THRUSH has targeted for death. Paluzzi also appeared in the debut episode of the short-lived espionage-related program *The Girl from U.N.C.L.E.* in 1966, in the episode "The Dog-Gone Affair," playing Tuesday Hajadakis (9/13/66). *Variety* commented that, "Miss Paluzzi should adorn more TV shows" and that, "she adds dimensions..." In this episode, U.N.C.L.E. agent April Dancer (Stefanie Powers) delivers a canine named Putzi to a Greek isle where fellow agent Mark Slate (Noel Harrison) is battling a man-made THRUSH disease. The dog carries the antidote.

Paluzzi also appeared in a very low budget Italian-Yugoslavian-British co-production titled *The One-Eyed Soldiers* (a.k.a. *Il Segreto dei Soldati d'Argilla*) in 1966. In this espionage thriller she co-stars alongside once-popular American television western star Dale Robertson and becomes involved with him, as together they are chased across Eastern Europe by enemy agents. Although it has an intriguing premise of an American adventurer searching Eastern European locales for the killer of a U.N. delegate, the film's leading man is not able to display the kind of heroic feats of derring-do that international audiences have become accustomed to via the James Bond series, and the mature Robertson makes for a rather taciturn hero. Paluzzi tags along as his love interest.

She reunited with *U.N.C.L.E.* co-star Robert Vaughn in the film *The Venetian Affair* (1967), a confusing and heavy-handed espionage thriller. A former CIA operative (Vaughn) who has become a reporter for an international news agency has been assigned to cover a terrorist bombing that killed delegates of a U.N. peace conference in Venice. The flick is filled with double crosses and many twists and turns, leaving the viewers pondering the attractive locales, femme fatales (Paluzzi and Elke Sommer), twilight career performance by aging horror film star Boris Karloff (as a political analyst) and slow pacing.

Much more effective as an espionage thriller clearly based on the success of the James Bond formula was OSS 117 Murder for Sale (a.k.a. Niente Roses per OSS 117, a.k.a. No Roses for OSS 117, 1968) which starred American actor John Gavin as an effective hero based on a popular series of novels by French novelist Jean Bruce (his books were influenced by the popular Ian Fleming–James Bond novels). In this film, secret agent OSS 117 (Gavin) is ordered to trade identities with an assassin in order to infiltrate the secret criminal organization headed by "the Golem" (Curt Jurgens), a megalomaniac intent on world domination via his cadre of well-trained assassins. Paluzzi appears as the chief medical doctor for the Golem's henchmen and the love interest for our globetrotting hero. Seldom-seen nowadays, the film is interesting for showcasing the actress, after resisting the romantic wiles of James Bond as one of Thunderball's main villains, coming full circle and finally becoming the love interest for an action hero modeled on the Bond character.

Luciana Paluzzi parlayed the international financial success and public interest in these espionage films into a career that lasted for another ten years. She followed the above roles with parts in a variety of films. She appeared in the Italian crime thriller A Black Veil for Lisa (a.k.a. La Morte Ha Sesso, 1968) as the wife of embittered and jealous police official John Mills, and in the enjoyable Japanese-American co-production about alien creatures infesting an orbiting space station, The Green Slime (1969). She also appeared in Spanish exploitation filmmaker Jesus Franco's 99 Women (a.k.a. 99 Mujeres) in 1969, playing the role of a terrorized inmate in a women's prison located in a jungle.

The seventies began with an appearance in the underrated Captain Nemo and the Underwater City (1969) and in the Spanish-produced film A Soldier Named Joe (a.k.a. El Hombre Que Vino del Odio, a.k.a. Run for Your Life, 1970), in which she co-starred with American actor Lang Jeffries as the love interest to an amoral smuggler. She appeared in the film Black Gunn (1972), an early black exploitation movie about a man (Jim Brown) who seeks revenge against the criminals who murdered his brother; Paluzzi provided the interracial love interest (as well as her first extensive nude scenes in a film). In 1973 she appeared as the character Carla Luchese in an episode of the TV series Search (1/10/73), about a crack team of experts searching for a missing heiress who has four days left to inherit a $4 billion estate.

In 1974 she returned to the scene of one of her earliest roles (as an Amazon) when she reunited with Thunderball director Terence Young for War Goddess (a.k.a. La Guerriere dal Seno Nudo, a.k.a. The Amazons). In this film, which relies on the nudity and sensual acrobatics of its sword swinging supporting cast of female stars, Paluzzi has a key role of an Amazon leader. She continued through the seventies with appearances in a few minor Italian crime thrillers and the American film The Klansman (1974), starring alongside Richard Burton and Lee Marvin. Her most recent roles were in the Italian sex comedy The Sensuous Nurse (a.k.a. L'Infermiera, 1976) and in The Greek Tycoon (1978), the film that dramatized the romance between Jacqueline Kennedy and Greek billionaire Aristotle Onassis.

Luciana Paluzzi is still active on the fringes of the film scene and still involved in the entertainment industry. In 1999 she was photographed (alongside other former Bond actresses) by the esteemed photographer Annie Liebovitz for a *Vanity Fair* magazine layout documenting the "Bond Girls" in preparation for the release of the nineteenth film in that series, *The World Is Not Enough* (2000). For whatever she is remembered, Luciana Paluzzi will surely be recalled as the one Bond girl who got her man, rather than the other way around.

Other films include: *Colpo Grosso, Grossissimo ... Anzi Probabile* (1972), *Manhunt: The Italian Connection* (a.k.a. *La Mala Ordine, Medusa,* a.k.a. *To Kynighitis Medhoussa,* 1973) and *Il Commissario Verrazzano* (1974).

Trina Parks

Diamonds Are Forever's Trina Parks was the first African-American actress to be featured in a James Bond movie. To this day, the scene where Parks, as the athletic five-foot-eight-and-a-half-inch, bikini-clad bodyguard Thumper, gives 007 a thrashing is one of the most exciting fight sequences the series has to offer. She truly left an indelible impression on fans of spy films.

Trina Parks grew up in the Bedford-Stuyvesant section of Brooklyn, New York. Her mother died was she was very young so she was raised by her father, Chuck Frazier, who played saxophone and flute for such renowned superstars as Cab Calloway, Duke Ellington and Billie Holiday. Recognizing talent in his daughter, he enrolled her in the Brooklyn Academy of Music. She majored in music, but she also was trained in dance, which turned out to be her forte. She studied under the tutelage of Katherine Dunham and Martha Graham, among others. Parks was the featured dancer in the Katherine Dunham Revue when it opened in Paris in 1964. She remained in Paris for awhile, where she appeared in a TV special with Michel Legrand and made her film debut in *Deux Anges Sont Venus*.

Returning to New York, Parks was cast in a few off–Broadway roles before she decided to give Hollywood a try. She did stunt work in *Beyond the Valley of the Dolls* (1970) and danced with James Earl Jones in *The Great White Hope* (1971). While performing at the Flamingo Lounge in Las Vegas, she learned that the producers of *Diamonds Are Forever* (1971) were looking for a girl to do this "wild scene." Parks remarked to *Ebony Magazine* in 1972, "I didn't know what kind of 'wild scene' they were talking about but I decided to go over and check it out anyway." After impressing the producers enough to cast her in the role, Parks had to finagle two weeks off to shoot the movie. "James Bond only comes into a girl's life once—if she's lucky, so I just had to have that leave."

Parks was cast in what turned out to be one of the most infamous scenes in James Bond movie history. Toward the end of *Diamonds Are Forever* (1971), Bond discovers villain Ernst Blofeld's desert hideaway and goes there looking for kidnapped millionaire Willard Whyte (Jimmy Dean). As he sneaks into the house, he encounters Amazonian bodyguards Bambi (stuntwoman

In *Diamonds Are Forever* (United Artists, 1971), Sean Connery (James Bond) gets a lesson in female brutality from Trina Parks as Blofeld's deadly bodyguard, Thumper.

Donna Garrett) and Thumper (Parks) in Blofeld's huge open-air living room. After greeting him ("Is there something we can do for you," asks Thumper), the agile Amazonians beat the stuffing out of Bond, with Thumper kicking Bond first in the groin. After they give him a thorough thrashing, the hellions toss him into the swimming pool. However, when they jump in to finish him off, Bond gets the advantage and holds their heads under water until Bambi gasps and tells him where Dean is being held. Parks is especially menacing as Thumper, moving with the grace of a feline on the prowl and ready to pounce on her next victim. Recalling the fight scene, the lithesome dancer commented to *Ebony*, "Just about everything was choreographed in detail by stunt producer Paul Baxley."

Regarding Parks' infamous kick to Sean Connery's groin, John Koch wrote in *Boston After Dark*, "...Ms. Parks said that during the first few takes she simply couldn't perform with adequate realism. When Connery assured Ms. Parks ... that he was reinforced with 'double protection' she continued to demur. Finally, when Connery offered to display his prophylactic credentials, she dug into the part, preferring to avoid the exhibition."

Though *Diamonds Are Forever* gave Parks much exposure and reams of publicity, she never achieved major stardom, despite revealing to *Ebony* that her dream was to "make it really big in all three fields ... big hit records, good film roles, top club dates, even concerts." Alas, her film career never caught fire. Parks interviewed for the female leads but did not get cast in the sequels to both *Shaft* and *Cotton Comes to Harlem*. The parts she did land included a member of an African-American female biker gang in *Darktown Strutters* (1974) and a hardened prisoner at a jungle prison farm in *The Muthers* (1976).

Today Trina Parks is a choreographer and teacher. She instructs both the Katherine Dunham and Martha Graham dance techniques in various venues around Southern California while still finding the time to act and sing, most recently in the touring company of *I Don't Want to Cry No More*, which was billed as "an inspirational musical drama."

Other films include: *The Big Rip-Off* (1974—TV), *The Blues Brothers* (1980) and *Liquid Sky* (1982).

Joanna Pettet

Joanna Pettet was born Joanna Jane Salmon on November 16, 1944, in London, England. She and her mother relocated to Canada after her father, a British RAF pilot, was killed during World War II. Joanna took the surname of Pettet from her stepfather. She moved from Montreal to New York City at age 16 and studied acting at the famed Neighborhood Playhouse. Commenting to a British news correspondent in 1967 while promoting the film *Robbery*, she said, "I went to New York City with one thousand dollars in my pocket. I thought it would last me up to two years,

I'd never really fended for myself before and didn't realize how fast money could go. The whole nest egg was gone in three months." However, Pettet's acting talents landed her a scholarship and soon after roles in plays like *Take Her, She's Mine*, *The Chinese Prime Minister* and *Poor Richard*, all of which garnered the actress strong positive reviews from New York's theatrical community press. Now, the five foot, seven inch, 117-pound actress with green eyes, red hair and a 34-24-34 figure was ripe for the movies.

Leaving the Lincoln Center Repertory theatrical company, Joanna Pettet made her film debut in *The Group* (1966), in the central role of Kay Strong, the bright theater major at a Vassar-type women's college whose marriage to a drunken lout (Larry Hagman) leads her to a tragic fate. She next appeared with Peter O'Toole in the jarring *The Night of the Generals* (1967) as the daughter of a German officer (Charles Gray) suspected of murdering prostitutes.

Being sexy, long-legged and blonde, it was no surprise that Joanna Pettet was signed by producer Charles Feldman to play Mata Bond (Pettet described the character as "campy") in *Casino Royale* (1967), the multi-million dollar James Bond spoof. She made quite an impression on male audiences as the barely clothed spy, the daughter of Sir James Bond (David Niven) and Mata Hari. After surviving an attack on his life by an agent impersonating M's widow (Deborah Kerr), Sir James tracks down his daughter, now living in a foreign temple. Bond persuades her to do a little spy work ("Do I get an exploding briefcase and a secret transmitter?" she asks). Her mission, to infiltrate the International Mother's Help, a spy school in Berlin run by Frau Hoffner (Anna Quayle) and Polo (Ronnie Corbett), who immediately accept the revered German spy's offspring. Mata Bond spies an auction of chief villain Le Chiffre's "unique art treasures" of compromising photos of army officers which Le Chiffre is staging to help pay back his gambling debts to SMERSH. To prevent Le Chiffre from raising the money, Mata swipes the photos, disposes of Hoffman and Polo, and combats the auction bidders in a melee reminiscent of the fight scenes from the TV series *Batman*, complete with "Pows" and Zonks" uttered by Pettet's character. With the help of Carlton Towers (Bernard Cribbens) of the Foreign Office, Mata escapes with the photos and returns to London. Unfortunately, this is the last we see of her until the film's disjointed finale.

Pettet stayed in the UK to co-star (with Stanley Baker) in the thrilling crime film *Robbery* (1967) as Kate, a London housewife. She followed this role with one in a violent western called *Blue* (1968), which co-starred Terence Stamp. In conjunction with this film, Joanna Pettet joined the long list of Bond girls to disrobe for *Playboy* magazine. In December of 1967 she remarked to Christina Kirk, writing in *The New York Daily News*, "The photographs are in good taste, I think. I know I'm not a sex bomb. But I am—I hope—feminine. Young people today have a more down-to-earth idea of what's beautiful." She then attempted lighter parts in minor British comedies (including *The Best House in London*, released in 1969 with an undeserved X rating) before returning to the U.S. She married actor Alex Cord in 1968, and their son Damien was born shortly thereafter. Sadly, the marriage ended in 1976 and Damien tragically passed away in 1995.

Pettet's final espionage appearance was in *The Delphi Bureau* (1972), a made-for-television feature that introduced a short-lived series starring Laurence Luckinbill. He starred as Glenn Garth Gregory, an agent with a photographic memory who reports directly to the President of the United States and gets his assignments from a Washington, D.C., society hostess

(Celeste Holm). In the pilot feature, Pettet played the role of April Thompson, the secretary to a mute agriculturist (Dean Jagger) who has created a special grain to feed the world. Spies (Bob Crane and David Sheiner) infiltrate his farm to use as a cover to smuggle stolen military aircraft out of the country. At first suspecting of her duplicity, Gregory falls for Thompson, who turns out to be the heroine and helps him foil the plot. However, though the film ends with their blossoming romance, it was never explored further when the pilot was picked up as a series. Joanna Pettet's character was nowhere to be found.

In the seventies Pettet's career seemed mired in a seemingly endless array of American television films, where her roles ran the gamut from a nun who works as a pistol-packin' probation officer in *The Weekend Nun* (1972) to a widowed Wyoming homesteader in *Pioneer Woman* (1973). Pettet was also a fixture on a number of seventies cop and detective series, including *Mannix, Banacek, McCloud, Harry O, Police Story, Police Woman* and *Charlie's Angels*, among others.

The nadir of Pettet's once promising career came with Laurence Harvey's directorial debut, *Welcome to Arrow Beach* (1974), an unpleasant film about cannibalism in contemporary America (funded by the men's cologne company, Brut) which remained unreleased for years, only to surface in a heavily reedited version. Pettet played the human flesh–eating sister of Harvey's cannibal. Continuing in the horror realm, Pettet made four TV guest appearances on Rod Serling's *Night Gallery*. On the big screen she screamed her way through the chilling *The Evil* (1978), as one of the new inhabitants of a haunted mansion, and *Double Exposure* (1982), as the love interest of Michael Callan, who played a photographer who foresees the murders of his models. Later, an attempt to regain prestige backfired when she appeared in the

Joanna Pettet as Mata Bond in the outrageous spy spoof *Casino Royale* (Columbia, 1967).

little-seen film *Othello* (a.k.a. *Othello, the Black Commando*, 1982) in the role of Desdemona.

After playing the recurring role of a detective on the hit primetime soap *Knots Landing* in 1983, Pettet, Lana Wood and Britt Ekland played themselves on an episode of *The Fall Guy* in 1984. The three actresses are hired to play roles in the fictitious James Bond movie *Always Say Always*, on which series star Lee Majors and his crew are working as stuntmen as a cover to locate stolen art work. Thereafter, she worked occasionally, with the feature *Terror in Paradise* (1990) being her last known credit. Joanna Pettet had beauty, talent and poise and deserved better than being a TV movie-of-the-week actress. Reportedly, she resides in the desert outside of Los Angeles.

Other films include: *To Catch a Pebble* (1972), *Footsteps* (1972—TV), *A Killer in Every Corner* (1974—TV), *A Midsummer Nightmare* (1975—TV), *The Dark Side of Innocence* (1976—

TV), *The Hancocks* (1976—TV), *Two-Minute Warning* (1976—TV) [uncredited scenes in extended TV version], *Sex and the Married Woman* (1977—TV), *The Return of Frank Cannon* (1980—TV) and *Sweet Country* (1987).

Nyree Dawn Porter

Nyree Dawn Porter was born Ngaire Dawn Porter in New Zealand on January 22, 1940. She made her first appearance on the stage at age three, playing the role of a bird in an amateur production of *Noah's Ark*. She recalls today how, walking onto that stage for the first time she was delighted "...to hear the applause of the audience." Years later Porter pursued an acting career, but was still appearing in amateur productions until her big break. She told an Internet reporter from New Zealand, "I was acting in a local amateur production when a woman came to my dressing room and asked me if I ever considered acting as a career. She was the wife of a leading actor at the New Zealand National Theatre."

For the young woman, who also had an interest in reading, painting and ballet, the theater was a true love. She had grown too tall for ballet and became stuck in amateur theater productions due to an accident and an illness that prevented her from accepting starring roles in other productions. Husky-voiced and honey-skinned, the blonde actress was dubbed "Miss New Zealand Cinema" by 1958, although she had never made a film.

Nyree Dawn Porter left New Zealand for London, England, and stage roles led to appearances on a variety of television programs, including such espionage series as *Danger Man* (in "The Island," 1960), *The Avengers* (in "Death on the Slipway," 6/24/61) and *The Saint* (in "The Scorpion," 10/29/64).

Porter also appeared in a number of mediocre British films before finding international fame on the BBC television series *The Forsyte Saga* in 1967. After the program's run, she auditioned for the leading female role in the film *McKenna's Gold* (1968) opposite star Gregory Peck, but he felt that she was too young for the part. A role in a British television production of *Jane Eyre* (1970) won her the attention of other film producers, and she was quickly signed for a memorable role in the horror anthology movie *The House That Dripped Blood* (1970). In that film she played a nanny to one horrible little bewitching child. Porter's big break came with her being cast as the third lead in the ITC television show *The Protectors* in 1972.

The Protectors was a series that involved the world's three top agents, Harry Rule (Robert Vaughn of *The Man from U.N.C.L.E.* fame), Lady Caroline Ogilvie, the Contessa di Contini (Porter) and Paul Buchet (Tony Anholt), who were assigned the most dangerous missions around the world by agency head Rule, a leading investigator in semi-retirement who operates out of a luxurious modern office in London. His partners, the Countess and Buchet, operate primarily in France and Italy, with Rule joining them on the assignments. Together they were known as *The Protectors*.

Nyree Dawn Porter as the sophisticated agent Lady Caroline Ogilvie in the British adventure series *The Protectors* (ITC, ca. 1971).

Nyree Dawn Porter spent the majority of the series' two-year run clad in an incredible array of the finest clothes, driving the finest cars and traveling around the world, filming in some of the most beautiful locations that Europe had to offer. Being a seemingly stern scion of haute couture, her character, the Contessa, really itched to get into scu·es ... and often did.

The show lasted for an astounding 52 episodes, despite star and producer Robert Vaughn's unhappiness with the first season's story lines. In each episode the trio performed the usual feats of derring-do, but more often than not this was an old-fashioned espionage program, frequently with convoluted scripts and plots knee deep in Cold War ethics. This was an interesting device for an action show; however, audiences weaned on high adventure movies in the cinema (like the Bond series) were not that interested in it.

The program's lack of support from U.S. television networks meant that it all came to an end in 1974. Nyree Dawn Porter returned to her stage work and had roles in a small selection of films, some on television (most notably, *The Martian Chronicles* miniseries in 1979). She most recently appeared in the film *Hilary and Jackie* (1998). Sadly, she passed away on April 10, 2001.

Other films include: *Sentenced for Life* (1960), *Part-Time Wife* (1961), *The Man at the Carlton Tower* (1961), *Two Left Feet* (1963), *The Cracksman* (1963) and *From Beyond the Grave* (1973).

Stefanie Powers

No more than a competent actress, pretty, athletic Stefanie Powers (born Stefania Zofia Federkiewicz on Nov. 2, 1942, in Hollywood, California) has had a surprisingly successful and lengthy career. After being fired as one of the dancers in *West Side Story* when the producers realized that she was underage, this graduate of Hollywood High School went on to appear in *The Young Sinner* in 1960, but it was shelved. Her official film debut, using the name Taffy Paul, was in the Sandra Dee/Bobby Darin romantic comedy *If a Man Answers* (1962). Shortly thereafter she changed her name again, signed with Columbia Pictures and won kudos for her performance as the kidnapped younger sister of Lee Remick in the harrowing thriller *Experiment in Terror* (1962). An all-American beauty, Powers was typecast as the good girl in such routine films as *The Interns* (1962), *Palm Springs Weekend* (1963) and *The New Interns* (1964), the same year she was voted a "Star of Tomorrow." So it is no wonder that, after being cast as April Dancer in *The Girl from U.N.C.L.E.*, she commented to *Look* magazine, "It's a cop-out for an actress but it's flamboyant, and flamboyant I've never been." Powers looked fantastic as the U.N.C.L.E. agent armed with a pocketbook full of gadgets, but a beautifully coiffured spy does not a successful series make.

The press release for *The Girl from U.N.C.L.E.* touted Stefanie Powers' April Dancer as "the swingingest, coolest agent ever to tote an 'U.N.C.L.E.' special. Don't let her beauty mislead you. She is five-feet, five-inches of dark-haired danger." The character (originally to be named Cookie Fortune) was first introduced in "The Moonglow Affair" episode during the second season of *The Man from U.N.C.L.E.* The producers originally wanted Powers to play the role but she was making a movie, so Mary Ann Mobley took the part. When the producers decided to launch *The Girl from U.N.C.L.E.* as a series, they again went to Powers first, who eagerly accepted.

The Girl from U.N.C.L.E. was scheduled for the 7:30 P.M. timeslot on NBC opposite *Daktari* on CBS and *Combat* on ABC. To assure its success, U.N.C.L.E. agents April Dancer and her partner Mark Slate (Noel Harrison, Rex's son) reported to Mr. Waverly (Leo G. Carroll), as did their *Man from U.N.C.L.E.* counterparts Napoleon Solo and Illya Kuryakin, in the same New York headquarters. The show premiered on 9/13/66 with "The Dog Gone Affair," one of the series' better efforts. April jets off to Greece to stop THRUSH agent Apollo Zakinthios (Kurt Kaszner) from unleashing a slow-motion gas. Accompanying her is a dog whose fleas contain the antidote to the gaseous mixture. Though a bit preposterous, the show received favorable reviews. *Variety* remarked, "A team to be celebrated was formed in the debut of *Girl from U.N.C.L.E.* Only the mad power thrust of THRUSH, if ever successful, could tear Stefanie Powers and Noel Harrison asunder." Or bad reviews and low ratings.

As the show continued, it delved deeper and deeper into the silliness that also plagued *The Man from U.N.C.L.E* during its third season. It was not unexpected, since one of the show's original press releases focused exclusively on the gadgets found in April's handbag—"a lipstick that's a hypodermic, a rattail comb that's very handy as a stiletto and bubble gum with a

Stefanie Powers starred as U.N.C.L.E. agent April Dancer in the short-lived series *The Girl from U.N.C.L.E.* (MGM-TV, 1966).

bang." One of the series' best episodes pitted Powers' April Dancer against Gena Rowlands as a Baroness who has developed a formula retarding the aging process in "The Fountain of Youth Affair" (2/7/67). Sillier efforts included April dressed in a Shakespearean costume while tangling with Boris Karloff in drag in "The Mother Muffin Affair" (9/27/66), being kidnapped into Fernando Lamas' harem in "The U.F.O. Affair" (1/3/67) and masquerading as a go-go dancer to uncover a song that could spark an avalanche in "The Drublegratz Affair" (1/31/67). But the most embarrassing predicament April found herself in was when she was placed (à la *Batman*) in "this giant toaster to be cooked to crumbs" in "The Carpathian Caper Affair" (2/14/67). It was episodes like these that prompted *TV Guide* critic Cleveland Amory to comment that *The Girl from U.N.C.L.E.* is "about as believable as women's wrestling. And it has about as much wit as a roller derby." As for the cast, he wrote, "To fault all the actors equally in this show isn't fair—when everybody's that bad, the director deserves first blame." Ouch!

With reviews like that, and ratings falling, it was no surprise that the series was cancelled after only one season. Powers made two more stabs at the spy genre, playing Mona, Al Mundy's (Robert Wagner) companion, who vanishes when they get stranded in an old western town called "Fortune City" (2/2/70) on *It Takes a Thief*. The spy series *Search* featured her as Jill Davenport in the episode entitled "One of Our Probes Is Missing" (9/20/72). Tony Franciosa, as Probe agent Nick Bianco, searches for a missing agent who was investigating a counterfeiting ring.

During the seventies Stefanie Powers continued appearing in a number of mediocre features (in 1972's *Crescendo* she is a grad student terrorized by a dead composer's family) and even less-than-mediocre TV movies (in 1974's *Skyway to Death* she is trapped on a stalled sky tram high up in the mountains with Bobby Sherman). Her career was resurrected somewhat when she was cast as an attorney teamed with Harold Gould (as her reformed conman father) in the short-lived series *The Feather and Father Gang* in 1976. Though the series flopped, Powers received good notices. This indirectly led to her being cast opposite Robert Wagner as the super rich, adventurous sleuths Jennifer and Jonathan Hart in the breezy detective series *Hart to Hart*. The third time proved the charm for Powers, as the series was a huge commercial success, running for five seasons. Powers even received two Emmy nominations for "Outstanding Actress in a Drama Series" in 1981 and 1982.

After a brief marriage to actor Gary Lockwood during the sixties, Powers became a longtime companion of actor William Holden. After his untimely death and the cancellation of *Hart to Hart* during the mid-eighties, she concentrated most of her time championing the William Holden Wildlife Foundation to establish a permanent wildlife preserve in Kenya. She still finds time to accept an acting role or two, and most recently starred in a series of made-for-TV *Hart to Hart* reunion movies and the tele-feature *Someone Is Watching* (2000).

Other films include: *McLintock!* (1963), *Die! Die! My Darling* (1965), *Stagecoach* (1966), *Warning Shot* (1967), *The Boatniks* (1970), *Sweet, Sweet Rachel* (1971—TV), *Five Desperate Women* (1971—TV), *No Place to Run* (1972—TV), *The Magnificent Seven Ride!* (1972), *Herbie Rides Again!* (1974), *Nowhere to Run* (1978—TV), *A Death in Canaan* (1978—TV), *Escape to Athena* (1979), *Deceptions* (1985—TV), *At Mother's Request* (1987—TV), *When Will I Be Loved?* (1990—TV) and *Hart to Hart Returns* (1993—TV).

Dorothy Provine

Energetic Dorothy Provine (born on January 20, 1937, in Deadwood, South Dakota) is remembered most for her singing and dancing abilities, and as a talented comedienne. So it may come as a surprise that this beautiful blonde had the female lead in two spy movies—*The Man from U.N.C.L.E.* film *One Spy Too Many* (1965) and the James Bond rip-off *Kiss the Girls and Make Them Die* (1966). Provine's expert comedic performances are the films' high points and she steals the spotlight away from her male co-stars.

Before becoming a spy heroine supreme, Provine's acting career began after she left the University of Washington and accompanied a friend to Hollywood. She appeared on the debut episode of *77 Sunset Strip* and played a juvenile delinquent in *Live Fast, Die Young* (1958) before signing a seven-year contract with Warner Bros. Her first TV series, *The Alaskans*, got her noticed, but playing flapper Pinky Pinkham in her second series, *The Roaring Twenties*, made her a star. When the show ended in 1962, she returned to films, appearing to good effect in *It's a Mad, Mad, Mad, Mad World* (1963), *Good Neighbor Sam* (1964) and *The Great Race* (1965) before becoming part of the sixties spy craze.

In *One Spy Too Many*, Provine played Tracey Alexander, the ex-wife of maniacal Alexander (Rip Torn), who is intent on taking over the world as his namesake Alexander the Great tried to do. To that end, he steals the Army's top secret "will gas" (which "could chemically reduce an opponents' will to win") from the U.S. Army Biological Warfare Department. To their chagrin, Tracey joins U.N.C.L.E. agents Napoleon Solo (Robert Vaughn) and Illya Kuryakin (David McCallum) in their search for her husband. She is determined to get Alexander to sign her settlement papers to get back her million-dollar inheritance. Her character was a perfect example of the determined "innocent" who would get in the way despite their good intentions as the agents try to foil the villain's diabolical plot. However, Provine's performance made Tracey one of the show's more memorable innocents. (*Variety* raved that Provine "cavorts with expert charm, displaying fine style as an actress.") Through the course of the film, Tracey gets walled up in a tomb, tied up with Illya and suspended over a bottomless pit while a candle burns away at the rope, slapped by her husband and held at knifepoint. After all that he puts her through, the kooky Tracey is at first rueful when she learns Alexander has perished in a plane explosion. "I'm going to miss him," she says sadly. "All in all he gave me a pretty fast three years." "Even if he was a liar, a thief and a murderer?" asks an incredulous Solo. "He was *never* dull," she replies before going off to find another incredibly wealthy man to romance.

Provine played British agent Susan Fleming masquerading as a flighty socialite with a fussy chauffeur (Terry-Thomas), in *Kiss the Girls and Make Them Die* (a.k.a. *Se Tutte le Donne del Monda*), directed by Dino Maiuri and Henry Levin. Produced by Dino De Laurentiis, the Italian-Portuguese co-production was shot on location in Brazil in 1966. It was released in Italy that same year but didn't surface in the U.S. until 1968. In the film, Michael Connors plays an American agent named Kelly in Rio de Janeiro on assignment to investigate mysterious industrialist Mr. Ardonian (Raf

Vallone), who has perfected a satellite that emits ultrasonic waves that can sterilize mankind. While monitoring Ardonian, Kelly learns that the villain has collected a stable of beautiful women—each from a different country. At first Kelly assumes Susan Fleming is just another one of Ardonian's girlfriends. They agree to work together to bring him down. Ardonian discovers that Susan is a spy, and Kelly saves her from becoming part of his "hibernation harem" before dispatching the madman.

Though *Kiss the Girls and Make Them Die* is colorful and fast moving, Mike Connors lacks the sexiness of Sean Connery, James Coburn or even Paul Mantee (in *A Man Called Dagger*) to make a completely convincing secret agent. As Susan Fleming, Provine's forced British accent is off-putting and annoying. Critic William Peper wrote, "Henry Levin has directed for the easy laugh and Miss Provine, with her phony accent, shamelessly goes after every one." The *New York Times* was more complimentary and remarked that, "Miss Provine is quite the brightest thing about the picture." Accent aside, Provine acquits herself quite well as a prim and proper spy who doesn't use a gun but relies on some outlandish gadgets (including a mascara tube that emits knockout gas and a ring laced with poison) to waylay her enemies. Provine also displays quite a voluptuous figure when she strips down to her jungle shorts outfit. It is no wonder she was offered the role of Jean Harlow in the Bill Sargent production of *Harlow*, which she wisely turned down.

Provine starred in a few more films, including the comedies *Who's Minding the Mint?* (1967) with Jim Hutton, and *Never a Dull Moment* (1968) with Dick Van Dyke, before calling it quits. She married cinematographer Robert Day (who also directed many episodes of *The Avengers*) in 1967 and had a son shortly thereafter. In 1971, she told *Look* magazine, "I'm sort of retired now. I'm not doing anything—except a commercial.... When you decide to become a parent, you have to devote your full time to it and take care of your child." She died on April 25, 2010.

Dorothy Provine as the outrageously costumed British spy Susan Fleming in *Kiss the Girls and Make Them Die* (Columbia, 1966).

Other films include: *The Bonnie Parker Story* (1958), *The 30 Foot Bride of Candy Rock* (1959), *Riot in Juvenile Prison* (1959), *Wall of Noise* (1963), *That Darn Cat* (1965) and *The Sound of Anger* (1968—TV).

Eva Renzi

Eva Renzi was born Evelyn (Eva) Renziehausen on November 3, 1944, in Berlin, Germany. At age 16 she enrolled in the Berlin Actors' Studio and afterwards began appearing in plays on the German stage. During this period, an early acting career high point was playing a maid in an eight-month run of (a German translation of) Noel Coward's *Dinner at Eight*. Following this, Renzi married and had a daughter, Anoushka. When the marriage proved short-lived, she took to a modeling career to support herself and her child.

Modeling fashionable clothes and becoming a sort of glamour girl (she was 5'10" and 122 luscious pounds) for the German newspapers and journals led to her first film role as a free-spirited, sexually expressive woman in the movie *Playgirl* (a.k.a. *Berlin Ist Eine Suende Wert*, 1965). Renzi met fellow actor Paul Hubschmid (himself a star of the 1965 spy movie *Upperseven: The Man to Kill*) on the set of this film, and the two were romantically linked and then married. Hubschmid introduced his wife to James Bond series co-producer Harry Saltzman, who was casting for the second Harry Palmer film, *Funeral in Berlin*, featuring Michael Caine in the leading role as the reluctant but ingenious British spy. Apparently, Anjanette Comer was signed to play the female lead, Samantha Steel, but withdrew from the production near the beginning of shooting, so Saltzman replaced her with Eva Renzi.

In *Funeral in Berlin* (1966), secret agent Harry Palmer (Michael Caine) investigates the possible defection of the head of the Russian security for the KGB (Oskar Homolka), leading to a variety of mishaps and deadly espionage games. Renzi performed well enough in the film for Saltzman and fellow Bond series co-producer Albert Broccoli to offer her a leading role in the next planned James Bond film, *You Only Live Twice* (1967), but she declined (the part went to fellow German actress Karin Dor instead). Renzi told James Meade, a *Newark Evening News* reporter, in the fall of 1967 about her decision to pass on the Bond film, "Bond pictures are good for pretty girls but not for actresses. I would rather sell shoes."

Unfortunately, the choice to refuse the Bond movie meant that Eva Renzi appeared in a number of mediocre films like *Die Zeit der Kirschen Ist Vorbel* (1967), *Pink Jungle* (1968) and *That Woman* (1968). The obscure mystery thriller *Why Would Anyone Want to Kill a Nice Girl Like You?* (1968) was a welcome change of pace, with Renzi starring as a beleaguered woman who becomes embroiled in an assassination plot with bizarre results. However, the film, directed by Don Sharp, became, for one reason or another, something of an immediate nonentity, and over the years it has become a lost film, doing little for her career. She fared slightly better as a psychologically troubled woman in Italian horror director Dario Argento's debut feature *The Bird with the Crystal Plumage* (a.k.a. *L'Uccello dalle Piume di Cristallo*, 1969) as Monica Ranieri. The film is highly regarded by genre film aficionados, and its healthy video and DVD shelf life has made it a popular entry with European horror fans. The European (but primarily Greek) co-production *The Night of the Assassin* (a.k.a. *Appuntamento Con il Disonore*, a.k.a. *Rendezvous with Dishonor*, 1970) is a World War II thriller co-starring Michael Craig and Klaus Kinski (as a priest!), but the slow, laborious film ultimately has little to recommend it.

Renzi next appeared in the obscure German softcore sex film *Bite Me, Darling* (a.k.a. *Beiss Mich, Liebling*, a.k.a. *Love, Vampire Style*, 1970) as one of the lovely playthings that a comical vampire Count seduces. Today the film is little remembered, aside from some mediocre reviews at the time of its release, and has yet to surface on video or DVD in English speaking countries. Another thriller in the mold of *The Bird with the Crystal Plumage* was *Death Occurred Last Night* (a.k.a. *La Morte Risale a Leri Sera*, 1971), but this movie, primarily a mystery about a father (Raf Vallone) searching for the killer or killers of his daughter, is remembered today mainly for the amount of skin showed by the female cast members and its often brutal scenes of violence. Renzi attempted to break into the American market by appearing in the U.S. television pilot *Primus* (1971) in the role of Toni Hayden. However, the adventure show had a short life on the small screen after the original program was aired, and apparently she decided to return to Europe and spend the majority of her career (at least until the mid-eighties) acting in films and television productions in both France and Germany. She died on August 16, 2005.

Eva Renzi as Samantha Steel becomes involved in international intrigue in *Funeral in Berlin* (Universal, 1966).

Other films include: *Tatort–Kressin und der Tote Mann im Fleet* (German TV, 1971), *Das Blaue Palais: Der Gigant* (German TV, 1976), *Das Blaue Palais: Unsichtblichkeit...?* (German TV, 1976), *Papa Poule* (French TV, 1980), *La Fille Prodigue* (1981), *Jager Des Herzens* (1984) and *Dario Argento's World of Horror* (a.k.a. *Il Mondo dell'Orrore di Dario Argento*, documentary, 1985).

Janine Reynaud

Biographical details on Janine Reynaud are sketchy, in national and international reference sources and on-line databases, and sometimes inaccurate. Reynaud remains today as enigmatic a personality as she was in her heyday in the late sixties and early seventies when she appeared in numerous films. She was born in France in 1946, and she had a variety of career interests before meeting her future husband, the actor and filmmaker Michel Lemoine.

Lemoine had appeared on the stage in the late 1940s as an actor playing the part of Lenny in an adaptation of John

Steinbeck's *Of Mice and Men*. He journeyed to Italy in 1961, where he began a lucrative career as a film actor, appearing in dozens of movies in occasionally brief but memorable roles. Also that year he began an association with the French erotic filmmaker Jose Benazeraf and co-starred in his film *L'Eternite pour Nous* (1961). In the following years he appeared in other films by Benazera.

Lemoine met erotic film bit player Reynaud (after she began modeling for the French designer Jean Patou) on one of Benazera's film sets. After Reynaud met Lemoine, the two became inseparable, often to the point where he would surface (in minor roles) in the films in which she starred.

One of Janine Reynaud's earliest roles in a non-erotic film was in the espionage movie *Operation: White Shark* (a.k.a. *A.D. 3 Operazione Squalo Blanco*, 1965). In this rather obscure Italian production, secret agent AD 3 (Rodd Dana) is sent on a mission to recover a missing scientist, as well as important documents, from an undersea atomic laboratory. This rather tepid adventure film fell far below the low-budget espionage movie efforts from other European filmmakers of the period. In its eagerness to clone the Bond film formula, it forgot to have at its central axis an interesting hero.

What the film is remembered for chiefly is the introduction of the startling Reynaud to international cinema audiences. She was tall, with bright red hair, a figure that can be described as mature and sensually exciting, full, rich lips and narrow cheekbones that seemed to have sprung from her sharp, nearly Asiatic eyes. Reynaud gave the impression of a woman who is sensually enticing and at the same time ... dangerous. She possessed an unusual and exotic appearance for sure, and one which would cement her future roles, for Reynaud displayed that quality which today is referred to as androgynous.

In the obscure spy spoof *Special Mission in Caracas* (a.k.a. *Mission Speciale a Caracas*, 1965) about French agents who discover plans for a deadly nerve gas that will start a war between France and Russia, Reynaud appears as a treacherous femme fatale. A much larger role as a dominant, seemingly bisexual assistant to the leader of a sinister criminal organization in *Secret Agent Fireball* (a.k.a. *A 077 Sfida al Killers*, a.k.a. *The Killers Are Challenged*, 1966) brought even more attention to her. In this tale, three scientists (from Russia, the U.S. and West Germany) are selected for kidnapping and eventual assassination by a criminal organization. American secret agent Bob Fleming (Richard Harrison) goes to Casablanca to locate the missing scientists, and in order for his mission to succeed, he must impersonate yet another scientist who is to be assassinated.

In *Cifrato Speciale* (a.k.a. *Message Chiffre*, 1966), a French-Italian-German-Spanish co-production, Reynaud portrays the shapely but evil assistant to criminal mastermind Eduardo Fajardo. A special agent for C.U.R.D. (Lang Jeffries) is sent to Istanbul to discover who has stolen a secret anti-gravity formula developed by enemy agents.

In the all but forgotten espionage tale *The Spy Who Came from the Sea* (a.k.a. *La Spie Che Viene dal Mare*, 1966), Reynaud has a more prominent role in the tale of Italian counterespionage services that learn that a spy will appear in Italy within the next 48 hours to cause a disaster, with repercussions felt throughout the entire world. Many people who arrive in Italy during this time are suspected as being the spy, but the Italian Secret Service sends an American, Agent 027 (John Elliott), to San Marino to infiltrate the gang that has sent the special secret agent. Less convoluted was the Italian-Spanish film *Ypotron* (a.k.a. *Agente Logan, Missione Ypotron*, 1966). In this one, secret agent Lemmy Logan (Luis

Davila) is assigned to investigate the suspicious activities of an ex–Nazi atomic scientist named Professor Morrow who has been kidnapped by an East German organization. Agent Logan is sent to retrieve him, and, together with the professor's daughter, they follow the trail that leads to a secret missile base in Morocco. As in *Secret Agent Fireball*, Janine is on hand as an attractive but deadly agent for the other side.

Reynaud then appeared in a trio of films for Spanish director Jess Franco, who was just then closing out the sixties and entering into his second era of filmmaking. In *Necronomicon* (a.k.a. *Succubus*) she finally had a starring role, as the tortured succubus Lorna Green. Cast as a stripper, her character lures men (and women) to their deaths via her androgynous appearance, sensuality and Franco's bizarre mis-en-scene where the streets are always empty and nearly everything takes place (as in most of his later period films) in a bizarre, surreal, hallucinatory dream-like plane of existence.

Much more fun was to be had in Franco's second film with the actress, *Two Undercover Angels* (a.k.a. *El Caso de los Dos Bellazas*, a.k.a. *Rote Lippen*, 1967). As Diana, one of the duo of female private eyes (and strippers—for some reason, Franco had to have his gun-toting female private eyes also be strippers!), Reynaud, along with Rossanna Yanni (as Regina) form the Red Lips Detective Agency. In this bizarre espionage-horror hybrid, the women are hired to investigate the mysterious disappearances of nightclub dancers and fashion models, leading them to a bizarre artist (Adrian Hoven) who uses a werewolf-like killer (Michel Lemoine) to murder his victims.

In *Kiss Me Monster* (a.k.a. *Besame Monstruo*, 1967), the characters of Diana and Regina (Reynaud and Yanni) inhabit an even more surreal and strange landscape. The incoherence of the plot only adds to the lunacy onscreen as the two female private eyes again find themselves investigating murder on a sunny isle, encountering mutant male body builders in red bikinis and a dangerous group of feminist lesbian killers.

Reynaud then disappeared from the screen for a short time before she returned in the French sex film *I Am a Nymphomaniac* (a.k.a. *Je Suis une Nymphomane*, a.k.a. *Libido*, a.k.a. *Forbidden Passions*, 1970), directed by erotic filmmaker Max Pecas. Reuniting with Jose Benazeraf, she became his muse for his sexually explicit film *Frustration* (a.k.a. *Frustrated Women*, a.k.a. *The*

As Diana, one half of the Red Lips Detective Agency, Janine Reynaud investigates corruption, espionage, murder, white slavery and a werewolf killer in *Two Undercover Angels* (Atlas International, 1967).

Chambermaid's Dream, 1971). As Adelaide, a sexually impotent and tortured soul whose day and nightmares cross the boundaries of reality, resulting in total confusion and hysteria (even for the audience), she became the newest star of erotic cinema in France.

In the seventies, with the advent (and underground success) of hardcore pornography, American distributors demanded product for their exploitation grindhouses, so more of the Continental European sex films were marketed to major cities. Janine Reynaud became a familiar face in a number of them (with either originally produced hardcore footage or with the aid of sometimes clumsily edited hardcore inserts). After appearing in a few more of these type of films, Reynaud retired in 1974 and married a wealthy Texan, eventually relocating to America. Michel Lemoine, her former partner, continued on as a filmmaker into the eighties, directing hardcore pornographic features (some under a variety of pseudonyms).

Finally, the last word on Janine Reynaud comes from French journalist Henri Rode for the publication *Les Stars du Cinema Erotique*: "You couldn't mistake her for anyone else, a smoldering mouth, a shock of red hair imbued with a mysterious life."

Other films include: *Castle of Bloody Lust* (a.k.a. *Im Schloss der Blutigen Begierde*, 1967), *The Case of the Scorpion's Tail* (a.k.a. *La Coda dell Scorpione*, 1971), *Human Cobras* (a.k.a. *Cobras Humanas*, a.k.a. *L'Uomo Piu Velenoso del Cobra*, 1971), *I Am Available* (a.k.a. *Les Desaxees*, 1972), *Penelope* (a.k.a. *Penelope, Ou L'Hiver a Kermarec*, 1972), *Marianne Bouquet* (a.k.a. *Les Dexaxees*, 1972), *The Felines* (a.k.a. *Les Chiennes*, a.k.a. *The Bitches*, 1973) and *Invitation to Bed* (a.k.a. *Les Confidences Erotiques d'Un Lit Trop Accueillant*, 1973).

Diana Rigg

Diana Rigg was born on July 20, 1938, in Doncaster, Yorkshire, England. She was raised in an industrial town, and when she was two years of age her father, a railroad engineer, moved the family to India. Six years later she was back in Yorkshire attending classes at a private school while her father was working for the state railroad. After graduating school she tried her hand at modeling, but decided on acting (over parental objections) at age 17 when she auditioned for the Royal Academy of Dramatic Arts and was accepted into its roster. She then went on to the Royal Shakespeare Company, where she continued her studies in dramatics and acting. Diana's auburn red hair and 5'8" height combined to make her a stunning addition to productions such as *Twelfth Night*, where she played Viola, and *King Lear*, where she played Cordelia. Acting in productions for the RSC did not pay much money, but the chance to perform in prestigious roles gave her a greater hunger to act, leading her to "moonlight" in television in minor roles. One of her earliest small screen appearances was in an episode of the British series *The Sentimental Agent* about a rogue agent named Carlos Borella (portrayed by Carlos Thompson) who lets himself become the victim of a financial swindle in order to catch an international gang of villains. The two-part episode, "A Very Desirable Plot," was marketed to U.S. television as the movie *Our Man in the Caribbean* (1962). The reedited series episodes featuring Rigg are also notable for an appearance by Shirley Eaton.

In December of 1963 producers of the espionage-themed television series *The Avengers* knew that co-star Honor Blackman would not be returning as Cathy Gale, the well-loved, sexy, leather-wearing martial arts fighting partner against crime assisting agent John Steed (Patrick Macnee). The show's producers came up with the Emma Peel name before they even had an actress to portray the role. Apparently, the name arose when senior executives of the show brainstormed that Emma Peel came from the term "man appeal," shortened to "M-appeal"; they also mandated that Ms. Peel's character would be every bit as emancipated as her predecessor, Cathy Gale.

In December of 1964, after a search for the actress to play the part, the producers signed Elizabeth Shepherd, and two episodes of the new *Avengers* series were completed, "The Town of No Return" and "The Murder Market." However, production executives concluded that there was a spark missing, and production on the show halted until they found a suitable replacement. Enter Diana Rigg, who had just appeared on British television in an *Armchair Theatre* production of the play *The Hothouse*. Although she was 28 years old, Rigg decided to screen test for the role and won the part. However, with two unusable episodes in the can, the producers took a little extra time and completely overhauled the show, moving from the videotape format to film. This allowed them to move more easily from the studio to location shoots in the countryside. The show would also undergo a change in dramatic structure, from a primarily espionage-themed program to wildly fantastic plots involving killer cults, invaders from space, man-eating plants and killer robots.

Diana Rigg re-filmed both "The Murder Market" and "Town of No Return," and the new *Avengers* series (its fourth season) premiered on October 1965, after the show had been off the air for 1½ years. With two months of extraordinary press, the ABC network in America agreed to purchase the program for the United States if the show's creators could guarantee that the series would switch to color film. In March 1966 *The Avengers* premiered on American television with "The Cybernauts" episode, and viewers were glued to their sets awaiting the opening narration. Beginning with a staccato bass beat, then a martial drum roll, a narrator intones, "Extraordinary crimes against the people and the state have to be avenged by agents extraordinary. Two such people are John Steed, top professional, and his partner, Emma Peel, talented amateur. Otherwise known as *The Avengers*."

By April of 1967 Rigg decided to leave the show, which by that time had quite a following of fans in America, but was convinced to stay on and finish the season. Linda Thorson was signed on as Rigg's replacement and the last Rigg episode, "The Forget-Me-Knot" (a transition one in which she leaves and Thorson is introduced), was shown in March 1968. In her years on the program, Diana Rigg managed to surpass the appeal and media attention bestowed upon Honor Blackman. Although Rigg was thinner and more austere in appearance, she seemed sexier, with herself constrained in a variety of revealing, skin-tight leather pant suits and the like for most of the first two seasons. Utilizing Ray Austin's instructions as the show's fight choreographer, the people behind the show made Rigg look great. Hence, viewers tuned in to see not only what kind of light double entendres she and Macnee would exchange in their seemingly never consummated

The most popular female secret agent of all time, Diana Rigg's Emma Peel character assisted partner John Steed on numerous adventures in television's *The Avengers* (Assoc. British Picture Corp., ca. 1967).

role as Emma Peel, in the spring of 1994 she commented to the *New York Times*, "In Soho, there are pictures of me in black leather in very dubious sex shops. The photos are so old, nobody would recognize me now, thank God."

Among her finest episodes in the series are "A Touch of Brimstone," "The Joker," "Murdersville," "A Surfeit of H20," "The Gravediggers," "The Hidden Tiger," "Dial a Deadly Number" and "Too Many Christmas Trees." Despite this, Rigg herself claims to have no personal favorite episodes, as she told journalist Huw Rossiter, "I can never remember making the individual episodes. It's like seeing something for the first time. Mrs. Peel is a stranger to me now, but still one I enjoy bumping into from time to time."

The Avengers received Emmy nominations for "Outstanding Drama Series" in 1967 and 1968, while Rigg was nominated both years for "Best Actress in a Drama Series." Coincidentally, the show lost both times to *Mission: Impossible*, and Rigg lost twice to *Mission: Impossible*'s Barbara Bain.

relationship (although they do kiss, somewhat chastely, in "The Forget-Me-Knot" episode and often in "Who's Who?," but their bodies have been exchanged with those of dangerous Eastern European spies), but how she was going to fight her way out of a battle with her (studio trained) karate chops, light kicks and intelligence. Unlike most of the women in the Bond films (which *The Avengers* preceded), Emma Peel kicked butt, creating a new kind of emancipated woman for teenage girls to emulate (and someone for teenage boys to slobber over). Reflecting on her *Avengers*

Now concentrating on films, Diana Rigg's role as Miss Winters in the delectable and unfairly maligned period adventure film *The Assassination Bureau* (1969) showed more of her comedic skills than many television fans had noticed during her stint on *The Avengers*. The lighthearted romp, about a turn of the century organization of villains who assassinate people for the highest bidding person or country, costarred Oliver Reed and Telly Savalas.

Rigg became the second of *The Avengers*' leading female co-stars to appear as a leading lady in a James Bond film when she signed to appear as Tracy in the sixth James Bond adventure, *On Her Majesty's Secret Service* (1969). Being the first film without Sean Connery in the role, the movie faced many uphill battles in the theaters and with the media. Leading actor George Lazenby (who was nominated for a Golden Globe as "New Star of the Year in a Motion Picture" for his performance) had been an Australian model and was chosen for his rugged good looks. (The other actors considered for the role at the time were John Richardson, Anthony Rogers, Robert Campbell and Hans de Vries.) However, the movie, being the most realistic and violent in the series since the second film (*From Russia with Love* in 1963) was saddled with a nearly three hour running time and a climax where the spy hero finally weds, only to have his love cut down on their wedding day by a maniacal villain named Blofeld (played with odd mannerisms by Rigg's *Assassination Bureau* co-star Telly Savalas). The melancholy end of the film inclined the series' producers to convince former Bond Sean Connery to return for the next film (*Diamonds Are Forever* in 1971). This left Lazenby as the only actor in the "official" series to portray the role only once (although Timothy Dalton runs a close second with his two portrayals in the late eighties).

For Diana Rigg, however, more prestigious roles were offered. She co-starred with George C. Scott in Paddy Chayefsky's satire *The Hospital* (1970), appeared with Charlton Heston (as Portia) in *Julius Caesar* (1970), had her first starring role in an American sitcom television show with *Diana* (during the 1973-74 season) and received raves as Edwina Lionheart (the daughter of a former Shakespearean actor now gone mad, as played by Vincent Price) in the murderous but entertaining and macabre horror film *Theater of Blood* (1973).

In the eighties Rigg appeared in roles as diverse as a cameo in *The Great Muppet Caper* (1981), a murder suspect in *Agatha Christie's Evil Under the Sun* (1982) and back to Shakespeare (in the role of Regan) with *King Lear* (1984) for British television. In 1982 she published her first book, *No Stone Unturned*, an acclaimed collection of some of the worst theatrical critical reviews given her and other actors, a droll anthology of clippings. Diana Rigg has been nominated three times for Broadway's esteemed Tony Award (for *Abelard and Heloise*, *The Misanthrope* and *Medea*, for which she won in 1994). Beginning in 1989 Rigg took over as host for the PBS series *Mystery!*, a compilation of mostly British thrillers and detective stories. She was knighted in 1994 and is now known as Dame Diana Rigg.

Other films include: *In This House of Brede* (1975—TV), *A Little Night Music* (1977), *Witness for the Prosecution* (1982—TV), *Bleak House* (1985—TV), *Snow White* (1986—TV), *Mother Love* (1989—TV), *Genghis Cohn* (1993—TV), *A Good Man in Africa* (1994), *Running Delilah* (1994—TV), *Rebecca* (1997—TV), *Mrs. Bradley's Mysteries: The Speedy Death* (1998—TV), *Mrs. Bradley's Mysteries* (1999—TV), *Victoria and Albert* (2001—TV) and *Cinderella* (2002—TV).

Salli Sachse

Actress Salli Sachse was born Salli Vining on June 25, 1944, in San Diego, California. A former model, she had just married folk singer Peter Sachse and was working as a bank receptionist when she came to the attention of American International Pictures. She went on to appear in practically every beach movie, from *Muscle Beach Party* (1964) to *The Ghost in the Invisible Bikini* (1966). She was part of the beach contingent (including Patti Chandler, Mike Nader, Mary Hughes and Ed Garner) who surrounded Frankie Avalon and Annette Funicello as beach bunnies and surfer boys in most of their films.

Sachse also appeared in a few non-beach AIP movies, beginning with *Dr. Goldfoot and the Bikini Machine* (1965). Directed by Norman Taurog, it was a blatant take-off of the huge James Bond hit *Goldfinger*. Vincent Price (whom Sachse describes as being "a lot of fun; he was a jokester and loved teasing us girls") starred as Dr. Goldfoot, who is using his army of female robots to marry the world's wealthiest men and ensnare their fortunes. His plan goes awry when agent Craig Gamble (Frankie Avalon) falls in love with Dr. Goldfoot's prize robot, Diane (Susan Hart). Sachse was one of his other bikini-clad robots (along with Patti Chandler, Mary Hughes, Deanna Lund, Pamela Rodgers, Marianne Gaba, China Lee, etc.). As No. 4, she was assigned to marry and assassinate a rich Greek shipping magnate. "We had to wear gold lame bikinis and stiletto heels," remembers Sachse. "When Norman Taurog wanted us on the set, he'd yell [mimics voice], 'Bikini girls! Bikini girls!' We were used as product and I felt a bit exploited." To promote the film, most of the young cast was featured in the special *The Wild World of Dr. Goldfoot* (11/18/65).

Sache was also featured in *The Million Eyes of Su-Muru* (1967) from producer/screenwriter Harry Alan Towers, which was shot on location at the Shaw Brothers Studio in Hong Kong. The film starred Frankie Avalon and George Nader as American agents trying to keep the sadistic Su Muru (Shirley Eaton) and her army of women from taking over the world. Sachse and Patti Chandler played her two closest bodyguards, Mikki and Louise. "It was an incredible experience being in Hong Kong," remembers Sachse. "Patti Chandler and I stayed at the Hilton. The day I got there the producers had a costumer come to take my measurements. The next day my costume arrived. They made my clothes and shoes for the film overnight! I was totally astounded." While filming on location, the American stars were kept segregated from their Chinese co-stars because the Shaw brothers "didn't want their stars and contract players to see how well we were treated. One day Patti, Frankie and I ate at the Shaw Brothers Studio commissary. It was huge, with table after table of Chinese men eating rice dishes. There were dogs all over the place running in and out of the kitchen. And the men were feeding their scraps to them. Our eyes were just wide with amazement!"

Sachse's screen time is minimal in *The Million Eyes of Su-Muru* because after only five days of shooting she was notified that her husband, folk singer Peter Sachse, had been tragically killed in a plane crash. AIP executive Louis B. "Deke" Heyward had accompanied his cast to Hong Kong, and he arranged for her to fly home. She was unable to return to finish her scenes.

After appearing in a few biker films, and most notably as the LSD freak-out girl in *The Trip* (1967), starring Peter Fonda, Sachse quit acting in the early seventies. She modeled and made commercials but spent most of her time with Crosby, Stills, Nash, and Young as their personal photographer. Her photos were featured on their albums and in *Rolling Stone Magazine*. Today Salli Sachse resides in La Jolla, California. Though she has a master's degree in psychology, Sachse hasn't totally abandoned acting. She still finds time to act in regional theater productions and television commercials.

Other films include: *Bikini Beach* (1964), *Beach Blanket Bingo* (1965), *How to Stuff a Wild Bikini* (1965), *Ski Party* (1965), *The Ghost in the Invisible Bikini* (1966), *The Devil's Angels* (1967) and *Wild in the Streets* (1968).

Curvy Salli Sachse, co-star of many AIP films, including the spy spoofs *Dr. Goldfoot and the Bikini Machine* (1965) and *The Million Eyes of Su-Muru* (1967). (*Courtesy of Salli Sachse*)

Jill St. John

Jill St. John was born Jill Oppenheim on August 19, 1940, in Los Angeles, California. Raised by her "stage mother," who took the young girl to many auditions as a young child, the young Jill Oppenheim was acting by age five. Her mother even had her take ballet lessons, where her classmates included Natalie Wood and Stefanie Powers. By the late 1940s she was a semi-regular on the radio show *One Man's Family*, and shortly thereafter, at age 11, her mother changed Jill's last name to St. John, a more fanciful and lugubrious moniker for a young would-be star. By the age of 16, her mother even talked her into plastic surgery and had her change the shape of her nose. Away from her parent, whom some sources labeled domineering and others benign, Jill

St. John attended UCLA, where she was assessed by professors as having an IQ of 162, a high degree of intelligence that would later get her admission into MENSA.

As a young child, St. John admired the comedienne Kay Kendall and dreamed of attaining a career like her idol. But, although she attempted comedy (the radio show that she performed on as a child was a comedy-drama), it seems that she garnered a contract with 20th Century–Fox in 1958 on the basis of her voluptuous, outrageously curvy body (that made strong men drool) rather than any comedic or dramatic talents. Her first film role on loan to Universal was as Erica in *Summer Love* (1958), followed by other nondescript parts in other movies until she appeared in *The Lost World* (1960) as Jennifer Holmes. In this science fiction adventure film (directed by Irwin Allen, of television's *Land of the Giants* and *Lost in Space* fame), she became the Victorian heroine (but still shapely, despite her costume's inability to confine her large breasts) who accompanies Professor Challenger (Claude Rains), Lord Roxton (Michael Rennie) and young Malone (David Hedison) to a land inhabited by prehistoric monsters. The film did well at the box office, becoming a major hit. On the strength of her performance in *The Lost World*, St. John then received roles in more diverse fare, such as *The Roman Spring of Mrs. Stone* (1961) and the comedy *Come Blow Your Horn* (1963), starring Frank Sinatra. For the latter, she received a Golden Globe nomination for "Best Actress in a Comedy or Musical Motion Picture."

Her first appearance in an espionage film was in *The Liquidator* (1965). As Iris, a young woman hired by the British Secret Service to keep new star agent Boysie (Rod Taylor) in line (if not in bed), she shines. The film, about an ex-soldier (Taylor) mistaken for an adventuresome hero and then hired to be the Secret Service's best agent after World War II, is an enjoyable but sometimes oddly disjointed film, fluctuating unevenly between comedy and stark drama. Featuring a fine supporting cast of British film veterans (including Trevor Howard and Wilfred Hyde-White), the movie showcased one of St. John's best adult performances. Her next outing in a similar role was in the TV pilot *Fame Is the Name of the Game* (1966). In this mystery thriller with overtones of espionage, an investigative journalist (Anthony Franciosa) checks on the murder of a call girl. St. John (as Leona Purdy) makes a stunning appearance in the program as a seductive but bitchy woman.

The next two years were busy ones for St. John. She reunited with Frank Sinatra in the adult-themed thriller *Tony Rome* (1967) and wore elaborate costumes for the high adventure comedy *The King's Pirate* (1967). It was back to spy adventures for Jill St. John when she journeyed to England to appear in the American co-production *The Spy Killer* (1969). She portrayed Mary Harper, an international fashion model and girlfriend of John Smith (Robert Horton), an ex–secret agent brought back into the fold (by Sebastian Cabot, his former boss) to untangle a deadly web of murder and deceit involving double and enemy agents. Directed and written by British horror film veterans Roy Ward Baker and Jimmy Sangster, *The Spy Killer* still remains an entertaining, if elaborately scripted, espionage thriller, much more adult than the standard television fare of the time. (It was co-produced by the ABC network in a bid to recapture some of the success of their previous UK co-production, *The Avengers*.) St. John performed well but really had little to do except to act glamorous (as usual) and terrified when the need came.

St. John and Horton reunited for the sequel tele-feature *Foreign Exchange* in 1970. Exhibiting a touch of nihilism that feature films like *The Spy Who Came in from the Cold* (1962) and *The Quiller Memorandum* (1966) showed, *Foreign Exchange* continued the story of former agent Smith (Horton) and his attempts to leave his life as a spy in the past. In this movie he is blackmailed into an assignment behind the Iron Curtain; otherwise, his glamorous model girlfriend (St. John) will be defamed and deported.

It is most likely without a doubt that the reason Jill St. John was offered the role of duplicitous Tiffany Case in the James Bond movie *Diamonds Are Forever* (1971) was because of her work in the previous two films. This alternately appreciated and hated entry in the series featured the last "official" appearance by Sean Connery as the British secret agent 007, who is sent to Las Vegas, Nevada, to investigate the disappearance of diamonds. Along the way he discovers that his old arch nemesis Ernst Stavros Blofeld (Charles Gray) is once again involved. Blofeld and his criminal empire are planning to use a large cache of stolen diamonds to affect an orbiting satellite system.

There were many problems with *Diamonds Are Forever*. It reveals the beginning of a distinct, formulaic structure and a comedic, sometimes campy tone in the series that carried over to and remained throughout all of the Roger Moore Bond entries. Much of the film looks cheap, garish and ugly, and Connery, appearing world weary and older than he does now, even at age 71, delivers a strange performance (stranger still, considering that he was involved in a protracted battle between the Bond film producers over his high fee for the film; they nearly decided on American actor John Gavin as the new Bond before giving Connery his millions). As for St. John, the results are mixed. She was not only the first American woman to portray a Bond girl, but definitely one of the most voluptuous (though for a majority of the film she is attired in a tight, form-fitting, sometimes not entirely flattering bikini). But for fans of feminine pulchritude, she lends a heavenly touch to such a marred

Fiery redhead Jill St. John, as Tiffany Case, brandishes an automatic weapon in *Diamonds Are Forever* (United Artists, 1971).

and disjointed film. However, acting-wise, St. John delivers a shrill, often one-note performance at odds with her earlier work, placing her alongside Tanya Roberts (of *A View to a Kill*, 1983) and Denise Richards (of *The World Is Not Enough*, 2000) as one of the worst of the Bond girls.

St. John followed *Diamonds Are Forever* with what is essentially her best dramatic film performance in the brutally violent UK movie *Sitting Target* (1972). In this film she has the role of Pat, the wife of the imprisoned Oliver Reed, a criminal who, having learned that she and his ex-partner and friend (Ian McShane) had worked together to have him found guilty of a crime and sent to jail, escapes for his revenge. As the terrified and terrifying woman who alternates between each man for her survival, St. John delivered a powerhouse performance. Unfortunately, she took off time from acting for a few years and returned to the small screen with the abysmal television movie *Brenda Starr* (1976), based on the popular daily comic strip. The failure of this pilot film to find an appreciative audience (or kind critics) sent the film into instant obscurity, and it has rarely been seen since its initial telecast. It also sent St. John (as with most of her sixties contemporaries) into the acting realm of B-films, made-for-TV movies and episodic television (i.e. *The Love Boat*, *Vega$*, etc.).

In recent years Jill St. John has acted infrequently. She appeared in the TV pilot for *Hart to Hart* (1979) with former ballet school classmate Stefanie Powers, and rekindled her friendship with Natalie Wood, her other former classmate. On November 29, 1981, Wood died in a tragic drowning incident, and two months later St. John and Wood's widower husband (and *Hart to Hart* co-star) Robert Wagner began dating. They were wed in 1990. She had previously been married to Lance Reventlow, heir to the F.W. Woolworth fortune, and singer Jack Jones. Currently, St. John and Robert Wagner live on an estate in the Pacific Palisades, California, where together they tend to her stable of horses. One of her passions is also cooking. A gourmet cook, she has written two cookbooks and has served as a cooking specialist on television morning news and entertainment shows.

Other films include: *Tender Is the Night* (1962), *Who's Minding the Store?* (1963), *Who's Been Sleeping in My Bed?* (1963), *The Oscar* (1966), *Eight on the Lam* (1967), *Telethon* (1977—TV), *The Concrete Jungle* (1982), *The Player* (1992), *Something to Believe In* (1998), *The Trip* (2001) and *The Calling* (2001).

Tura Satana

After her cinematic accession to cult icon status via appearances in low-budget movies that achieved their own brand of cult status, Tura Satana became known to many genre film fans in the seventies, eighties and nineties for starring in Russ Meyer's *Faster, Pussycat! Kill! Kill!* (1966) and T.V. Mikels' *The Astro-Zombies* (1967) and *The Doll Squad* (1973). The dark eyed, jet black–haired beauty with exotic appeal, accentuated by her extraordinarily pronounced bustline and the sultry combination of her American Indian and Japanese heritage, had also appeared on some American spy television programs, as well as in *Our Man Flint* (1967), before disappearing in 1973 to private life. She journeyed through a number of positions, ultimately becoming a security chief, before fans found her and she, in turn, discovered that there was a whole cadre of aficionados for her work. In the 1990s Tura Satana came out of retirement to accept the accolades and interest bestowed upon her by her fans.

Tura Satana began her career in entertainment by becoming a stripper. "I started out as an interpretative dancer," she said, "but I was offered more money if I took my clothes off, so I did." What is unusual is that Satana started out at a very early age. "I started dancing at the age of thirteen years old. I became a professional dancer at the age of fifteen years old. If the owners of the clubs I had worked in ever knew that I was only fifteen, I think that they would have had a heart attack."

Her first film role was in a Billy Wilder film called *Irma La Douce* (1963), starring Jack Lemmon and Shirley MacLaine. "I was working at the Pink Pussycat nightclub in West Hollywood," remembers Satana. "Wilder and his wife came in. His wife was the one who told him that he had finally found his Suzette Wong. After that, we were great friends. He always loved my professionalism." It was this role that led to her appearance in the legendary *Faster, Pussycat! Kill! Kill!* "Russ Meyer approached me about *FPKK* [while] I was working on *Irma La Douce* at the time. I came in for the interview in my costume of the bridesmaid from the Church in *Irma*. It was hard to be tough and bitchy while I was wearing pink and flowers." The movie became a quiet cause célèbre at the time, with Satana and her female companions becoming three of the deadliest women on Earth that you would never want to meet: voluptuous vixens who would beat, terrorize and murder, all the while finding time to sexually get off on—and then abuse—their (mostly male) captives. This was B—movie entertainment at its height. Satana was immediately elevated to a special status as Varla, the leader of the bad girls. She flipped, karate chopped and killed men. "I took a lot of my anger that had been stored inside of me for many years and let it loose. I helped to create the persona of Varla and helped to make her someone that many women would love to be like."

Tura Satana guest starred on *The Man from U.N.C.L.E.* and its sister-show, *The Girl from U.N.C.L.E.* In between TV appearances, she turned up (uncredited) in the Bond spoof *Our Man Flint* (1966), starring James Coburn. ("I played both of the dancers in the nightclub where Flint [Coburn] finds a Bond clone and they stage a fight.") In "The Finny Foot Affair" (11/24/64) on *The Man from U.N.C.L.E.*, the agents are on the move against a strange disease that has aꞏicted an entire British coastal village. In "The Moulin Ruse Affair" (1/17/67) on *The Girl from U.N.C.L.E.*, agents April Dancer (Stefanie Powers) and Mark Slate (Noel Harrison) journey to a Caribbean isle where the insane Dr. Toulouse (Shelley Berman) is threatening to market a super-strength pill to THRUSH.

"I had a great deal of fun doing the shows and being able to associate with the caliber of stars that I did work with," recalls Tura Satana fondly. "In *The Man from U.N.C.L.E.* one of the guest stars was a very young Kurt Russell. I played a female spy and heavy in that show. In *The Girl from U.N.C.L.E.* I played Rabbit, the leader of the female guards in the house of the sinister Dr. Toulouse."

In 1973 Tura Satana co-starred with a bevy of gorgeous women in T.V. Mikels' *The Doll Squad*, a film that some genre aficionados claim partly inspired the *Charlie's Angels* television show. In *The Doll Squad*, Satana and others (including star Francine York) assemble to defeat a corrupt villain from a foreign country. While the low-budget movie was bereft of Hollywood-type production values, it was far and away (in terms of quality and story) better than the previous T.V. Mikels film in which Satana had appeared. In that film, *The Astro-Zombies*, she essayed the role of Satana, a sultry and dangerous enemy agent and head of a group of villains working for a foreign power that turns American lawmen into robots.

As for *The Doll Squad*, Satana recalls, "I suggested he [Mikels] hire Francine York for the lead, since he wanted a more notable name than mine to be starring with Michael Ansara. I remember that we had a lot of fun doing the film with the gals that we had. All of the ladies were professional actresses, and we had our friendly little power plays, but they were all great to work with. I remember inviting Aaron Spelling

Noel Harrison (U.N.C.L.E. agent Mark Slate) flips for sultry Tura Satana as evil bodyguard Rabbit in "The Moulin Ruse Affair" from *The Girl from U.N.C.L.E.* (MGM-TV, 1967).

to the screening of *The Doll Squad*. He thoroughly enjoyed seeing it. Shortly thereafter came *Charlie's Angels*."

For years afterward Satana had declined to be involved with the movie business for a variety of reasons, but now plans a comeback. "I have been asked on several occasions to revive my career," says Satana. "I was basically retired because my husband didn't care for show business in general. Since he passed away in October of 2000 I have received numerous offers to resume my career as an actress and have three film projects pending at this time. I even helped write one of them. ... I will play the head mistress for a school of female assassins. The role I will play is very similar to some of the *FPKK* role, but in a more subtle way. I hope that all of my fans enjoy it as much as I will in making it." First up though for Satana is Ted V. Mikels' *Mark of the Astro-Zombies* (2002). She died on February 4, 2011.

Other films include: *Who's Been Sleeping in My Bed?* (1963).

Jane Seymour

Jane Seymour was born Joyce Penelope Wilhelmina Frankenberger in Hillingdon, England, on February 15, 1951. The daughter of a well-to-do physician, her life growing up in a modest home was far from wanting. At age 13 the young woman made her stage debut as a member of the London Festival Ballet, which was soon followed by theatrical training with the Arts Education School. In 1969 the 5'4" black-haired beauty made her film debut (as part of a huge ensemble cast) in director Richard Attenborough's flawed, satiric anti-war film *Oh! What a Lovely War*, which today is chiefly remembered for one of ex–Beatle John Lennon's rare dramatic movie roles. Seymour's next film appearance came in *The Only Way* (1970), a now-forgotten British film, and then she married Richard Attenborough's son, Michael, in 1971 (they were divorced in 1973). Afterwards she appeared in a popular UK television series titled *The Onedin Line* about the British shipping industry in the 1800s. By this time she also had played numerous bit parts on radio dramas presented by the BBC.

After portraying Pamela Plowden in Richard Attenborough's revered, fictionalized docudrama *Young Winston* (1972), Seymour was chosen by James Bond film producers Albert R. Broccoli and Harry Saltzman to play the role of the tempting Solitaire in *Live and Let Die* (1973). This was the eighth official Bond film and the first to star new leading man Roger Moore. However, Seymour's interpretation of the role differed somewhat from what the producers, the writers and director Guy Hamilton had envisioned for the film. During the earliest stages of the shooting of the movie, Seymour delivered her lines in a stilted, heavily accented British stage voice, forcing the producers to consider re-dubbing all of her lines. Co-star Roger Moore dubbed her "Baby Bernhardt" on and off the set (in reference to the renown actress Sarah Bernhardt and to Seymour's affected readings of her *Live and Let Die* lines). The

Jane Seymour, as Solitaire, joins Roger Moore (James Bond) in a dangerous adventure in *Live and Let Die* (United Artists, 1973). (*Courtesy of Michael Monahan*)

movie's producers wanted a sexier interpretation of her character, a psychic and sex object for the film's chief villain, Mr. Big/Dr. Kananga (Yaphet Kotto); and they began altering her performance to suit their needs, and re-shot the now useless footage they deemed ruined by her early performance. Achieving this, the *Live and Let Die* staff then began to alter the physical appearance of the character, changing her from an initially stiff seductress (as envisioned in the original shooting script) to an almost living doll.

Seymour commented to author Steven Jay Rubin in *The Complete James Bond Movie Encyclopedia*, "When I'm introduced at Mr. Big's headquarters in Harlem, they covered me with glitter and false eyelashes and they gave me an exotic hairdo. That was their way of bringing in the Occult. I was far more interested in the Voodoo element in the story because I had actually attended a ceremony in Jamaica with Geoffrey Holder, who knew a great deal about the supernatural. The Solitaire character could have been much more interesting if this Voodoo element was brought out. After all, she was respected by everyone as having the power of second sight, as did her mother before her, and [originally in an early draft of the shooting script] she lived all alone in that house on the cliff. It had fascinating possibilities. Unfortunately, all I was given were breathlessly sexy lines and tons of eye makeup."

If the seemingly haughty Seymour appeared problematic during the initial filming of *Live and Let Die*, she relaxed enough to let the film crew suspend her over a pool filled with live sharks, have live snakes thrust into her face and sit as a passenger on a double-decker bus as its top portion is sheared completely off during one of the movie's more elaborate stunts. The film, on its initial theatrical release, was well-received and theater audiences reacted well to Moore's portrayal of Bond, although in later films in the series his characterization would become a satirical portrait of the suave agent as seen in the Connery films and this movie. Only in *For Your Eyes Only* (1981) and portions of *Octopussy* (1983) will the Bond of *Live and Let Die*, as enlivened by Roger Moore, make an appearance.

As for Jane Seymour, the role of Solitaire drew respectable praise from critics, but she did become the first of the new breed of Bond women. The voluptuous, shapely vixens of old were now out, to be represented by thin runway model types. Although Seymour came from a background of classy British film and television roles, with an extensive array of radio work, it was obvious that Bond fans missed a little of the daring "kiss and play" so apparent in earlier features in the series. Possibly this is why Gloria Hendry's Rosie Carver character (a CIA agent who briefly beds and assists Bond/Moore) is more fondly remembered than Seymour as far as the women in *Live and Let Die* are concerned.

Jane Seymour next appeared in the British–U.S. television miniseries *Frankenstein: The True Story* (1973) in the role of Agatha, and then followed this well-regarded interpretation of the Mary Shelley novel with many roles in television films and series on both sides of the Atlantic. She appeared in *The Four Feathers* (1977) and on the science fiction TV show *Battlestar Galactica* (1978), and managed to marry again in 1977. That same year she co-starred (with Patrick Wayne) in *Sinbad and the Eye of the Tiger* (1977), an adventuresome family film with special effects supplied by Ray Harryhausen, who had worked on virtually all of the Sinbad films since the late 1950s. Her next feature film of note, *Somewhere in Time* (1980), was a flawed but highly romantic tale of time travel and lost love (featuring co-star Christopher Reeve). Based on the book *Bid Time Return* by Richard Matheson, the film, since its release, has garnered an immense cult appreciation.

Unfortunately, the once promising career of Jane Seymour became mired in prime-time American television, where she became a mainstay on all the major networks throughout the remainder of the seventies and all through the eighties, appearing in films, miniseries and episodic TV. In between her hectic television work schedule she managed to squeeze in a divorce from Geoffrey Planer, another marriage (to David Flynn, from 1981 to 1993) and the occasional (failed) theatrical feature, like *Oh, Heavenly Dog!* (1980), with Chevy Chase, and *Lassiter* (1984), with Tom Selleck.

In 1988 Jane Seymour won the prestigious Emmy award for her portrayal of Maria Callas in the television miniseries *Onassis, the Richest Man in the World*. In 1993 she finally became the star (and producer) of her own television series. Titled *Dr. Quinn, Medicine Woman*, the homespun show of a female doctor named Michaela "Mike" Quinn working in the wild west captured the hearts and attention of aging TV fans mourning the cancellation of the likewise treacly *Little House on the Prairie*. The successful show was finally canceled in 1999, but Seymour resurrected it in the guise of occasional television "event" movies, the most recent one telecast late in 1999, with more apparently on the way. Jane Seymour married actor James Keach in 1993 and they have sired two children, Johnny and Kris (named after family friends Johnny Cash and Kris Kristofferson). In 1999 England's Queen Elizabeth named Jane Seymour an Officer of the Order of the British Empire (OBE).

Other films include: *The Hanged Man* (1974—TV), *The Story of David* (1976—TV), *The Dallas Cowboy Cheerleaders* (1979—TV), *Jamaica Inn* (1982—TV), *The Scarlet Pimpernel* (1982—TV), *The Phantom of the Opera* (1983—TV), *Heidi* (1993—TV), *The New Swiss Family Robinson* (1998—TV), *Yesterday's Children* (2000—TV), *Dr. Quinn, Medicine Woman: The Heart Within* (2001—TV) and *Touching Wild Horses* (2002).

Nancy Sinatra

During the early sixties, Nancy Sinatra (born Nancy Sinatra, Jr., on June 8, 1940, in Jersey City, New Jersey) was a familiar face on television, popping up on variety and talk shows. One of her earliest appearances was on the legendary *Frank Sinatra Timex Show* in 1960 where she welcomed home Elvis Presley from his stint in the army. At that time her only claim to fame was that she was the daughter of crooner Frank Sinatra and the wife of teen heartthrob Tommy Sands. In 1964 Sinatra made her film debut in the beach movie *For Those Who Think Young* (1964), starring James Darren and Pamela Tiffin, and was voted a "Star of Tomorrow."

After taking a few more supporting roles in teenage movies, Nancy Sinatra's first movie lead—and only spy film appearance—was in the very funny farce *The Last of the Secret Agents?* (1966), starring the nightclub and TV comedy team of Steve Rossi and Marty Allen, the poor man's Dean Martin and Jerry Lewis. Nancy played a French cutie named Micheline, whose father, Papa Joe (Lou Jacobi), disapproves of her romance with Steve Donovan (Rossi). With his pal Marty Johnson (Allen), Donovan is forever looking for work. They are recruited by the agency GGI (Good Guys, Inc.) when they unwittingly get involved in the operations of THEM, an international organization of art thieves headed by Zoltan Schubach (Theo Marcuse). Disguised as entertainers hired to perform at Schubach's soiree, the duo learn that THEM is planning to steal the Venus de Milo. Sinatra isn't given much to do, as most of her scenes revolve around the restaurant that her father owns. (The scene where her dressed is ripped off is very cute.) But she is part of the big finale in the cellar of Schubach's mansion filled with stolen art objects. As for her reviews, most critics ignored her performance to comment on her singing, though she only gets to warble the brassy title tune over the credits. *Variety* remarked that the song, "has a good sound," while Frederick H. Guidry, writing in the *Christian Science Monitor*, commented, "Her best contribution is the defiantly loyal title song, delivered in tones that twang like a steel guitar." Sinatra was supposed to film a production number, singing a song by Burt Bacharach and Hal David, but due to budget limitations it was cut.

In "The Take Me to Your Leader Affair" (12/30/66) on *The Man from U.N.C.L.E.*, a now totally blonde Sinatra played the feisty, wisecracking Coco Cool, a clear sign of the silliness ahead. But that was what the third season of *The Man from U.N.C.L.E.* was all about as it tried to out do *Batman*, its competition on ABC-TV. Coco disappears just as her scientist father, Adrian Cool (Woodrow Parfrey), spots an approaching UFO. This turns out to be a ruse by power-mad industrialist Simon Sparrow (Paul Lambert), who is controlling an asteroid whose "aliens" name him their representative on Earth. Sparrow has the bikini-clad Coco kidnapped to make everyone believe Cool's discovery. U.N.C.L.E. operative Illya Kuryakin (David McCallum) is also captured as he tries to save Coco, and they are taken to Sparrow's base of operations in the Louisiana Bayou and locked in the attic. Their playful, innuendo-laced banter is amusing, and they even sing a duet entitled "Trouble," which was composed by David McCallum. Coco tries to entice Illya into performing with her pro-

Publicity shot of Nancy Sinatra (as Micheline) from *The Last of the Secret Agents?* (Paramount, 1966).

fessionally ("Do you want to be a nothing all your life?") but gets nowhere with the stoic secret agent ("I'm sorry but you can't win me by flattery"). The episode is full of inane devices—Illya uses a metal rod hooked into the sole of his shoe as a jackhammer and the elastic waistband from his underpants as a slingshot. Sparrow's disgusted fiancée Corinne (Whitney Blake) joins U.N.C.L.E. agent Napoleon Solo (Robert Vaughn) to expose Sparrow, and she shoots him dead. Though Sinatra gives a one-note performance, she has a sincere quality about her that comes across, making her fun to watch and listen to.

Sinatra toughened her image when she was cast as a biker chick opposite Peter Fonda in *The Wild Angels* (1966). Grossing over $6 million, this film single-handedly started the wave of biker movies that played drive-ins throughout the country. Sinatra then came into her own when her recording career (begun in 1961) finally took off in the U.S. Her single "These Boots Are Made for Walking" became a number one record in 1966 and won her a Grammy nomination. The press played up her new image as a tough talking, mini-skirted, go-go boot wearing hellcat. She made a few more film appearances, culminating in a lead role as a sexy tax collector opposite Elvis Presley in *Speedway* (1968). She also starred in her own TV variety specials, winning Golden Globe nominations for each—the Emmy-winning *Movin' with Nancy* and *The Nancy Sinatra Show*. And she continued releasing hit records, including "Sugar Town," "Summer Wine" with Lee Hazelwood, "Somethin' Stupid" with Frank Sinatra (receiving a second Grammy nomination), plus the theme songs from the films *You Only Live Twice* and *Tony Rome*.

Nancy Sinatra retired in 1974 to raise her two daughters from a second marriage to Hugh Lambert. In 1989 she made an appearance as herself on the hit TV drama series *China Beach*. She launched a full-scale comeback in 1995, which included a new album with original songs, a national tour and a nude layout in *Playboy*.

Other films include: *Get Yourself a College Girl* (1964), *Marriage on the Rocks* (1965), *The Oscar* (1966), *The Ghost in the Invisible Bikini* (1966) and *Mayor of Sunset Strip* (2001).

Sylvia Solar

Sultry and sexy with a flowing mane of red hair (sometimes brunette, according to the roles), Sylvia Solar (often credited as Sylvie Solar or Silvia Soler) appeared in numerous European films from 1957 onward. Her career highpoints include roles in a number of espionage-themed films, comedies and the occasional thriller.

Solar first appeared onscreen in the French film *C'Est Arrive a 36 Chandelles* (1957), and her very next role was in the French-German spy movie *Hoopla—Jezt Kommt Eddie!* (1958). In this comical thriller, a secret agent named Eddie Peterson (Eddie Constantine) investigates the kidnapping of a scientist's daughter, as well as the stolen formula for a new cheaper form of fuel. A surprisingly affable adventure, this is one of the few movies that Constantine made outside of France (it was filmed in West Germany) during this time period and is virtually interchangeable with one of his Lemmy Caution films. Sylvia Solar plays an enemy agent temptress. She was in the Spanish musical comedy *Vampiressas 1930* (1962), director Jesus Franco's remake of *Singing in the Rain*, and returned to work with Constantine in the private eye adventure *As If It Were Raining* (a.k.a. *Comme S'Il en Pleuvait*, 1963). In 1964 she journeyed to Italy to co-star in the comical spy satire *The Two Mafiosi* (a.k.a. *I Due Mafiosi*) about two bumbling idiots (comedians Franco Franchi and Ciccio Ingrassia) who land in a variety of mishaps because of mistaken identities.

Solar returned to West Germany to appear in *Manhattan Night of Murder* (a.k.a. *Mordnacht in Manhattan*, a.k.a. *100 Dollar Gang*, 1965), an entry in a series of German films about an American FBI agent (George Nader); the movies were based on a number of popular pulp novels written by German authors featuring American characters and familiar landscapes. In *Manhattan* a criminal gang of violent felons goes nuts and attacks small businessmen in New York City. FBI man Jerry Cotton (Nader), the Nation's top agent, battles them in an all-out war. Solar appears in a small but pivotal role as one of the criminal gang's gun molls. In *Agent Sigma 3: Mission Goldwather* (1966) she had a major role as a sultry vixen whose shapely body spelled danger for CIA agent Sigma 3 (Jack Taylor), who travels throughout Europe to rescue a kidnapped scientist held by a criminal organization.

In the obscure *The Man from Interpol* (a.k.a. *L'Homme de L'Interpol*, 1966) Solar was damning men to their end by using her body and evil mind to corrupt heroic agents. In *Coplan Takes a Vacation in Mexico* (a.k.a.

French poster for German film *Manhattan Night of Murder* (1965), co-starring Sylvia Solar, which was released in France as *Les Gangs de Manhattan*.

Coplan Ouvre le Feu a Mexico, a.k.a. *Mexican Slayride*, 1967) she was another nasty woman, seducing French agent Coplan (Lang Jeffries). His mission is to track the building of an atomic bomb and a missing nuclear scientist, which takes him to Mexico where a terrorist organization seeks to rule the world ... or destroy it. That same year she appeared in other European espionage movies, like *Spy Today, Die Tomorrow* (a.k.a. *Mister Dynamit—Morgen Kuss Euch der Tod*, a.k.a. *Mr. Dynamite, You'll Enjoy It More*). As Natascha, Solar was a tempting (and deadly) lovely who assisted the chief villain in his plot to rule the world through the use of a new laser weapon. Several NATO agents have been put on the case, including (former *Tarzan*) Lex Barker from the U.S. and Interpol Inspector Brad Harris. The villain plots to destroy Washington, D.C. unless a huge ransom is paid. The hugely entertaining (but low-budget) *Danger Death Ray* (a.k.a. *Il Raggio Infernale*, 1967) is about a secret agent named Bart Vine (or Mike Morris, for the German print of the movie is titled *Mike Morris Jagt Agenten in die Holle*), played by another former small-screen *Tarzan*, Gordon Scott, battling a nefarious criminal organization. Traitorous Alberto Dalbes, who has kidnapped a scientist who has invented a deadly laser ray, is the chief villain. Scott traces the group to Istanbul, where Sylvia Solar, as Dalbes' sexy but deadly chief henchgirl, eliminates any interlopers.

In 1968 Sylvia Solar reunited with George Nader for *Death and Diamonds* (a.k.a. *Dynamit in Gruner Seide*, a.k.a. *Dynamite in Green Silk*), another Jerry Cotton FBI adventure. In this film, a vicious gang of criminals goes on the rampage, and agent Cotton (Nader) infiltrates the organization to put an end to their schemes. Solar co-starred as the head of the gang of nasty criminals.

In the seventies, Sylvia Solar became the object of attraction for European (particularly Spanish) horror genre filmmakers and appeared in a number of thrillers and horror movies before fading from the spotlight. She died on May 17, 2011.

Other films include: *La Redada* (a.k.a. *Barcelona Kill*, 1971), *Crimson* (a.k.a. *Las Ratas No Duerman de Noche*, 1973), *Horror Story* (1973), *The House of Lost Women* (a.k.a. *La Maison des Filles Perdues*, 1973), *Wide-eyed in the Dark* (a.k.a. *Gatti Rossi in un Labirinto di Ventro*, a.k.a. *Eyeball*, 1975), *The Night of the Howling Beast* (a.k.a. *La Maladicion de la Bestia*, a.k.a. *The Werewolf and the Yeti*, 1975), *The Wicked Caresses of Satan* (a.k.a. *La Perversa Caricia de Satan*, 1975), *Terror Canibal* (a.k.a. *Terror Canibal*, 1981), *Sinatra* (1988—TV) and *Makinavia, el Ultimo Choriso* (1990).

Elke Sommer

Elke Sommer was born Elke Schletz on November 5, 1940, in Berlin, Germany. The pretty blonde was the daughter of a Lutheran minister named Peter Schletz (who died when she was 14) and his wife, Renata Topp. Raised by her widowed mother in a modest home, the young Elke Schletz studied in the prestigious Gymnasium School in Erlangen, where she excelled in Greek and Latin histories and culture. Within a student body of 500, she was one of only two females attending. At

17 years of age she worked as a nursemaid in London, England, where she perfected her command of the English language. Afterward she returned to Germany and attended college, planning on becoming a diplomatic translator for the United Nations (she now spoke seven languages, including German, English, Italian, Spanish, French, Swedish and Yugoslavian). Her intended profession was sidetracked by a new career as an actress, as the young woman had now become quite a "looker," filling out her frame with pounds of attractive, voluptuous flesh and a 36-22-36 figure. She soon landed her first film role, while on vacation in Italy, when a representative of the famed Italian director Vittorio De Sica invited her to appear in a movie. This came as a complete surprise because only days before she was sitting in a café in Viareggio, Italy, when someone planted a ribbon on her blouse and asked her to stand. The entire café erupted into applause, as she had been chosen "Miss Viareggio."

As she commented to journalist Steve Swires in an interview for the publication *Fangoria* in March 1992, "I was on holiday with my mother and somebody saw me and said, 'We need someone just like you for a movie we're making.' They offered me the equivalent of $2,000. I had been living on $70 a month in England. So I did it and missed a semester of school..." Elke also explained (in the same interview) how her family surname was changed from Schletz to Sommer: "When I first started out filming in Italy, everybody had trouble pronouncing Schletz. They called me 'Skittle' and 'Sklitz' and 'Skultz.' I didn't want that to be done to my good family name, so I changed it to 'Sommer.' It seemed to go well with my blonde hair."

The Italian film was called *The Defenders of the Jaguar* (a.k.a. *L'Amico del Giaguaro*, 1958). In the same year, other Italian features followed, including (in the role of Julia) Lucio Fulci's tale of juvenile delinquents and rock and roll music called *The Jukebox Girls* (a.k.a. *La Raggazi del Juke Box*), as well as the similar themed film *Howlers of the Dock* (a.k.a. *Urlatori alla Sbarra*), also directed by Fulci and co-starring American Jazz legend Chet Baker. Returning to Germany, she began appearing in movies made in her homeland, reappearing as the new starlet Elke Sommer. Called to France to make a movie, she starred in erotic filmmaker Max Pecas' *Daniela by Night* (a.k.a. *De Quoi Tu Te Meles, Daniela*, a.k.a. *Daniela, Criminal Strip-Tease*, 1961), playing the title role. Ostensibly her first espionage credit, this feature was about a beautiful woman (Sommer) involved with stolen microfilm and international spies. As well, the movie made sure to show off its shapely star in form-fitting dresses, underwear and a few early provocative nude scenes. She made her English language acting debut in the 1961 British film *Don't Bother to Knock* as Ingrid.

Another role in another Max Pecas French sexploitation movie *Sweet Ecstasy* (a.k.a. *Douche Violence*, 1961), followed. Her first big international break came with the World War II film, *The Victors* (1963), as Helga; and the fact that she filmed some of her controversial scenes twice, once in the nude (for Continental versions) and once clothed, garnered her plenty of press coverage at the time. Following *The Victors* (in which Senta Berger also appeared), Sommer co-starred in *The Prize* (1963), as Inga Andersen, with Paul Newman. This thriller, filmed in Europe, used the attractive pairing of Newman and Sommer to keep audiences from being distracted by the convoluted plot involving an attempt to kidnap a Nobel Prize winner in Stockholm during a peace conference. Sommer was awarded a Golden Globe for her performance in this film as one of the "Most Promising Newcomers—Female" of 1963 (along with Ursula Andress and Tippi Hedren).

She then co-starred (with Peter Sellers)

in *A Shot in the Dark* (1964). As Maria Gambrelli, a beautiful, shapely and possibly deadly suspect in a string of murders, Sommer became the love interest of bumbling French policeman Inspector Clouseau (Sellers). One of the uproarious film's highlights is the sequence where Sommer and Sellers find themselves stuck in a nudist colony, definitely calling attention to her non-acting assets. The film did quite well financially in international markets, and Sommer won raves for her performance. She was named one of *Film Daily*'s "Finds of the Year" and the number one "Star of Tomorrow" by *The Motion Picture Herald*. Afterwards, Sommer found herself cast in a string of mediocre comedies emphasizing her beauty and comedic talents as an actress.

As her career began to steady itself, with many major film roles being offered, Elke Sommer jumped into one of the leading lady roles in the British espionage satire *Deadlier Than the Male* (1967). As Irma Eckman, a sadistic and voluptuous killer, she nearly stole the film (with fellow assassin and implied lesbian lover Sylva Koscina as Penelope). The movie is about Bulldog Drummond (Richard Johnson), a freelance insurance agent, soldier of fortune and spy for hire investigating murders committed by two female assassins (Sommer and Koscina). One of the film's highlights is a sequence where Sommer attempts to seduce and murder Drummond in the luxurious castle of villain Carl Petersen (Nigel Green), only to fail. Minutes later Koscina enters the boudoir and succeeds in at least bedding the hero, forgetting to murder him in the throes of passion. The sequel, *Some Girls Do* (1969), replaced Sommer and Koscina with Daliah Lavi and Beba Loncar (as Helga and Pandora), two similar characters.

That same year (1967), Sommer appeared in the obscure espionage adventure film *The Corrupt Ones* (a.k.a. *The Peking Medallion*, a.k.a. *Die Holle von Macao*) as Lilly Mancini. The movie is about an adventurer (Robert Stack) who is given a valuable medallion by a secret agent on the run, leading to run-ins with Chinese agents and seductive femme fatales (including Nancy Kwan) who chase him all over the Orient. After co-starring in *The Oscar* (1966), a failed movie about Hollywood hopefuls and their dreary lives, Sommer returned to espionage films with a leading role in *The Venetian Affair* (1967). As Sandra Fane, she assisted the film's leading man (Robert Vaughn) in ferreting out enemy agents endangering a noble scientist (Boris Karloff) in Europe. Essentially, an often plodding and overly pretentious portrayal of Vaughn's Man from U.N.C.L.E. persona, the film showed that he may have been too stiff a leading man to carry such a movie. But Elke Sommer and fellow glamorous star Luciana Paluzzi were certainly eye candy enough for the spy film fans who turned out to see the film during its initial theatrical run.

Sommer then followed this role with the female lead in the obscure Italian-French-Spanish caper film *They Came to Rob Las Vegas* (a.k.a. *Radiografia di un Colpo d'Oro*, 1968), and then co-starred in the European produced film *The Invincible Six* (1968), where, as Zari, a European woman living with Iranian fighters in the desert, she becomes the catalyst for a series of battles with a band of heroes (led by Stuart Whitman and James Mitchum) aiding a village of peasants. What is essentially a rehash of *The Magnificent Seven* becomes an enjoyable (if dark) action thriller offset by rousing gunfights and Elke's full frontal nude scenes (one of the highlights of the film). A starring role in the comedy *The Wicked Dreams of Paula Schultz* (1968) as a defecting Eastern European athlete did little for her career, as the film was a box-office bomb.

She returned to the spy cinema as the

slinky and seductive Linka Karensky in the Hollywood movie *The Wrecking Crew* (1969), the last of the Dean Martin–Matt Helm features. *The Wrecking Crew*'s fans are torn between the movie being either the second best film in the series (after *The Silencers*) or the worst. Depending on your own opinion, it is certainly colorful and filled with glamorous starlets (Sommer, Nancy Kwan, Sharon Tate and Tina Louise appear), even if star Dean Martin appears inebriated for most of the running time. Notable is the scene in which the bosomy Sommer saunters directly into the camera while the lens lowers and ends up focused solely on her crotch! Oddly enough, Sommer's *Deadlier Than the Male* co-star Nigel Green is the villain in *The Wrecking Crew*.

Elke Sommer entered the seventies working with Italian horror film director Mario Bava on one of his weakest films, *Baron Blood* (a.k.a. *Gli Orrori del Castello di Norimberga*, 1972) and on one of his best films, *Lisa and the Devil* (a.k.a. *Lisa e il Diavolo*, 1972), in the title role of Lisa. However, the latter film became mired in legal and financial entanglements, leading to it being severely reedited and released in a truncated form in the mid-seventies as *The House of Exorcism*, with new footage turning the dreamy, darkly macabre movie into another *Exorcist* clone. Also that year, Sommer appeared in the U.S. TV film *Probe* (a.k.a. *Search*), a pilot for a series about a hi-tech group of government secret agents aided by the latest technology available. Her role in the film was a small, thankless part. In *The Swiss Conspiracy* (1977), a former American

A promotional pose from *The Venetian Affair* (MGM, 1968), with Elke Sommer and Robert Vaughn. (Courtesy of Michael Monahan)

justice official (David Janssen) working as a private detective in Europe is hired by a Zurich bank to protect its customers from blackmailers.

In the eighties Elke Sommer found herself appearing in a number of small, independently financed films like *Death Stone* (1986), and worked quite often in American and internationally financed miniseries like *The Winds of War* (1983). In 1986 she appeared in the documentary *Hollywood Ghost Stories* (1986) as herself, talking about the home that she and her ex husband Joe Hyams shared that she claimed had been haunted by an actual ghost. Apparently, she and Hyams lived in this house from 1964 to 1968 before leaving because of repeated mysterious occurrences. While the couple maintained that they never actually saw a ghost, several of their guests did see the apparition of a middle-aged man wearing a white shirt and tie. After remodeling the home, loud banging sounds in the middle of the night and a mysterious fire caused Sommer and Hyams to flee. Since then, the house has changed owners several times, and over 30 people have encountered the mysterious forces within.

In the mid-nineties Elke Sommer made international headlines again when a public battle between her and Zsa Zsa Gabor turned ugly. Gabor remarked to a German magazine (in 1990) that Sommer was "over the hill and spending her nights in sleazy bars, as well as being broke, balding and looking like a 100-year-old grandmother" (according to articles published in *The New York Post* in the winter of 1993). In return, Sommer claimed in public (in the same magazine) that Gabor had "a fat rear end." After the smoke cleared, a Los Angeles, California, jury awarded Sommer $3.3 million in a libel suit.

In recent years Elke Sommer has concentrated on painting. She is an accomplished artist whose work has been critically acclaimed and shown in over 40 one-woman shows in major art galleries throughout the world. She has also hosted a PBS series, *Painting with Elke*, and authored a book on the subject. Athletic too, Sommer is a prize-winning race car driver and was once a hostess of the nationally syndicated television show *The World of Speed and Beauty*. She has also been dubbed by *Sports Illustrated* magazine "The Brute" because of her playing on the tennis courts of the world, where she is a top-ranked celebrity tennis player. Elke Sommer has returned to Germany, where she has appeared in a number of films. But movie fans will not forget her visage or body, for she truly was one of the most glamorous and sexy of the international starlets during the sixties and seventies.

Other films include: *Femmine di Lusso* (1960), *The Heroes of Telemark* (1964), *Percy* (1971), *Zeppelin* (1971), *Percy's Progress* (a.k.a. *It's Not the Size That Counts*, 1974), *Ten Little Indians* (1974), *Carry On Behind* (1975), *Pronto Ad Uccidere* (1976), *The Prisoner of Zenda* (1978), *The Double McGuffin* (1979), *A Nightingale Sang in Berkeley Square* (a.k.a. *The Mayfair Bank Caper*, 1979), *Stunt Seven* (1979), *Jamaican Gold* (a.k.a. *The Treasure Seekers*, 1979), *Anastasia: The Mystery of Anna* (1986—TV), *Peter the Great* (1986—TV), *Severed Ties* (1992), *Alles Nur Tarnung* (1997), *Flashback—Morderische Ferien* (2000) and *Nicht mit Uns* (2000).

Stella Stevens

Curvaceous Stella Stevens has had a staggeringly long career due to her stunning looks and ability to play both comedic and dramatic roles (though it seemed she was always cast as a floozy or prostitute). Stevens was born Estelle Eggleston on October 1, 1936, in Yazoo City, Mississippi. She was married at 15, had a child, Andrew, at 16 and was divorced the following year. She went on to study drama at Memphis State and landed the lead role of Cherie in a regional stage production of

Bus Stop. While she was working as a model in the tearoom of Goldsmith's Department Store, a press agent promoting the film *God's Little Acre* encouraged her to go to New York. She did, and he introduced her to executives from 20th Century–Fox who signed her to a contract.

Needing money to support her son after Fox passed on her option, Stevens agreed to pose semi-nude for *Playboy* as a playmate. Promised $3,000, she only received $500 and had to work *Playboy* parties to get the rest. She balked, especially when she was cast at the last minute to play Appassionata Von Climax in *Li'l Abner* (1959) after Paramount executives could not convince Tina Louise to reprise her Broadway role. She begged *Playboy* not to run the photos, but seeing that she was now going to co-star in a big movie, they made her Miss January 1960, tagging her "Bella Stella." Though she was bitter about this experience, Stevens later did two more layouts for *Playboy*—in May 1965 and January 1968. In 1972 she remarked to *Show* magazine that the layouts contained "beautiful pictures" and that "you can't buy publicity like that." Ten years later she changed her opinion and commented to an interviewer, "I feel they [*Playboy*] used me. I never did like them, and we just never had a good relationship. It never did me any good."

Li'l Abner launched Stella Stevens' film career, as she was a hit as the sexy, squeaky-voiced social climber and shared the Golden Globe Award for "Most Promising Newcomers—Female" with Angie Dickinson, Janet Munro and Tuesday Weld. She also landed a contract at Paramount and gave competent dramatic performances in *Man-Trap* (1961) and *Too Late Blues* (1961), but neither were hits. The studio then forced her to co-star opposite Elvis Presley in *Girls! Girls! Girls!* (1962). She faced suspension if she refused to do the film.

Nineteen sixty-three was a bigger year for Stevens, as she proved herself a top drawer comedienne in *The Nutty Professor* (playing a coed named Stella Purdy) and *The Courtship of Eddie's Father* (as shy beauty contest winner Dollye Daly). Theater owners finally took note of her, and she was voted a 1963 "Star of Tomorrow." She voluntarily left Paramount in 1964 for more varied roles and was signed by Columbia Pictures.

The tagline for the first Matt Helm film, *The Silencers* (1966), exclaimed, "Follow his secret from bedroom to bedlam, with guns, girls and dynamite!" For once the studio's PR department did not over hype. As delineated in a series of novels by Donald Hamilton, Matt Helm (played by Dean Martin) is a boozing, philandering rake of a spy, now a playboy photographer, enticed out of retirement by his ex-partner Tina Batori (Daliah Lavi). Their assignment is to travel to Phoenix to thwart Tung-Tze (Victor Buono), the leader of the Big O organization, from starting World War III by sabotaging an atomic missile—Operation Fall Out. Stevens played red-haired Gail Hendrix, the innocent, wide-eyed girlfriend of Big O operative Sam Gunther (Robert Webber). The first glimpse of Gail is of her shapely derriere as she is clumsily drying herself off poolside after accidentally getting Helm wet. ("That is not a girl, Tina" Helm says, "that's a disaster area!") Soon after, she spills her drink on him. At the Slaygirl Club, dancer Sarita (Cyd Charisse), who has in her possession a defecting scientist's computer tape, is assassinated on stage. During the confusion, the dying Sarita passes the capsule to the innocent Gail and tells her where Big O is located. Helm immediately suspects that Gail is also an enemy agent when she denies having the tape. He literally strips her dress off of her and finds the tape stashed in her cleavage. To prove her innocence, Gail accompanies Helm to "Wig Wam at San Juan" to locate Big O's headquarters. Gail

The Silencers (Columbia, 1966) starred Stella Stevens as the shapely klutz Gail Hendrix, foil to Dean Martin's super cool Matt Helm.

is, in fact, only an innocent bystander, while the real double agent is Tina. The bungling Gail helps Helm destroy the equipment controlling the missile, kill the enemy agents and return to his life as a retired spy.

Recalling *The Silencers*, Stevens commented to *Filmfax Magazine* in 2000 that, "Dean Martin was wonderful to work with. We became buddies ... Phil Karlson was a great comedy director." As for her character of Gail Hendrix, she described her to *Femme Fatales* in 1999 as "a fiery red-head who wasn't dumb but accident prone. I thought of myself as a female Jerry Lewis to Dean Martin's straight man."

Stevens' performance was the standout in *The Silencers*. Her portrayal was so memorable that she unknowingly set the tone for every actress playing the innocent kook in spy films and TV for the rest of the decade. She proved she had superior comedic timing, and her chemistry with Martin was fabulous, though this role typecast her as the sexpot. The only minor quibble is that Phil Karlson lets her drunken scene in the rain run on too long. Critics though, praised Stevens to the hilt. "Zany and refreshing," "superb," and "outstanding," were just a few of the accolades thrown her way. With reviews like that, it is no wonder that she touted herself for an Oscar nomination for "Best Supporting Actress." This was at a time when putting ads in the trades was not as common a practice as it is nowadays. However, for the most part, Academy members do not take seriously comedic roles, especially ones played by sex goddesses. Alas, Stevens was snubbed.

After teaming again with Dean Martin in the sex comedy *How to Save a Marriage—and Ruin Your Life* (1968), Stevens returned to the spy genre in *Sol Madrid* (1968). The results this time were much less successful than with *The Silencers*. David McCallum (fresh from his long run on *The Man from U.N.C.L.E.*) is cast as Interpol agent Sol Madrid, who is assigned to find the missing Harry Mitchell (Pat Hingle), the former right hand man to Mafia crime boss Dano Villanova (Rip Torn), who has absconded with $500,000. Stevens (who yells most of her lines and gives one of her worst performances) played the crass, shrill Stacey Woodward, Villanova's former mistress, whom Mitchell paid half his take to for her silence. Madrid threatens Stacey that he will inform Villanova of her whereabouts unless she accompanies him to Acapulco to convince Mitchell to testify against the Mafia. In Mexico she is kidnapped by Villanova, becomes hooked on heroin and has a wild psychedelic dream while under the drug's influence.

Stevens ended the sixties by giving her finest performance to date as Hildy, a perky prostitute with a heart-of-gold who falls in love with a grizzled old prospector (Jason Robards), in the comic western *The Ballad of Cable Hogue* (1970), directed by Sam Peckinpah. Though she gives a very fine performance, the indelible image that is left with moviegoers (especially males) is her infamous nude bathing-in-a-barrel scene. Never has Stevens looked more sensual than at that moment.

The seventies kept Stevens busy with roles as a women's libber in *Stand Up and Be Counted* (1972), *Slaughter* (1972) and, most memorably, ex-prostitute Linda Rogo in the granddaddy of all disaster films, *The Poseidon Adventure* (1972). Though co-star Shelley Winters took all the accolades as an overweight Jewish grandmother who saves the survivors and dies in the process, Stevens gives an equally good performance as the foul-mouthed wife of Ernest Borgnine, who meets a deadly end high up on a catwalk. Continuing on in the decade, Stevens was featured in many forgettable made-for-TV quickies, episodic television shows and low-budget movies. Among the few highlights from this period were *Cleopatra Jones and the City of Gold* (1974), as the Dragon lady, *Nickelodeon* (1976), with Ryan O'Neal, and the TV movie *Friendship, Secrets and Lies* (1979).

The eighties found Stella Stevens co-starring as Lute-Mae in the turgid nighttime soap *Flamingo Road* (1981–1982). She ended the decade on daytime's *Santa Barbara*, playing card dealer Phyllis Blake. In between, Stevens appeared in many less-than-mediocre films and direct-to-video productions (a few directed by her son Andrew Stevens), never lacking for work even as she got older. Though it is wonderful that she has remained so active and does not lack for work, the word "selective" is obviously not part of her vocabulary, based on the titles alone of some of her nineties' movies—*The Terror Within II* (1990), *Little Devils: The Birth* (1993), *Attack of the 5'2" Women* (1994), *The Granny* (1995) and *Bikini Motel* (1997).

Stella Stevens has branched out into other areas. She directed a documentary called *The American Heroine* examining the women of the eighties, but it has never been released. She also directed a low-budget film entitled *The Ranch* (1989) starring her son Andrew. In the mid-nineties she appeared in two CD-ROM games—*Pandora's Poker Palace* and *Phantasmagoria*. Stella acted non-stop until 2010 and returned to her recurring role of Jake on *General Hospital* for a period. She co-wrote (with William Hegner) the novel *Razzle Dazzle*, in 1999. Her last film was the direct-to-video *Megaconda* in 2010. She has also launched her own series of fragrances, called Sexy with Gold Label for women, and Black Label for men.

Other films include: *Say One for Me* (1959), *Advance to the Rear* (1964), *The Secret of My Success* (1965), *Rage* (1966), *Where Angels Go, Trouble Follows* (1968), *In Broad Daylight* (1971—TV), *Climb an Angry Mountain* (1972—TV), *Linda* (1973—TV), *Arnold* (1973), *The Day the Earth Moved* (1974—TV), *The New, Original Wonder Woman* (1975—TV), *Kiss Me, Kill Me* (1976—TV), *Las Vegas Lady* (1976), *Murder in Peyton Place* (1977—TV), *The New Love Boat* (1977—TV), *Cruise Into Terror* (1978—TV), *The Manitou* (1978), *Twirl* (1981—TV), *Wacko* (1981), *Women of San Quentin* (1983—TV), *Chained Heat* (1983), *Amazons* (1984—TV), *Monster in the Closet* (1986), *Man Against the Mob* (1988—TV), *Mom* (1990—Video), *Down the Drain* (1990—Video), *South Beach* (1992—Video), *Point of Seduction: Body Chemistry III* (1994), *Star Hunter* (1995—Video), *Invisible Mom* (1995—Video), *Body Chemistry 4: Full Exposure* (1995—Video), *In Cold Blood* (1996—TV), *The Dukes of Hazzard: The Reunion!* (1997—TV), *By the Dawn's Early Light* (2000—TV), *Size 'Em Up* (2001) and *The Long Ride Home* (2001).

Yoko Tani

Yoko Tani was born on May 2, 1932, in Paris, France. The Eurasian actress (she is half–Japanese and half–French) began her career in the performing arts modeling. She then followed that with small (sometimes uncredited) roles in films, beginning with an appearance in the costume melodrama *Ali Baba and the Forty Thieves* (a.k.a. *Ali Baba et les Quarante Voleurs*, 1954). Her heritage and schooling in England made her a favorite among the haute couture scene in Paris, and she followed the costume melodrama with a part in *Mannequins in Paris* (1956).

Following a minor role (as an unnamed bar hostess) in *The Quiet American* (1958), Yoko Tani graduated to a leading part in the international European co-production *The First Spaceship on Venus* (1959) as Space Commander Sumiko Ogimara. A role in *The Savage Innocents* (1959) led to costume adventures such as the Italian film *Samson and the Seven Miracles of the World* (a.k.a. *Maciste Alla Corte del Gran Khan*, a.k.a. *Maciste in the Court of the Great Khan*), where she had the leading female role of Princess Lei Ling. Similarly, Tani also played princesses in *Marco Polo* (1961) and

Ursus and the Tartar Princess (a.k.a. *Ursus e la Ragazza Tartara*, 1962).

As the popularity of the peplums, or sword and sandal movies (as they became known as in the United States and England), waned, the success of the James Bond films all over Europe meant that similarly espionage-themed motion pictures would soon be in production. Many starlets, like Tani, soon found themselves in a number of these films. Her first spy movie role was in *Last Plane to Baalbeck* (a.k.a. *Un Aero per Baalbeck*, a.k.a. *FBI Operazione Baalbeck*, 1963), a little known adventure film about a female Interpol agent (Rossana Podesta) who is sent to Lebanon to stop a criminal organization engaged in arms and weapons trafficking in the Middle East.

A minor role, as Isami Hiroti, in the Dean Martin comedy *Who's Been Sleeping in My Bed?* (1963) became Tani's only brush with Hollywood, but that same year she journeyed to Britain to co-star (as the seductive Lin Sivan) in the mystery thriller *The Partner* (a.k.a. *Edgar Wallace Mysteries: The Partner*). Before long, she went to Germany to appear in *The Death Ray of Dr. Mabuse* (a.k.a. *Die Todesstrahlen des Dr. Mabuse*, 1964). In the role of Mercedes, a seductive spy, she confounded an Interpol agent (Peter Van Eyck) who is assigned to protect the inventor of a new super weapon that the criminal mastermind Dr. Mabuse is after.

On the strength of this characterization, many European filmmakers were hiring the lithe, black-haired actress for similar parts in espionage films. Her next role in such a movie was in the Italian *OSS 77: Operation Lotus Flower* (a.k.a. *OSS 77–Operazione Fior di Loto*, 1965). In this film, a Secret Service agent named Robert Kent (Stanley Kent, real name: Sandro Moretti) is assigned to save a famous Chinese scientist who escaped from an atomic power station in Pakistan. It seems that Russian jets shot down his escape plane, and Kent must rescue both the plane's pilot and the scientist, who are also being stalked by a neo–Nazi spy ring called "NZ 2," as well as Tani and her agents.

In *Desperate Mission* (a.k.a. *Agente Z55 Missione Disperata*, 1966), she was back on familiar ground; when dueling bands of Chinese agents kidnap a nuclear scientist, Agent Z55 (German Cobos) is sent to retrieve him. In the obscure *Goldsnake "Killer's Company"* (a.k.a. *Goldsnake "Anonima Killers,"* a.k.a. *Operation Goldsnake*, 1966), Secret Service agent Kurt Jackson (Stanley Kent, rn: Sandro Moretti) is sent to Singapore, where a fugitive Chinese scientist (who has created bombs of a very small size) is sought by yet more Chinese agents and Middle Eastern spies.

Tani was the slinky and seductive Chinese agent in *The Spy Who Loved Flowers* (a.k.a. *Le Spie Amano i Fiori*, 1966), where a British secret agent named Martin Stevens (Roger Browne) receives orders from his superiors to assassinate three individuals who form part of an international criminal organization that has carried out the theft of a deadly Gamma ray. After the elimination of the third figure, the agent finds out that the chief of the criminal empire is someone in his own agency.

The entertaining, psychedelic pop failure *The Seven Golden Chinamen* (a.k.a. *Le Sette Cinesi d'Oro*, 1967), about a U.S. secret agent named Mark, who is sent to Rome to investigate an Armenian scientist who has created a new powerful weapon in liquid form, is a complete disaster. In no time at all, Mongolian Chinese agents (including Yoko Tani) are also on the trail. The obscure film is little more than a low-budget, Ed Wood–type mess from no-talent Italian auteur Vincenzo Cascino (who also made the equally bizarre but slightly more entertaining *Sette Donne d'Oro Contro Due 07* in 1966 with Mickey Hargitay).

Yoko Tani also appeared in the 1966–1967 British television series *Man in a Suit-*

case. In the two-part episode "Variation on a Million Bucks" (1967) she played Taiko, the lovely actress-model who had once had a love affair with ex–secret agent McGill (Richard Branford). Unlike her other spy film appearances, here she just appears on the fringes of a story where McGill, now a private detective, investigates the death of a defecting Russian agent and is drawn into a complicated search for money and valuable secret documents. The reedited episodes were then released to U.S. television as *To Chase a Million* in 1967.

In 1960 British television was introduced to the pre-cinematic James Bond adventures of a special secret agent named John Drake. As played by actor Patrick McGoohan, the series, titled *Danger Man* (and later *Secret Agent* in the United States), had several incarnations during 1960–1961, 1964–1965 and 1965–1966. A proposed fourth series was set in motion, but only two episodes were filmed in January of 1968. Yoko Tani was in both of them (although as two entirely different characters). In the first, entitled "Koroshi," she played a woman named Ako Nakamura who assists McGoohan's John Drake character as he battles a deadly cult of assassins. In the episode "Shinda Shima" she played Miho, as Drake continued his battle against the sect and infiltrates their island headquarters. The two episodes were then reedited, and Yoko Tani's role was made that of a single character; then they were combined (they were also the only episodes of *Danger Man/Secret Agent* that were filmed in color) and released as a feature film titled *Koroshi*. The movie also has the interesting theme

In *Goldsnake "Killer's Company"* (Arce Films, 1966), Yoko Tani shows that she means business.

of a British agent working in tandem with Japanese counterparts to battle corrupt international villains within a secret base located in Japan, which sometimes echoes the James Bond film *You Only Live Twice* (1967).

Yoko Tani then returned to France, the place of her birth, where she appeared in a few minor movies before she died in July of 1999 due to cancer.

Other films include: *Walk, Don't Run* (1966), *Le Fils du Ciel* (French TV, 1972) and *Ca Fait Tilt* (1977).

Sharon Tate

Sharon Tate was one of the most breathtakingly beautiful blondes to ever grace the silver screen. Adored by everyone who had the pleasure of knowing her, this stunning Texan was one of the most photographed starlets of her time. Her style and look epitomized what the sixties were all about, and with her young life cut short she remains a true tragic icon of that decade.

She was born Sharon Marie Tate on January 24, 1943, in Dallas, Texas. Her father was a Major in the army so the family moved around a lot. They resided for short periods of time in such cities as Tacoma, Houston, El Paso and San Francisco. When Tate was 16 years old her father was shipped overseas to Europe. The blossoming beauty began entering pageants and playing bit roles in Italian films such as *Barabbas* (1961). She was voted Prom Queen during her senior year at Vincenza American High School, and she headed for Hollywood in 1961 after receiving encouragement from actor Richard Beymer (whom she met while he was filming *Hemingway's Adventures of a Young Man*) and his agent.

Tate's first acting job in the States was in a cigarette commercial, though she had never smoked before. She was spotted in the reception area of Filmways Studios by executive Martin Ransohoff, who was so dazzled by the young beauty that he immediately signed her to a seven-year contract. Tate was the frontrunner for the role of Billie Jo Bradley in *Petticoat Junction* until the network discovered that she had posed for *Playboy* magazine and instead gave the role to Jeannine Riley. After taking a series of acting and singing lessons, Tate was cast in the recurring role of Janet Trego, one of Mr. Drysdale's secretaries, on *The Beverly Hillbillies*. She made close to 15 appearances on the show between October 1963 to October 1965, hidden under a dark wig. Ransohoff was waiting until the right part came along to unleash the beautiful blonde Texan on the American public.

One of Tate's few TV guest shots during this time was in the episode entitled "The Girls of Nazarone Affair" (4/12/65) on *The Man from U.N.C.L.E.* Tate and Kathy Kersh (another Filmways contract player) portrayed beautiful THRUSH agents working for Lucia Nazarone (Danica d'Hondt), who is after a serum that provides great strength and has resurrection capabilities. The two blonde beauties team up against Robert Vaughn's Napoleon Solo and beat the stuffing out of him.

After playing minuscule roles in *The Americanization of Emily* (1964) and *The Sandpiper* (1965), Tate's big break came when Ransohoff persuaded director Roman Polanski to cast her over his original choice of Jill St. John in the horror-comedy spoof *The Fearless Vampire Killers* (1967). Polanski at first balked, but he relented after seeing Tate in costume as the naïve innkeeper's buxom daughter. He not only got a more talented leading lady than St. John, but a wife as well. (They were married on January 20, 1968.) But it was *Valley of the Dolls* (1967) which made Tate a star. In this camp classic, while most of her fellow actors overplayed it to the hilt, Tate brought pathos to her role as a desperate starlet who does nudie European "art" films to pay for her husband's medical expenses. Thinking her looks and body are her only marketable assets, when she learns she has breast cancer she commits suicide. As the ad proclaimed,

Sharon Tate was truly one of the 1960s' most beautiful actresses ever to grace a spy film or any film for that matter.

"Jennifer ... International sex symbol—victimized by everyone. She took the blue pills." For her performance, Tate received a Golden Globe nomination for "New Star of the Year—Female," and she was voted a "Star of Tomorrow."

Luckily for Tate, she got to prove *she* wasn't just a body by giving a standout comedic performance as Freya Carlson, the bungling agent assigned to assist Dean Martin's Matt Helm in *The Wrecking Crew* (1969). Of all the Matt Helm movies, this one by far featured the most outrageously mod sixties fashions and futuristic gadgets. Dressed in mini-dresses with her hair up and wearing big glasses, Freya masquerades as an employee of the Danish tourist office who is delegated to help "vacationer" Matt Helm during his stay in Denmark. But he has been sent there by ICE to track down Count Contini (Nigel Green) who stole a billion dollars in gold. Helm is constantly trying to lose Freya (even after he finds out that she works for ICE), but she is doggedly persistent in aiding him. Her determination and bumbling actually save Helm's life twice when beautiful enemy agents Linka Karensky (Elke Sommer) and Yu-Rang (Nancy Kwan) try to seduce and assassinate him. After Linka is gunned down in a trap set for Helm, Freya has a martial-arts fight with Yu-Rang. (Bruce Lee coached Tate and Kwan for this scene.) Freya gets the best of Yu-Rang, who is killed on an exploding bed. Helm and Freya escape in Matt's portable folding mini-copter and board the train Contini is on. During a melee, Contini falls to his death, the gold is retrieved, and the accident-prone Freya lets down her hair and seduces a very willing Helm.

Though *The Wrecking Crew* received tepid reviews, Tate received good notices as Freya, which was reminiscent to Stella Stevens' part in *The Silencers*. *Variety* found Tate "very pleasant" and the *New York Times* commented, "the only nice thing is Sharon Tate." Edward Sothern Hipp wrote in the *Newark Evening News*, "If there is any acting plus in *The Wrecking Crew*, it must go to Miss Tate. She's cute, she's learning how to act and her effort adds up to considerably more than a mere leg-show."

Sadly, Tate never had a chance to prove Hipp or any of the other critics correct. On August 9, 1969, Charles Manson's drugged-out followers brutally murdered an eight-month pregnant Tate, hairdresser Jay Sebring, heiress Abagail Folger and two others at her rented home on Cielo Place in Beverly Hills. The Manson clan cut short a very promising career. Her last film *12+1* (a.k.a. *The Twelve Chairs*), in which she co-starred with Vittorio Gassman, was released after her death, in 1970.

Other films include: *The Wheeler Dealers* (1963), *Eye of the Devil* (1966) and *Don't Make Waves* (1967).

Linda Thorson

Linda Thorson was born Linda Robinson on June 18, 1947, in Toronto, Ontario, Canada. She moved to Great Britain in 1965, where she trained as a dancer. Gaining an interest in drama, she became an alumnus of the Royal Academy of Dramatic Arts. As a teenager, Thorson studied all the great and classic dramas of the world and performed in an indeterminate amount of productions at the Academy, but in order to make ends meet she went on auditions for television shows.

At age 20 she was signed to replace Diana Rigg (who co-starred as Emma Peel) on the hit television show *The Avengers*. Thorson was selected out of over 200 applicants, and told to dye her brunette hair blonde and lose weight. Before that, the 20-year-old actress had never stepped in front of a camera. During studio brainstorm sessions to introduce Rigg's replacement, it has been reported that Thorson chose the name Tara King for her character because of her love for the film *Gone with the Wind* and King for "King and Country." The first *Avengers* episode in which the tall, brunette (Thorson stood a full 5'9" in 1968) and bosomy actress appeared was "The Forget-Me-Knot," which was telecast March 20, 1968, in the U.S. and on September 25, 1968, in the UK. This episode was an emotional one for *Avengers* co-stars Rigg and Patrick Macnee because it was their swan song together. But the episode was also tying in the next generation, when at its finale Rigg's character, Mrs. Peel, passes Thorson's Tara King on the stairs to John Steed's flat and tells her to "take care" of the roguish spy.

Unlike Honor Blackman's lovable, agile Cathy Gale and Diana Rigg's sexy, delightful Mrs. Peel, Thorson's Tara King had an uphill battle with audiences and the show's producers. Both thought her too emotional at times. As well, the show's stories were beginning to show signs of apparent fatigue and wear. Thorson, through her character, seemed to inject more sexual tension into her and Macnee's working relationship and seemed to generally react more fearfully than the fighting female stars that came before her. Regardless, some good episodes came out of the Thorson/Macnee *Avengers* team, including "All

Linda Thorson as Tara King with Patrick Macnee as John Steed in *The Avengers* (Assoc. British Picture Corp., 1968).

Done with Mirrors," "Wish You Were Here," "Love All" and "Take-Over."

Years after the cancellation of the show, it has only recently been uncovered that the show's creators attempted to introduce the Tara King character via a special 90-minute episode titled "Invitation to a Killing" instead of "The Forget-Me-Knot." However, "Invitation" was cut down to "Have Gun, Will Haggle."

In 1983 Thorson told author Dave Rogers (*The Avengers*, ITV Books), "I had eighteen months as Tara and she was the only one of Steed's girls to be single. I used a lot of wigs and changed from blonde to brunette and redhead. I decided that she was in love with Steed. Any girl who would risk her life and spend that much time with a man must be in love. I think my interpretation influenced the producers and they let me play it my way."

However, whether it was the lack of

mostly prime scripts, or the May-December romance hinted at, or that the program was just showing signs of weariness, audiences and the network alike agreed that the time had come for The Avengers to end. It was canceled in 1969. "Before this series, you never really saw a girl making much of a fuss with Steed," commented Thorson to author Dave Rogers. "But in this series, I kiss him now and again, and I look at him devotedly. We took the sex relationship for granted. By the mid-sixties Emma Peel was part of life, so we took it for granted that Steed and Tara, and Emma before her, had slept with Steed, but simply didn't dwell on it."

In 1975 executives in France contacted Brian Clemens, the show's original producer, because the program was still very popular in their country. They were unaware that The Avengers was no longer being produced (it had been six years since its cancellation) and requested if Tara King (Thorson) would be available for a commercial spot. Clemens persuaded Thorson and Patrick Macnee to reunite for a one-off champagne advertisement for French television, and this was shot in the summer of 1975. The ad was a hit, and Clemens and Macnee were back in Avengers-land when the same French TV company co-financed and co-produced an entirely new program called The New Avengers, which lasted for two seasons.

Linda Thorson went on to appear in a variety of films, like Valentino (1977) and The Greek Tycoon (1978), but also concentrated on the stage, appearing in Noises Off and Steaming, winning theatrical awards from the New York critics for her roles in both. On television she has appeared in "The Roman Touch" episode (12/3/78) of The Return of The Saint (with Ian Oglivy) and a variety of programs, like the situation comedy Marblehead Manor in 1986, Star Trek: The Next Generation in 1987 and The Hoop Life in 1999. Finally, soap opera fans will remember Linda Thorson as the scheming Julia Medina from the show One Life to Live, which she appeared on from 1989 through 1992.

Other films include: Curtains (1983), Joey (1985), Sweet Liberty (1986), The Other Sister (1999), Mind Prey (1999—TV), Straight into Darkness (2001) and Half Past Dead (a.k.a. Lockdown, 2002).

Maggie Thrett

Dark-haired, fresh-faced Maggie Thrett was born Diane Pine on November 18 in New York City. She began working as a model, gracing the pages of many magazines, including the cover of Harper's Bazaar, to help finance her singing career. Thrett made her Off-Broadway debut in Out Brief Candle in 1962 and had a modest hit record with "Soupy," produced by Bob Crewe. The song rose to number 36 on MCA's Fabulous 57 in June of 1965, and Thrett headlined at a few clubs including the Basin Street East.

Soon after, Maggie Thrett headed West after landing a contract at Universal when she accompanied her then husband to his audition. She got in but he didn't. She made her film debut in a small role as "the second sister" in Dimension 5 (1996) starring Jeffrey Hunter and France Nuyen.

Maggie Thrett, as hired assassin Wipeout, shows off her karate skills in *Out of Sight* (Universal, 1966). (*Billy Rose Theatre Collection, The New York Library for the Performing Arts, Astor, Lenox and Tilden foundations*)

Her first film for Universal was the beach/spy spoof *Out of Sight* (1966), in which she played the karate-chopping F.L.U.S.H. assassin Wipeout who arrives in Malibu on a surfboard from Hawaii. She's hired by Big D (John Lawrence) to terminate secret agent John Stamp (Jonathan Daly). Thrett plays her role amusingly. When Big D's henchman Mousie (Jimmy Murphy) asks her, "Wipeout, did you come all the way from Hawaii on that board?" she replies drolly, "Sure, I caught a good wave." Norman Grabowski's big-and-stupid character named Huh! falls for her after she knocks him out with a powerful karate chop to the neck. He becomes smitten because she is stronger than he is. After dancing on the shore to the sounds of the rock group The Astronauts and attracting the beach kids' attention ("She must be at least 22!"), Wipeout sets her sights on her mission. She lures Homer (who's impersonating Agent Stamp) to a private pad where she tries to kill him. Just as she is about to finish Homer off with a karate chop, a jealous Huh! walks in and sees lipstick on Homer's cheek. He goes to karate chop Homer also, and knocks out Wipeout, thwarting her objective.

On television Maggie Thrett turned up twice on *The Wild Wild West*. With her dark brown hair and olive complexion, she was able to essay a variety of ethnic roles. In "The Night of the Freebooters" (4/1/66) she played soft-spoken Rita Leon, a Mexican whose husband is being held prisoner by the Freebooters, a renegade army, led by Thorald Wolfe (Keenan Wynn), set to invade and claim Mexico's Baja, California. "The Night of the Running Death" (12/15/67) gave Thrett more to do as a dancer named Dierdre (a.k.a. Topaz) who has a passion for molasses-covered Cherries Jubilee and is the girlfriend of assassin Enzo (played by female impersonator T.C. Jones). She fakes her death in order to aid Enzo, masquerading as a female British schoolteacher, in killing a princess. As a disguised Dierdre goes to shoot her, agent Artemus Gordon (Ross Martin) comes up from behind and grabs her arm, deflecting the shot. He then says to his partner James West (Robert Conrad), "Let me present our dear friend Topaz to you, James. We know her better as Dierdre." Artemus then rips off her veil and quips, "And we gave you *such* a nice funeral."

Reportedly, Maggie Thrett withdrew her life savings to buy out her contract with Universal. Her most memorable role thereafter was in the box-office hit *Three in the Attic* (1968), playing a Jewish hippie who is making it with college Lothario Christopher Jones, along with coeds Yvette Mimieux and Judy Pace. When they all discover that Jones is having sex with them simultaneously, they tie him up in their dorm's attic and try to drain him of his virility. After playing a prostitute in the feature film *Cover Me Baby* (1970), starring Robert Forster, she disappeared from the Hollywood scene.

Other films include: *I Love a Mystery* (1967—TV) and *The Devil's Brigade* (1968).

Marilu Tolo

Marilu Tolo was born in 1943 in Rome, Italy. The actress with brunette hair, green eyes and a wispy (she stood a tall 5'10") "Glamour Girl" figure first appeared onscreen in an unknown Italian television program at age 16. One year later she landed on the big screen with a role in *The Adolescents* (a.k.a. *I Dolci Inganni*, 1961). Within three years she appeared in *Marriage, Italian Style* (1964) and then numerous films in sultry minor roles. Subsequent screen roles were in sexy costume adventures such as *Messalina vs. the Son of Hercules* (a.k.a. *L'Ultimo Gladiatore*), *Hercules and the Ten Avengers* (a.k.a. *Il Trionfo di Ercole*) and *The Terror of Rome Against the Son of Hercules*, all low-budget adventure films made between 1964 and 1965.

Her first role in an espionage film was in the Italian-Spanish co-production *Espionage in Lisbon* (a.k.a. *Mision Lisboa*, a.k.a. *Mission Lisbon*, 1965), where an agent (Brett Halsey), sent after a secret formula that neutralizes electricity, finds that the scientist who had originated the formula has been murdered and a cadre of mysterious, sinister enemy agents are circling. Tolo appeared as a femme fatale, who attempts to murder, then seduce, our hero. As Virgia in *The Poppy Is Also a Flower* (a.k.a. *The Opium Connection*, 1966) an international co-production funded by the U.N., the actress is

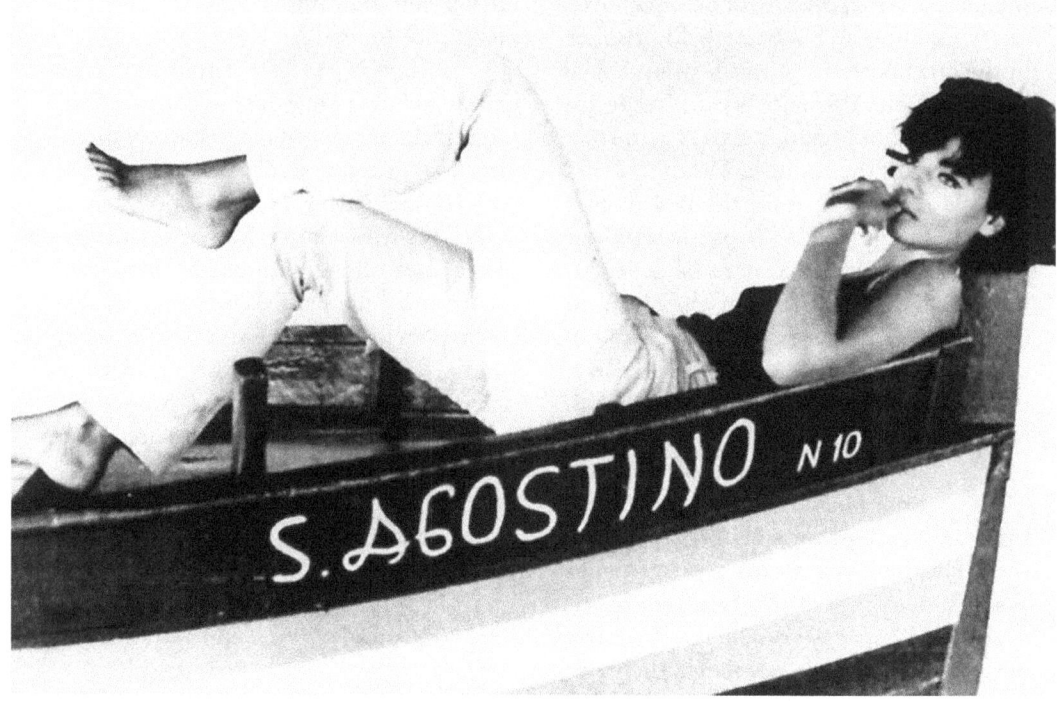

The seductive Marilu Tolo was lusted after by many male fans of sixties spy films.

lost amidst the all-star cast populated by Hollywood names and European superstars. As Gioia in *Kiss the Girls and Make Them Die* (a.k.a. *Se Tutte le Donne del Mondo*, 1966), Tolo was but one of a bevy of beautiful women who were waiting for CIA agent Mike Connors to put an end to villain Raf Vallone and his plan to sterilize the world and have a select group of women (Tolo included) for himself. In the Bond spoof *Operation Oro* (a.k.a. *Baleari Operazione Oro*, a.k.a. *The Balearic Caper*, 1966), she appears with hero agent Jacques Sernas, who does battle with *Goldfinger* villain Harold Sakata over a magical golden scepter.

Tolo also appeared as Paola in *Perry Grant, Agent of Iron* (a.k.a. *Perry Grant, Agente di Ferro*, a.k.a. *The Big Blackout*, 1966), an obscure espionage thriller, and as Prinzi in the equally obscure *A Stroke of 100 Millions* (a.k.a. *Un Colpo da Mille Milliardi*, a.k.a. *The Suez Intrigue*, 1966), where she assisted the secret agent hero, played by Rik Van Nutter (American CIA contact Felix Leiter to James Bond in *Thunderball*), as he battled a sadistic madman bent on infecting the Suez Canal with radioactive waste. Afterwards, Tolo appeared in the little-seen French spy film *Casse-Tout Tete Chinois pour le Judoka* (1967) and co-starred as a medical professional who ends up embroiled in a convoluted assassination plot in *The Killer Likes Candy* (a.k.a. *Un Killer per Sua Maesta*, 1968).

Marilu Tolo ended the decade by appearing in the mega-star abomination *Candy* (1968), and then began to appear in more prominent films, such as the dark Richard Burton thriller *Bluebeard* (1972) and *The Greek Tycoon* (1978). She received some of the best critical reviews of her career for her starring role in the supernatural Swedish film *Inn of the Flying Dragon* (a.k.a. *Onskans Vardshus*, a.k.a. *The Sleep of Death* (1981), but had last been seen appearing in American and European co-financed miniseries made for television, including *Marco Polo* (1982) and *The Last Days of Pompeii* (1984), as well as the pilot for the show *The Countess and the Cowboy* in 1980.

Other films include: *The Thief of Baghdad* (1961), *Le Streghe* (1966), *Django Kill* (a.k.a. *Se Sei Vivo Spara*, 1972), *Mio Caro Assassino* (1971), *Themroc* (1972), *Le Cinque Giornate* (1973), *Prigione di Donne* (1974) and *Vacanze di Natale* (1983).

Irene Tsu

Chinese actress Irene Tsu (born on November 4, 1944, in Shanghai) played sweet and not-so-sweet Asians in a number of spy-themed film and television programs during the sixties. After fleeing Shanghai with her family when the Communists took over, Tsu landed in New York. As a teenager she began taking ballet classes and landed a role in the touring company of *The World of Susie Wong*. Her friendship with the play's star, Nancy Kwan, led to an audition as one of the teenage dancers in *Flower Drum Song* (1961). Tsu got the job, and this led to a variety of minor exotic roles in such films as *Take Her, She's Mine* (1963), *The Sword of Ali Baba* (1965) and *How to Stuff a Wild Bikini* (1965).

Tsu's first TV spy show was an episode of *The Man from U.N.C.L.E.* titled "The Hong Kong Schilling Affair" (3/15/65), in which she played the small role of Jasmine, an U.N.C.L.E. agent based in Hong Kong. Her only contribution was to sew a hidden microphone into the suit jacket of an innocent tourist (Glenn Corbett) who gets entangled with an organization that sells top secret military secrets to the highest bidder. Oscar winner William Tuttle received special credit for his make-up creations for David McCallum, who, as U.N.C.L.E. agent Illya Kuryalin, is disguised as a Mongolian warlord. "I remember working with David McCallum and he was a very precise actor," remarks Tsu. "In one scene we were playing Chinese checkers. He didn't want me to come in and say my line until he did a certain move. The first couple of times I goofed it up. He said sternly, 'Don't say *anything* until I make my move!' I finally got it right."

After appearing as "the Girl" in "A Cup of Kindness" on *I Spy* (9/22/65), Tsu made a second appearance on *The Man from U.N.C.L.E.* in the second half of the two-part "The Five Daughters Affair" (4/7/67), which was released overseas as the feature *The Karate Killers*. Tsu perkily played Reiko, a geisha girl who helps Kim Darby's character, named Sandy, escape from THRUSH, who are after her dead father's secret formula to turn seawater into gold. ("This was a fun part to play," says Tsu. "By this time I think I was doing some *real* acting.") Sandy confides in Reiko, who tries to contact U.N.C.L.E. in New York for her, with no luck. Knowing that THRUSH could come any minute, Reiko has her fellow geishas make up Sandy to be one of them. U.N.C.L.E. agents Napoleon and Illya get to Sandy first, but Reiko mistakes them for THRUSH agents, and she and her fellow geishas knock them out with a karate chop to their necks. When they come to, Reiko apologizes to the impressed agents

Irene Tsu (left), as geisha girl Reiko, with Robert Vaughn (Napoleon Solo), Kim Darby (Sandy) and David McCallum (Illya Kuryakin) in the *The Man from U.N.C.L.E.* episode "The Five Daughters Affair," which was released theatrically as *The Karate Killers* (MGM, 1968).

and asks if U.N.C.L.E. would consider her for a position as an agent.

Next up for Irene Tsu was the unsuccessful spy spoof *Caprice* (1967), directed by Frank Tashlin, and starring Doris Day (whom Tsu describes as being "very talented, with a sparkling, animated personality") as an industrial spy caught between two rival cosmetics companies. They are both after a secret formula developed by Stuart Clancy (Ray Walston) that prevents hair from getting wet when under water. Tsu played model Su Ling, Clancy's mistress, who holds the key to the secret formula.

The part of Su Ling is one of Tsu's sexiest and most enjoyable roles. One of *Caprice*'s funniest moments, in the best slapstick tradition, is when Day tries to clip a lock of a bikini-clad Tsu's hair. Her orange and white swimsuit presented her with a lot of trouble during those scenes. "I had to dive into a swimming pool, and the bottom half of my bikini kept dislodging," says Tsu with a laugh. "It was so embarrassing. I couldn't swim very well, so I would hold it with one hand and dive with the other. But Tashlin [the director] said, 'Don't dive with one hand. It looks ridiculous.' They promised me that they wouldn't use it if my bathing suit came down. It did and naturally they used it. Luckily they were forced to cut it for the U.S. version."

On "The Night of the Samurai" episode of *The Wild Wild West*, which aired on 10/13/67, Tsu once again played a character named Reiko, but unlike the character in the aforementioned *Man from U.N.C.L.E.* episode, this one is no heroine. At first she comes across as a docile Japanese woman who helps agents James West (Robert Conrad) and Artemus Gordon (Ross Martin) retrieve the Sword of Kuniyoshi. She even saves West from being killed by villain Hannibal Egloff (Thayer David) by slipping him "The Kiss of a Friend," which is actually a dagger. It is a surprise to learn at the end that she was running the dirty tricks department. When West guesses that she killed Hannibal, Reiko coldly replies, "Of course. He was just a fat bloated slug. Why should I have given second thoughts?" Tsu's icy performance helps make this episode quite entertaining.

In 1968 Irene Tsu appeared as a Vietnamese spy, opposite John Wayne, in *The Green Berets*. Though reviled by critics, the film was a box-office smash. She journeyed to Hong Kong to star opposite newcomer Jeff Bridges in the spy spoof *The Yin and Yang of Mr. Go* (1970). Bridges, in his first starring role, played a writer/CIA agent assigned to work with a Russian scientist to retrieve a set of stolen plans that blocks anti-ballistic warheads which criminal mastermind Mr. Yin-Yang Go (James Mason) plans to sell to the highest bidder. Tsu was cast as Bridges' love interest, Tah Ling. Since this was directed by actor Burgess Meredith and also featured such esteemed thespians as Broderick Crawford and Jack MacGowran, Tsu thought "that this would be my breakout film." However, the problem-laden production was first hindered by the tremendous dislike Mason had for Meredith. "At one point they weren't even speaking to one another," reveals Tsu. "When Jeff and I would go to dinner, Mason and Meredith would be eating at separate tables. They would try to coax us to sit with them, but we wouldn't take sides and sat by ourselves." When the Canadian bankers financing the film went bankrupt, the production was closed down and the movie was never completed. Surprisingly, years later *The Yin and Yang of Mr. Go* was released on video with animated sequences added to bridge the gaps of the plot.

During the seventies Irene Tsu married Hungarian director Ivan Nagy. She shed her cute sixties persona (along with her long hair) and began playing more hardened roles, beginning with her last spy appearance, in "Double Dead" (2/12/72) on *Mission: Impossible*. On the big screen Tsu could be found playing a stewardess in *Airport 1975* (1974), a terrorist in *Paper Tiger* (1975) and a police detective in *Hot Potato* (1976). After a respite from acting in the late seventies (to concentrate on a career in fashion), Tsu returned to the acting profession with a supporting role in *Down and Out in Beverly Hills* (1986). She has never lacked for roles since, and also works as a Beverly Hills realtor.

In 2001 Irene Tsu reprised her role as the mother of Ensign Harry Kim (Garrett Wang) on an episode of *Star Trek Voyager*. She had previously played this part in a 1997 episode entitled "Favorite Son." Tsu continues to act but her main focus is on her adopted daughter. "I am now a new mom," exclaims Irene Tsu. "It's the best role I ever had!"

Other films include: *Seven Women* (1966), *Women of the Prehistoric Planet* (1966), *Paradise, Hawaiian Style* (1966), *Three the Hard Way* (1974), *Steele Justice* (1987), *Mr. Jones* (1993), *Snap Dragon* (1993), *Widow's Kiss* (1994), *Comrades: Almost a Love Story* (1997) and *Tell Me No Secrets* (1997—TV).

Sigrid Valdis

Buxom Sigrid Valdis was the obligatory blonde in the spy spoof *Our Man Flint* (1966), starring James Coburn as Derek Flint. As the only flaxen-haired Flint girl, her physical appearance alone made her a standout. Valdis was born Patricia Olson on September 21, 1935, in Bakersfield, California. After graduating high school she relocated to New York and sold sports cars on Park Avenue. From the money she earned, she began studying acting with Stella Adler.

After returning to California, Valdis landed a role as a scantily clad girl in the film *Marriage on the Rocks* (1965), starring Frank Sinatra and Dean Martin. Two episodes of *The Wild Wild West*, playing Miss Piecemeal, followed. According to Susan E. Kesler, writing in *The Wild Wild West: The Series*, "in the tradition of Miss Moneypenny, Piecemeal is the governor's secretary and basically a bitch." In her first episode, entitled "The Night the Wizard Shook the Earth" (10/1/65), she is a cohort of Dr. Miguelito Loveless (Michael Dunn), who steals a formula for a new explosive that he helped develop with Professor Nielsen (Harry Bartell). Valdis returned as Miss Piecemeal, who was still up to her dirty tricks, in "The Night of the Torture Chamber" (12/10/65). Now secretary to Governor Bradford (Henry Beckman), she helps engineer her boss' kidnapping for the evil Professor Bolt (Alfred Ryder). Bolt replaces Bradford with look-alike actor Sam Jamison (also Beckman), so the "Governor" can get his hands on the millions of dollars in the state's treasury to finance Bolt's art collection.

In the successful spy spoof *Our Man Flint*, Valdis (resembling a younger, zaftig Doris Day) is beautifully costumed as Anna, one of the assistants to filmdom's slickest secret agent, Derek Flint (James Coburn). The girls pamper Flint as they shave, dress and massage him—a feminist's worst nightmare. Anna rubs Flint's neck in his apartment, dances the rumba with him at an elegant restaurant, and, after Flint's superior Lloyd Kramden (Lee J. Cobb) is hit with a poison dart, asks, "Why would anyone want to kill Mr. Kramden?" Soon after, Flint is off to France to find out, leaving his girls behind. As Flint evades Galaxy's plot to assassinate him, the villains kidnap his girls (Anna is abducted at a dress shop) and take them to a remote volcanic island off of Italy to be programmed as pleasure units. Anna is brainwashed to be a Roman slave girl but is rescued by Flint, who defeats Galaxy and restores world order.

As with the rest of the Flint girls— Shelby Grant, Gianna Serra and Helen Funai—Valdis has little to do but look pretty, fawn over Flint and act scared. However, she and the other actresses do it in a stylish, graceful manner, giving the film a boost. Though the "Flint Girls" never reached the levels of the "Bond Girls," they helped *Our Man Flint* and *In Like Flint* become hits and made an indelible impression on filmgoers during the sixties.

In the fall of 1966 Valdis joined the cast of *Hogan's Heroes* during its second season. As Helga, Colonel Klink's secretary, she had little more to do than recite lines such as, "Herr Kommandant, Colonel Hogan to see you." Off-screen she began an affair with the show's married star, Bob Crane. In 1970 Valdis and Crane were wed on the set of the sitcom. After the show

Super sleuth James Coburn, as Derek Flint, is flanked by his consorts (starting at lower right) Sigrid Valdis (Anna), Helen Funai (Sakito), Shelby Grant (Leslie) and Gianna Serra (Gina) in *Our Man Flint* (20th Century–Fox, 1967).

was cancelled, Sigrid Valdis retired from acting to raise their son Scott. They were still married as of Crane's death in 1978, though Valdis had started and then stopped divorce proceedings against him due to his proclivity for pornography. Found bludgeoned in his Scarsdale, Arizona, hotel room (amid a number of homemade porn tapes, most starring him), Crane's murder remains unsolved to this day. Soon after, Valdis dropped completely from the limelight. Today her son Scott Crane is a DJ on KQBZ 100.7 FM in Seattle, partnered with fellow DJ Little Johnny Seattle. Their program, *Shaken, Not Stirred*, is one of Seattle's highest rated radio shows. Purportedly, Sigrid Valdis has participated in some of their comedy bits though she rarely makes public appearances. She passed away on October 14, 2007.

Other films include: *The Two Tickets to Paris* (1962) and *The Venetian Affair* (1967).

Monica Vitti

Monica Vitti was born Maria Luisa Ceciarelli on November 3, 1931, in Rome, Italy. Interested in drama at an early age, she attended the famed Academy of Dramatic Arts, and by age 14 she made her official stage debut (playing a 40-year-old woman) in the production *The Enemy* by Nicodemi. Upon her graduation, she joined other esteemed Italian dramatic schools, like the Orazio Costa Company and the Tofano-Ninchi Company, ending with an acclaimed performance in Arthur Miller's *After the Fall* in 1956, directed by Franco Zeffirelli. By now she was known as Monica Vitti. In 1986 she told a journalist for *Andy Warhol's Interview* magazine, "Directors at that time didn't want actors to act, especially actresses. They were expected to be pretty. So they told me I should stick to the theater. They said, 'Your nose is too thin.' My whole family went away to America to live ... they said, 'How can you stay alone in Italy?' But I used their absence to become an actress. That's how I became Monica Vitti. When they came back, my parents had to call me Monica. They had to acknowledge what had happened."

Monica Vitti's cinema debut came in the late 1950s when she found work dubbing American and French actresses into the Italian language for productions filmed abroad and released in that country. Her onscreen film debut came in the 1958 movie *Le Dritte*, but her career really got a boost when she was discovered by Michelangelo Antonioni, and her first starring role in a film came in 1960. This role was an acclaimed one for her, in Antonioni's *L'Avventura*. Roles in other Antonioni films followed, and the two became romantically linked, but in actuality they were already living together before *L'Avventura* finished principal photography. For the next five years she continued in a succession of highly regarded films (some of them, including *The Eclipse* [a.k.a. *L'Eclisse*, 1962] and *The Red Desert* [a.k.a. *Il Deserto Rosso*, 1964], under Antonioni's direction). Unlike other Italian starlets of the day, Vitti was not interested in playing the comely bimbo next door. In fact, those roles were hardly offered to her in a country where sex is considered a favorite cinematic subject. "I'm blonde, with freckles and I don't have a big chest. In the beginning, all this made it very difficult for me, but in retrospect, it allowed me to do my own thing."

She had her first role in an English language film in 1966 when she was chosen as the lead in the American-British co-production of *Modesty Blaise*, directed by Joseph Losey. In this film, Vitti stars as a sexy super-super agent named Modesty Blaise who becomes involved in all kinds of intrigue and espionage when her nemesis, Gabriel (Dirk Bogarde), and his psychopathic female sidekick (Rossella Falk) plan on creating a crisis in the Middle East. The British government asks the retired Modesty Blaise to return to active service, which she will do, considering they pay her a high fee. Blaise is weary of being the "Queen of International Adventure," with its accompanying elegance and luxury, and seeks monetary payment for all her troubles. Based on a European comic strip, the film, a pop art extravaganza populated by surreal vignettes and bizarre dialog, was a critical success but a commercial failure.

Vitti returned to Italy where she continued to work, winning several acting honors for her role in the film *The Girl with a*

Alluring and dangerous are just two words used to describe Monica Vitti as *Modesty Blaise* (20th Century–Fox, 1966).

Pistol (a.k.a. *La Ragazza con la Pistola*, 1968). (She had won the Italian Best Actress "Silver Ribbon" award previously in 1961 for the Antonioni film *The Night* [a.k.a. *La Notte*].)

Monica Vitti spent the majority of her cinematic career acting in the Italian cinema. Her diverse skills as an actress garnered her critical acclaim, and her attractive form even made sure that she was cast in a number of sexy comedies. She returned to English language moviemaking in 1978 with a role in the Michael Ritchie film *An Almost Perfect Affair*. In recent years Monica Vitti has reunited with Michelangelo Antonioni for the film *The Mystery of Oberwald* (1980) and has prospered on the business side of the cinema, going into production and even attempting directing (*Scandalo Secreto*, 1989); her films have received positive critical reactions in her native Italy.

Other films include: *The Flying Saucer* (a.k.a. *Il Disco Volante*, 1964), *The Queens* (a.k.a. *Le Fate*, 1966), *The Chastity Belt* (a.k.a. *La Cintura di Castita*, 1967), *The Phantom of Liberty* (a.k.a. *The Fantom de Liberte*, 1974), *Mimi Bluette* (1974), *Blonde in Black Leather* (1977), *Letti Salvaggi* (a.k.a. *Tigers in Lipstick*, 1979), *Flirt* (1983), and *Francesca e Mia* (1986).

Ira von Furstenberg

Ira von Furstenberg was born on April 18, 1940, in Rome, Italy. Her family was of noble origins and gained great wealth by dealing with rare antiquities during and immediately after World War II. Most of the von Furstenberg siblings (there were a number of brothers and sisters) went on to become fashion designers, and in some manner or form managed to keep themselves near the pinnacle of European society's haute couture.

As an actress, Ira von Furstenberg was not lauded by any critical accolades, but she seemed to have turned in serviceable performances in a small number of movies like *The Battle of El Alamein* (a.k.a. *La Battaglia di El Alamein*, 1968) and *Five Dolls for an August Moon* (a.k.a. *5 Bambole per la Luna D'Agosto*, 1970). However, two of her most notable (and finest) performances were in two espionage films. In the Italian film *Matchless* (1966) she played the delectable Arabella, a thorn in the side of Patrick O'Neal's beleaguered journalist who is chased all over Europe by Red Chinese spies seeking the invisibility formula that he was given by a dying scientist. Von Furstenberg managed to infuse her character with equal parts sexy charm and danger.

In the West German–French co-production *Dead Run* (a.k.a. *Das Geheimnisse in Goldenen Nylons*, a.k.a. *The Secret of the Girl in the Gold Nylons*, 1967), she was the leading lady (named Suzanne), an apparently innocent woman who, by a mere coincidence, is chased all throughout France and Germany by Eastern European agents because they believe that she knows the identity of an assassin on the run. Her only hope lay with Interpol Inspector Peter Lawford (in an uncharacteristic dour perfor-

In the Italian feature *Matchless* (United Artists, 1966), sexy Ira von Furstenberg (Arabella) matches wits with an invisible agent. (*Courtesy of Michael Monahan*)

mance), as enemy agents besiege her and attempt to murder her.

Von Furstenberg tried to send her acting career into overdrive with appearances in a number of Italian sex comedies and dramas from the late sixties to the mid-seventies (among them, *Calde Notti di Don Giovanni* [1971] and *Homo Eroticus* [1971]). But her career as an actress petered out. During the late seventies she became a public relations manager for fashion designer Valentino. The nineties found her hosting her own TV talk show in Germany, where she presented former and current members of the European aristocracy. Today she is also known as Princess Virginia Carolina Theresa Pancrazia Galdina von Furstenberg, and is well known as a socialite and partygoer who is mentioned in gossip columns among the rich, famous and powerful.

Other films include: *J'ai tué Raspoutine* (a.k.a. *I Killed Rasputin*, 1967), *A Qualsiasi Prezzo* (a.k.a. *The Vatican Affair*, 1968), *Giornata Nera per l'Ariete* (a.k.a. *Evil Fingers*, a.k.a. *The Fifth Cord*, 1971), *Los Amigos* (a.k.a. *Deaf Smith and Johnny Ears*, 1972), *O Amante de Minha Mulher* (1978) and *Plus beau que moi, tu meurs* (1982).

Lesley Ann Warren

Lesley Ann Warren was born on August 16, 1946, in New York City. She began ballet training as a very young child, and by the time she was 13 years old she was good enough to win a scholarship to study with the esteemed choreographer George Balanchine. Two years later, the now wide-eyed teenager quit dancing to become an actress. She enrolled in New York's Professional Children's School and studied for a time at the Actor's Studio with Lee Strasberg. She made her Broadway debut in the 1963 musical *110 in the Shade*. She was an immediate sensation and was chosen to play the lead role in the musical TV special *Cinderella* in 1965. Warren returned to Broadway in 1966 to co-star with Elliot Gould in *Drat the Cat* before signing a contract with Walt Disney, who championed her as an ingenue who could sing and dance. Warren made her film debut in *The Happiest Millionaire* (1967), and appeared in more films for Disney before wisely severing her ties to the studio, as the big Hollywood musical was a dying breed.

Warren married hairdresser Jon Peters in 1967. She appeared in the TV movie *Seven in Darkness* (1969) before signing on as a regular in the TV series *Mission: Impossible*. The hiring of Lesley Warren (billed sans the Ann) caused quite a stir with the show's creator, Bruce Geller. The season following Barbara Bain's departure featured a number of sophisticated actresses cast as IMF agents. Among the ones who made a great impact on television audiences were Lee Meriwether, Jessica Walter, BarBara Luna and Anne Francis. However, the producers wanted to draw some younger viewers, so Warren (all of 23) was added to give the show a "now" and "with it" look. Warren concurred and told *TV Guide*, "I believe in being natural. I want a contemporary, hippie, braless, now kind of thing."

Warren's character, Dana Lambert, made her *Mission: Impossible* debut with lots of fanfare and fair reviews. For example, *Variety* remarked early on that, "Pretty Lesley Warren lacks the exotic sophistication of former femme lead Barbara Bain but, in addition to being a pleasure to the eye ... proves to be a facile actress." Some of the episodes that headlined her included "The Killer" (9/19/70), where she masquerades as a bag lady who is the contact for hired killer Eddie Lorca (Robert Conrad). She supplies him with all the information from his boss regarding his next hit but has inserted a picture of IMF agent Barney (Greg Morris) in place of the real intended victim. When Dana is "shot" by the IMF, she confesses to Lorca that he was the real intended victim before she "dies," setting up a showdown between the contract killer and his associates. In "The Amateur" (11/14/70) Dana goes undercover as a cocktail waitress working for schemer Eric Schilling (Anthony Zerbe) in an Eastern bloc country to aid local priest Father Bernard (Peter Brocco) in his mission to smuggle out a rocket laser and list of Western operatives. In "The Hostage" (12/19/70) Dana pretends to be the girlfriend of condemned PRF prisoner Luis, being held by the U.S., who pleads with his father to let kidnapped IMF agent Paris (Leonard Nimoy) go free so the U.S. will spare Luis' life.

Warren fared best in the youth-oriented episode entitled "Takeover" (1/2/71), as her character Dana masquerades as a notorious college activist whom fellow demonstrator Billy Walsh (Richard Kelton) bails out of jail. He has been bribed by the backer of a political candidate to stage some violent protest marches to embarrass the incumbent state governor.

Unhappy with the way her *Mission: Impossible* character was progressing (or not progressing) throughout the season, Warren and the producers mutually parted ways. Though she received a Golden Globe nomination as "Best Supporting Actress in a TV Series," she never really caught on with the fans—or the critics. Her young, hip character seemed very much out of place with the rest of the "older" IMF agents. John L. Wasserman wrote in *TV Guide*, "[Warren] was about as convincing as the Marines being led into combat by a female impersonator." Author Patrick White commented about Warren in *The Complete Mission: Impossible Dossier* that, "watching her work in the series, one occasionally senses the feeling of untapped potential, but most often she seems miscast as an international trade diplomat or simply too young for a glamorous jet-setter or hardened bank robber."

After exiting *Mission: Impossible* in 1970, Lesley Ann Warren (playing Cathy Lange) made one more journey into spydom opposite Roy Scheider in the glossy TV movie *Assignment: Munich* (1972), a pilot for a proposed series shot on location in Europe. Scheider played an American operative working as the manager of a club in Munich who agrees to help the government locate a cache of gold stolen by the Nazis during the war. When the pilot was picked up as a series beginning in the fall of 1972, the locale was changed to Vienna (hence the title change to *Assignment: Vienna*) and Robert Conrad took over for Scheider who had taken another acting job in the interim.

Lesley Ann Warren became a mainstay in forgettable TV movies and miniseries throughout the seventies. However, for *79 Park Avenue* she won a Golden Globe for "Best Actress in a Television Series—Drama" in 1978. She finally got a film role that highlighted her shapely body and made full use of her comedic abilities when she was cast in *Victor/Victoria* (1982), starring James Garner and Julie Andrews. Her performance as the dumb blonde gun moll Norma earned her Academy Award and Golden Globe nominations for "Best Supporting Actress." But Warren followed this by giving a downright embarrassing per-

IMF agents Lesley Ann Warren, as Dana, and Leonard Nimoy (Paris) go undercover as performers in "Flip Side" on *Mission: Impossible* (Paramount Television, 1971).

formance as an unhappily married college professor who has an affair with one of her students (Christopher Atkins), who works as a stripper, in the awful *A Night in Heaven* (1983). This became a pattern in Warren's career, as she was cast numerous times as the older woman who gets involved with much younger men. Luckily, Warren saved her reputation by giving well-received performances in *Songwriter* (1984), as an up and coming singer, and *Choose Me* (1984), as a bar owner.

As life often imitates art, after divorcing husband Peters in the seventies, Lesley Ann Warren was involved for real with a younger man, dancer Jeffrey Hornaday—ten years her junior. Today she is happily married to ad executive Ron Taft, whom she met in 1991. Still sexy and gorgeous, Warren recently co-starred in the thrilling but overlooked drama *The Limey* (1999). Terence Stamp played a British career criminal, just released from prison, who journeys to Los Angles to investigate the mysterious circumstances of his daughter's death. Warren is simply splendid as Elaine, an older actress who knew his daughter and helps Stamp discover who his child really was. Based on this performance alone, Lesley Ann Warren should never have to lack for work again, and she appeared in a few episodes of *Will and Grace* as the kooky mistress of Will's father.

Other films include: *The One and Only, Genuine, Original Family Band* (1968), *The Daughters of Joshua Cabe* (1972—TV), *The Letters* (1973—TV), *The Legend of Valentino* (1975—TV), *Harry and Walter Go to New York* (1976), *Portrait of a Stripper* (1979—TV), *Portrait of a Showgirl* (1982—TV), *Clue* (1985), *Baja Oklahoma* (1987—TV), *Burglar* (1987), *Cop* (1987), *Life Stinks* (1991), *Pure Country* (1992), *Bird of Prey* (1995), *Going All the Way* (1997), *Teaching Mrs. Tingle* (1999), *Twin Falls Idaho* (1999), *Trixie* (2000), *Delivering Milo* (2000), *The Quickie* (2001), *The Myersons* (2001), *Losing Grace* (2001) and *Secretary* (2002).

Raquel Welch

Actress Raquel Welch was *the* sex goddess of the sixties. There is no denying that the curvy brunette with the measurements of 39-22-33 (as touted in the trailer for *Fathom*) was a stunning beauty. Men lusted after her, while women envied her. But her screen persona as a sex symbol and pin-up girl contrasted with her real life role of hard working actress and loving mother. She was always trying to prove that she not only possessed a pretty face and a voluptuous body but real acting talent as well.

Raquel Welch was born Jo Raquel Tejada on September 5, 1940, in Chicago, Illinois. Her family relocated to San Diego, California, when she was three. While a student at La Jolla High School, the buxom beauty was crowned "Miss Photogenic," beating out over 150 other young girls. She went on to be crowned "Miss La Jolla," "Miss San Diego" and "Maid of California." After graduating high school she entered San Diego State College on a Theatre Arts scholarship and married boyfriend James Welch. Their son Damon was born the following year. Pursuing her desire to become an actress, Welch worked as a weather girl on a local morning program titled *Sun Up* and began modeling. The demands of being a new mother, wife and student caught up to Welch and she dropped out of school. Her daughter Tahnee was born in 1961, and her marriage ended soon after. Welch then packed up her children and moved to Hollywood. To support her family, she began working as a fitting model. A chance encounter with former child actor Patrick Curtis, whom she met at a coffee shop, would change her life forever. His publicity talents aided the ambitious, self-determined young actress in becoming a star. A stint as "the Billboard Girl" on the variety series *Hollywood Palace* in 1963 led to bit roles in a few movies, including *A House Is Not a Home* (1964) and *Roustabout* (1964), with Elvis Presley. Though onscreen only briefly, she nevertheless made an impression and was voted a Hollywood Deb Star in 1965, the year she landed her first major role—in the youth-oriented film *A Swingin' Summer* (1965).

Welch's first two forays into spydom never panned out. In 1965 producer Saul David tested her for the female lead in the spy spoof *Our Man Flint* (1966), but the film's production was delayed. Welch told columnist Sheila Graham in 1966 that, "I almost played one of the leads in *Thunderball* [1965]. Someone sent my photograph to producer Cubby Broccoli. He sent me a ticket to come to London ... but nothing came of it." Reportedly, when the head of 20th Century–Fox, Richard Zanuck, heard that producer Broccoli was pursuing Welch, he signed her to a contract. She was cast as a surgeon's assistant who is part of a medical team that is miniaturized and injected into the blood stream of a dying scientist in the hit film *Fantastic Voyage* (1966). Welch won raves—not for her emoting, but for her voluptuous body encased in a tight diving suit. Exhibitors, voting in *The Motion Picture Herald*, named her a "Star of Tomorrow" for 1966. But wary of her acting ability, Fox loaned her to Hammer Studios for the remake of *One Million Years B.C.* (1967). The image of a now blonde Welch clad in a fur bikini appeared all over the world, catapulting her to the top echelon of international sex symbols. Her poster adorned many a wall of adolescent boys. Raquel Welch remained in Europe to make a few more films, including the spy movie *Fathom* (1967), shot on location in Malaga, Spain.

Fathom is a breezy, light-hearted spy spoof directed by Leslie H. Martinson. The movie opens with a camera pan across the bikini-clad Raquel, immediately taking advantage of her curvaceous figure as she readies her parachute for a jump while the title credits roll. After performing a free-fall at a fiesta in Malaga, Spain, the sexy skydiver/dental hygienist is offered a ride back into town by a man named Timothy (Richard Briers), who takes her to meet Colonel Campbell (Ronald Fraser). She is duped into retrieving the "Fire Dragon" (thinking it is a failsafe device that can trigger a hydrogen bomb) before Red Chinese agents Peter Merriweather (Tony Franciosa, sporting bleached strawberry blond hair) and Jo-May Soon (Greta Chi) get ahold of it. She parachutes into Merriweather's villa, activates a bugging device and discovers the dead body of a man named Kurt. As she picks up the bloodied statuette beside his corpse, Merriweather and Jo-May startle her. Fathom sweet talks her way out of the situation ("I'm just a skydiver with a lousy sense of direction"). As Merriweather escorts her on horseback back to town, he stops to dispose of the body. Over the course of the film, as she doggedly searches for the "Fire Dragon," a bikini-clad Fathom is lusted after by mysterious millionaire Serge Serapkin (Clive Revill), pursued by a helicopter, run down by a speedboat and trapped in a bullring with a stampeding bull.

After surviving myriad attempts on her life and not being able to determine the good guys from the bad guys, a conned Fathom discovers the "Fire Dragon" in her make-up case as she packs her suitcase to leave town. At the finale, Fathom and all the agents converge on the train. During a wild melee for the "Fire Dragon," the make-up case is thrown out the window and Peter jumps out after it. Fathom and Timothy escape from the train with the "Fire Dragon," but guards detain Serapkin. They rendezvous with Campbell and attempt to fly to Paris. In the air, Campbell reveals that they are flying to Ankara and admits that, "your friend Merriweather spoke the truth. He is the detective—I'm the thief." When she attempts to jump from the plane she finds that her parachute has been rigged. Peter, who is in pursuit by plane, shoots Campbell. Fathom struggles with Timothy, who falls from the plane. As Peter gives Fathom desperate instructions to land the out-of-control aircraft, he is surprised to learn that she can fly. Fathom determines that Peter wants to sell the "Fire Dragon" to the highest bidder, but Fathom returns it to its rightful owners and drops it out of the plane, landing it in Jo-May's birthday cake. Fathom and Peter then fly off to meet later that night.

As spy spoofs go, *Fathom* is fast-moving fun. It is colorful, gorgeously photographed, and features a witty screenplay by Lorenzo Semple, Jr. (of *Batman* fame). One of the film's running jokes is that Fathom is always being asked how she got her unusual name—and always responds differently. "Fathom is six feet. Papa was hoping for a tall son. Papa was disappointed." "First initials for uncles—Freddie, Arthur, Tom, Harry, Oscar, Milton. They were all rich and Papa wasn't taking any chances." And, "It's short for Elizabeth." Of course, *Fathom* is greatly helped by the stunning presence of the sultry sex goddess. When Welch emerges from her hotel wearing a bright green bikini and makes her way through the streets of Malaga, her unearthly beauty takes your breath away. Martinson gets a skillful per-

Stunning Raquel Welch as Fathom Harvil, skydiver/spy, in *Fathom* (20th Century–Fox, 1967).

formance from Welch, and she plays her part tongue-in-cheek.

Raquel Welch remarked to *Newsday* in 1967, "I think what saved a mediocre picture like *Fathom* was that the photography was good, I looked sexy and the character was charming. At times like that, I'm grateful that I have the sexiness to fall back on. It's not satisfying, however." Most critics disagreed with Welch's assessment of herself and didn't take to her as a reluctant agent. She was described in *Time* as being "an antiseptic Barbie doll ... painful enough to make Modesty Blaise cry U.N.C.L.E." Like most of Welch's movies, *Fathom* was not a hit at the box office, grossing only a paltry $1 million.

Post-*Fathom*, Welch married Patrick Curtis (they divorced in 1972) and appeared in a number of high profile films valiantly playing a variety of characters. Her roles included Lillian Lust, one of the Deadly Sins, in *Bedazzled* (1968), a go-go dancer in *Flare-Up* (1967), a boozy socialite in *Lady in Cement* (1968) and a Mexican woman in *100 Rifles* (1969). Welch stretched her acting muscles by playing a transsexual in *Myra Breckenridge* (1970), but the movie was a disastrous flop. As James Ankeny writes on the *All Movie Guide* database, "Her situation was unusual; she was certainly a star and a household name, yet few people ever went to see her movies." Though the critics usually savaged her in film after film, Welch insisted she had acting talent and deserved better material. She finally got a chance to prove herself right by giving a first-rate comedic performance as the klutzy Lady Constance in *The Three Musketeers* (1973). She won a Golden Globe award for "Best Actress in a Motion Picture Musical/Comedy." During her acceptance speech, between shrieks of joy she stammered, "There are a lot of people for really good reasons who kind of don't like to take awards because—well that's for them—I've been waiting for this one since *One Million Years B.C.*" Though more confident with her talent and her status in Hollywood, the then 35-year-old sex goddess wasn't able to follow this up with anything substantial on the big screen. The bottom fell out for her when she was cast opposite Nick Nolte in *Cannery Row* (1980) and was fired by MGM after three weeks of shooting for "not fulfilling the terms of her contract." Welch sued, and her lawsuit languished in the courts for years.

With her movie career at a standstill, Raquel Welch accepted an offer to replace Lauren Bacall in the hit Broadway musical *Woman of the Year* and won rave reviews. But still the film offers did not materialize for her. Welch kept busy promoting her very successful book and video entitled *Raquel: Total Beauty and Fitness*. In 1986 she finally got her day in court and emerged victorious against MGM, and she was awarded $11.8 million. Welch then turned to television and gave an impressive performance as a woman with Lou Gehrig's Disease in *Right to Die* (1987), for which she was nominated for a Golden Globe. Raquel Welch finally returned to the big screen with a role opposite Leslie Nielsen in *The Naked Gun 33⅓: The Final Insult* (1994). She has been working consistently ever since, and there seems to be no stopping the sixties icon of the silver screen who can currently be seen in the feature film *How to Be a Latin Lover* (2017).

Other films include: *Shoot Loud, Louder... I Don't Understand* (1966), *The Oldest Profession* (1967), *Bandolero!* (1968), *The Biggest Bundle of Them All* (1968), *Hannie Caulder* (1971), *Fuzz* (1972), *Kansas City Bomber* (1972), *Bluebeard* (1972), *The Last of Sheila* (1973), *The Wild Party* (1974), *The Four Musketeers* (1975), *Mother, Jugs & Speed* (1976), *L'Animal* (1977), *Trouble in Paradise* (1988—TV), *Tainted Blood* (1993), *Chairman of the Board* (1998), *What I Did for Love* (1998), *Tortilla Soup* (2001) and *Legally Blonde* (2001).

Lana Wood

Much to her dismay, actress Lana Wood is best remembered by fans for her brief appearance as the golddigging Plenty O'Toole in the James Bond adventure *Diamonds Are Forever* (1971), starring Sean Connery. Onscreen for only a few scenes, she is one of the most popular Bond girls in the history of this series. "Isn't that *bizarre*," exclaims Wood with a laugh. "*I'm only in the movie for three minutes!*"

Natalie Wood's younger sister was born Svetlana Zacharenko Gurdin on March 1, 1946, in Santa Monica, California. She followed her older sister into the acting profession and made her film debut at eight years old in John Ford's classic western *The Searchers* (1956). Wood received good notices and went on to appear in a few television dramas with Jack Lemmon and Charlton Heston, among others. But unlike Natalie, Lana didn't want to act as a child and she waited until she was 18 before re-starting her career with an episode of *Dr. Kildare*. Sexier and more rounded than her more famous sibling, Wood found herself typecast in sexpot roles. After playing a coed in *The Girls on the Beach* (1965), Wood was signed to play sexy Eula Harker in the short-lived soap opera *The Long, Hot Summer* (1965-66). When the series was cancelled midway through its first season, 20th Century-Fox immediately moved Lana Wood into their hit soap opera *Peyton Place*. As Sandy Webber, a slinky temptress from the wrong side of the tracks, Wood was an immediate hit with the viewers and played the role for close to two years.

Lana Wood's foray into spydom began with two appearances on *The Wild Wild West*. In her first episode, entitled "The Night of the Firebrand" (9/15/67), she is amusing as the cleverly named character Vixen O'Shaughnessy, a runaway from finishing school seeking to help those less fortunate than her. Living up to her name, the misguided Vixen aids outlaw Sean O'Reilly (Pernell Roberts), who has captured Fort Savage on his way to incite a revolution in Canada, purportedly to help that country's repressed people. On "The Night of the Plague" (4/4/69), *The Wild Wild West*'s last original episode (aired before the show's cancellation), Wood played Averi Trent, the spoiled, headstrong daughter of the state's governor. Outraged when she and her fellow passengers are told to disembark from their stagecoach, she sneaks back on, determined to make her destination of Fort Cordovan, unaware that James West is using it as a decoy to trap a group of bandits. West's plan works until Averi makes her presence known and is taken hostage by the crooks, who are a troupe of Shakespearean actors infected with a fatal disease.

"I loved doing *The Wild Wild West*," says Lana Wood. "What this show afforded me—that most of the other series that I did didn't—was that it gave me the chance to be humorous. I am a *very* funny person with a terrific sense of humor. I love doing comedy, and *The Wild Wild West* was not a serious western. It was very tongue-in-cheek. A fan recently sent me copies of my episodes, and those are about the only shows that I thought I was very good in. I got to show a side of myself that I wasn't always allowed to." Regarding Robert Conrad, whom a number of actresses had problems with, Wood found him to be "adorable. I had known Robert Conrad for many years because he was Natalie's friend. I never had a problem with him. And Ross Martin was a very sweet, intelligent man."

After playing a swinging bachelorette in *For Singles Only* (1968), and a mini-skirted biker babe in *Free Grass* (1969), Wood posed semi-nude for *Playboy* magazine. Her pictorial appeared in the April 1971 issue, accompanied by some of her poetry. These photos indirectly helped Wood land her most famous role—Plenty O'Toole. In *Diamonds Are Forever* (1971), secret agent James Bond (Sean Connery) is assigned to pose as a diamond smuggler, leading him and jewel thief Tiffany Case (Jill St. John) from Amsterdam to Las Vegas in pursuit of 50,000 carats of diamonds. Bond meets bar girl Plenty O'Toole (Wood) at a crap table in a Vegas casino. After introducing herself to Bond, who has been winning, she goes with him up to his room. Their tryst is interrupted as thugs try to kill Bond and toss Plenty out the 15-story window. ("We filmed this at night. I was topless. The crowd got a nice view of me in nothing but a pair of pale blue panties.") Fortunately, Plenty lands in the hotel's pool. A short time later she is discovered murdered and floating face down in Tiffany's pool.

Lana Wood found Sean Connery very "charming and attentive" and "very relaxed and easy to work with." She also admits to "an interlude" with him. What's more revealing is that Wood also had a number of scenes that were excised from the final print due to "running time." Wood discloses that, "there were scenes of Sean and me having dinner before we went up to his room that established the attraction be-

Sean Connery's James Bond puts the moves on Lana Wood, as Plenty O'Toole, in *Diamonds Are Forever* (United Artists, 1971).

tween us, and of me going back to the hotel room, finding Sean in bed with Tiffany, and rifling through her wallet. Another scene [which was never shot] had me going to Tiffany's house trying on her clothes and putting on her wigs. I was flabbergasted that they cut all this out. I didn't even realize it until I had come back from a world tour promoting *Diamonds Are Forever*. I went to the Grauman's Chinese Theatre in Hollywood to watch it with a friend because I was so busy promoting the film I never had time to see it. I literally bent over to get some popcorn as the thugs threw me out the window, and by the time I had straightened up my character was dead. I thought, 'Wow, all of a sudden I have this little part.' I actually asked why they cut most of my scenes and I was told that they didn't have much relevance to the plot." These missing scenes finally explain how and why Plenty O'Toole is found murdered in Tiffany Case's swimming pool wearing her wig. The assassins mistook her for Tiffany and killed her.

Though *Diamonds Are Forever* was a huge box-office smash, it is considered one of the lesser Bond films. Though Connery looks tired and paunchy in the early scenes, he expertly handles some of the witty lines of the script during the rest of the film. While Connery is impressive as usual, his performance cannot overcome the convoluted plot. The screenwriters retained the characters of Tiffany and the homosexual hit men Wynt and Mr. Kidd from Ian Fleming's original novel, but their new plot, involving Blofeld, is confusing. The casting of the supporting roles doesn't help either, but Lana Wood received kudos from the fans and the critics. *Variety* remarked, "Lana Wood ... gets good mileage from her brief exposure as Plenty O'Toole." While the critic in *The New York Post* stated that, "a girl so pretty [as Lana] deserves a better fate than the one she meets."

Wood's last entry in the spy arena was a guest appearance on *Mission: Impossible*. The prolific Leslie H. Martinson directed her episode, entitled "The Deal," airing on 9/30/72. Lana Wood played bad girl Marcy Carpenter, girlfriend of Charles Rogan (Robert Webber), a syndicate big shot financing a coup on the small island of Camagua. By backing British soldier of fortune General Oliver Hammond (Lloyd Bochner), Rogan and his cronies will control the island's gambling and prostitution rings. Rogan heads to the island to pass on to Hammond a key to a safety deposit box containing $5 million dollars. It is up to the IMF team to intercept the key and identify the bank.

Wood continued acting through the seventies and early eighties. She is most proud of her role as Ben Gazzara's mistress in the acclaimed miniseries *QB VII* (1974). Unfortunately, she is remembered most for her role as a lesbian prison guard in *Nightmare in Badham County* (1976—TV) and for her topless nude scenes in the low-budget horror film *Demon Rage* (1982). Wood retired from acting after a year's stint on the CBS soap *Capitol* in 1984 to work in production and casting. One of her last acting credits was as herself on an episode of *The Fall Guy* in 1984. Three former Bond girls (Wood, Joanna Pettet and Britt Ekland) are hired to play roles in the fictitious James Bond movie *Always Say Always*, on which series star Lee Majors and his crew are working as stuntmen as a cover to locate stolen art work.

Lana Wood returned to the limelight in 1999 and posed with other former Bond girls for layouts in *Vanity Fair* and *TV Guide*, as well as a solo spread for *Femme Fatales* magazine. To this day she is flabbergasted at the amount of fan mail she receives from around the world regarding *Diamonds Are Forever*. "Overall, I wasn't crazy about *Diamonds Are Forever*," reveals Wood. "I always find it amazing that this is the one film everybody talks about when they meet me. I loved meeting the people and working on the film but I wasn't happy with the end result. I hope someday that they release it on DVD with my missing scenes." Wood's wish has recently come true, as the new DVD version does, in fact, include her missing scenes as well as other outtakes and a "making of" documentary.

Other films include: *Five Finger Exercise* (1962), *Black Water Gold* (1970—TV), *A Place Called Today* (1972), *Who Is the Black Dahlia?* (1975—TV), *Little Ladies of the Night* (1977—TV), *Speedtrap* (1978) and *Grayeagle* (1978).

Celeste Yarnall

Celeste Yarnall is a classic beauty who had talent but could never find the one role that would catapult her to super stardom. She was born on July 26, 1944, in Long Beach, California. Always having a bit of "ham" in her, she began modeling for Max Factor as a teenager and was discovered by Ozzie Nelson while passing through the studio lot where his TV series was shot. She made her film debut as a coed in the Jerry Lewis comedy *The Nutty Professor* (1963), but her acting career was put on hold for a year when she was selected by millions of voters across the Northeast to become the last elected Miss Rheingold. For one year she toured and did promotion for Rheingold Beer. Returning to Hollywood in 1965, she began landing minor roles in film and on television (in *Burke's Law*, *Mona McCluskey*, *The Smothers Brothers Show*, *Bewitched*, *Gidget* and the *Star Trek* episode "The Apple").

Yarnall's first spy production was in "The Night of a Thousand Eyes" on *The Wild Wild West* (10/22/65), playing the very minor role of Miss Purviance. She later grabbed a lead guest role on *The Man from U.N.C.L.E.* in "The Monks of St. Thomas Affair" (10/14/66) and gave a very convincing performance as Andrea Fouchet. She is a young French girl (engaged to a nice, ordinary young man) who, while searching for her missing uncle, an Abbott of the St. Thomas Monastery, gets entangled with U.N.C.L.E. agent Napoleon Solo (Robert Vaughn) and a THRUSH agent (David J. Stewart) masquerading as Abbott Simon who plans to operate a ray gun from the monastery to wipe out half the capitals of Europe. "There is a great story of how I won this role," says Celeste Yarnall. "They were only auditioning French actresses like Claudine Longet for this part. I just signed with a new agent and told him I did dialects. He sent me to MGM to interview for this role. When I walked in I said in a French accent, 'Bon jour. My name is Celeste Yarnall and I'm from Paris.' The producer [Boris Ingster], who was foreign, started speaking to me in French. I know only a little bit of French, so I said, using a French accent, 'No, no, no. I am in this country to practice my English. Don't speak French to me. I will read the script in English and you tell me how I do.' One of the words in the script was The Beatles. When I got to it, I pronounced it 'The Be-a-tles.' They fell on the floor laughing and I got the part almost on the spot. After we started shooting, I said to Boris Ingster, using my normal American accent, 'You know I'm really not French.' His jaw dropped and he said that I had totally convinced them that I was from France."

"The Monks of St. Thomas Affair" is fast moving, wittily written by Sheldon Stark and features an exciting musical score by Gerald Fried. Stewart makes a menacing villain, and Celeste Yarnall is stunning as the innocent caught in the plot. The scenes where Solo and Andrea await their fate at the hands of THRUSH, and Solo helps Andrea to realize that she really does love Randolph ("And he is sweet; you know, you don't have to swing to be sweet"), are touchingly enacted, enhanced by director Alex March, who shoots most of it in close-up, concentrating on Yarnall's expressive eyes. "Overall, doing *The Man from U.N.C.L.E.* was an excellent experience for me," says Yarnall. "Robert Vaughn was wonderful to work with. He is a very elegant and intelligent man. I must have done a good job because it lead to many more acting offers for me."

In 1967, unhappy in the direction her career was going—or not going, Celeste Yarnall risked her life savings, dyed her hair blonde and traveled to the Cannes Film Festival, with her husband Sheldon Silverstein acting as her manager. She was chosen by the foreign press at Cannes as "The Most Photogenic Beauty of the Year." And producer Harry Alan Towers picked Yarnall to play a female Tarzan in *Eve* (1968). Though Yarnall made a stunning vine swinger, the film played mostly drive-ins. She next portrayed a slinky fashion model opposite Elvis Presley in *Live a Little, Love a Little* (1968). Yarnall received nice reviews for both films and was voted a "Hollywood Deb Star" and the "Most Promising New Star of 1968" by the Association of Theatre Owners.

Celeste Yarnall essayed the role of another foreigner on *It Takes a Thief*. She played Ilsa Malenska in the episode titled "Locked in the Cradle of the Keep" (4/15/68). The SIA pulls off a charade to convince a communist named Boris (Joe Bernard) that Robert Wagner's Al Mundy is a defector and traitor. Boris believes the ruse and connects Mundy to the "underground," enabling him to infiltrate an Eastern block country to meet his contact. The beautiful Ilsa (a double agent posing as Mundy's girlfriend) then informs him that his contact (a professor) was murdered. Nobody knows what Mundy is supposed to steal. They only know where it is located (State Museum) and that it could cause great turmoil for most Iron Curtain countries if it falls into the wrong hands. Ilsa leads Mundy to the museum and tells him the only clue to the object: As the professor lay dying, he whispered to her, "The keep, the crib in the keep..."

Recalling her appearance, Celeste Yarnall comments, "Robert Wagner was very friendly and professional. But he had a nasty habit of changing the dialog right before we were to begin shooting our scenes. Learning new lines that quickly is hard enough, but it is extremely difficult when you have to do it with an accent. I thought this was a bit inconsiderate of Wagner."

In 1971 Yarnall gave a chilling performance as *The Velvet Vampire*, directed by Stephanie Rothman for New World Pictures. After playing two supporting roles in films by Michael Winner, Yarnall, now divorced, realized she needed a steady paycheck and a new career to support her daughter Camilla. Yarnall founded her own very successful commercial real estate company called Celeste Yarnall and Associates in the late seventies, and in 1987 she started a new company representing young and upcoming screenwriters and directors. At this time she was coaxed into returning to acting. She appeared in such films as *Fatal Beauty* (1987), *Funny About Love* (1990), directed by Leonard Nimoy, and *Born Yesterday* (1993), starring Melanie Griffith and Don Johnson. Her TV appearances included episodes of *Knots Landing*, *Melrose Place* and *Sisters*.

Recently, Celeste Yarnall's acting career has been sidelined due to her interest in nutrition and love for animals. She authored her first book in 1995, called *Cat Care Naturally: Celeste Yarnall's Complete Guide to Holistic Health Care for Cats*, combining nutrition and holistic health care with a bit of pet astrology. She has since bred six generations of Tonkinese and Oriental Shorthair cats on her natural regime, and has released an updated version of her book entitled *Natural Cat Care*, as well as a new book called *Natural Dog Care*. She also received her Ph.D. in Nutrition from Pacific Western University in 1997 and is now working on a book for people, stressing the importance of nutrition. Despite her many endeavors, the always–terrific looking Celeste Yarnall still finds time to go

Celeste Yarnall, outfitted in typical sixties spy girl fashion. (*Courtesy of Celeste Yarnall*)

on acting auditions and attend autograph shows around the country.

Other films include: *Under the Yum Yum Tree* (1963), *Around the World Under the Sea* (1966), *Bob and Carol and Ted and Alice* (1969), *Beast of Blood* (1970), *Ransom for a Dead Man* (1971—TV), *The Mechanic* (1972), *Scorpio* (1973), *Fatal Beauty* (1987), *Daughters of Privilege* (1991—TV), *Driving Me Crazy* (1992) and *Midnight Kiss* (1993).

Francine York

Standing 5-foot-8 and measuring 38-23-35, beautiful, statuesque Francine York was usually cast in bigger-than-life roles. She was born Francine Yerich on August 26, 1938, in Aurora, Minnesota. The acting bug bit her as a child and she appeared in all her elementary and secondary school plays. Upon graduating high school, York began modeling sweaters around the country for Dayton's department stores. After deciding to reside in San Francisco, she appeared in print ads wearing ladies undergarments for Macy's and began entering beauty pageants. She won the Miss San Francisco contest and placed first runner-up in the Miss California rung of the Miss USA pageant. A stint as a showgirl at a San Francisco nightclub led her to landing a manager, who convinced her to give Hollywood a try. She was spotted by a producer in an acting class and was signed to play the owner of a scandal sheet in *Secret File: Hollywood* (1961), starring Robert Clarke. Though the film was a low-budget mess, York proved she had the screen presence (and the drive) to make it in Hollywood, and soon she was appearing in minor film roles opposite Jerry Lewis, Marlon Brando and Elvis Presley. Her physical attributes and authoritative qualities seemed to have hampered her efforts to land lead roles in major motion pictures, but she copped the female leads in two AIP programmers, *Space Monster* (1965) and *Curse of the Swamp Creature* (1966).

Television made much better use of York's beauty and talent as she appeared in sitcoms, drama series and variety programs with an equal amount of felicity. Her sojourn into the spy craze began with "The Old Flame" (3/10/66), an episode of *The Double Life of Henry Phyfe* in which she convincingly played Italian agent X-22 (a.k.a. Gina). Red Buttons' mild-mannered Henry Wadsworth Phyfe gets in trouble with his fiancée's mother (Marge Redmond) when she discovers a photograph of the glamorous spy in his apartment. She immediately jumps to the conclusion that Phyfe is two-timing her daughter. Regarding Buttons, York remarks, "He was adorable. We've been friends ever since. He just thought I was so great." So did a number of producers and directors, as York began landing lead guest shots on such popular series as *Death Valley Days*, *Batman*, *Lost in Space* and *Gomer Pyle, USMC*.

On *The Wild Wild West* episode "The Night of the Pelican" (12/27/68), a blonde York played Dr. Sara Gibson, the only woman stationed on Alcatraz Island, which is occupied by a master criminal named Chang (Khigh Dhiegh) in his scheme to control all of San Francisco Bay.

"When I did *The Wild Wild West* it was during its last season," recalls Francine York. "I read for director Alex Nicol and he told me, 'We have this problem with Robert Conrad. He's not that tall and we're trying to protect him.' So I went home a bit discouraged. The next day he called me back and said, 'I just read forty girls and you've become the shortest girl in town.' What they needed for the part was something that I don't even have to try at—authority. I played a doctor and had to boss these guards around. It's a strong role and I just looked gorgeous. In one scene, Robert Conrad and I are standing together on the firing squad about to get shot, and Charles Aidman (he replaced Ross Martin, who was recovering from a heart attack)

Va-va-voom! Spy babe Francine York lets it all hang out. (*Courtesy of Francine York*)

comes running in with this box full of gas that knocks everybody unconscious. The episode turned out great and Bob said to me, 'Gee, how come we haven't used you before?' Of course, I didn't tell him. Someone asked me later how I got away with walking next to Bob Conrad in the firing squad scene. I said, "I walked in the holes and he walked on the hills.' Years later I ran into him at a party. I said, 'Hi Bob. I worked with you once on *The Wild Wild West*.' He said, 'How did you work with me? You're too tall.' He wasn't too nice at that moment."

On *It Takes a Thief* Robert Wagner played Al Mundy, a former thief who works as an SIA agent. Francine York briefly played his Girl Friday in a few early episodes. It was a role reminiscent of Lovey Kraveszit in the Matt Helm films, and the Flint girls in *Our Man Flint*. York recalls, "I played Miss Amanda Agnew. I would come in at the beginning of each episode, and just as our characters would get romantic, Wagner would be called away by his boss [played by] Malachi Throne. It was sort of like the parts I played on *Burke's Law* with Gene Barry. I stupidly left *It Takes a Thief* when my agent convinced me to take a part in a pilot Irwin Allen was producing. I could have done both, especially since working with Robert Wagner was so wonderful. He was very kind to me and he has a great sense of humor."

After co-starring with George Peppard in the western *Cannon for Cordoba* (1970), and bringing Venus de Milo delightfully to life on *Bewitched* in 1972, York played a waitress on *Mission: Impossible*'s opening episode during its last season. "Break," airing on 9/16/72, was set in the gaming world of billiards and was one of the better later episodes. The IMF needs to infiltrate the large illegal gambling empire run by Dutch Krebbs (Carl Betz) and his lieutenant, Press Allen (Robert Conrad), to locate the murdered body of an undercover agent who has the evidence in a wristwatch camera to convict them. Phelps poses as a pool shark (with the help of Barney's computer-guided cue balls) as a way to get Krebbs' attention. York worked in the pool joint where most of the action takes place. Recalling this show, Francine York exclaims, "Peter Graves was darling! I love that man. We are good friends until this day. I used to date his brother Jim Arness.

I think Peter and his wife would have loved if things had gotten more serious with Jim and I. Peter Lupus was a handsome hunk and Greg Morris was very nice. He looked at me and said, 'Pretty lady.'"

By 1973 the sixties spy craze had practically run its course. One of the last genre films during this time period was the action B-film *The Doll Squad*, directed by Ted V. Mikels. Francine York energetically played Sabrina, a CIA agent and leader of the Doll Squad. She is assigned by CIA operative Connolly (Anthony Eisley) to stop a madman who plans to overthrow the governments from around the world by unleashing thousands of rats infected with the bubonic plague. After Sabrina contacts two of her members to re-join the Doll Squad, they are ambushed and killed. Realizing that there is a mole in Connolly's office, Sabrina deduces that it is his secretary, which leads to a catfight—complete with hair pulling. Sabrina gets the vixen to reveal that the mastermind is Eamon O'Reilly (Michael Ansara), a former agent and Sabrina's lover. After rounding up four more deadly dolls, including Cat (Sherri Vernon) and Lavelle (Tura Satana), the Doll Squad, decked out in black jumpsuits and white go-go boots, heads to O'Reilly's island fortress. After a series of explosions and gun battles, O'Reilly captures Sabrina. As he is about to eliminate her, the wily agent sprays him with her mace ring and stabs him with a sword.

The Doll Squad was one of Mikels' (who had previously directed *The Astro-Zombies*) bigger budgeted films. Even so, it was still low-budget; and with a little more funding for special effects and extra time for shooting, Mikels could have had a winner. However, it was good enough for ABC to "borrow" the idea for their new series *Charlie's Angels*. Or that is what Mikels claims, and York wholeheartedly agrees. "Ted went to the producers with the premise," states Francine York emphatically.

"They even asked me to audition for *Charlie's Angels*, and I would have been perfect for it. Charlie Grauman made a pass at me, I turned him down, and that was the end of that!

"Ted Mikels is an incredible man—very talented—and a real filmmaker who loves his work," continues York. "Everybody has their own little idiosyncrasies. One of Ted's was that he loved to do movies about women beating up guys. He is a very good person but he had a rough time on this shoot. He was fighting with his girlfriend Sherri Vernon, who played one of the Doll Squad members, during the picture and she slugged him on the way to Catalina on this nine-passenger plane. And he was smarting all day. The poor guy had to direct fifty scenes and he was very angry. Ted and I fought tooth and nail over a couple of things too, particularly the film's conclusion. He wanted his girlfriend's character to save me and kill the villain played by Michael Ansara. But I thought Sabrina should kill him. I said to Ted, 'Ted, who's the leader of the Doll Squad? *I* am the star of this picture and don't forget it.' He and I laugh about this. We've been very good friends all these years. The whole ending was my idea and it turned out great."

As for her co-stars, York comments, "Michael Ansara is just a doll—a real professional and a sweet, wonderful man. I couldn't say anything nicer about him. I met Anthony Eisley when we appeared in a Christian anthology TV show together. I recommended him for *The Doll Squad* and that's how he got the part. After he got into it though, I don't know how happy he was! [Laughs] Tura Satana was nice. She was a wonderful stripper before she became an actress. And she does this interesting dance in the film."

Francine York continued working at a steady pace throughout the seventies and eighties. Her roles have ranged from a sweet nurse in the made-for-TV disaster movie *Flood* (1976), to blackmailing vixen Lorraine Temple on the soap opera *Days of Our Lives* in 1978, to Jerry Lewis' foil in the comedy *Cracking Up* (1983).

Looking fabulous, the ageless Francine York's career is hotter than ever as she most recently appeared in *Family Man* (2000), starring Nicolas Cage and Téa Leoni. Between auditioning and accepting acting roles, her days are spent prepping a new movie about bigotry in the South with her good friend, director Vincent Sherman.

Other films include: *Sergeant Was a Lady* (1961), *It's Only Money* (1962), *The Nutty Professor* (1963), *Bedtime Story* (1964), *Tickle Me* (1965), *Mutiny in Outer Space* (1965), *Welcome Home, Soldier Boys* (1972), *Centerfold Girls* (1974), *Time Travelers* (1977—TV), *The Underachievers* (1987), *Marilyn Is Alive* (1992), *Counter Measures* (1998) and *The Big Tease* (1999).

Bibliography

Amis, Kingsley. *Colonel Sun*. New York: Bantam, 1969.
Balbo, Lucas, Peter Blumenstock, Christian Kessler, and Tim Lucas. *Obsession—The Films of Jess Franco*. Germany: Graf Haufen & Frank Trebbin, 1993.
Brooks, Tim, and Earle Marsh. *The Complete Directory to Prime Time Network and Cable TV Shows, 1946–Present*. 4th ed. New York: Ballantine Books, 1995.
Castleman, Harry, and Walter J. Podrazik. *Harry and Wally's Favorite TV Shows*. New York: Prentice Hall Press, 1989.
Craig, Yvonne. *From Ballet to the Batcave and Beyond*. Venice, CA: Kudu Press, 2000.
Crenshaw, Marshall. *Hollywood Rock*. New York: Harper Perennial, 1994.
Eaton, Shirley. *Golden Girl*. London: BT Batsford Ltd, 2000.
Espions a L'Italienne. France, Monster Bis, Joel Cabanes–editor, 199?.
Fleming, Ian. *Casino Royale*. New York: Macmillan, 1954.
———. *Live and Let Die*. New York: Permabooks, 1956.
———. *From Russia, with Love*. New York: Macmillan, 1957.
———. *Goldfinger*. New York: Macmillan, 1959.
———. *Moonraker*. New York: Signet, 1960.
———. *Diamonds Are Forever*. New York: Signet, 1961.
———. *Dr. No*. London: Pan, 1961.
———. *For Your Eyes Only*. New York: Signet, 1961.
———. *Thunderball*. New York: Viking, 1961.
———. *On Her Majesty's Secret Service*. New York: Signet, 1963.
———. *The Spy Who Loved Me*. New York: Signet, 1963.
———. *You Only Live Twice*. London: Pan, 1966.
Gardner, John. *License Renewed*. New York: Berkeley, 1982.
———. *For Special Services*. New York: Berkeley, 1983.
———. *Icebreaker*. New York: Berkeley, 1984.
———. *Role of Honor*. New York: Berkeley, 1985.
———. *Nobody Lives Forever*. New York: Charter, 1987.
———. *No Deals, Mr. Bond*. New York: Charter, 1988.
———. *Scorpius*. New York: Charter, 1990.
———. *Win, Lose or Die*. New York: Berkeley, 1990.
———. *Brokenclaw*. New York: Berkeley, 1991.
———. *The Man from Barbarossa*. New York: Berkeley, 1992.
———. *Death Is Forever*. New York: Berkeley, 1993.
———. *Never Send Flowers*. New York: Berkeley, 1994.
———. *SeaFire*. New York: Berkeley, 1995.
———. *Cold Fall*. New York: Berkeley, 1997.
Gebert, Michael. *The Encyclopedia of Movie Awards*. New York: St. Martin's Press, 1996.
Gerani, Gary, and Paul H. Schulman. *Fantastic Television*. New York: Harmony Books, 1977.
Gianakos, Larry James. *Television Drama Series Programming: A Comprehensive Chronicle, 1959–1975*. Metuchen, NJ: Scarecrow Press, 1978.
———. *Television Drama Series Programming: A Comprehensive Chronicle, 1947–1959*. Metuchen, NJ: Scarecrow Press, 1980.

_____. *Television Drama Series Programming: A Comprehensive Chronicle, 1975–1980.* Metuchen, NJ: Scarecrow Press, 1981.

_____. *Television Drama Series Programming: A Comprehensive Chronicle, 1980–1982.* Metuchen, NJ: Scarecrow Press, 1983.

_____. *Television Drama Series Programming: A Comprehensive Chronicle, 1982–1984.* Metuchen, NJ: Scarecrow Press, 1987.

_____. *Television Drama Series Programming: A Comprehensive Chronicle, 1984–1986.* Metuchen, NJ: Scarecrow Press, 1992.

Gomarasca, Manlio and Davide Pulici. *99 Donne.* Italy: Nocturno Press-Media Word, 1999.

Green, Joey. *The Get Smart Handbook.* New York: Collier Books, 1993.

Heitland, Jon. *The Man from U.N.C.L.E. Book: The Behind-the-Scenes Story of a Television Classic.* New York: St. Martin's Press, 1987.

Helt, Marie and Richard. *West German Cinema Since 1945: A Handbook.* New York: Scarecrow Press, 1987.

Holston, Kim. *Starlet.* Jefferson, NC: McFarland, 1988.

Homage a Eurocine. France, Monster Bis, 2000.

Die Italienische Produktion 1965, 1966. Unitalia Film, 1965, 1966.

Kesler, Susan E. *The Wild, Wild West: The Series.* Downey, CA: Arnett Press, 1988.

Krafsur, Richard P., ed. *The American Film Institute Catalog of Motion Pictures: Feature Films 1961–1970.* New York & London: R.R. Bowker Company, 1976.

_____. *The American Film Institute Catalog of Motion Pictures: Feature Films 1961–1970 Indexes.* New York & London: R.R. Bowker Company, 1976.

Langman, Larry and David Ebner. *Encyclopedia of American Spy Films.* New York: Garland Publishing, 1990.

Lisanti, Tom. *Fantasy Femmes of Sixties Cinema: Interviews with 20 Actresses from Biker, Beach, and Elvis Movies.* Jefferson, NC: McFarland, 2001.

Lopez, Daniel. *Film by Genre.* Jefferson, NC: McFarland, 1993.

Macnee, Patrick and Marie Cameron. *Blind in One Ear—The Avenger Returns.* San Francisco: Mercury House, 1989.

Maltin, Leonard. *Leonard Maltin's Movie and Video Guide 1995.* New York: Penguin Books USA, 1994.

Marill, Alvin H. *Movies Made for Television: The Telefeature and the Mini-Series, 1964–1984.* New York: New York Zoetrope, 1984.

McNeil, Alex. *Total Television: The Comprehensive Guide to Programming from 1948 to the Present.* New York: Penguin Books, 1996.

Morton, Alan. *The Complete Directory to Science Fiction, Fantasy and Horror Television Series: A Comprehensive Guide to the First 50 Years 1946 to 1996.* Peoria, IL: Other World Books, 1997.

Parish, James Robert and Michael R. Pitts. *The Great Spy Pictures.* Metuchen, NJ: Scarecrow Press, 1974.

_____ and Vincent Terrace. *The Complete Actors' Television Credits, 1948–1988 Volume 2: Actresses.* Metuchen, NJ: Scarecrow Press, 1989.

Paul, Louis. "The European Spy Film of the 1960s: A Filmography." *Blood Times,* Vol. 2 No. 1, 1992.

Pearson, John. *James Bond: The Authorized Biography of 007.* New York: Pyramid, 1975.

Perry, Jeb H. *Universal Television.* Metuchen, NJ: Scarecrow Press, 1983.

Pfeiffer, Lee and Dave Worrall. *The Essential Bond: The Authorized Guide to the World of 007.* New York: Harper Collins, 1999.

Phillips, Mark, and Frank Garcia. *Science Fiction Television Series: Episode Guides, Histories, and Cast and Credits for 62 Prime Time Shows, 1959 through 1989.* Jefferson, NC: McFarland, 1996.

Pollmar, Norman and Thomas B. Allen. *Spy Book: The Encyclopedia of Espionage.* New York: Random House, 1998.

Poppi, Roberto and Mario Percorari. *Dizionario Del Cinema Italiano—I Film Vol. 3— 1960-1969.* Italy: Gremese Editore, 1992.

La Produzione Italiana 1963, 1964, 1965, 1966, 1967, 1968, 1969–1970, 1971–1972. Italy: Unitalia Film, various years.

Prouty, Howard H., ed. *Variety Television Reviews 1923–1988.* 15 volumes. New York: Garland Publishing, 1989.

Rogers, Dave. *The Avengers.* ITV Books: Great Britain, 1983.

Rubenstein, Leonard. *The Great Spy Films.* New York: Lyle Stuart, 1981.

Rubin, Steven Jay. *The Complete James Bond Movie Encyclopedia.* Chicago: Contemporary Books, 1990, 1995.

Strodder, Chris. *Swingin' Chicks of the '60s.* San Rafael, CA: Cedco, 2000.

Thompson, Howard, ed. *The New York Times Guide to Movies on TV.* Chicago: Quadrangle Books, 1970.

TV Guide. January 1, 1958–December 31, 1978. Weekly.

Variety Film Reviews 1907–1980. 16 volumes. New York: Garland Publishing, 1983.

Variety Portable Movie Guide. New York: Berkley Boulevard Books, 1999.

Ward, Jack. *Television Guest Stars: An Illustrated Career Chronicle for 678 Performers of the Sixties and Seventies*. Jefferson, NC: McFarland, 1993.

_____. *The Supporting Players of Television, 1959–1983*. Cleveland: Lakeshore West Publishers, 1996.

Weldon, Michael. *The Psychotronic Encyclopedia of Film*. New York: Ballantine, 1983.

_____. *The Psychotronic Video Guide*. New York: St. Martin's Griffin, 1996.

White, Peter J. *The Complete Mission: Impossible Dossier*. New York: Avon Books, 1991.

Willis, John. *Screen World*. New York: Crown, annual.

Wood, Lana. *Natalie: A Memoir by Her Sister*. New York: Putnam, 1984.

Index

A.D. 3 Operazione Squalo Blanco see Operation: White Shark
ABC Monday Night Football 107
Absolutely Fabulous 194
Absurd Person Singular 90
Acker, Sharon 205
Across 110th Street 147
Adams, Beverly 19, 33–36, 179, 319
Adams, Don 27, 126, 127, 233
Adams, Julie 88
Adams, Nick 122, 218
Addams, Tom 99
The Adolescents 291
The Adventurer 28, 54, 133
Adventures in Rainbow County 209
The Adventures of a Casanova 36
The Adventures of Ozzie and Harriet 150
Un Aero per Baalbeck see Last Plane to Baalbeck
Against All Odds see The Blood of Fu Manchu
Agatha Christie's Evil Under the Sun 259
Agent 8¾ 161
Agent for H.A.R.M. 80, 139, 217
Agent Sigma 3: Mission Goldwather 273
Agente 003 Operazione Atlantide see Operation Atlantis
Agente 077 Dall'Orient con Furore see Fury in Istanbul
Agente 077: Missione Bloody Mary see Mission Bloody Mary
Agente Logan, Missione Ypotron see Ypotron
Agente Segreto 777 Invito ad Uccidere see Secret Agent 777: Invitation to Murder

Agente Z55 Missione Disperata see Desperate Mission
Aghayan, Ray 137
Aidman, Charles 314, 315
Airport 67
Airport 1975 295
The Alaskans 250
Aldrich, Robert 121
Alexander, Peter 170
Alfie, Darling 100
The Alfred Hitchcock Hour 123, 140
Alfred Hitchcock Presents 53, 109
Ali Baba and the Forty Thieves 282
Allen, Irwin 19, 199, 262, 316
Allen, Marty 84, 270
Allen, Steve 1, 20
Allen, Valerie 118
Allen, Woody 143, 176
Almodovar, Pedro 186
An Almost Perfect Affair 299
Altman, Robert 193
Always on Sundays 63
L'Amantide 76
Ambler, Eric 10
The Ambushers 19, 33, 35, 59, 168
The American Heroine 282
An American in Rome 36
American Scene Magazine 171
The Americanization of Emily 89, 158, 285
Ames, Totty 141
Amis, Kinsley 13
L'Ammazzatina 76
Amory, Cleveland 129, 249
Amos Burke, Secret Agent 2, 3, 26, 93, 139, 169, 195, 198, 229, 232
Amuck! 83
Andalousie 109
Anderson, Barbara 107
Anderson, Gillian 227
Anderson, Herbert 171

Andress, Ursula 14–17, 19, 36–39, 66, 67, 275, 319
Andrews, Dana 186
Andrews, Harry 200
Andrews, Julie 302
The Andy Griffith Show 171
Angeli, Pier 39–41
Angels from Hell 204
Anholt, Tony 30, 245
Annis, Francesca 227
Anniversary Waltz 200
Ann-Margret 14, 15, 19, 21, 41–43, 106, 319
Ansara, Michael 192, 265, 316, 317
Anthony, Robert 93
Antonelli, Laura 44–46, 181
Antonioni, Michelangelo 81, 95, 298, 299
Any Given Sunday 43
Apache's Last Battle 175
L'Arcangelo 44
Arden, Eve 124
Ardisson, Giorgio 18, 92
Are You Being Served? 193
Arent, Eddie 225
Argento, Dario 122, 252
The Argoman Fantastic Superman 78
Arizona Colt 224
Arkin, Alan 117
Armored Command 191, 192
Arness, James 316
Arnie 174
Around the World Under the Sea 120
Arriva Dorellik see Here Comes Dorellik
Arrivderci, Baby 167
Art Linkletter's House Party 84
Arthur, Maureen 233
As If It Were Raining 273

Index

L'Asino D'Oro: Processo per Fatti Strani Contro Lucius Apuleius Cittadino Romano 82
Asner, Ed 191, 195
Assassination 154
The Assassination Bureau 258, 259
Assignment: Munich 302
Assignment Terror 115
Assignment: Vienna 28, 131, 204
Asso di Picche: Operazione Controspionaggio see Operation: Counterspy
Astor, Mary 236
The Astro Zombies 264, 265, 316
The Astronauts 155, 290
Atkins, Christopher 303
Attack of the 5'2" Women 282
Attenborough, Richard 267
Auger, Claudine 15, 16, 46–48, 61, 238
Aumont, Jean-Pierre 49
Aumont, Tina 49, 50, 319
Austin, Ray 257
Austin Powers: International Man of Mystery 30, 71, 147
Austin Powers: The Spy Who Shagged Me 30
Avalon, Frankie 120, 145, 146, 198, 260
Avenger X 185
The Avengers (TV series) 24, 30, 53, 54, 69–71, 118, 129, 133, 167, 186, 208, 245, 251, 257–259, 262, 288, 289
L'Avventura 298
Ayres, Lew 230

Bacall, Lauren 307
Bacharach, Burt 17, 38, 270
Bachelor Father 171
Bad Day at Black Rock 128
Badgers Bend 227
Baer, Max, Jr. 232
The Baileys of Balboa 89
Bain, Barbara 28, 50–53, 131, 197, 220, 258, 301, 302, 319
Bain, Conrad 220
Baker, Carroll 76, 185
Baker, Chet 275
Baker, Joby 131
Baker, Roy Ward 54, 262
Baker, Stanley 38, 188, 243
Le Bal des Voyous 217
Balch, Vivi 225
Baldini, Renato 208
Baleari Operazione Oro see Operation Oro
Balin, Ina 167, 192
The Ballad of Cable Hogue 281
The Ballad of Josie 155
Banacek 174, 244
Banco a Bangkok Pour OSS 117 see Panic in Bangkok for OSS 117
Bang! Bang! You're Dead! 16, 58, 178, 179

Barabbas 285
Baraka X-77 161
Bardot, Brigitte 47, 170, 216
Barich, Richard 235
Barker, Lex 114, 115, 175, 178, 274
Barnaby Jones 207
The Baron 186–188, 209
Baron Blood 277
Barray, Gerard 161
Barris, George 155
Barry, Ann 195
Barry, Gene 3, 26, 28, 54, 59, 99, 128, 133, 139, 150, 169, 182, 195, 198, 220, 229, 232, 316
Bartell, Harry 296
Bastedo, Alexandra 53–55
Batman 104
Batman (TV series) 101, 157, 160, 168, 249, 270, 306, 314
Battle Cry 128
Battle for the Planet of the Apes 231
The Battle of El Alamein 300
The Battle of the Bulge 40
Battlestar Galactica 205, 269
Bava, Lamberto 39, 76
Bava, Mario 48, 74, 98, 147, 163, 175, 179, 214, 223, 277
The Bawdy Adventures of Tom Jones 100
Baxley, Paul 242
Bay of Blood 48
Be Our Guest 218
Beach Ball 155
Beach Blanket Bingo 216
Beach Party 102, 120, 146
The Beast of Morocco 139
Beat the Clock 163
The Beatles 70, 89, 183, 311
Beatty, Warren 214
The Beauty Centre Show 83
Beckman, Henry 296
Bedazzled 307
Bedtime Story 80
Beir, Fred 40
The Bellboy and the Playgirls 114
Belmondo, Jean-Paul 38, 45
Ben Casey 157, 158, 205
Benazeraf, Jose 254, 255
Benson, Raymond 13, 144
Berenger, Tom 59
Bergen, Candice 82
Berger, Senta 14, 16, 19, 24, 56–60, 124, 169, 175, 178, 218, 220, 275, 319
Bergerac, Jacques 65
Bergere, Lee 153, 232
Berghof, Herbert 133
Bergonzelli, Sergio 83
Berlino Appuntamento per le Spie see Spy in Your Eye
Berman, Shelley 265
Besame Monstruo see Kiss Me Monster
The Best House in London 243

Beswicke, Martine vii, 14, 60–63, 139
Betz, Carl 168, 316
The Beverly Hillbillies 1, 122, 157, 232, 285
Beverly Hills Brats 223
Bewitched 93, 164, 203, 204, 311, 316
Beymer, Richard 285
Beyond the Valley of the Dolls 240
Bianchi, Daniela 16, 37, 63–66, 92, 185, 189
The Big Game 231
Big Guns 226
The Big Test 113
The Big Valley 129
Bikini Motel 282
The Billy Barnes Revue 205
The Bird with the Crystal Plumage 252, 253
Bisset, Jacqueline 17, 66–69
The Bitch 100
Bite Me Darling 253
Bixby, Bill 232, 233
Black Belly of the Tarantula 48, 122
Black Belt Jones 148, 150
Black Caesar 147, 150
Black Gunn 239
A Black Veil for Lisa 239
Black Venus 186
The Blackboard Jungle 128
Blackman, Honor 16, 24, 67, 69–72, 115, 120, 164, 202, 257, 288
Blain, Gerard 40
Blake, Whitney 272
Blanc, Erika 14, 16, 19, 73–77, 185
The Blancheville Monster 184
Blast-Off 176
Blazing Sands see Brennender Sands
The Blood of Fu Manchu 97, 120
The Blood Splattered Bride 54, 55
The Bloody Judge 181
Blow-Up 81, 95
Blue 243
Blue Denim 200
The Blue Max 39
Bluebeard (1972) 292
Bob Hope Presents the Chrysler Theatre 111, 140, 155
Il Bocconcino 93
Bochner, Lloyd 310
The Bodies Bear Traces of Carnal Violence 50
Body Puzzle 76
Boeing, Boeing 182
Bogarde, Dirk 21, 49, 121, 161, 298
Bonanza 50, 107, 171, 192, 205
Bond, Diane 141
Bond, Samantha 208
Boone, Brendon 157, 231
Borman 77
Born Yesterday (1993) 312
Boschero, Dominique 19, 77–79

Bouchet, Barbara vii, 15, 17, 66, 79–83, 139, 200, 202, 226
Bower, Antoinette 111
Bowie, David 97
The Boy Friend 90
Boyd, Stephen 169, 214, 231
Bracken's World 156
Brando, Marlon 80, 97, 314
Brandt, Thordis 14, 84–86, 137, 141
Branford, Richard 283, 284
Brass, Tinto 49, 73
Brave Soldier Schwik 213
Brazzi, Rossano 63, 73, 229
Breakout 154
Brenda Starr 264
Brennender Sands 174
Brett, Jeremy 48
Brice, Pierre 57, 115, 175, 178
The Brides of Fu Manchu 95
Bridges, Jeff 295
Bridges to Heaven 228
Bridget Jones' Diary 72
Briers, Richard 305
Brigadoon (TV special) 207
Brocco, Peter 302
Broccoli, Albert "Cubby" 1, 16, 18, 19, 36, 38, 81, 236, 252, 267, 305
The Broken Hearts Club: A Romantic Comedy 213
Brolin, James 67
Bronson, Charles 38, 154
Brook, Claudio 180
Brooks, Mel 27, 126, 196
Brooks, Richard 175
Brosnan, Pierce 13, 22, 121, 208
Brotherhood of Satan 88
Brown, Jim 148, 239
Brown, Les 104
Brown, Les, Jr. 89
Browne, Roger 74, 78, 184, 185, 224, 225, 283
Bruce, Eve 141
Bruce, Jean 14, 239
Brynner, Yul 48, 58, 177
Buchholz, Horst 161
A Bullet for Pretty Boy 170
A Bullet for the General 61
Bullet to Beijing 188
Bullitt 67
Bunny Lake Is Missing 200
Buono, Victor 35, 279
Burke's Law 3, 24, 33, 128, 150, 157, 164, 218, 220, 232, 311, 316
Burnett, Carol 191
Burns, George 155
Burton, Richard 111, 210, 239, 292
Bus Stop 198
Butterfield 8 140
Buttons, Red 2, 27, 164, 233, 314
Buzzanca, Lando 224
By Love Possessed 102
Bye Bye Birdie 41

C.C. and Company 43
Cabot, Sebastian 262, 263
Cage, Nicholas 317
Caiano, Mario 184
Cain, Dean 213
Caine, Michael 186, 188, 252
Calamity Jane 104
Calde Notti di Don Giovanni 83, 301
Caldwell, Erskine 210
Call to Danger 192
Callan, Michael 202, 244
Calloway, Cab 240
Cameron, James 69
Campbell, Robert 259
Can Hieronymus Merkin Ever Forget Mercy Humppe and Find True Happiness? 99, 100
Canavari, Cesare 76
A Candidate for the Killing 180
Candide ou l'Optimisme au Xxe Siecle 174
Candy 292
Cannery Row 307
Cannon 142, 197
Cannon, J. D. 195
Cannon for Cordoba 316
Cantrell, Lana 91
The Cape Town Affair 67
Capitol 310
Capri, Anna 24, 86–89
Caprice 15, 21, 104–106, 294
Captain Nemo and the Underwater City 239
The Cardinal 200
Cardone, Alberto 115
The Caretakers 210
Carla and Lola 214
Carnal Knowledge 43
Carne, Judy 89–91
Carol, Cindy 109
Carousel 207
The Carpet of Cruelty 114
Carradine, David 154
Carre de Dames pour un As 161
Carrera, Barbara 238
Carroll, Kathleen 35
Carroll, Leo G. 24, 27, 102, 126, 151, 152, 247
Carroll, Victoria 151
Carry On Constable 118
Carry On Nurse 118, 153
Carry On Sergeant 118
Carter, Dixie 220
Cascino, Vincenzo 283
Cash, Johnny 269
Casino Royale 12, 14, 16, 38, 54, 66, 68, 81,82, 176, 243
Casse-Tout Tete Chinois pour le Judoka 292
El Caso de los dos Bellazas see *Two Undercover Angels*
Cast a Giant Shadow 58
Castle, William 53
The Castle of Fu Manchu 97

The Cat and the Canary (1978) 72, 202
Catlow 177
Cavelli, Joseph 124
Ce Kim Novak al Telefono 163
Celli, Adolfo 47, 65, 66, 178, 189, 238
C'Est Arrive a 36 Chandelles 272
Chamberlain, Richard 65
The Champions 54, 228
Chan, Jackie 295
Chandler, Jeff 236
Chandler, Patti 120, 145, 146, 260
Chanel, Helen see Hélène Chanel
Chanel, Hélène 19, 91–93
Channing 33
Chaplin, Geraldine 188
Chapman, Leigh 150
Charisse, Cyd 279
Charles, Arlene 151
Charles in Charge 207
Charlie's Angels 212, 244, 267, 316, 317
Chase, Chevy 269
Chatterbox 205
Chayefsky, Paddy 50, 259
Cheers 127
Chevie, Edmund 101
Cheyenne 86
Chi, Greta 23, 93, 94, 229, 305
Chin, Tsai 95–97
China Beach 152, 272
The Chippy Kids 183
CHiPs 36, 197
Chisum 107
Chomsky, Marvin 204
Choose Me 304
Christie, Julie 36, 47, 169, 218, 238
The Christmas Path 213
Ciannelli, Eduardo 84
Cifrato Speciale 184, 254
Cilento, Diane 144
Cimber, Matt 160
Cinderella (1965) 301
Cinque Marines per Cento Ragazze 92
Cioffi, Charles 131
City of Fear 213
La Ciudad sin Hombres see *Rio '70*
Clanton, Jimmy 232
Clark, Ken 18, 65, 74, 178, 184, 185, 189
Clark, Norman 185
Clarke, Robert 314
Clash of the Titans 39
Claudelle Inglish 210
Clemens, Brian 54, 167, 289
Cleopatra Jones and the City of Gold 281
CNN Presents 127
Cobb, Lee J. 136, 141, 142, 296
Cobos, German 18, 75, 283
The Cobra 59
Coburn, James 19, 22, 84, 89,

Index

103, 135–137, 140, 142, 158, 179, 251, 265, 296, 297
Cocteau, Jean 46
Code Name Red Roses 40
Codename 54
Cohen, Larry 147
Cold Comfort Farm 194
Cole, Corinne 35
Coleman, Dabney 140
Collins, Gary 220
Collins, Jackie 101
Collins, Joan 98–101, 182, 183, 319
Un Colpo da Mille Milliardi see *A Stroke of 100 Millions*
Colpo in Canna see *Loaded Guns*
Colpo Maestro Al Servico di Sua Maesta Britannica see *The Great Diamond Robbery*
Colpo Rovente 82
Colpo Sensazionale Al Servizio del Sifar see *Master Stroke in the Service of the Sifar*
Columbo 205
Come Back, Little Sheba 221
Come Blow Your Horn 262
The Come Rubare la Corona d'Inghilterra see *Argoman Fantastic Superman*
Come Spy with Me 15, 21, 117, 118
Comer, Anjanette 252
Con la Muerte e el Espalda see *Elektra One*
The Concrete Jungle 197
Conde, Jose Antonio Nieves 214
Connery, Neil 65, 209
Connery, Sean 1, 11, 16, 18, 19, 36, 47, 61, 62, 64, 65, 72, 81, 95, 96, 115, 119, 132, 138, 139, 143, 144, 149, 172, 208, 209, 238, 241, 242, 251, 259, 263, 308–310
Connor, Kenneth 118, 119
Connors, Mike 179, 250, 251, 292
Conrad, Joseph 10
Conrad, Robert 27, 28, 88, 102, 124, 131, 140, 147, 156, 170, 172, 195, 196, 210, 291, 295, 302, 308, 309, 314–316
The Conspirator 69
Constantine, Eddie 95, 272, 273
Contest Girl 139
Conway, Gary 199
Cooper, Stan 185
Cooper, Terence 81
Cop Story 48
Coplan Ouvre le Feu a Mexico see *Coplan Takes a Vacation in Mexico*
Coplan Sauve Sa Peau see *Coplan Saves His Skin*
Coplan Saves His Skin 180
Coplan Takes a Vacation in Mexico 273, 274
Coppola, Francis Ford 114

Il Coraggioso, lo Spietato il Traditore see *The Courageous Merciless and the Traitor*
Corbett, Glenn 293
Corbett, Ronnie 243
Cord, Alex 111, 206, 243
Cord, Damien 243
Corey, Jeff 93
Corey, Wendell 80
Cornthwaite, Robert 229
The Corrupt Ones 167, 276
Corruption 188
Cosby, Bill 25, 88, 109, 206, 231
Cotten, Joseph 226
Cotton Comes to Harlem 242
The Countess and the Cowboy 293
The Courageous, the Merciless and the Traitor 92
The Courtship of Eddie's Father 279
Cover Me Baby 291
Cox, Wally 84
Cracking Up 317
Craig, Michael 252
Craig, Yvonne 24, 27, 101–104, 147, 150, 319
Crane, Bob 244, 296
Crane, Scott 297
Crawford, Broderick 139, 295
Crawford, Joan 210, 211
Creasy, John 188
Cremaster 5 39
Crescendo 249
Crewe, Bob 289
Cribbens, Bernard 243
Crime Doctor's Diary 208
Cristal, Linda 191
Crosby, Bing 99
Crosby, Bob 104
Crosby, Stills, Nash, & Young 261
Cross of Iron 59
The Crowded Sky 128
The Crucible 198
Cruise, Tom 53, 317
Cruise Into Terror 108
Cry Chicago 41
Cukor, George 142
Culp, Robert 25, 53, 88, 109, 171, 172, 206, 207, 229–231
Cummings, Robert 180
The Curse of the Pink Panther 194
Curse of the Swamp Creature 314
Curtis, Donald 232
Curtis, Patrick 304
Curtis, Tony 30, 100, 182, 188
Cushing, Peter 55, 185, 188, 193
Cyclone 63

The Dagora Space Monster 143
Dalbes, Alberto 274
Dallas 131
Dalle Ardenne all'Inferno see *Dirty Heroes*
Dalton, Timothy 13, 22, 259
Daly, Jonathan 155, 198, 199, 290
Damon, Mark 226

Damon, Stuart 54
Damone, Vic 40
Dana, Rodd 254
Danger: Death Ray 19, 274
Danger: Diabolik see *Diabolik*
Danger Man 61, 70, 133, 208, 245, 284
Danger Route 15, 16, 18, 82, 200, 201
Daniela by Night 275
Danilova, Alexandra 101
Danton, Ray 18, 178, 189, 214, 226
Darby, Kim 152, 153, 212, 293, 294
Darin, Bobby 247
Dark Places 100
Dark Shadows 157
Dark Tower 203
Darktown Strutters 242
Darren, James 109, 180, 270
Da Silva, Howard 109
David, Hal 270
David, Saul 140, 305
David, Thayer 295
Davies, Robert-Hartford 60
Davila, Luis 254, 255
Davis, Sammy, Jr. 82
Day, Doris 14, 15, 21, 80, 104–106, 155, 294, 296, 319
Day, Robert 231, 251
Day for Night 67
Day of the Outlaw 191
Day George, Lynda 28, 106–109, 142, 206
Days of Our Lives 212, 317
Dead Run 300
Deadlier Than the Male 16, 18, 189, 161, 162, 176, 177, 182, 276, 277
The Deadly and the Beautiful see *Wonder Women*
The Deadly Bees 182
Dean, James 40, 41
Dean, Jimmy 240
Death and Diamonds 274
Death Knocks Twice 93
Death Occurred Last Night 253
The Death Ray of Dr. Mabuse 283
Death Scream 192
Death Valley Days 314
Deathmoon 231
Il Debito Conjugale 83
Decameron Nights 98
Dee, Sandra 86, 140, 247
The Deep 67
The Defenders of the Jaguar 275
Dehner, John 89, 172
Deighton, Len 11, 13, 188
Deiha Tsing 97
Dekker, Albert 117
De Laurentiis, Dino 33, 73, 179, 214, 250
Delevanti, Cyril 220
Delon, Alain 38, 48, 49, 59, 214, 226

Index

The Delphi Bureau 243, 244
The Delphi Bureau (TV series) 28, 131, 204, 205
The Delta Factor 212
De Martino, Alberto 185
Demme, Jonathan 63
Demon Rage 310
Il Demonio 175
De Metz, Danielle 24, 109–111
Deneuve, Catherine 140, 214
Dennis, Sandy 35, 202
Department S 30, 54,188, 209, 227, 228
Derek, Bo 36
Derek, John 36
De Sade 59
De Sica, Vittorio 275
Desperate Mission 16, 18, 283
The Detective (1968) 67
Un Detective (1969) 44
Detournement de Mineurs 91
Deuel, Peter 90
Deux Anges Sont Venus 240
The Devil at Four O'Clock 195
Devil Dog: The Hound from Hell 63
Devil in the Flesh 44
The Devil Within Her 100
The Devils 107
The Devil's Daffodil 213
The Devil's Nightmare 76
The Devil's Wedding Night 226
De Vries, Hans 259
Dhiegh, Khigh 314
D'Hondt, Danica 158, 159
Diabolically Yours 59
Diabolik 14, 179, 180, 214, 215
Diagnosis: Murder 53
The Diamond Connection 83
Diamond Head 229
Diamonds Are Forever 12, 15, 16, 18, 208, 240–242, 259, 263, 308–310
Diana 259
Diary of a Madman 163
Diaz, Cameron 43
Dick, Andy 127
Dick Smart 2.007 178, 179
The Dick Van Dyke Show 50, 111, 171
Dickinson, Angie 58, 279
Diff'rent Strokes 220
Diffring, Anton 57
Digging Up Business 104
Dillard, Mimi 14, 111–113
Dillman, Bradford 84, 202
Dimension 5 14, 198, 229, 289
Dino, Desi and Billy 43
The Dinosaurs 127
Dirty Heroes 66
Il Disco Volante 73
Disney, Walt 3, 301
The Divine Nymph 50
DM Killer 175
Doctor at Large 118

Dr. Goldfoot and the Bikini Machine 145, 146, 198, 260
Dr. Goldfoot and the Girl Bombs 44, 45
Doctor in the House 118
Dr. Jekyll and Sister Hyde 63
Dr. Kildare (TV series) 33, 65, 205, 308
Dr. No 3, 12, 15, 18, 24, 36, 37, 60, 132, 208
Dr. Quinn, Medicine Woman 269
The Doll Squad 15, 21, 264, 265, 267, 316, 317
A Doll's House 98
Donahue, Troy 117, 118, 210
Donlevy, Brian 180
The Donna Reed Show 1, 53
Don't Bother to Knock 275
Don't Just Lie There, Say Something 193
Don't Look in the Attic 189, 191
A Doppia Faccia 181
Dor, Karin 15, 16, 95, 113–116, 224, 252
Dorelli, Johnny 180, 181
The Doris Day Show 106
Doris Day's Best Friends 106
Double Exposure 244
Double Face 181
The Double Life of Henry Phyfe 2, 27, 164, 233, 314
Douglas, Gordon 141, 142
Douglas, Kirk 58, 80, 174, 175
Doversola, Gordon 129, 141, 142
Down Among the Z Men 132
Down and Out in Beverly Hills 295
Dragnet (TV series) 85, 155, 156
Dragon: The Bruce Lee Story 168
Drat the Cat 301
Le Dritte 298
Dromm, Andrea 15, 21, 117, 118
Drowning on Dry Land 203
Due Mafiosi Contro Goldginger see *Two Mafiosi Against Goldginger*
I Due Mafiosi see *The Two Mafiosi*
Due Samurai per Centro Geisha 177
Due Sosia in Allegria 223
Duell Zu Dritt 177
Duello Nel Mondo see *Ring Around the World*
Duggan, Andrew 86, 141
Dunaway, Faye 47, 238
Dunham, Katherine 240, 242
Dunn, Michael 140, 229, 296
Duvall, Robert 154
Dynamit in Gruner Seide see *Death and Diamonds*
Dynamite Jim 224
Dynasty 98, 101, 207
Dynasty: The Reunion 101

Eastham, Richard 41
Eaton, Shirley vii, 16, 24, 111, 118–121, 257, 260
The Eclipse 298

L'Edera 76
Edmonds, Louis 117
Edwards, Blake 75, 188
Edwards, James 111
Edwards, Vince 35, 157, 158
Egan, Richard 191
Eighteen and Anxious 102
The '80s Woman 127
Eisley, Anthony 129, 137, 316, 317
Ekberg, Anita 37, 93
Ekland, Britt 244, 310
Elektra One 225
Ellery Queen 166
Ellington, Duke 240
Elliott, John 254
Ellison, Harlan 99, 124
Empire of the Ants 100
Enter Laughing 165
Enter the Dragon 89, 150
Ercole e la Regina di Lidia 160
Ericson, John 27, 73, 129
Erode di Grande 160
The Eroticist 45
Es Muss Nicht Immer Kaviar Sein see *Operation Caviar*
Espionage in Lisbon 19, 74, 291
Estevez, Luis 202
Esther and the King 98, 223
Estigma 55
Estrada, Erik 203
L'Eternite pour Nous 254
Eurotica 76
Eve 312
Everett, Chad 137, 139
Evers, Jason 131
Every Mother's Son 153
The Evil 244
The Evil That Men Do 154
The Executioner 100
Experiment in Terror 247

The F. B. I. 107, 165
Fabiani, Joel 30, 181, 227, 228
Faccia di Spia 79
Face of Fire 208
The Face of Fu Manchu 95, 114
Fade Out, Fade In 191
Fair Exchange 89
Faith, Dolores 86
Fajardo, Eduardo 254
Falcon Crest 39, 220
Falk, Peter 205
Falk, Rossella 16, 21, 49, 121, 122, 298, 319
The Fall Guy 244, 310
Fame Is the Name of the Game 262
Fame Is the Spur 69
Family Affair 165
Family Man 317
Fancher, Hampton 210
Fanfare for a Death Scene 191
Fangs of the Underworld 143
Fantaghiro II, III, IV 39
Fantastic Journey 220
Fantastic Voyage 47, 136, 305

Index 328

Fantasy Island 202, 220
Farewell to Manzanar 94
Farrell, Sharon 24, 122–125
Farrow, Mia 135, 218
Faster, Pussycat! Kill! Kill! 264, 265, 267
Fatal Beauty 312
Fathom 15, 21, 23, 93, 94, 305, 306
Le Fatiche di Ercole 160
Fax, Jesslyn 88
The Fearless Vampire Killers 285
The Feather and Father Gang 249
Feldman, Charles 16, 38, 81, 82, 243
Feldon, Barbara 27, 125–128, 164
Feldon, Lucien Verdoux 125
Felicia 140
Fell, Norman 218, 219
Fellini, Federico 121, 161
Fellini's Casanova 50
Fellini's 8½ 121
Fellini's Satyricon 44, 49
Felony Squad 107, 113
Fenech, Edwige 76
Ferrer, Mel 93
Ferrial, Francois 50
Ferroni, Giorgio 214
Feuer Frei auf Frankie see *Target: Frankie*
Fickling, Forest G. "Skip" 128
Fickling, Gloria 128
Fifteen and Pregnant 207
The Fifth Cord 122
Fimberg, Hal 141
Finch, Peter 121
A Fine Madness 172
Finney, Albert 97
The First Spaceship on Venus 282
Fisher, Terence 57
A Fistful of Diamonds 75
Five Dolls for an August Moon 300
Five Fingers (TV series) 236
Five Gates to Hell 93
Five Golden Dragons 180
The Five Sinners 213
Flamingo Road (TV series) 281
Flare-Up 307
Fleming, Ian 1, 7, 10–13, 16, 19, 24, 37, 38, 47, 64, 71, 72, 81, 144, 149, 150, 169
Fleming, Rhonda 88
The Flintstones in Viva Rock Vegas 101
Flipper 107
Flood 317
Flower Drum Song 167
The Flying Nun 113, 204
Folger, Abagail 287
Fonda, Jane 106
Fonda, Peter 261, 272
Fontaine, Joan 98
For Amusement Only 89
For Singles Only 309
For the Love of Ivy 147

For Those Who Think Young 270
For Your Eyes Only 12, 208, 268
Forbidden Planet 128
Ford, John 102, 308
Ford, Patrick 102
Foreign Exchange 262, 263
The Forger of London 113
Forrest, Steve 186–188
Forster, Robert 168, 291
The Forsyte Saga 245
Forsyth, Rosemary 135
Forsythe, Stephen 78
Forte, Fabian 44, 170
Foster, Gloria 25
The Four Feathers 269
Four for Texas 37
The Four Just Men 69
Four Queens for an Ace 161
Franchi, Franco 44, 177, 224, 273
Franchi, Regina 76
Franciosa, Anthony (Tony) 23, 28, 88, 93, 94, 111, 262, 305, 306
Francis, Anne 25, 28, 128–131, 153, 301, 319
Francisci, Pietro 236
Franciscus, James 63, 135, 165, 207
Franco, Jesus (Jess) 74, 97, 120, 180, 181, 189, 226, 239, 255, 273
Franco & Ciccio 92
Franju, Georges 161
Frank Sinatra Timex Show 270
Frankenstein Conquers the World 143
Frankenstein: The True Story 269
Fraser, Ronald 93, 305
Frazier, Chuck 240
Freda, Riccardo 91, 181
Freddy & the Dreamers 155
Free Grass 309
Fregonese, Hugo 98
French Dressing 213
Fried, Gerald 311
Friendship, Secrets and Lies 281
Frobe, Gert 72, 114, 119, 175
Froebe, Gert see Frobe, Gert
From Noon to Three 154
From Russia with Love 12, 16, 37, 60–64, 66, 92, 132, 138, 139, 150, 185, 208, 259
Frost, David 200
Il Frusta e il Corpo 175
Frustration 255, 256
Fuchsberger, Joachim 75, 95, 114, 213, 225
The Fugitive (TV series) 107, 122, 205
Fujikawa, Jerry H. 231
Fulci, Lucio 177, 214, 275
The Fuller Report 189
Fun in Acapulco 37
Funai, Helen 136, 296, 297
Funeral in Berlin 252, 253
Funicello, Annette 146, 260

Funny About Love 312
Funny Girl 85, 129
Furia a Marrakech see *Fury in Marrakesh*
Further Up the Creek 118
Fury in Istanbul 15, 178
Fury in Marrakesh 19, 78

Gaba, Marianne 145, 260
Gabor, Zsa Zsa 278
Gaburro, Bruno 73
Gangs of New York 83
Gangster's Law 93
Gardner, John 13
Garner, Ed 260
Garner, James 104, 125, 302
Garrett, Donna 242
Garrison's Gorillas 157
Garroway, Dave 163
Gary Lewis & the Playboys 155
Gaspard-Huit, Pierre 46
Gassman, Vittorio 65, 189, 287
Gaunt, William 54
Gavin, John 18, 180, 225, 239, 263
Gaynor, Mitzi 228, 229
Gayson, Eunice 24, 131–133
Gazzara, Ben 310
Gazzolo, Nando 114, 224
Geeson, Judy 100
Das Geheimnis der Chinesischen Nelke see *The Secret of the Chinese Carnation*
Geheimnis der Gelben Monche see *Target for a Killing*
Das Geheimnisse in Goldenen Nylons see *Dead Run*
Geller, Bruce 51, 301
The Gemini Affair 157, 160
Gemini Rising 131
Gemma, Giulliano 38
The Gene Krupa Story 102
General Hospital 199, 212, 282
Genitori in Blue-Jeans 91
Gen-O and Prince Fudomyo 143
The Gentle Rain 107
George, Christopher 107, 212
Gern Habich die Frauen Gekillt see *Spy Against the World*
Get On with It! 118
Get Smart 1, 27, 51, 125–127, 139, 152, 164, 213
Get Smart, Again! 127
Get Yourself a College Girl 218
The Ghost in the Invisible Bikini 147, 260
The Ghoul 55
Gidget 102
Gidget (TV series) 311
Gidget Goes to Rome 109
Giler, David 168
Gilligan's Island 191, 192
The Girl from U.N.C.L.E. 27, 84, 110, 218–220, 247–249, 265, 266
Girl Happy 218

The Girl Hunters 119
The Girl in the Red Velvet Swing 98
A Girl Named Tamiko 229
Girl of the Night 128
The Girl Who Knew Too Much 168
The Girl with a Pistol 298, 299
The Girls on the Beach 86, 308
Girls! Girls! Girls! 279
Giuletta degli Spiriti 161
Gleason, Jackie 171
A Global Affair 80
The Glory Guys 57
God's Little Acre 191, 279
Golan, Gila 16, 19, 133–135, 137
The Golden Arrow 77
Goldeneye 22
Goldfinger 12, 15, 16, 65, 66, 71, 72, 78, 115, 119–121, 133, 145, 150, 155, 164, 208, 260
Goldsmith, Jerry 141
Goldsnake "Anonima Killers" see *Goldsnake "Killer's Company"*
Goldsnake "Killer's Company" 19, 283, 284
Gomarasca, Manlio 226
Gomer Pyle, U.S.M.C. 129, 314
Gone with the Wind 182, 288
Good Neighbor Sam 250
Goodbye Charlie 216
Gould, Harold 249, 301
Goulet, Robert 207
Grabowski, Norman 155, 198, 199, 290
The Graduate 106
Graham, Martha 240, 242
Graham, Sheila 305
Grandpa Goes to Washington 174
Granger, Farley 83
Granger, Stewart 65, 98, 114, 115, 178
The Granny 282
Grant, Cary 97, 104
Grant, Shelby 14, 135–137, 296, 297
The Grasshopper 67
Grauman, Charlie 317
Graves, Peter 52, 53, 99, 100, 108, 192, 206, 316
Gray, Charles 243, 263
Gray, Janine 89
The Great Diamond Robbery 178
The Great Muppet Caper 259
The Great Race 250
The Great White Hope 240
The Greatest Show on Earth (TV series) 51
The Greek Tycoon 239, 289, 292
Green, Nigel 95, 114, 161, 167, 168, 186, 189, 192, 276, 277, 287
Green Acres 137
The Green Archer 113
The Green Berets 295
The Green Hornet 107
The Green Slime 239
Greene, Graham 10

Greene, Richard 97
Gregory, James 34, 108
Grieco, Sergio 185
Gries, Tom 192
Griffith, Hugh 228
Griffith, Melanie 312
Die Grosse Freiheit 116
The Group 243
Guest, Val 38, 81
Guida, Gloria 181
A Guide for the Married Man 172
Gulager, Clu 192
The Guns of Navarone 227
Gunsmoke 122, 171
Gur, Alicia see Gur, Alizia
Gur, Aliza see Gur, Alizia
Gur, Alizia 61, 137–139

Hagen, Ross 168
Hagman, Larry 243
Hale, Jean vii, 16, 19, 22, 84, 140–142
Haley, Jack, Jr. 3
Hall, Juanita 229
Halsey, Brett 18, 40, 74, 109, 291
Hama, Mie 16, 115, 143, 144
Hamilton, Donald 14, 19, 168, 279
Hamilton, George 47, 102
Hamilton, Guy 133, 148, 267
Hamilton, Kipp 158
Hamlin, Harry 39
Hammerhead 35, 158
The Hangman 191
Hanin, Roger 65, 161, 178
Hanold, Marilyn 141
The Happiest Millionaire 301
Happy Days 157
The Happy Hooker Goes to Hollywood 63
Hard Times for a Vampire 161
Hardly Working 199
Hargitay, Mickey 283
Hargrove, Dean 126, 202, 218
Hari, Mata 9, 10, 93
Harlow (Lynley version) 251
Harrington, Pat, Jr. 110
Harris, Brad 75, 274
Harris, Richard 105
Harrison, Noel 27, 99, 110, 238, 247, 265, 266
Harrison, Richard 18, 78, 92, 178, 254
Harry O 244
Harryhausen, Ray 135, 269
Hart, Susan 145–147, 198, 260
Hart to Hart (TV movie) 249
Hart to Hart (TV series) 249
Hartman, Ena 111
Harum ScaruM 169
Harvey, Laurence 161, 175, 229, 244
Hawaii Five-O 125, 142, 165, 197
Hawk 107
Hawkins, Jack 98

Hazelwood, Lee 272
Heatherton, Joey 86
Hedison, David 262
Hedren, Tippi 37, 275
Hefner, Hugh 223
Heisser Hafen Hong Kong see *Hong Kong Hot Harbor*
Heitland, Jon 220
The Helicopter Spies 25, 84, 202
Hell Up in Harlem 147
Hell's Belles 170
Hemingway's Adventures of a Young Man 285
Hemsoborna 174
Henderson, Maye 111
Hendry, Gloria vii, 16, 147–150, 269
Hendry, Ian 70
Henry, Buck 126
Henry, Mike 139
Hepburn, Audrey 169
Hercules 160, 236
Hercules and the Ten Avengers 291
Hercules Unchained 160
Here Comes Dorellik 180
Herod the Great 160
Hershey, Barbara 203
Herzog, Werner 213
Heston, Charlton 57, 182, 229, 259, 308
Heyward, Louis M. "Deke" 260
Hickman, Dwayne 145, 198
The High Commissioner 176
High Heels 45
Hilary and Jackie 245
Hill, James 167
Hill, Steven 196, 220
Hiller, Wendy 202
Hillyer, Sharon vii, 24, 150–152
Hilton, George 224
Hingle, Pat 281
Hirt, Al 191
Hitchcock, Alfred 116
Ho, Linda 150, 229
Hogan's Heroes 85, 204, 296
Holbrook, Hal 207
Holden, William 167, 229, 249
Holder, Geoffrey 268
Holiday, Billie 240
Die Holle von Macao see *The Corrupt Ones*
Hollywood Ghost Stories 277
Hollywood Palace 305
Holm, Celeste 244
Holocaust 2: The Memories, Delirium and the Vendetta Part Two 50
Holt, Seth 202
L'Homme de l'Interpol see *The Man from Interpol*
L'Homme de Marrakech see *The Man from Marrakech*
L'Homme d'Istanbul 161
Homo Eroticus 301
Homolka, Oscar 252
Honey West 25, 128–130, 164

Hong, James 216
Hong Kong Hot Harbor 77
The Hoop Life 289
Hoopla—Jezt Kommt Eddie! 272
Hope, Bob 47, 99
Hopper, Hedda 136, 137
Hornaday, Jeffrey 304
Hornet's Nest 163
Horror 184, 185
Horror at 37,000 Feet 231
Horror Express 185
Horten, Rena 155
Horton, Robert 262, 263
The Hospital 259
Hossein, Robert 40
Hot Money Girls see The Treasure of San Teresa
Hot Potato 295
Hotel der Toten Gaste 114
A House Is Not a Home 305
House of Insane Women 185
The House That Dripped Blood 245
Hoven, Adrian 255
How Now Dow Jones 207
How to Frame a Figg 104
How to Save a Marriage—And Ruin Your Life 281
How to Seduce a Playboy 170
How to Stuff a Wild Bikini 33, 293
Howard, Duke 21
Howard, Trevor 58, 169, 262
Howard Hughes: His Women and His Movies 223
The Howl 49
Howlers of the Dock 275
Hubschmid, Paul 114, 224, 252
Hud 150
Hudson, Rock 104, 163
Hughes, Howard 221
Hughes, Ken 38, 81
Hughes, Mary 260
Hunt, Gareth 30, 193
Hunter, Jeffrey 198, 229, 289
Hunter, Tab 66, 77, 145
Hunter, Thomas 75
Huston, John 38, 81
Hutton, Jim 166, 251
Hutton, Robert 100
Hyams, Joe 277, 278
Hyde-White, Wilfred 262
Hyer, Martha 229
Hysteria 186

I Am a Nymphomaniac 255
I Dream of Jeannie 111, 122, 204
I, Emmanuelle 76
I Hate My Body 55
I Have Seven Daughters 236
I Love Vienna 216
I Pinguini Ci Guardino 223
I Spy 25, 53, 84, 109, 164, 206, 207, 217, 229–231, 293
I Tre Nemici 177
I Was a Teenage Werewolf 147
Ice Palace 210

If a Man Answers 247
Iguana with a Tongue of Fire 79
Ihnat, Steve 84, 141
Im Stahlnetz des Dr. Mabuse 175
In Harm's Way 80
In Like Flint 16, 19, 22, 84, 85, 103, 135, 140–142, 296
In the Folds of the Flesh 41
Incontrera, Annabella 181
The Indian Tomb 236
Ingrassia, Ciccio 44, 177, 224, 273
Ingster, Boris 151, 311
Inhat, Steve 141
Inn of the Flying Dragon 292
Innocent Bystanders 188
International Secret Police: Key of Keys 143
The Interns 247
The Invaders 107
Invasion 95
The Invincible Six 276
The Invisible Dr. Mabuse 114
The Invisible Strangler 277
The Ipcress File 186–188
Ireland, Jill 128, 153, 154
Irma La Douce 265
The Iron Mask 46, 160
Ironside 107, 192
Istanbul Express 59, 220
It Conquered Hollywood! 147
It Happened at Lakewood Manor 108
It Happened at the World's Fair 102
It Takes a Thief 28, 29, 59, 61, 88, 104, 107, 116, 164, 170, 192, 202–204, 249, 312, 316
It's a Mad, Mad, Mad, Mad World 250

Jackson, Horace 111
Jacobi, Lou 270
Jaekin, Just 76
Jagger, Dean 205, 244
Jagger, Mick 188
James, Edith 101
James, Sid 118, 119
James and the Giant Peach 194
James Tont: Operation Goldsinger 224
James Tont: Operazione U.N.O. see James Tont: Operation Goldsinger
Jane Eyre (TV series) 245
Janssen, David 60, 116, 277
Jason and the Argonauts 71, 163
Jason King 54, 227, 228
Jeffreys, Anne 205
Jeffries, Lang 18, 75, 184, 239, 254, 274
Jeffries, Lionel 175
Jensen, Karen 155–157
Jergens, Diane 232
Jewison, Norman 117
Jigsaw (TV series) 131
Joan of Arc (1999) 69
The Joe Pyne Show 232

The Joey Bishop Show 145
Johann Strauss: The King Without a Crown 116
John Goldfarb, Please Come Home 80
John the Bastard 61
Johnny Banco 161
Johnny Tiger 198
Johnson, Don 312
Johnson, Richard 18, 82, 161, 176, 177, 182, 193, 200, 201, 218, 276
Jones, Christopher 291
Jones, Jack 264
Jones, James Earl 240
Jones, T.C. 291
Jordan, Lewis 92
Jordan, Patrick 156
Jourdan, Louis 58, 98
Journey to the Lost City 236
The Joy Luck Club 97, 231
Judd for the Defense 168
Judex 161
The Juggler 174
The Jukebox Girls 275
Jukebox Jury 89
Julia 113
Juliet of the Spirits 161
Julius Caesar 259
Jurgens, Curd see Jurgens, Curt
Jurgens, Curt 66, 110, 115, 225, 239

La Kali Yug Dea della Vendetta 46
The Karate Killers 110, 153, 211, 293, 294
Karina, Anna 156
Karloff, Boris 239, 276
Karlson, Phil 280, 281
Kaszner, Kurt 199, 247
Katzin, Lee H. 156
Kaufman, Maurice 72
Kaufman, Robert 145
Kaufmann, Christine 80
Kaye, Celia 218
Kaye, Danny 97
Keach, James 269
Keaton, Michael 104
Keel, Howard 191
Kelly, Gene 3
Kelly, Jim 150
Kelton, Richard 303
Kendall, Kay 262
Kendall, Tony 75
Kennedy, Jacqueline 239
Kenny, Paul 180
Kent, Robert 77, 283
Kent, Stanley 283
Kerr, Deborah 243
Kerr, John 229
Kersh, Kathy vii, 89, 157–160
Kiel, Richard 1, 140
Kill, Baby, Kill 74
Kill Panther Kill 75
The Killer Is on the Telephone 122
The Killer Likes Candy 292

Un Killer per Sua Maesta see *The Killer Likes Candy*
The Killers Are Our Guests 181
Killing Game 48
Kim Novak Is on the Telephone 163
Kincaid, Aron 146
The King and I 195
King Kong Escapes 143
King Kong vs. Godzilla 143
King Lear (TV) 156, 259
The King's Pirate 262
Kinski, Klaus 179–181, 213, 252
Kirk, Christina 243
Kirk, Tommy 102
Kiss Her Goodbye 122
Kiss Me Monster 255
Kiss the Girls and Make Them Die 14, 33, 179, 250, 251, 292
Kisses for My President 86
Kissin' Cousins 102
Kitten with a Whip 41
The Klansman 239
The Knack ... And How to Get It 66
The Knickerbockers 155
Knots Landing 244, 312
Knotts, Don 104
Kohner, Susan 191
Kokusai Himitsu Keisatsu: Kagi No Kagi see *International Secret Police: Key of Keys*
Kommissar X—Drei Blaue Panther see *Kill Panther Kill*
Koroshi 284
Koscina, Sylva 19, 160–163, 177, 182, 276, 319
Kotto, Yaphet 148, 268
Kovack, Nancy 19, 27, 163–166, 175
Kovacs, Laszlo 20
The Kraft Music Hall 90, 220
Kraft Suspense Theatre 191
Kramer, Stanley 133
Kristen, Marta 157, 160
Kristofferson, Kris 269
Kruger, Christiane 181
Kruschen, Jack 105
Kuluva, Will 24
Kung Fu 197
Kwan, Nancy 16, 19, 158, 166–169, 276, 277, 287, 293

Laberinto de Pasiones 186
Lady Frankenstein 226
Lady Godiva Rides Again 98
Lady in Cement 307
Lady in the Corner 209
Lady in the Fog 208
Lamas, Fernando 249
Lambert, Hugh 272
Lambert, Paul 270
Lamour, Dorothy 99
Lanchester, Elsa 102, 164
Land of the Giants 197, 199, 262
Land of the Pharaohs 98
Landau, Cecil 169

Landau, Martin 28, 50–53, 93, 196, 220
The Landlord 147
Landy, Hanna 141
Lane, Jocelyn 27, 104, 135, 169–171
Lane, Mara 169
Lang, Fritz 57, 114, 236
Langdon, Sue Ane vii, 21, 27, 171–174, 221, 233
Lansbury, Angela 211
Lansbury, Bruce 107
Lassiter 269
The Last Chance 38
The Last Days of Pompeii 293
The Last of the Renegades 114
The Last of the Secret Agents? 84, 270, 271
Last Plane to Baalbeck 283
The Last Time I Saw Archie 229
The Last Tomahawk 114
Laugh-In see *Rowan and Martin's Laugh-In*
Lavi, Daliah 16, 17, 19, 57, 66, 164, 174–177, 189, 190, 193, 276, 279, 319
Law, John Philip 214, 215
Lawford, Peter 300
Lawrence, John 155, 198, 199, 290
Lazenby, George 17, 61, 193, 208, 209, 259
Leave It to Beaver 1
Le Carré, John 7, 10, 11, 13
Lee, Anna 141, 142
Lee, Bernard 65, 209
Lee, Bruce 89, 135, 150, 158, 168, 287
Lee, China 145, 260
Lee, Christopher 57, 95, 97, 114, 115, 161, 175, 180, 181, 185, 193, 213
Lee, Margaret 14, 15, 19, 33, 177–181, 226
The Legend of Forrest Tucker 109
The Legend of Lylah Clare 121
Legrand, Michel 240
Leigh, Janet 118, 135
Leigh, Suzanna 181–183, 227, 319
Leigh, Vivien 182
Lembeck, Harvey 146
Lemmon, Jack 200, 265, 308
Lemoine, Michel 253–255
Lennon, John 267
Lenya, Lotte 64
Lenzi, Umberto 76, 185, 214
Leo e Beo 76
Levin, Henry 43, 179, 250, 251
Lewis, Jerry 44, 135, 182, 199, 270, 311, 314, 317
La Ley del Deseo 186
Libido 79
License to Kill 22
Das Licht der Liebe 213
Liebovitz, Annie 239
Lt. Robin Crusoe, U.S.N. 167

Life at the Top 72
The Light in the Forest 200
Li'l Abner 191, 279
The Limey 304
Die Lindenwirtin Vom Donaustrand 56
Line, Helga 19, 65, 184–186
The Liquidator 54, 262
Lisa and the Devil 163, 277
Little Devils: The Birth 282
Little House on the Prairie 269
Live a Little, Love a Little 85, 312
Live and Let Die 12, 16, 22, 148–150, 208, 267–269
Live Fast, Die Young 250
Living Between Two Worlds 111
The Living Daylights 22
Lloyd, Sue 24, 186–191
Lo Strano Ricatto di Una Ragazza per Bene 226
Loaded Guns 38
Lockwood, Gary 168, 249
Lodge, John 85, 155
Logan, Joshua 228, 229
Lollobrigida, Gina 236
Lom, Herbert 110, 178, 179
Loncar, Beba 16, 19, 189–191, 177, 193, 276
The Long, Hot Summer (TV series) 308
The Long Ships 189
Longet, Claudine 311
Longstreet (TV movie) 63
Longstreet (TV series) 111, 207
Lord Jim 175
Loren, Sophia 236
Losey, Joseph 49, 121, 298
The Lost Continent 182
Lost in Space (TV series) 157, 262, 314
The Lost World (1960) 262
Louise, Tina vii, 16, 19, 168, 191–193, 277, 279
Love, American Style 174, 192, 199, 220
Love and Bullets 154
The Love Boat 220, 264
Love Me or Leave Me 104
Love on a Rooftop 90
Lover Come Back 104
The Loves and Times of Scaramouche 39
Loving 235
Luckinbill, Laurence 28, 204, 243
The Lucky, el Intrepido see *Lucky Inscrutable*
The Lucky Inscrutable 189, 226
Lumley, Joanna 30, 193, 194, 319
Luna, BarBara vii, 24, 27, 28, 195–197, 301, 319
Lund, Deanna vii, 145, 197–200, 260, 319
Lupus, Peter 52, 108, 316
Lust for a Vampire 182
Lye, Reg 94

Lynley, Carol 16, 25, 200–203, 210, 236, 319
Lynn, Robert 115
Lyons, Robert 131

M.M.M. 83 40
Mabry, Moss 35
MacGowran, Jack 295
Machiavelli, Nicoletta 33
Maciste in Hell 91
MacLachlan, Janet 25
MacLaine, Shirley 82, 182, 265
Macnee, Patrick 24, 30, 53, 70, 71, 193, 257, 288
Macready, George 89
Mad About You 127
Mademoiselle Striptease 236
The Magnificent Seven 276
The Magnificent Tony Carrera 75
El Magnifico Tony Carrera see *The Magnificent Tony Carrera*
Major Dundee 57
A Majority of One 232
Majors, Lee 244, 310
Making It 207
Malden, Karl 41
Malicious 45, 50
Malicious 2000 45
Mallet, Tania 15
Man Against the Mob: The Chinatown Murders 39
A Man Called Dagger 1, 14, 15, 20, 21, 112, 172–174, 221–223, 232–235, 251
The Man from Interpol 273
The Man from Marrakech 47
The Man from O.R.G.Y. 113
The Man from U.N.C.L.E. 11, 19, 24, 27, 53, 58, 80, 84, 86, 87, 89, 90, 99, 102, 109, 110, 112, 123, 124, 126, 139, 150–154, 157, 158, 164, 169, 171, 196–197, 202, 203, 205, 211, 212, 216, 218–220, 229–231, 238, 245, 247–250, 265, 270, 281, 285, 293–295, 311, 312
Man in a Suitcase 228, 283, 284
The Man in the Looking Glass 187, 188
The Man Who Knew Too Much 104
The Man with the Golden Gun 12, 208
The Man with the Icy Eyes 83
Man Without a Memory 59
Man, Pride and Vengeance 49
The Manchurian Candidate 111
Manhattan Night of Murder 273
The Maniacs 177
Manimal 39
Mann, Delbert 140
Mann, Larry D. 164, 232
Der Mann mit den 1000 Masken see *Upperseven: The Man to Kill*
Mannequins in Paris 282
Mannix 85, 152, 165, 212, 244

Manson, Charles 287
Mantee, Paul 21, 112, 172–174, 221–223, 233–235, 251
La Mantilla de Beatriz 184
Man-Trap 279
Marais, Jean 214
Marblehead Manor 289
March, Alex 311
Marchal, Xiol 92
Marco Polo (1961) 282
Marco Polo (1982) 293
Marcus Welby, M.D. 137, 207, 212
Marcuse, Theo 124, 270
Markham, Robert see Amis, Kingsley
Marlowe 125
Marooned 165
Marquand, Christian 49
Marquand, Tina see Aumont, Tina
Marriage, Italian Style 291
Marriage on the Rocks 296
Mars Needs Women 103
Marshall, Dodie 150
Marshall, Don 199
Marshall, E.G. 58, 169
Marshall, Joan 84
Marta 214
Martel, Arlene vii, 24, 203–205, 319
Martha, Ruth and Edie 209
The Martian Chronicles 245
Martin, Dean 14, 19, 21, 33, 34, 37, 41, 43, 44, 49, 59, 99, 164, 167, 175, 192, 270, 277, 279–281, 283, 287, 296
Martin, George 225
Martin, Ross 27, 88, 140, 156, 170, 195, 291, 295, 309, 314, 315
Martin, Strother 88
Martino, Sergio 39
Martinson, Leslie H. 305, 310
Marvin, Lee 239
Maryland 221
Mason, James 236, 295
Mason, Marlyn vii, 24, 63, 205–207
Masquerade 213
Massaccesi, Aristede 214, 216
Master Stroke in the Service of the Sifar 185
Mastroianni, Marcello 38, 169
Matchless 19, 300
Matheson, Don 199
Matheson, Murray 233
Mathews, Kerwin 40, 41
Matinee Theater 205
A Matter of Who? 71
Mauri, Dino 179, 250
Maxwell, Lois 16, 65, 208–210
Maxwell, Paul 213
McBain, Diane vii, 24, 27, 210–213
McCallum, David 24, 25, 86, 87, 90, 95, 99, 109, 112, 139,

151–154, 159, 169, 171, 196, 197, 203, 206, 211, 212, 218, 231, 238, 250, 270, 281, 293, 294
McCallum, Jason 154
McCarey, Leo 229
McCarthy, Kevin 218
McCay, Peggy 86
McClory, Kevin 47
McCloud 244
McClure, Doug 28, 88, 127, 195, 220
McDowall, Roddy 202
McGavin, Darren 206
McGiver, John 86
McGoohan, Patrick 284
McGrath, Joe 38, 67, 81
McHale's Navy 140
McHale's Navy Joins the Air Force 140
McKenna's Gold 245
McNair, Barbara 25
McQueen, Steve 67, 125
McShane, Ian 263
The Mechanic 154
Medical Center 137
Mehta, Zubin 166
Mein Freund, der Lippizanner 116
Melcher, Marty 106
Mell, Marisa 14, 180, 213–216, 319
Melody in the Dark 131
Melrose Place 312
Melvin and Howard 63
The Memoirs of Sherlock Holmes 48
The Men 204
Meredith, Burgess 191, 295
Meriwether, Lee 28, 301
Merrill, Bob 91
Merrill, Dina 28
Message Chiffre see *Cifrato Speciale*
Messalina vs. the Son of Hercules 291
Metzger, Radley 72, 202
Meyer, Russ 264, 265
Michael, Mary 141
Michaels, Kay 151
Michelle, Donna 139, 216, 217
Midnight in St. Petersburg 188
Mifune, Toshiro 38
Mighty Joe Young (1949) 221
Mighty Joe Young (1998) 223
Mikels, Ted V. 21, 264, 265, 316, 317
Miles, Vera 86
Milland, Ray 98, 231
Miller, David 35
A Million Dollars for an Assassin 74
The Million Eyes of Su-Muru 120, 260
Millione di Dollari per Sette Assassini see *A Million Dollars for an Assassin*
Mills, Hayley 167
Mills, John 239
Mimieux, Yvette 210, 212, 291
Minardos, Nico 195

Mineo, Sal 102
Minsky, Harold 205
Mision Lisboa see *Espionage in Lisbon*
Mission Bloody Mary 19, 65, 74, 184
Mission: Impossible (TV series) 27, 51–53, 99, 100, 107–109, 131, 196, 197, 204, 206, 220, 258, 295, 301–303, 310, 316
Mission Speciale a Caracas see *Special Mission in Caracas*
Missione Mortale Molo 83 see *M.M.M. 83*
Missione Speciale Lady Chaplin see *Special Mission Lady Chaplin*
Mister Dynamit—Morgen Kuss Euch der Tod see *Spy Today, Die Tomorrow*
Mister X 185
Mit Eva Fing die Sunde 113
Mitchell, Cameron 231
Mitchum, James 276
Mitchum, Robert 229
Mobley, Mary Ann 24, 59, 218–221
The Mod Squad 142
Modesty Blaise 14–16, 21, 49, 121, 122, 298, 299, 306
Moglie Pericolose 223
Molina, Jacinto see Naschy, Paul
Mona McCluskey 311
Mondo Cane 179
The Monkees 204
Monroe, Marilyn 56, 98, 142
Montalban, Ricardo 82, 231
Montez, Maria 49
Moonraker 12, 208
Moore, Alvy 137
Moore, Barbara 152
Moore, Roger 13, 21, 22, 24, 30, 70, 100, 113, 119, 148, 149, 182, 186, 188, 208, 209, 263, 267–269
Moore, Terry 14, 21, 221–223, 234, 235
Moorehead, Agnes 211
Mordnacht in Manhattan see *Manhattan Night of Murder*
The Morecambe and Wise Show 193
Morgan, Sherill see Chanel, Hélène
Moriarty, Michael 203
Moritz, Louisa 113
Morley, Robert 99
Morris, Greg 52, 108, 302, 316
Mortuary 108
Moss, Arnold 139
The Mountain of the Cannibal God 39
Movin' with Nancy 272
Mrs. Harris und der Heirattschwindler 177
Mulargia, Edoardo 92
Muldaur, Diana 192

Mulhare, Edward 105, 135
The Mummy's Vengeance 185
Munro, Janet 279
Murder, She Wrote 109
Murderers' Row 15, 19, 21, 33–35, 41–43, 168
Murphy, Jimmy 155, 290
Murphy's Law 154
Murray, Jan 172, 173, 221, 222, 233, 235
Muscle Beach Party 236, 260
The Muthers 242
My American Vacation 97
My Dear Killer 185
My Fair Lady 99
My Favorite Martian 157, 232
My Three Sons 33, 111, 122
Myers, Mike 30, 147
Myra Breckenridge 307
Mystery! (TV series) 259
Mystery Island 187
The Mystery of Oberwald 299

Nader, George 120, 260, 273, 274
Nader, Mike 260
Nagy, Ivan 295
Naked Gun 168
The Naked Gun 33⅓: The Final Insult 307
The Naked Truth 118
Namath, Joe 43
The Nancy Sinatra Show 272
Naschy, Paul 115
Neal, Patricia 85
Nearly a Nasty Accident 118
Necronomicon 255
Ned Kelly 188
Neilson, John 157
Nelli, Barbara 74
Nelson, Ed 107
Nelson, Ozzie 33, 150, 311
Neopolitan Sting 181
Neri, Rosalba 19, 83, 98, 115, 189, 223–227
Never a Dull Moment 251
Never Say Never Again 238
The New Adventures of Charlie Chan 69
The New Avengers 30, 193, 194, 289
The New Interns 247
New York Chiama Superdrago see *Secret Agent Super Dragon*
Newley, Anthony 99
Newman, Barry 156
Newman, Paul 40, 163, 275
Nichols, Mike 43
Nicholson, James H. 145
Nickelodeon 281
Nico-Icon 50
Nicols, Rosemary 30, 227, 228
Niebelungen, Teil 1: Siegfried 115
Niebelungen, Teil 2: Kriemhilds Rache 115
Nielsen, Leslie 168, 307

The Night 299
Night Creature 168
Night Gallery 244
A Night in Heaven 303
The Night of the Assassin 252
The Night of the Blood Monster 181
The Night of the Generals 243
The Night of Violence 92
The Night That Evelyn Came Out of the Grave 76
A Night to Remember 69
Nightmare Castle 184
Nightmare in Badham County 192, 310
Nillson, Harry 183
Nimoy, Leonard 302, 303, 312
99 Women 239
The Ninth Circle 189
Niven, David 38, 66, 67, 81, 82, 99, 243
The Nobody Runs Forever see *High Commissioner*
Nolte, Nick 307
Non Ho Sonno 122
Noriega: God's Favorite 197
Norris, Chuck 148, 168
North, Jay 211
La Notte 299
Novak, Kim 121
The Nude Bomb 127
La Nuit la plus Chaude 217
Number One of the Secret Service 188
The Nutty Professor 279, 311
Nuyen, France 14, 24, 93, 166, 167, 198, 228–231, 289, 319

O.C. and Stiggs 193
O. K. Connery see *Operation: Kid Brother*
Oates, Simon 188
O'Brian, Hugh 3, 28, 88, 131
O'Brien, Chuck 140
Octaman 41
Octopussy 13, 209, 268
O'Donnell, Peter 14
The Offspring 63
Oglivy, Ian 289
Oh, Heavenly Dog! 269
Oh, Rosalinda 153
Oh, What a Lovely War 267
O'Hara, Maureen 73
O'Herlihy, Dan 206
Old Shatterhand 175
Olga and Her Children 226
On Her Majesty's Secret Service 12, 15, 16, 17, 61, 193, 208, 209, 259
Onassis, Aristotle 239
The Onassis Richest Man in the World 269
The One-Eyed Soldier 238
100 Rifles 307
100 Shot, 100 Killed 143
One Life to Live 197, 289

Index

One Million Years B. C. 61, 305, 307
One of Our Spies Is Missing 24, 86, 102
One on Top of the Other 214
One Spy Too Many 24, 102, 103, 216, 217, 250
The Onedin, Line 267
O'Neal, Patrick 300
O'Neal, Ryan 281
O'Neill, Eileen vii, 1–3, 15, 21, 25, 26, 27, 173, 221, 232–235
The Only Way 267
Opatoshu, David 204
Operation Atlantis 19, 73
Operation Caviar 57
Operation: Counterspy 18, 92
Operation Doublecross 214
Operation: Entertainment 235
Operation: Kid Brother 65, 209
Operation Masquerade see *Masquerade*
Operation Oro 65, 292
Operation Poker 184
Operation: White Shark 254
Operazione Poker see *Operation Poker*
The Opium Connection see *Poppy Is Also a Flower*
The Oprah Winfrey Show 101
L'Optimisme au Xxe Siecle 174
The Oscar 140, 276
A 077 Sfida Al Killers see *Secret Agent Fireball*
OSS 77: Operation Lotus Flower 77, 283
OSS 77—Operazione Fior di Loto see *OSS 77: Operation Lotus Flower*
OSS 117 Murder for Sale 19, 180, 225, 238
Othello 244
O'Toole, Peter 125, 243
Our Agent Tiger 178
Our Man Flint 16, 19, 134–137, 140, 168, 264, 296, 297, 305, 316
Our Man in Marrakech see *Bang! Bang! You're Dead!*
Our Man in the Caribbean 118
Out of Sight 155, 198, 199, 290
The Outer Limits 203, 231
The Outlaws Is Coming 163

Pace, Judy 111, 291
Page, Geraldine 202
Pajama Party 145
Palance, Jack 38
Palm Springs Weekend 247
Paluzzi, Luciana 16, 24, 61, 180, 226, 236–240, 276
Panic in Bangkok for OSS 117 40, 41
Panic in the Parlor 118
Paper Tiger 295
Paradise, Hawaiian Style 182
Parfrey, Woodrow 231, 270

Parks, Trina 240–242
Parrish 210
Parrish, Robert 38, 67, 81
The Partner 283
The Partridge Family 220
The Party 110, 111
Pas de Roses pour OSS 117 see *OSS 117 Murder for Sale*
Password: Kill Agent Gordon 185, 224
Password: Uccidere Agente Gordon see *Password: Kill Agent Gordon*
Patou, Jean 254
Patterson, James 131
Paulsen, Albert 169
Pavan, Marisa 39
Peau d'Espion see *To Commit a Murder*
Pecas, Max 255, 275
Peck, Gregory 83, 245
Peckinpah, Sam 59, 281
Peep 209
The Peking Medallion see *Corrupt Ones*
The Penthouse 61
Peppard, George 39, 100, 316
Percy 188
Perfect Friday 38
Perry Grant, Agent of Iron 292
Perry Grant, Agente di Ferro see *Perry Grant, Agent of Iron*
Perry Mason 109, 111, 164, 171, 218
Perschy, Maria 180
The Persuaders 30, 100, 182, 188, 209, 228
Peter the Great 39
Peters, Jon 301
Pettet, Joanna vii, 14, 17, 66, 206, 242–245, 310
Petticoat Junction 285
Peyton Place 221
Peyton Place (TV series) 308
Philips, Lee 88
Pickard, John 172
Pickup on South Street 67
Pieces 108
Pillow Talk 104
The Pink Jungle 252
Pinza, Ezio 195
Pioneer Woman 244
Platt, Edward 139, 233
Playboy 170, 172, 216, 217, 223, 272, 279, 285
Playgirl 252
Pleasance, Donald 115, 119, 168
Please Don't Eat the Daises (TV series) 152
The Pleasure Girls 227
The Pleasure Seekers 136
Pock, Bernie 169
A Pocketful of Miracles 41
Podesta, Rossana 283
Poitier, Sidney 189
Polanski, Roman 214, 285
Poli, Maurice 75

Police Story 174, 244
Police Surgeon (TV series) 70
Police Woman 244
The Poppy Is Also a Flower 58, 169, 291, 292
Porel, Marc 38
Porter, Nyree Dawn 30, 70, 181, 245, 246
La Portiera Nuda 76
Portrait of a Bourgeois in Black 60
The Poseidon Adventure 202, 281
The Potting Shed 200
Powers, Stefanie 27, 218, 238, 247–249, 261, 264, 265
Prehistoric Women 61
Der Preis der Liebe 116
Preiss, Wolfgang 57
Preminger, Otto 80, 81, 200
Premonition 125
Presley, Elvis 37, 41, 85, 102, 103, 169, 172, 182, 183, 207, 212, 218, 270, 272, 279, 305, 312, 314
Price, Vincent 44, 145–147, 163, 198, 260
Primo Baby 157
Primus 253
Prince Valiant 118
La Principessa Nuda 50
Printemps a Paris 77
The Prisoner 54
Prisoner in the Middle 116
The Prize 275
Probation Officer 69
Probe 277
Project: Kill 168
Prosperi, Franco 179
The Protectors 30, 181, 245, 246
Provine, Dorothy 14, 216–218, 250, 251
Psychomania 140
Pulici, Davide 226
Purdom, Edmund 108

QB VII 90, 310
Qingmei Zhuma 97
Quarry, Robert 80
Quayle, Anna 243
Quest for Love 100
Quest for the Mighty Sword 216
The Quiet American 282
The Quiller Memorandum 58, 202, 262
Quincy 36

Raft, George 180
The Rag Trade 89
Il Raggio Infernale see *Danger Death Ray*
Raid on Rommel 111
Rains, Claude 262
The Ranch 282
Randall, Tony 58, 178
Ransohoff, Martin 157, 285
Rapporto Fuller, Base Stoccolma see *The Fuller Report*

Index

Ray, Fred Olen 63
Ray, Jacki 141
The Red Desert 298
The Red Skelton Hour 33
Red Sun 38
Redmond, Marge 314
Reed, Oliver 258, 263
Reese, Tom 41
Reeve, Christopher 269
Reeves, Steve 160, 236
La Reina del Chantecler 93
Reiner, Carl 165
Reinl, Harald 115
The Reivers 125
The Reluctant Saint 236
Remick, Lee 247
Rennie, Michael 66, 115, 262
Rentadick 97
Renzi, Eva 252, 253
Requiem for a Secret Agent 65
Requiem per un Agente Segreto see *Requiem for a Secret Agent*
The Return of Dr. Mabuse 175
The Return of Mr. Moto 186
The Return of the Fly 109
The Return of the Saint 289
Return to Peyton Place 200, 236
Revenge 72, 100
The Revenge of Frankenstein 132
The Revenge of the Pink Panther 188
Reventlow, Lance 264
Revill, Clive 305, 306
Rey, Alejandro 204
Rey, Fernando 224
Reynaud, Janine 19, 253–256
Reynolds, Burt 91, 191
Reynolds, Debbie 3
Reynolds, Sheldon 115
Rhino! 120
Rhodes, Hari 88
Ricco 48
Rich Man, Poor Man 108
Richards, Denise 22, 263
Richardson, John 61, 180, 259
Richman, Peter Mark 80, 139, 142, 217
Ricky and Barrabas 163
Ride the Wild Surf 145
Rider on the Rain 154
Rigg, Diana 14–16, 24, 118, 209, 256–259, 288
Right to Die 307
Rigo, Vincenzo 181
Riley, Jeannine 285
Rilla, Walter 57, 95, 114
Rimini, Rimini 163
Ring Around the World 19, 78, 92
Rio '70 120
Riptide 131
Risi, Dino 181
Ritchie, Michael 127, 299
La Rivolta dei Sette 184
The Road to Hong Kong 99
The Roaring Twenties 250
Roarke, Adam 170

Robards, Jason, Jr. 107, 281
Robbery 242, 243
Roberts, Pernell 308
Roberts, Tanya 263
Robertson, Cliff 213
Robertson, Dale 238
Robinson, Edward G. 98
Robinson, Smokey 117
Rock, Pretty Baby 101
Rode, Henri 256
Rodgers, Pamela 260
Rodriguez, Percy 107
Rogers, Anthony 259
The Rogues 93, 109, 205
Rohm, Maria 180
Rollin, Jean 50
Roma Bene 59
Roman, Leticia 84
The Roman Spring of Mrs. Stone 262
Romance on the High Seas 104
Romero, Alex 3
Romero, Cesar 160
Rondi, Brunello 175
Room for One More 86
Room 13 114
Roots 108
Rose Girl Resli 113
Rose Rosse per il Fuehrer see *Code Name Red Roses*
Rosenhaus, Marty 135
Rossellini, Roberto 191
Rossi, Steve 84, 113, 270
Rothman, Stephanie 312
Rouge et le Noir 48
The Rounders 172
The Rounders (TV series) 150
Roustabout 172, 305
Route 66 203
Rowan and Martin's Laugh-In 89–91
Rowlands, Gena 249
Ruhman, Heinz 213
Run for Your Life 155
Run for Your Wife 198
Rush, Richard 20, 172, 235
Russell, Ken 213
Russell, Kurt 265
Russell, Rosalind 232
Russell, Tony 75
The Russians Are Coming, the Russians Are Coming! 117
Ryan, Robert 210
Rydell, Bobby 168
Ryder, Alfred 296

Sabato, Antonio 83
Sachse, Pete 260
Sachse, Salli vii, 120, 145, 260, 261
Safari Express 38
The Saint (TV series) 19, 21, 24, 54, 70, 100, 119, 133, 182, 186, 188, 209, 245
St. Elsewhere 231
Saint James, Susan 59

St. John, Jill 16, 197, 261–264, 285, 309, 310
The St. Valentine's Day Massacre 142
Saints and Sinners (TV series) 122
Sakata, Harold 65, 72, 120, 229, 292
Salon Kitty 50
Saltzman, Harry 1, 16, 18, 19, 81, 148, 236, 252, 267
Salvatori, Rene 170
The Salzburg Connection 156
The Sammy Davis Jr. Show 129
Samson and the Sea Beast 177
Samson and the Seven Miracles of the World 91, 282
Samurai Pirate 143
The Sandpiper 285
Sands, Diana 25
Sands, Tommy 270
Sangster, Jimmy 262
Sansone Contro I Pirati 177
Santa Barbara 281
Santoni, Espartaco see Anthony, Robert
Sapphire and Steel 194
Sarafian, Richard 210
Sargent, Bill 251
Sargent, Joseph 126, 218
Sarrazin, Michael 67
Sassoon, Beverly see Adams, Beverly
Sassoon, Vidal 33, 35, 36
Satan Never Sleeps 229
Satana, Tura vii, 264–267, 316, 317, 319
The Satanic Rites of Dracula 193
Saturday Night Out 60
Saut d'Ange see *The Cobra*
The Savage Innocents 282
Savage Sisters 150
Savalas, Telly 191, 193, 211, 212, 258, 259
Sax, Arline see Martel, Arlene
Saxon, John 59, 220
Scacco Internazionale see *The Last Chance*
Scandalo Secreto 299
The Scarlet and the Black (TV miniseries) 83
Scheider, Roy 302
Schell, Maria 181
Schubert, Karin 186
Schusse im Dreivierteltakt see *Spy Hunt in Vienna*
Der Schweigende Engel 80
The Scorpio Letters 111, 120
Scorsese, Martin 83
Scott, George C. 259
Scott, Gordon 274
Scott, Pippa 164
Scusi, Lei e Favorale o Contrario? 44, 49
Se Tutte le Donne del Mondo see *Kiss the Girls and Make Them Die*

Index

Sea Fury 236
Search see Probe
Search (TV series) 28, 88, 127, 131, 199, 220, 239, 249, 277
Search for Tomorrow 197
The Searchers 308
Sebring, Jay 158, 287
Secret Agent see Danger Man
Secret Agent Fireball 18, 78, 254, 255
Secret Agent 777: Invitation to Murder 99
Secret Agent Super Dragon 19, 20, 178, 214
Secret File: Hollywood 314
The Secret of My Success 72
The Secret of the Black Trunk 57
The Secret of the Black Widow 114
The Secret of the Chinese Carnation 77
The Secret War of Harry Frigg 163
The Secret Ways 56, 57
Le Sedicenni 44
Segal, George 59, 142, 235
Il Segno di Zorro 184
Il Segreto dei Soldati d'Argilla see The One-Eyed Soldier
Seizure 63
Selleck, Tom 269
Sellers, Peter 38, 67, 81, 99, 110, 111, 132, 188, 194, 275, 276
Selsman, Mike 200
Semple, Lorenzo, Jr. 306
Send Me No Flowers 104
The Sensuous Nurse 39, 239
The Sentimental Agent 186, 256
The Sentimental Spy 118
Serato, Massimo 225
Serling, Rod 244
Sernas, Jacques 65, 292
Serra, Gianna 136, 137, 296, 297
Sesso E Volontieri 181
Le Sette Cinesi d'Oro see The Seven Golden Chinamen
Sette Donne d'Oro Contro Due 07 283
The Seven Golden Chinamen 283
Seven in Darkness 301
Seven Orchids Stained in Red 214
Seven Thieves 98
Seven Ways from Sundown 186
77 Sunset Strip 157, 171, 250
79 Park Avenue 302
Sex with a Smile 83
Sex with a Smile 2 83
Sex with a Will 181
The Sexual Revolution 44
Seymour, Jane 16, 149, 267–269, 319
Shack Out on 101 221
Shaft 242
Shalako 72
Shane (TV series) 154
Sharif, Omar 169
Sharp, Don 252

Shatner, William 99, 229
Shattered 59
Shaw, Bobbi 146
Shaw, Robert 64
She 37
Sheiner, David 244
Shelyne, Carole 155
Shepherd, Elizabeth 257
Sherlock Holmes and the Deadly Necklace 57
Sherman, Bobby 129, 249
Sherman, Vincent 317
Shindig 146
Ship of Fools 133
Shirley Valentine 194
Shonteff, Lindsay 188
A Shot in the Dark 276
Siamo Uomini O Caporali? 160
The Siege of Syracuse 191
The Sign of Zorro 184
The Silencers 15, 16, 19, 33–35, 41, 164, 165, 168, 175, 277, 279, 280, 287
The Silent Force 107, 142
Silva, Henry 186
The Silver Chalice 40
Silverstein, Sheldon 312
Simonelli, Giorgio 224
Sinatra, Frank 37, 43, 67, 99, 195, 198, 262, 270, 272, 296
Sinatra, Nancy 270–272
Sinbad and the Eye of the Tiger 269
The Sinister Monk 114
Sisters 312
Sitting Target 263
The Six Million Dollar Man 197, 205
The Sixth Sense 220
$64,000 Question 125
Skala, Lilia 105
Ski Party 102
Skyway to Death 249
Slalom 65, 189
Slate, Jeremy 170
Slaughter 281
Slaughter Hotel 226
Slaughter's Big Rip-Off 147
The Slime People 145
Smile 127
Smith, Kent 156
The Smothers Brothers Show 311
So Long as You Live 113
So Sweet, So Perverse 76, 185
Sodom and Gomorrah 40
Sol Madrid 281
Solar, Sylvia 19, 272–274
A Soldier Named Joe 239
Solvay, Paolo 226
Some Girls Do 16, 18, 19, 176, 189, 190, 193, 276
Somebody Up There Likes Me 40
Someone Is Watching 249
Somewhere in Time 269
Sommer, Elke vii, 14, 16, 19, 37, 161, 162, 167, 168, 177, 182, 192, 239, 274–278, 287, 319
Son of Dracula 183
Songwriter 303
Sorel, Jean 214
The Sound of Music 133
South Bureau Homicide 150
South Pacific 228
Southern, Terry 17
The Southern Star 38
Space Monster 314
Space: 1999 51
The Spartan Gladiators 184
Sparv, Camilla 43
Special Mission in Caracas 254
Special Mission Lady Chaplin 65, 185
The Specialist 89
Speedway 272
Spelling, Aaron 3, 128, 129, 232, 265
Le Spie Amano I Fiori see The Spy Who Loved Flowers
La Spie Che Viene del Mare see The Spy Who Came from the Sea
Spie Uccidono a Beirut see Secret Agent Fireball
Le Spie Uccidono in Silenzio see The Spy Kills Silently
La Spie Vengono dal Semifreddo see Dr. Goldfoot and the Girl Bombs
Spillane, Mickey 119, 212
Spinner, Anthony 152
Spinout 212
Spirit of '76 53
Spirits 203
Spy Against the World 115, 178
Spy Hunt in Vienna 57, 175
Spy in Your Eye 40
The Spy Killer 262
The Spy Kills Silently 16, 75
Spy Today, Die Tomorrow 274
The Spy Who Came from the Sea 19, 254
The Spy Who Came In from the Cold 57, 262
The Spy Who Loved Flowers 283
The Spy Who Loved Me 12, 298
The Spy with My Face 24, 58, 216
The Spy with the Cold Nose 175
Stack, Robert 111, 167, 210, 276
Stafford, Frederick 66
Stamp, Terence 49, 243, 304
Stand Up and Be Counted 281
Stangata Napoletana 181
Stanton, Harry Dean 88
Stanwyck, Barbara 129
Star Trek 82, 99, 117, 152, 164, 197, 203, 204, 231, 311
Star Trek: The Next Generation 289
Star Trek: Voyager 295
Stark, Ray 166, 167, 229
Stark, Sheldon 311
Starr, Ringo 183
State Fair (1962) 41

Steele, Barbara 177, 184
Steiger, Rod 98
The Stepford Wives 192
Stern, Howard 91
Sterne, Morgan 197
Stevens, Andrew 281
Stevens, Connie 155, 210
Stevens, Craig 88
Stevens, Paul 203
Stevens, Stella 15, 19, 175, 278–282, 287, 319
Stewart, David J. 311
Stockwell, Dean 139
Stone, Christopher 116
Stone, Leonard 112
Stone, Oliver 43, 63
A Storm in Summer 207
The Stranger and the Gunfighter 76
Strangers When We Meet 163
The Strangler of Blackmoor Castle 114
Strasberg, Lee 191
Streisand, Barbra 129
Stroka, Michael 157
A Stroke of 100 Millions 292
The Stud 101
The Stunt Man 125
Submarine Attack 208
Subterfuge 99, 182, 183
Un Sudario a la Medida see *A Candidate for the Killing*
Sullivan, Barry 202
Summer Love 262
Summertime Killer 48
Sunset Beach 197
Superseven Calling Cairo 224
Superseven Chiama Cairo see *Superseven Calling Cairo*
Surfside Six 171, 210
Swashbuckler 45
Sweet Charity 82
Sweet Ecstasy 275
The Sweet Ride 67
A Swingin' Summer 305
Swires, Steve 275
The Swiss Conspiracy 60, 277
The Sword of Ali Baba 169, 293
The Sword of El Cid 63
The Swordsman of Sienna 160

Tabori, Kristoffer 207
Taft, Ron 304
Take Her, She's Mine 243, 293
Tales from the Crypt 100
Tales That Witness Madness 100
The Talos Mummy 72
Tamba, Tetsuro 144
Tamblyn, Russ 189
Tani, Yoko 14, 16, 19, 95, 282–284
Tank Battalion 195
Tank Force 236
Target for a Killing 15, 115
Target: Frankie 75, 225
Target Gold Seven 75

Tarzan (TV series) 113
Tarzan and the Jungle Boy 139
Tashlin, Frank 104, 294
Tate, Sharon 14, 19, 157–160, 277, 285–287
Taurog, Norman 145, 260
Taylor, Elizabeth 69, 140
Taylor, Jack 273
Taylor, Robert 69
Taylor, Rod 176, 262
Teahouse of the August Moon 195
Tecnica di una Spia see *Target Gold Seven*
Teenage Millionaire 232
Tempi Duri per i Vampiri 161
Ten Little Indians (1965) 120, 175
Tender Is the Night 93
Tenney, Del 140
The 10th Victim 38
Der Teppich des Grauens see *The Carpet of Cruelty*
Teresa 39
The Terrible People 113
Terror in Paradise 244
Terror of Rome against the Son of Hercules 291
The Terror Within II 282
Terry-Thomas 153, 250
Das Testament des Dr. Mabuse see *The Testament of Dr. Mabuse*
The Testament of Dr. Mabuse 57
Testament of Orpheus 46
Testi, Fabio 38
Texas Across the River 49
The Texas Chainsaw Massacre 59
That Certain Summer 207
That Hagen Girl 208
That Lady from Peking 168
That Man from Istanbul 161
That Woman 252
Theatre of Blood 259
These Old Broads 101
They Came to Rob Las Vegas 276
The Thief Who Came to Dinner 67
13 Frightened Girls 53
Thompson, Carlos 118, 256
Thorson, Linda 257, 287–289, 319
Those Fantastic Flying Fools 176
The Three Avengers 77, 177
Three Coins in the Fountain 236
Three in the Attic 291
The Three Musketeers 72, 307
Three on a Couch 135
The Three Stooges 163
Thrett, Maggie 14, 289–291
The Thrill of It All 104
Thriller 109
Throne, Malachi 316
Thunderball 12, 14–16, 19, 46–48, 60, 61, 65, 66, 78, 208, 236–239, 292, 305
Tickle Me 169
Tiffin, Pamela 270
The Tiger Likes Fresh Blood 65

The Tiger of Eschanpur 236
Le Tigre Aime la Chair Fraiche see *The Tiger Likes Fresh Blood*
Le Tigre se Parfume a la Dynamite see *Our Tiger Agent*
Tinti, Gabriele 163
Titan A.E. 97
To Chase a Million 284
To Commit a Murder 58
To Love a Vampire 182
To the Devil—A Daughter 72
To Trap a Spy 24, 238
Tobias, Michael 142
The Today Show 163
Die Todesstrahlen des Dr. Mabuse see *The Death Ray of Dr. Mabuse*
Tolan, Michael 204
Tolo, Marilu 19, 33, 65, 291–293
Tom Dollar 75
Tommy 43
Tomorrow Is Too Late 39, 208
Tomorrow Never Dies 22
Tompkins, Angel 199
Tony Rome 199, 262, 272
Too Late Blues 279
Top Sensation 226
Topaz 116
Topol 227
Torn, Rip 216, 250, 281
The Torture Chamber of Baron Sadism 115
Torture Garden 35
Toto in Paris 161
Toto in the Moon 161
Toto Nelle Luna 161
Tous le Chemins Menent à l'Homme 79
Towers, Harry Alan 260, 312
Tracy, Spencer 195
The Trail of the Pink Panther 194
Train d'Enfer see *Operation Doublecross*
The Trap 191
The Treasure of San Teresa 95
The Treasure of Silver Lake 114
Trevillion, Dale 125
Trevor, Claire 67
Les Tribulations d'un Chinois en Chine see *The Tribulations of a Chinaman in China*
The Tribulations of a Chinaman in China 38
The Trip 261
Triple Cross 48
The Triumph of the Ten Gladiators 184
The Trouble with Girls 207
Trust Me 53
Tryon, Tom 57
Tsu, Irene vii, 105, 293–295, 319
The Turtles 155
Tuttle, William 293
Twelfth Night (TV) 256
The Twelve-Handed Men of Mars 177

Index

Twelve O'Clock High (TV series) 164
12+1 287
The Twilight Zone (TV series) 128, 203
A Twist of Sand 72
Two for the Road 66
The Two Mafiosi 273
Two Mafiosi Against Goldginger 224
The Two Orphan Vampires 50
Two Undercover Angels 255
Two Weeks in Another Town 175
Tyson, Cicely 25

Uggams, Leslie 25
UHF 174
Ullman, Elwood 145
Ultimo Tango a Zagarol 63
Uncle Was a Vampire 160
Under the Yum Yum Tree 200
Undermind 228
Die Unentschuldigate Stunde 56
The Unnaturals 79
Die Unsichtbaren Krallen des Dr. Mabuse see *The Invisible Dr. Mabuse*
The Unstoppable Man 208
The Untouchables 203
L'Uomo dal Pugno d'Oro see *A Fistful of Diamonds*
The Upper Hand 72
Upperseven: The Man to Kill 19, 114, 224, 252
Ursus and the Tartar Princess 283
Ustinov, Peter 207

Valdis, Sigrid 136, 296, 297
Valentine's Day 111
Valentino 289
Valley of Gwangi 135
Valley of the Dolls 142, 285
Valley of the Dragons 109
Vallone, Raf 33, 179, 250, 251, 253, 292
Vampiressas 1930 273
Van Ark, Joan 142
Van Der Zyl, Monica 37
Van Dreelen, John 128, 139, 170
Van Dyke, Dick 53, 251
Van Eyck, Peter 65, 283
Van Nutter, Rik 292
Vanzina, Stefano 180
Vaughn, Peter 35
Vaughn, Robert 24, 25, 30, 53, 80, 86, 90, 102, 103, 109, 112, 123, 139, 151–153, 157, 158, 169, 171, 181, 196, 197, 203, 206, 211, 212, 216–218, 231, 238, 239, 245, 250, 272, 276, 277, 285, 294, 311, 312
Vega$ 264
The Velvet Vampire 312
The Venetian Affair 238, 276, 277
The Vengeance of Lady Morgan 74
Venus in Furs 180

La Verdad Oculta 55
Verhoeven, Michael 59
Verhoeven, Paul 59
Vernon, Sherri 316, 317
Versatile Varieties 128
Victoire, ou la Douleur des Femmes 50
Victor, David 220
Victor/Victoria 302
The Victors 57, 58, 275
A View to a Kill 209, 263
Villa Fiorita 73
Villiers, James 176, 189
Violent Playground 95
The Virgin and the Gypsy 72
The Virgin Soldiers 97
The Virginian (TV series) 107, 155, 220
Vitti, Monica 15, 21, 49, 73, 121, 298, 299
Viva Las Vegas 41
Viva L'Italia 191
Vivendo, Cantando Che Male Ti Fo? 223
von Furstenberg, Betsy 90
von Furstenberg, Ira 19, 300, 301

Wagner, Robert 28, 29, 59, 88, 104, 107, 116, 164, 170, 192, 202, 204, 249, 264, 312, 316
Wagon Train 51, 122
The Waiting Room 150
Wakabayashi, Akiko 115
Walker, Robert 113
Walking the Edge 168
Wallace, Edgar 57, 69, 113, 114, 214
Wallach, Eli 38, 98
Walley, Deborah 146
Wallis, Hal B. 182, 183
Walsh, Raoul 98, 223
Walston, Ray 105, 233, 294
Walt Disney's Wonderful World of Color 57
Walter, Jessica 301
The Waltz King 57
Wanamaker, Sam 100, 200
Wang, Garrett 295
Wang, George 224
War Goddess 185, 186, 239
Ward, Burt 104, 157, 160
War-Gods of the Deep 145
Warner, Jack 155
Warren, Lesley Ann 28, 107, 301–304
Wayne, John 107, 295
Wayne, Patrick 269
Webb, Clifton 229
Webb, Jack 229
Webber, Robert 279, 310
The Weekend Nun 244
Weinrib, Lennie 155
Welch, Raquel 14, 15, 21, 23, 47, 61, 93, 94, 135, 304–307
Welcome to Arrow Beach 244

Weld, Tuesday 279
Welles, Mel 226
Welles, Orson 38, 67
Wendy and Me 155, 157
West, Adam 104, 168
Weston, Jack 80
What a Carve-Up! 118
What's Up, Tiger Lily? 143
When Women Had Tails 59
When Women Lost Their Tails 59
The Whip and the Body 175
White, Daniel 74
White, Slappy 113
White Slave Ship 40
The White Spider 114
Whitman, Stuart 276
The Who 43
Who Saw Her Die? 79
Who's Been Sleeping in My Bed? 283
Who's Minding the Mint 251
Why Would Anyone Want to Kill a Nice Girl Like You? 252
The Wicked Dreams of Paula Schultz 276
Widmark, Richard 56, 57, 189
Wilcoxon, Henry 88
The Wild Angels 272
The Wild Wild West (TV series) 27, 28, 88, 102, 124, 139, 140, 147, 155, 170, 172, 195, 196, 203, 210, 290, 291, 294–296, 308, 311, 314–316
Wild Wild Winter 155
The Wild World of Dr. Goldfoot 146, 260
Wilder, Billy 17, 265
Wilkin, Jeremy 228
Will and Grace 304
Williams, Esther 118
Williams, Kenneth 118
Williamson, Fred 147
Wills, Annika 227
Wilmer, Douglas 95
Wilson, Earl 125
Windom, William 205
The Winds of War 277
Winner, Michael 312
Winter a-Go-Go 33
Winters, Shelley 281
Winterstein, Frank 167
Wiseman, Joseph 36
The Witchmaker 85, 137
Without Apparent Motive 45
Woman in Hiding 208
Wonder Women 168
Wood, Ed 283
Wood, Lana vii, 15, 16, 244, 308–310, 319
Wood, Natalie 261, 264, 308–310
The World Is Not Enough 22, 239, 263
World of Speed and Beauty 278
The World of Susie Wong 93, 95, 166, 167, 229
Woyzek 213

The Wrecking Crew 14, 16, 19, 158, 167, 192, 277, 287
Wyler, Richard 120, 179
Wyler, William 129
Wynant, H. M. 202
Wyngarde, Peter 30, 54, 227, 228
Wynn, Keenan 291
Wynter, Dana 203

The X-Files 227
Xinfang, Zhou 95

The Yangtse Incident 95
Yankovic, Weird Al 174

Yanni, Rosanna 255
Yarnall, Celeste vii, 24, 29, 311–313, 319
The Yin and Yang of Mr. Go 295
York, Francine vii, 15, 21, 27, 28, 265, 314–317, 319
You Only Live Twice 12, 16, 19, 96, 115, 116, 119, 143, 144, 208, 252, 272, 284
Young, Terence 60, 61, 64, 132, 185, 239
The Young and the Restless 125
Young Dillinger 218
The Young Land 102

The Young Sinner 247
Young Winston 267
Ypotron 254

Zanuck, Darryl F. 128, 140
Zanuck, Richard 305
Zarak 132
Zeffirelli, Franco 298
Die Zeit der Kirschen Ist Vorbe 252
Zelle, Margaretha Gertrude *see* Hari, Mata
Zerbe, Anthony 156, 302
Zimmer mit Fruhstuck 60

Index

www.ingramcontent.com/pod-product-compliance
Ingram Content Group UK Ltd.
Pitfield, Milton Keynes, MK11 3LW, UK
UKHW050543150426
5217IPUK00026B/2053